Frontier's END

The Life &
Literature
of Harvey
Fergusson

ROBERT F. GISH

University of Nebraska Press: Lincoln & London

Copyright © 1988 by the University of Nebraska Press
Manufactured in the United States of America

The paper in this book meets the minimum require-
ments of American National Standard for Information
Sciences – Permanence of Paper for Printed Library
Materials, ANSI z39.48-1984.

Library of Congress Cataloging in Publication Data
Gish, Robert.
Frontier's end: the life and literature of Harvey
Fergusson / Robert F. Gish.
p.   cm.
Bibliography: p.
Includes index.
ISBN 0-8032-2121-5 (alkaline paper)
1. Fergusson, Harvey, 1890–1971.   2. Novelists,
American – 20th century – Biography.   3. Frontier and
pioneer life in literature.   4. Western stories –
History and criticism.   I. Title.
PS3511.E55Z67   1988
813'.52—dc19   87-30214   CIP

Frontispiece: Harvey Fergusson in Hollywood, 1932.
Courtesy of The Bancroft Library.

TO GEORGE ARMS — AND "GREEN FIELDS" . . .

Contents

ILLUSTRATIONS

Frontispiece:
Harvey Fergusson in
Hollywood, 1932

Preface

Anyone who attempts to write a literary biography faces countless decisions and difficulties which I have come to think of metaphorically as a "frontier." Geographical and topographical vocabularies are often resorted to when one is talking about lives, life writing, and biography. Biographers of all kinds often think of themselves as facing a "maze" of information, of confronting a "jungle" of papers and documents, of "searching," "exploring," and "questing" to find out all there is to know about their subjects. Certainly Leon Edel uses such vocabulary in his classic book on the theory and practice of literary biography.[1]

Because Fergusson's novels and his history, *Rio Grande*, deal so consistently with the settling of the American West, with the closing of the American frontier, and then with the replacement and recurrent frontiers which follow; and because his art reflects his life as a man born at the end of the nineteenth century—the very year, 1890, that the Census Bureau declared the frontier closed—I try to explain his life and his literature in relationship to the concept of "frontier's end."

Actually, what can be learned here is how I have reinvented Fergusson's life, his art, and their relationship. I have tried to be scrupulously factual and honest, and I have tried to extricate myself from the process. *Frontier's End* is intended as a literary biography of Fergusson, not as an autobiography of its author. But it is precisely here—somewhere between fact and fiction, between what Edel identifies so rightly as subject and self—that biography as "frontier" begins to take shape.

Biography was once thought of as among the purest forms of nonfiction, and easily classified as factual and historical, and usually laudatory. It is now seen as part fact, part fiction, somewhat akin to the new journalism's "faction," as much associated with the narrative techniques of the novel as with history. Such catchy but far from inane titles as *Telling Lives* and *Ultimately Fiction* reflect the state of biography.[2] Literary biography further complicates the matter because of its divided purpose—part literary history, part literary criticism. The warnings by the New Critics against the "biographical fallacy" have not entirely died out.

I do not claim to offer here *the* life of Harvey Fergusson—only *a* life, one person's attempt to understand who Fergusson was and what he accomplished. Similarly, my attempts at the reciprocal illumination of his life and his art represent only one way. One thing I am certain of: truth is relative and illusive. We cannot even be certain that Fergusson's own diaries reflect the "real" man, any more than we can assume that he is, completely, his fictional characters, narrators, and personae. I have confronted shadows—in his diaries, papers, and novels, and in the correspondence and interviews carried on with those near to him who "knew" him, or thought they did. Fergusson perpetuated a version of himself in his diaries just as surely as others had a version of him.

I am convinced that despite his utterances to the contrary, change inevitably meant loss for him. His books are elegiac in spite of themselves and in spite of his elaborate proclamations that change meant growth. A motif of this book is that the deaths of Franz Huning, H. B.

Fergusson, Frank Spitz, and Rebecca McCann all added to his sense of grief and, in the latter two instances, of guilt. I see him finally as a sad, regretful man, tending more and more in his diaries toward skepticism if not cynicism; always attempting to understand his present and larger ideas of history in terms of his and his family's past.

Such a reading of his life and literature is not without its ironies, ambivalences, and controversy. Fergusson believed in something he called "destiny": change would come and one would surely see what was to be. "Vamos a ver" was his credo. But for a man who ostensibly allied himself with change, Fergusson's patterns for coping with the present and attempting to judge it in fiction never drastically changed. They were cast in his youth as a Rousseauistic free spirit, roaming the rivers, mesas, and mountains of New Mexico.

Significantly, the division of Albuquerque into an Old Town and a New Town at the time of his birth programmed him for the rest of his life as a turn-of-the-century, transitional man with one foot in the nineteenth century and one in the twentieth. In this respect Fergusson is like Matthew Arnold and other moderns "Wandering between two worlds, one dead, / The other powerless to be born."[3] In a sense, Fergusson saw his world—the world of increasing industrialism and technology, of the emerging woman, of the anonymity and new morality allowed by the pull of big cities and by the enclosed privacy and mobility of the automobile—as replicating the changes of his grandfather's and his father's lives. The former headed west over the Santa Fe Trail, and the latter did his westering by railroad. His grandfather's identity as a "writer-adventurer" imprinted him, as did his father's life-myth as a "rebel's son."

The train and the car are ever-present symbols of change in Fergusson's fiction and are always tied to changes in relationships between race, gender, money, and the landscape. But all in all, Fergusson felt himself to be as free-spirited, as self-reliant and liberated, as anachronistic, as the mountain men who lost out to the forces of change and history. He was a part of the liberating urban and sexual revolutions of the 1920s and 1930s, yet too old for the newer morality and sexual freedom of the 1960s. In his young adulthood he turned back to the ways of his grandfather and father; in his middle and old age he turned back to his youth, when he had roamed uninhibited in nature, rebellious against small-town conventions.

In a sense, his life was one of self-imposed exile. In what can only be described as his compulsion for constant traveling Fergusson was in search of the freedoms of the past, known most completely in his youth and in the frontier myths lived out by his ancestors.

Alfred Kazin observes that most American writers "tend to project the world as a picture of themselves."[4] It is an essential premise of *Frontier's End* that Fergusson created both his sense of history and his sense of fiction out of his view of himself. His fiction is supremely autobiographical, and the patterns which originated and recurred in his life are transferred to his fiction time and again. Insofar as he changed his plots and cast of characters, he developed as a novelist, writing his best books last; but insofar as he did not change, his books tend to repeat each other.

This amounts to saying that Fergusson wrote one book and wrote it over and over again, at times perfecting it, at times lapsing, whether that book was fiction or was history. In his early phase he was relatively fashionable. Today, his attempts at modern, East-as-frontier novels seem even more old-fashioned than his West-as-frontier books—some of which read like modern Westerns. Whatever the case, Fergusson's historical fictions and fictional histories not only deal substantively with the themes of the frontier, and recurrent frontiers, but also serve as enactments of the frontier as process—just as this literary biography of Fergusson intends to do.

Many people have shared their knowledge with me in the making of this book, and I want to thank them. My interest in Harvey Fergusson and the Fergusson family is due largely to two influences: growing up in Albuquerque, where I attended kindergarten in Castle Huning in 1945, and reading Paul Horgan's stories, which reawakened my memories of Albuquerque when I was many miles away from New Mexico. By the time I came to write this book Francis Fergusson was the only surviving family member, and he graciously shared his memories and his home with me during a weekend. He granted me permission to use his brother's papers at the Bancroft Library; and his wonderful wife,

Peggy, gave me the best recipe for shortbread in existence. I am deeply indebted to Harvey Fergusson's niece, Lina Fergusson Browne's daughter, Li Caemmerer (Mrs. Alexander Caemmerer, Jr.) for her many letters, helpful information, and encouragement. Fred D. Huning, Jr., shared much Huning family lore with me in the office of his family mercantile business in Los Lunas, New Mexico. Harvey Fergusson, II reassured me at a crucial moment.

My gratitude to Quail Hawkins is difficult to express. She has inspired me and allowed me some small measurement of how very much Harvey Fergusson meant to her.

Other kindred spirits, with Harvey Fergusson and with New Mexico and the Southwest, I also want to thank: the late Irene Fisher, who although ill and in discomfort, granted me a long and, I fear, too tiring bedside interview in her Albuquerque home; Peggy Pond Church for our talk while looking east toward the Sangre de Cristos, and for "Return to a Landscape," which she read to me and which I knew was true; and Lawrence Clark Powell, who gave it to me straight during two lingering, gloriously air-conditioned interviews amidst the heat of a Tucson summer. Alfred A. Knopf patiently answered my letters when illness and age could have excused him.

My appreciation for the query responses, leads, and information relayed to me by the following individuals goes much beyond the mere mentioning of names: Allen Schares; Paul and Stanleigh Carey; Jesse Carmack; Roland Dickey; Donald S. Dreesen; Charles McDowell, *Richmond Times-Dispatch;* Henry Trewhitt and Carolyn J. Hardnett, *Baltimore Sun;* Virginius Dabney; Val Almendarez, National Film Information Service; Professor David Townsend, New Mexico State University; Professor Emeritus T. M. Pearce, University of New Mexico; Calvin Horn, publisher; Harold S. Head, University Registrar, Washington and Lee University; and Jim Acosta, Associate Registrar, University of New Mexico.

Four men who know much of what there is to know about Harvey Fergusson—Saul Cohen, James K. Folsom, John R. Milton, and William T. Pilkington—pointed me in the direction I needed to go, and sent along road maps. Frank Waters and Professor Deb Wylder helped in my appreciation of "mountain men." Professor Cecil

Robinson more than made up for missing our first appointment. William A. Koshland returned all of my calls and was always cordial and helpful.

Many libraries and other depositories, and their respective staffs, made an inquiry such as this possible. First, I owe much to the assistance afforded me by the Bancroft Library, University of California, Berkeley, and most especially by Professor James Hart, Director, Bonnie Hardwick, and Richard Ogar. I also wish to thank the following: James H. Hutson, Chief, Manuscripts Division, Library of Congress; Pat Murphy, Manager, Film Library, Metro-Goldwyn Mayer/ United Artists; Neil R. Jordan, Head, Humanities Department, Enoch Pratt Free Library, City of Baltimore; Averil J. Kadis, the Enoch Pratt Free Library; John Delaney, Manuscripts Cataloguer, Library, Princeton University; the Humanities Research Center, University of Texas at Austin; the New York Public Library; Laurel E. Drew and Darlene Leaman, Special Collections, Albuquerque Public Library; Donald Farren, Alice Tipton Seeds, and Mary Blumenthal, Special Collections, General Library, University of New Mexico; Larry Keefer, Ed Wagoner, Donald Gray, Tom Kessler, Gretchen Meyer, and Pat Wilkenson, Library, University of Northern Iowa; Donald A. Sinclair, Curator of Special Collections, Archibald Stevens Alexander Library, Rutgers, the State University of New Jersey; Giselle von Grunebaum, Gifts Librarian, University Library, University Research Library, University of California, Los Angeles; Roxanna Deane, Chief, Washington Division, Martin Luther King Memorial Library; Margery Fee and Chris Petter, Special Collections, Library, University of Victoria; Harold Merklen and Anastacia Teodoro, New York Public Library; and Captain J. J. Klopper, New Mexico Military Institute.

Credit is also due to the personnel of the United States Forest Service: Irving W. Thomas, Director of Personnel Management; Lou Armijo, Public Affairs Specialist; and Linda Brownlow, Secretary. Long-time New Mexico conservationists the late Elliott S. Barker and Homer C. Pickens answered many questions—as did former rangers Ed. C. Groesbeck, L. F. Cottam, and Lou Liedman.

I had the special help of my two daughters, Robin E. Butzier and

Annabeth Gish, both of whom worked as my research assistants at various times in Iowa, New Mexico, and California. My son, Tim, gave me the best advice I have ever had about writing.

I also owe thanks for funding and time to Professor Jan Robbins and Vice President James Martin, to Deans Thomas Thompson and John Downey, and to the Professional Development Leave Committee at the University of Northern Iowa. To Professor Leonard Dinnerstein and the National Endowment for the Humanities I owe my gratitude for their faith in my work. My friend and colleague George F. Day still helps me stand tall when the puzzlements and frustrations of biography start to shrivel my confidence. Kenyon Thomas, Jim Harris, Sandy Schackel, Tom Hill, and Paul Hutton all revived me with their special pats on the back. John Lavine and Ken Connelly introduced me into the unknown territory of word processing. Patricia Murphy readied the final manuscript, with the assistance of Ethelyn Snyder and Coleen Wagner. Doug Toft offered the finest of editorial advice.

To my wife, Judy, and our past frontiers, our own glory days, now twenty years into memory and the history of Albuquerque, I owe my hope for whatever frontiers still await us.

It goes without saying that any successes of this effort are shared by all of these individuals. Any failures are mine.

Fergusson, Frontier's End, and
the Modern West (1890–1971)

Mutability is a common theme in literature. The writings of Harvey
Fergusson are no exception. Regardless of how change is written
about, whether in celebration or in mourning, as elegy or as anthem,
one thing is certain: mutability is inevitable, and humanity is ambivalent in its perceptions and discussions of it.

Consider Fergusson's physical appearance. He was a handsome
man. Yet he regarded himself, particularly in his later years, as homely
and was reluctant to have any photographs taken: he was self-conscious about his large ears and his large nose, which became more
bulbous with age. He walked with a slight stoop—his father regarded
it as a slouch and sent him to military school to correct it. As Fergusson aged and became crippled by arthritis, the stoop became even
more pronounced, and he walked with a shuffle and needed a cane. He
lived a long life, and age worked its ways on him. Two accounts of
Fergusson by his younger sister, Lina, are to the point: "In his prime
he was a vigorous-looking man, 5' 11" in height, broad-shouldered and

rather rangey in build. He looked like the outdoorsman he was—hunter and fisherman—with a long stride suited to covering mountains either as game hunter or timber cruiser for the U.S. Forest Service. He had light hair (light brown rather than blond), gray-blue eyes, a rather florid complexion, in type clearly deriving from the Huning (German) side of the family."[1]

In the last year of Fergusson's life Lina wrote to Lawrence Clark Powell concerning the inadvisability of attempting to interview Fergusson. "I hope he need not be remembered as he now is—such a sad and distressing spectacle."[2] There is something of the will to preserve a finer memory if not a legend in Lina's letters regarding the change of her brother. She saw him as best represented, if anywhere, in *Wolf Song* (1927) and *The Conquest of Don Pedro* (1954). Hers is a natural enough inclination. Age needs reverence; but the truth of what age did to Fergusson, not just physically but psychologically, needs knowing too. The remarkable thing is that with some minor tatters his spirit held to the end.

Fergusson leaned toward both a nostalgic yearning for his past and a faith in his final "destiny." He passed through stages of longing for the past and of belief in the future; but, all in all, he seems to have found his future in the past, in "memories of the future." He was an Anglo born into a world which observation seemed to say belonged to Native Americans, and if not to them, then to the Hispanics who although they attempted to overthrow the Native American inheritance, nevertheless anticipated the Yankees. Fergusson's heritage was that of interlopers; although he was a native westerner, born to the Southwest, he was still alienated by his genealogy and his Anglo-European values. In this sense, as a marginal man in time and in culture, he qualified as a modern; and part of his modernity was his sense of loss, of nostalgia.

Novelist Marilynne Robinson speaks about what she calls the "nostalgic fallacy" in almost strident and angry terms, saying that all too many modern writers are enchanted by a venerable fable of the world once being what it was intended to be until catastrophe interrupted things and the Golden Age was lost.[3] Insofar as this is true,

Fergusson's catastrophe was the announced closing of the American frontier in 1890—the year of his birth.

Like all writers, Fergusson faced change and wrote about it. It was his heritage, his history, his *donnée*. The uniqueness he can claim in his treatment of mutability in his writing is how it affected his "destiny," as he was wont to call it. That destiny placed him in the American Southwest at the end of the American frontier and at the beginning of the modern West. His life story and how he grappled with it as "ordeal," how he sought to understand it, reshape it, and tell it in his books, is the story of change at an especially important transitional period in American history. To understand his life and his art, his various personal and temporal frontiers, is to better understand the Anglo ethnocentrism and maleness of a southwesterner looking back at the end of the American frontier in the nineteenth century and attempting to understand his present and future in the twentieth century.

Fergusson's life and literature provide the extra advantage of illustrating the myths which have come to be associated with the frontier in what are now classic works by Henry Nash Smith, Richard Slotkin, Leo Marx, John G. Cawelti, and others. Fergusson's need for wilderness and solitude was countered by an equal need for the stimulus and challenge of urban living. His identity as a hunter of wild game and as a city dweller "hunting" for his living and his loves, satisfying basic appetites for food and shelter and sex, make him an intriguing case study, almost a prototype of the American hunter-hero which Slotkin traces with such erudition in *Regeneration through Violence*. Fergusson fits, as well, considerations about technology and wilderness, and about the opening of "virgin land" which Marx and Smith have advanced.[4]

Fergusson's life begins at an ending. He was born January 28, 1890—a watershed year in all subsequent attempts to understand the ever-shifting idea and place known as the American West. Thus Fergusson's birth in an auspicious year, a year said to mark the end of both a time and a space, affords an apt vantage point for his life's telling.

In the early nineteenth century a frontiersman was considered one who lived "on the outlying districts of civilization."[5] Edwin Fussell notes that both the terms *frontier* and *West* are ambiguous but merit definition in relationship to each other and in relation to American civilization and westering: "The Westward Movement is . . . the inclusive term within which the more limited term the West must always be approached, as the West, so defined, is the inclusive term containing the still more restricted term the frontier."[6] Whether seen in relation to European perceptions of America as New World or in relation to American perceptions of its own West, *frontier* is not so much a word, Fussell insists, as it is a trope which should be extended to mean the "frontier metaphor": "The frontier was the imaginary line between American civilization and nature, or the uncreated future, and everything that came to depend upon that line was ironically reversible" (p. 17).

The historian who first advanced a theory about the significance of the American frontier and incorporated it into American historiography was Frederick Jackson Turner. Fergusson was to make Turner's theories an integral part of his historical novels largely because his grandparents, his parents, and he himself lived them. Turner first presented his ideas on "The Significance of the Frontier in American History" before the American Historical Association. He chose to begin his now famous essay with a quotation from a bulletin of the superintendent of the census for 1890. The superintendent announced the end of the frontier as a distinguishable "line" of settlement: "Up to and including 1880 the country had a frontier settlement, but at present the unsettled area has been so broken into by isolated bodies of settlement that there can hardly be said to be a frontier line."[7] The announcement of that ending, and Turner's use of it as a beginning for his essay, initiated a controversy among historians which extends to this day, for the frontier's disappearance is still disputed, even in lingering geographical terms, and in terms of new frontiers of science and technology.

For all official purposes, Fergusson was registered a child of the new West rather than the old; a citizen of the modern West, resident of a world gone beyond the frontier in time and space. He was born into one of the "isolated bodies of settlement" to which the superintendent of the census alluded. Still, the frontier lingered longer in New Mexico largely because of its historic ties with the older culture of the Spanish settlers, farmer Mexicans, and the ancient if not timeless cultures of Native Americans.

Born literally on the dividing line between Old Town and New Town, Fergusson had a fascinating but frustrating view of endings and beginnings. Albuquerque's Old Town was permeated by two centuries of Hispanic culture—the language, the dress, the food, the folkways and mores; by a lesser number of Native Americans; and by the horses and buggies, guns and boots, the pioneer/agrarian atmosphere of cattlemen and sheepmen. Its New Town was a boom town, occasioned by the arrival of the railroad and Anglo merchants bent on riding the momentum of prosperity and progress symbolized by the snorting of the "iron horse." As a child Fergusson roamed between both worlds—and beyond them, along the nearby Rio Grande, which ran to the west of Albuquerque; across the mesas which extended west to the volcanoes and east to the Sandia Mountains; and into those very mountains and others. He walked the landscape, rode his horse over it, peddled his bicycle to the limits of the town, frolicked in the river, hunted the wild game of the region. In short, the frontier landscape and cultural environment shaped his personality and his imagination. His older sister, Erna, describes the influences of the Rio Grande on her brother this way: "[He] writes of country as it can be known only to one who has absorbed it through every experience of his life. His *Rio Grande* is the river he has swum in, hunted along, jumped when it was low, fought when it was high. He grew out of it as truly as did the cattails along its margin; he comes back to it as surely as a migrating duck."[8]

The Rio Grande is also a metaphor for the influence of Albuquerque and all of New Mexico on his identity. He carried the influence of the Southwest with him throughout his life, even as he traveled to the recurrent frontiers of the East and the Far West—Washington, D.C., New York City, Hollywood, and Berkeley, California. Significantly, in one of his last works of fiction, Fergusson assumed the eponymic name "Mark West."

THE FAMILY FRONTIER

Fergusson lived until 1971, well into the new frontiers of the nuclear age. He lived through two world wars, the Korean War, the Cold War, and Vietnam. He lived through the time of reevaluated human and civil rights, the new morality of beatniks, flower children, and hippies, and the paradox of middle-class radicalism. Although he experienced world wars and their social and economic consequences as a citizen, he never fought in them—except vicariously in certain of his novels, like *The Life of Riley* (1937). The problems and horrors of world war led him to write two philosophical and social inquiries into historical change (*Modern Man*, 1936, and *People and Power*, 1947). But in his fiction and in his history, *Rio Grande* (1933), such cataclysms of change are conspicuous by their absence. They are ignored in preference for older frontier conflicts between wilderness and civilization, between primitivism and the assumed advancement of progress into the Southwest; for attention to older warfares between Native Americans, Hispanics, and Anglos; for attention to the new campaigns in the on-going battle of the sexes and the frictions inherent in the perennial rise and fall of older and younger generations, new technologies over old or nonexistent ones.

As Fergusson grew older and dedicated himself to becoming a writer, he was drawn into the past of his ancestors and the passing of the frontier as he knew it as a boy in Albuquerque. He was preoccupied with sexuality and the changes in sexual relationships which were part of the "new morality" that developed first in the 1920s and was given new impetus in the 1950s and 1960s. The emergent woman and the wandering, single male—all of the complex relationships associated now with the politics of sex—provided lifelong fascination for him. Born into small-town, status-quo Victorian values, he rebelled into his own brand of liberalism and libertinism, ironically in partial conformity with other iconoclasts like Witter Bynner, Mabel Dodge Luhan, Mary Austin, H. L. Mencken, Randolph Bourne, Sinclair Lewis, Theodore Dreiser, Floyd Dell, and Frank Harris. The eroticism which pervades all of his fiction, always affected by his ethnocentric assumptions about interracial sexual and cultural unions of Anglos and Hispanics, now seems not only distorted but at times boorish.

Largely because of his identity as a hunter and a "timber cruiser," because of his "Daniel Boone" image as a latter-day mountain man and the characterization of his protagonists as red-blooded, he-men lovers, adoring of and adored by women (by Fergusson's own count, he had intercourse with approximately eighty women),[9] Fergusson's personality and his persona now seem exaggerated and stylized, and if not heroic then chauvinistic—the identity of a bygone age rather than of the ideal of the 1980s. It is not so much his interests in wilderness and in women that make him and his novels seem old-fashioned; rather, it is his seemingly naive attitudes about solitude and sex, all offered in the midst of absolutist presumptions.

When the future of the 1950s and 1960s arrived, Fergusson was lost in the past, of a different vogue and generation, out of step with his times—ahead of them in his past, and behind them in his future. His perception of his future, when it came, was not the future of which futurists speak in the vocabulary of "megatrends," "future shocks," and "third waves." It was a much older future, if such a thing is possible—a future simultaneously envisioned and remembered from the vantage point first of an ending of the frontier in 1890, and then of an extended identification with the age of flappers and Prohibition, of passion spent in the back seat of a car on the mesa, of men around a campfire in the mountains talking about their sexual exploits.

Fergusson came to regard New Mexico as the vital center of the West—old and new. He experienced almost first-hand the mutability played out against the distant pasts of deteriorating Spanish dynasties and mountain men. He experienced, on the spot, the mutability occasioned by cars and trains replacing horses and wagons. Born a westerner—a "square" who soon wised up, to borrow a term from Wallace Stegner—Fergusson wrote about a West which changed so much that it became many things, confusing and contradictory—for the Wests of his grandparents and parents were not the West of his youth. In a world of accelerated change he stabilized himself by recreating and reliving the Wests of his ancestors. In his fictive projections of himself into the lives of his maternal and paternal grandfathers and to a lesser degree into the life of his father, he nurtured his family tree, transplanted in the soil of the Rio Grande Valley and the American frontier.

In New Mexico, during territorial days and after statehood, he witnessed ancient Native American cultures facing successive Hispanic and Yankee conquests across what he insisted on viewing as a changeless, eternal terrain. Almost of necessity, it was the Yankee perspective which he adopted and which he not altogether unconsciously helped mythologize as the rightfully dominant and heroic replacement for the one-time glorious era of the Spanish *ricos*. His was a home which saw the cliff dwellings of Frijoles Canyon and the development of the atomic bomb at Los Alamos within a few miles of each other.

Fergusson's maternal grandfather's new frontier had been that of a German immigrant heading by boat across the Atlantic to a new life in America, which manifested itself as his own new West, first in St. Louis and as a trader and bullwhacker on the Santa Fe Trail of 1849, then as a pioneer settler and founding father in Albuquerque at a propitious time for a "writer-adventurer" with considerable adeptness at merchandising. This grandfather, Franz Huning, outlived his time and experienced the end of the frontier as he knew it on the Santa Fe Trail and in early Albuquerque. Near the end of his life he withdrew to his "castle" and then took to his bed, waiting for death. Huning thus established a paradigm in the family of elegiac loss and nostalgia in regard to the frontier's end.

Fergusson's paternal grandfather, Sampson Noland Fergusson (who spelled his surname with one *s*), had been a Southern gentleman—a physician and a plantation and slave owner. His was the frontier of the Civil War and its aftermath, which contributed to an urge for westering in his son, Fergusson's father, Harvey Butler Fergusson, Sr. Sampson Noland Ferguson's frontier ended in the literal dissolution of his Old South and in his own comparative poverty. So it was that the life and fortune of his son, H. B. Fergusson, depended on another of American history's significant events. Identifying himself as a "Rebel's Son" in his own aborted attempt at a first novel, H. B.

Fergusson went west, like so many others, but with something of an edge as a charming, well-educated attorney sent to settle mining litigation. Promises and prospects held and were profitably realized when H. B. Fergusson outgrew his practice in the southeastern New Mexico town of White Oaks and moved north to Albuquerque to be closer to the business potential brought about by the arrival of the railroad. In one of the most fortunate chances of his life, he met and married Clara Mary Huning, the daughter of Franz Huning, by then one of the town's most prospering land owners and developers—a man destined to be a town legend as the designer and builder of a "castle" which served as a symbol of the man, his family, and his times, of old dreams and new resources. But like Huning's waning will to conquer anything more, H. B. Fergusson's new frontier rose and prospered for a time in politics, in association with William Jennings Bryan and Albert B. Fall, and then nosedived into depression and suicide.

Harvey Fergusson's own life at the turn of the century was filled with the echoes of these changes, of his heritage as a boy growing up in the at once backward, primitive, and isolated, civilized, social, and progressive spheres of Albuquerque. He was at first drawn away from the socializing aspect of the town, as allowed him by his family's prominence, back into the wilderness and solitude preserved by his grandfather Huning on the grounds surrounding his Castle Huning and extending to the Rio Grande on its western boundary; then in his adulthood Fergusson left the small-town isolation of Albuquerque for larger cities.

Fergusson in his youth saw the drama of new statehood for New Mexico from a front-row seat while his father served as a territorial representative and then, for a time, as an elected congressman. With the examples of the older generations of his family—the bullwhacking Franz Huning of the Santa Fe Trail and the Albuquerque merchant and entrepreneur; Sampson Noland Ferguson, the Confederate officer and aristocrat of the Old South; and his father, the frontier lawyer and politician who made it big out West, who literally struck it rich in a mine named "Old Abe"—Harvey Fergusson grew up surrounded by the lives and the legends of a family of frontier heroes, writer-adventurers, men on the move, travelers who stood and for a time made their mark. Those family legends formed Fergusson's own heroic ideals when he hit the trail of modern adventure, backtrailing across the continent, first as a journalist, then a novelist-historian whose motive and means soon became the retelling of his family's frontiers and their part in the story of the American frontier.

By the 1920s Fergusson confirmed for himself that his version of the life of a writer-adventurer was to give voice to the two worlds he knew, the ending of the frontier and the beginning of the modern West. It was a decision, a destiny, that would last half a century. The loss of the respective frontiers which came to Franz Huning, Sampson Noland Ferguson, and H. B. Fergusson initiated Fergusson into the realization that change is accompanied by loss. This became even more apparent with the accidental death by drowning of his closest friend, Frank Spitz. Another death, that of his second wife, Rebecca McCann, left him with even greater remorse and made it even more necessary for him to write.

Although Fergusson's wanderlust and his roaming life as a poet-adventurer in the tradition of his family took him away from the Southwest of his youth, that special romantic frontier of childhood, and catapulted him into the urban frontiers of Washington, D.C., and New York City, he regularly returned to New Mexico, to its wilderness and solitude, to measure the changes in the landscapes of his memory.

TURNER'S FRONTIER

In order to further understand the frontier as Fergusson knew it and the recurrent endings of it which he experienced, a closer look at Turner's "The Significance of the Frontier in American History" is in order.

In Turner's Darwinian conceptualization, American history was protean, "fluid," always moving, presumably until 1890, in recurrent waves and surges to the "great West." According to Turner, the motion and resulting changes and repercussions were not one constant, uninterrupted surge. Rather, the evolution of American history advanced and stopped in stages—pausing on "frontiers" of the frontier: "Thus American development has exhibited not merely advance along a single line, but a return to primitive conditions on a continually advancing frontier line, and a new development for that area. American social development has been continually beginning over again on the frontier.[10]

Such a process provides the plots of most of Fergusson's novels, and indeed, in his life—except for the point of view. Even when Fergusson is describing such a regenerative process, he is looking at it either retrospectively and elegiacally or as a present which is somehow felt to be only second best to the original move west. His nineteenth-century characters move west as part of the original exuberance; and his twentieth-century characters who backtrail to the East always compulsively head for the West and wilderness, only to find a semblance of what was there or a stylized primitivism which they mock and satirize. Only the landscape holds out some authentic satisfaction in its isolation and solitude. Even there, however, the railroad and the progress it symbolizes soon enter into the garden, the forests are cut, sawmills appear, mines gouge the earth, money and machines intrude. In the case of the train and the car, with the increased mobility they allow, and in the case of the anonymity and sexual freedom allowed by large cities, the loss is compensatory enough to be viewed as a gain. So although Fergusson abides by Turner's model of American history as frontier, he welcomes and regrets its advance and its end.

Turner pictures the frontier as an all-powerful "master" which reshapes and molds the colonist, stripping off his "garments of civilization" and reclothing him in buckskin, making him live in a log cabin and plant corn with a stick: "He shouts the war cry and takes the scalp in orthodox Indian fashion" (p. 29). There is much of the Boone myth in this kind of atavism. And there is much of Fergusson's fictional frontiersman here: his nineteenth-century mountain men Sam Lash and Jean Ballard, and his twentieth-century surrogate mountain men Morgan Riley and Alec McGarnigal. There is, too, much of Fergusson himself in such a shouting.

Turner compares the force of settlement, in its movement away from Europe, to sublime geological forces: "As successive terminal moraines result from successive glaciations, so each frontier leaves its traces behind it, and when it becomes a settled area the region still partakes of the frontier characteristics" (p. 30). If ever there was a description of the social forces at work in the interactions between Old Town and New Town Albuquerque, and known to Fergusson in his boyhood, this is it. According to Turner, it was the need for communication between the Far West and the East which caused the settlement of the Great Plains. By the time the Rocky Mountain West came to be settled in the last decades of the century, bodies of settlement were so scattered that, as the 1890 Census reported, there was no longer any identifiable frontier line. Thus, in Turner's explanation, each century, from the founding of the country to the time of Turner's generation, had its own particular defining frontier: "The fall line marked the frontier of the seventeenth century; the Alleghanies that of the eighteenth; the Mississippi that of the first quarter of the nineteenth; the Missouri that of the middle of this century (omitting the California movement); and the belt of the Rocky Mountains and the arid tract, the present frontier" (pp. 22–23).

In addition to assuming that the Rocky Mountain West and the "arid tract" between the Rockies and California were the last frontiers, Turner with unconscious ethnocentrism ignores the fact that the Southwest was, every bit as much as New England, also one of the first frontiers. He says nothing about the Spanish colonization of the Rio Grande Valley and the greater Southwest. Furthermore, American Indians are reduced to the "Indian question," political problems to be solved in "a series of experimentations on successive frontiers" (p. 33). Following the Darwinian assumptions of the Italian economist Loria, Turner sees the development of America up from savagery and barbarism toward "civilization" to be a universal progression. Here he changes his metaphor to that of the United States as a page in the book of time: "The United States lies like a huge page in the history of society. Line by line as we read this continental page from west to east we find the record of social evolution. It begins with the Indian and the hunter; it goes on to tell of the disintegration of savagery by the entrance of the trader, the pathfinder of civilization; we read the annals of the pastoral stage in ranch life; the exploitation of the soil by the raising of unrotated crops of corn and wheat in sparsely settled farming communities; the intensive culture of the denser farm settlement; and finally the manufacturing organization with city and factory system" (p. 34).

As a historian, and certainly as a novelist, Fergusson used Turner's "large-print" Darwinian page as if it were his very own. Turner's various passing frontiers of Indian, hunter, trader, rancher, farmer, and city worker offer an evolutionary system adapted by Fergusson line by line across the pages of his own books. Fergusson's scheme is not quite as one-directional and diachronic as Turner's, for Fergusson's frontiers overlap into anachronisms of one kind or another. His focus is more on Anglo and Hispanic cultural clashes and mergings than it is with Native Americans. But all the recurrent waves of frontiers are there—the hunter especially, the mountain man, the trader assuredly, the individual heading West and heading away from the West, all combining to dramatize the human and mythical sweep of change before and after the official ending of the frontier.

In Turner's view, the changes toward "civilization" started with Indian trade in relation to geographical factors: "The buffalo trail became the Indian trail, and this became the trader's 'trace'; the trails widened into roads, and the roads into turnpikes, and these in turn were transformed into railroads" (p. 37). Trails, roads, railroads, and travel along them are so omnipresent in Fergusson's novels as to qualify as a dominant motif. This is not because of Turner, for his thesis is in some ways as much descriptive as speculative. In any event, Fergusson's writings take from travel much of their thematic and plot structure as well as development of characterization based on numerous kinds of travelers.

Thanks to his portrayal of American Indians as a common danger to the settlement process, Turner argues by way of causality that common lines of defense were formed on the frontier, politically as well as militarily. A benefit of this action for Turner is his belief that the frontier served as a "military training school" which, in its constant resistance to Indian aggression, helped develop "the stalwart and rugged qualities of the frontiersman" (p. 38). Fergusson has no particular interest in military matters, in cavalry and Indian wars.

Nevertheless, there are signs in his fiction of ethnocentric attitudes toward American Indians as obstacles to Anglo settlement. Some would prefer to attribute this more to historical fact than to Fergusson's biases. Indeed, in Fergusson's characterization of Black Wolf, the southern Cheyenne warrior in *Wolf Song* (1927), and Kenyatch, the Ute chief in *Grant of Kingdom* (1950), the image of the Indian as enemy is balanced by the image of Indian as friend and ally.

Fergusson's historical novels and *Rio Grande* refine Turner's thesis and focus it on the Southwest. Others have refined Turner in ways more critical than narrational. Richard Hofstadter points out that one of Turner's major failings was his tendency to think of America as having a frontier rather than being one, a national safety valve not so much of free land, as Turner argued, as of freedom and a new beginning, and a destination for European immigration—place as future. In Hofstadter's view, "The mingling of peoples that took place in the United States must be placed alongside the presence of 'free land' in explaining American development."[11]

T. M. Pearce makes a similar point in his critique of Turner's frontier thesis. Pearce is concerned in particular with Turner's neglect of Hispanic and Native American "frontiers": "It can be said that the Anglo-American frontier was only one of many frontiers in the history of the United States. . . . And basic to all frontiers was the presence, on the other side, of the American Indian race. Thus there was never just one frontier at any one place or time, for the front was always opposite another front."[12]

Pearce's conclusion about Turner's neglect of the "other" frontiers is not applicable to Fergusson's novels in that Fergusson does not ignore the contacts of the Anglo frontier with other cultures; indeed, he emphasizes these contacts. But they do remain "others." Pearce insists that "the 'American frontier,' as described by Turner and explored by his many disciples, has had its intellectual limits—and the result has been that the human forces on frontiers other than the Anglo-American have been inadequately studied or completely overlooked" (p. 106). Pearce emphasizes that the Southwest was a complex and populated region long before waves of settlement moved West. From Cabeza de Vaca's explorations, through Juan de Oñate's colonization of the upper Rio Grande Valley in 1598, followed by Catholic missions and later the opening of the Santa Fe Trail in 1821 and its "influx of Anglo-American trappers, traders, soldiers, adventurers, health-seekers, and other colonizers," the Southwest's cultures were many and diversified (Pearce, p. 107).

Fergusson's assumptions, like Turner's, were ethnocentric and biased in favor of the Anglo culture's then-dominant values. Like Turner, he shared a belief in the evolutionary advancement of Anglo-European culture and Western European values. But he had greater empathy for and understanding of the Hispanic side of the frontier. And that empathy was tempered by his own sense of alienation and urge to explore whatever frontiers remained.

Two expositions of Fergusson's views about historical and social change in relation to the end of the frontier and the beginning of the modern world are *Modern Man: His Belief and Behavior* (1936) and *People and Power: A Study of Political Power in America* (1947).[13] Published just before and just after World War II, both books were written at a time of tremendous change in American life and during a time of continued soul-searching for Fergusson as a thinking man responding to change in his middle years. Many of Fergusson's early essays and articles demonstrate his inclination toward social commentary in expository prose and his ability for sustained argument. *Rio Grande* (1933) is a somewhat earlier panoramic view of the diverse cultural confrontations and mixings over the centuries from Spanish colonization to modern times along the Rio Grande. And Fergusson's own probing but still guarded autobiography, *Home in the West: An Inquiry into My Origins* (1944), is yet another exposition, albeit from a much more intimate perspective, on a similar subject: mutability as it affected a boy growing up in the Southwest. *Rio Grande, Home in the West, Modern Man,* and *People and Power* are all bound in autobiography and represent a decade's vacation from fiction (with the exception of *Proud Rider*, 1935–36, and *The Life of Riley*, 1937)—all readying him for his two masterworks of fiction, *Grant of Kingdom* (1950) and *The Conquest of Don Pedro* (1954). Because of their representative image of Fergusson's life as a modern frontiersman and his thought about the frontier, these works are considered here as autobiographies of a sort, illustrating just how important his own life and its retelling were to Fergusson.

MODERN FRONTIERSMAN

Modern Man, ironically, given its pertinence to Fergusson's other writings, has proved one of his least understood and least popular works. Completed and revised in California during a decade in which he wrote Hollywood screenplays for good financial gain, and the result of the matching good fortune of a Guggenheim Fellowship, *Modern Man* is the product of a somber eschatological reflection on historical change. Read against its own premises, the book is a willful act, Fergusson's attempt to put into practice just the kinds of concerns about which he is writing. His publisher at the time, Alfred A. Knopf, first rejected the book and then agreed to publish it out of deference to Fergusson. While later critics, particularly William T. Pilkington, tend to see Fergusson's conclusions as totally outdated if not misconceived and irrelevant to twentieth-century life, a handful of Fergusson's contemporaries hailed it as a significant although flawed attempt by a novelist at writing popular philosophy. Pilkington was the first to point out an ideological relationship between *Modern Man* and *People and Power* and Fergusson's novels—particularly his typology of men as "primitive," "mediaeval," "modern," and "great leaders" as the basis for the characterization of similar representative men in *Grant of Kingdom.*[14]

Even though some reviewers and critics have found *Modern Man* a relatively thought-provoking questioning of modernity, few are able to accept all of Fergusson's premises and conclusions. Pilkington, for example, says, "The relevance of [Fergusson's] ideas to a world only a few decades removed from the one he was writing about appears almost nil."[15] What readers of *Modern Man* generally see are Fergusson's extrapolations about the future, his optimism and wrong guesses. What is overlooked is the autobiographical connection between Fergusson's frontier heritage, his childhood while growing up in the sad shadow of the frontier's end, and the projection of that consciousness and its attitudes about the frontier into his view of what modern man faced.

Modern Man is something more than autobiography. It is a philosophical argument and a speculation. But its assumptions are so strongly tied to Fergusson's own experiences that it can be read for its autobiographical dimensions and for what insights it offers into Fergusson's beliefs and behavior, his pioneer background and how it contributed to his own identity as a "modern frontiersman." Fergusson's preface states that "modern thought is a wilderness of contention and contradiction" (p. vii), suggesting his authorial role as a frontiersman facing an ideational wilderness. His journey into the wilderness of conflicting ideas is very much dependent on his sense of self-necessity and self-reliance as his own best philosopher, his own best source and hope. Such a proclamation is cast implicitly, metaphorically, in terms of a newer installment of the same kind of impulse that led Fergusson's own ancestors west and similarly leads his favored protagonists on the road.

In their respective analyses of frontier mythology, Smith and Slotkin note that Daniel Boone, as the prototypic frontiersman, has historically been viewed as both a "harbinger of civilization and refinement" and a "cultural primitivist," and thus the image of the "Wild Western Hero could serve either purpose."[16] Fergusson's imagery and his persona project him into the wilderness of modernity via frontier conditioning and resolve. The conceit is clear, as is the voice behind it: Fergusson is engaged in a "long and painful struggle," not with bears and Indians and the elements, but with the idea of mutability; and he is bravely determined to follow the route to the answers of his quest wherever it leads. The result is a journal of just where he has traveled, what he has seen, and what has sustained him.

It is particularly indicative of Fergusson's identity as a writer-adventurer and of the autobiographical nature of *Modern Man* that he begins his speculations with a discussion of the importance of diaries and journals to a writer and the need for writers to judge and gauge the kinds of changes that take place in their own lives and careers. Fergusson was forty-six when *Modern Man* was published, and all of his books written between 1933 and 1947 have a decidedly middle-age cast to them. He speculates that whereas most people keep diaries in their youth and give them up in adulthood as their interests "lead the mind outside the egocentric circle," writers continue to need and keep diaries for the insights they allow on individual development: "Many writers have kept journals all their lives and have noted their own behavior with increasing volume and interest as they aged" (p. 3).

He continues this justification of keeping diaries as a means of furthering a writer's understanding of the world by saying that a writer's "peace" resides less in personal interest than "impersonal thought"; that a novelist's ability to create believable fictional characters depends on self-contemplation. The writer, for Fergusson, "is a narcissus who has found in his own image a key to the external world" (p. 4).

Fergusson began his diaries at the age of sixteen, recording in his first entry: "I have resolved to keep in this blank book a record of my daily doings, partly as a practice in writing, partly that I may remember what has happened and partly because I think it will be a pleasure to look over it in after years."[17] He kept the diaries, more or less devotedly, throughout his lifetime. Some entries amount to illegible scribbling. Others are neatly typed, with page after page of meaningful comments about his personal life, especially the women he knew, seldom fully identified; his health; his daily routine; his yearly resolutions and retrospective summaries; his aesthetic values; and intuitions and possibilities for his fiction. During the 1950s and early 1960s he set about to edit and organize the many yearly datebooks in which he recorded the scribblings of his heart and mind. Toward the end of his life, when writing became physically difficult for him because of arthritis, entries grow more sporadic and meager and serve mainly as evidence of determination, discipline, and years of habit. In the year just before his death Fergusson was happy if he could manage one sentence each day in his diary; and his last entry, recorded in the spring of 1970, is a simple instruction to call one of the persons employed to look after him.

In *Modern Man* he goes to unusual lengths to verify the source of himself found in the performance and substance of keeping years of diaries. He insists that he regards himself neither as the hero of a romance nor as the "victim of a tragedy" but that he acquired his record of himself by reflecting about his behavior and his "dreams, inspirations, plans, intentions, or resolutions"; this record allowed him to trace the relationships between "thought and action," "consciousness and behavior" (p. 4). In this respect, *Modern Man* as autobiography anticipates Fergusson's purest autobiographical work, *Home in the West,* which depends for much of its telling on the memoirs of his grandfather Huning. It is no surprise that Fergusson is so preoccupied with autobiography, since not only Huning but also his wife and their daughter, Fergusson's mother, kept journals about their frontier experiences. In all of their memoirs is the expectation that their children and grandchildren would naturally find these written life stories of value.

In *Modern Man* Fergusson argues that choice is an illusion and insists that he discovered, from the evidence of his own diaries, that at every stage of his life he never did what he intended. The same rationalizations he used to sustain his illusion of choice were also reflected more universally—or so it seemed to him—in the talk and printed justifications of others. Individually and collectively, modern man simply does not act on his reflections. At least one important inference can be drawn from such a belief: Fergusson's ideal was that action must be reconciled with and complemented by thought. For a writer, then, the act of writing is analogous to the ideal of a writer-adventurer—a frontiersman like Huning and the historical explorers and settlers before him, the Boone types—who, for whatever reason or as a result of whatever intended or capricious cause, found and shaped the frontier, America as serendipitous westering personified.

In terms of choice and action, intention and behavior, modern man needs an updated ideal, a new illusion which admits the disharmony in modern life between actual conditions and the state of knowledge. Change has been so rapid and overwhelming and disorienting in the modern period that he seeks a new balance. In trying to account for what he calls the "spiritual history of the Western European Stock from which I believe that I am sprung," Fergusson reductively establishes three types of humanity: "primitive man," "mediaeval or

Christian man," and "modern man" (p. 11). All of history is beyond his experience, but his own southwestern experiences allowed him to observe Pueblo Indians, penitentes, and Anglo-European middle-class merchants and professionals.

He further develops his scheme of things by referring to the split personality of modern man, who is on the one hand conditioned by habit and repetition and on the other desirous of spontaneity and freedom from convention. He believes that primitive and medieval societies found relatively easier ways to reconcile these antithetical urges. Basing much of his understanding of primitive societies on the work of Franz Boas, Fergusson comments that primitive societies solve the dilemma of divided desires by imposing the tribe over the individual and by worshiping the past and fearing spontaneity and change. Siding with the assumption that primitive societies can and should develop into civilized ones, he accepts the premise that to study such peoples as the Pueblo Indians is to study the essentials of modern man's "own cultural background" (p. 32). Thus, they are seen as anachronisms with which modern man can identify if he wishes. The primitive world is one of total conformity in Fergusson's mind. Of course, both the primitive and the civilized urges exist in many of his fictional characterizations and provide the basis of plot conflict and of setting in most of his novels.

In a line of thinking similar to Turner's, based on similar assumptions about the recurrency of frontiers, Fergusson asserts that "when men belonging to so called civilized races are found living under group conditions similar to those of tribal savages, they exhibit almost all of the characteristics that I have noted as distinguishing the primitive from the civilized man" (p. 37). Following such an assertion to its absurd conclusion, he states flatly that "primitive man . . . has little power to think" (p. 39). Since among primitive peoples individualized consciousness is discouraged, so goes his argument, there is no "conflict of impulse." It is conflict which both makes and breaks modern man.

Christian man shares some of the assumptions of primitive man. The violation of taboos and the resultant guilt became the road of primitive man toward civilization. In Fergusson's words, "Civilization is literally, like the Christian man, conceived in sin and born guilty" (p. 47). Christianity, he believes, was a means of dealing with two primary worries—guilt and death. In the development of modern man, the history of the individual repeats the history of the race. Primitive man saw his personality invaded by inexplicable external forces; however, Christian man saw his personality as split, intrinsically divided against itself: on the one hand good and on the other evil.

Fergusson equates Christianity with medievalism and more particularly with Catholicism. Drawing on his own experience, he speaks of knowing two kinds of Catholics—"primitive" Catholics and "more sophisticated types." The primitive Catholic, such as the penitentes which appear so often in his writings, impulsively sins to be forgiven. The "intellectual Catholic" is portrayed in a negative light as a "typically sad creature, inhibited in his emotional life, while his mental life is full of evasions and sophistries" (p. 510).

Protestantism holds even less appeal for Fergusson, who views it as a futile enterprise which rejected the emotionalism of Catholicism and replaced it with little else. In all, he dismisses Protestantism as "a working adjustment to life only on low levels of awareness, and it exists there chiefly as a primitive adaptation, notably among the Negroes and some classes of whites, who enrich it with primitive emotional elements, such as the camp-meeting and orgies of the Holy Rollers" (p. 52). The preacher, Daniel Laird, in *Grant of Kingdom* is an evangelical Protestant characterized by Fergusson with much more sympathy than such a condemnation of Protestantism would suggest.

Both primitive man and medieval man, then, says Fergusson, resisted change and believed life in all its essentials to be static. Modern man must accept change, and that is the cornerstone of Fergusson's house of history as constructed in *Modern Man*. When he speaks of modern man he also speaks of himself, a man born at the end of the frontier, between two worlds, past and future: "Modern man looks out, in helpless terror, upon a scene of upheaval and transformation. He is born in one world and dies in another. Change is the very stuff of his destiny" (p. 55). Although Fergusson insisted that he, as a modern man, must accept change, he nevertheless mourned his own youth and the world into which he was born insofar as he invariably returned to them in his fiction—a fiction which is almost entirely historical and partially tragic.

This ambivalence toward accepting and regretting his place in time as a modern frontiersman is seen throughout *Modern Man* in Fergusson's expressed bitterness toward the romanticizing of the frontier era and nineteenth-century pioneer life. Like Turner, he argues that the frontier is closed and that it was significant, but that as a *modus vivendi* its relevance to the modern world is over. Thus he justifies the end of the frontier by demythologizing pioneer life. However, in his criticism of frontier ruthlessness and inflexibility, an excessive bitterness is sensed, almost an anger working to rationalize his present predicament and the transferences he is expected to make as a modern frontiersman. Pioneering is no small force in his assessment of the belief and behavior of modern man. Not just American history but all of world history is viewed as a history of pioneering.

The history of modern Europe is the history of "industrial pioneering" just as certainly as the history of America is the history of "primary pioneering." In a sweeping generalization, one with a Turnerian ring, Fergusson says, "Almost all Western men are the descendants of pioneers as surely as they are descendants of mediaeval Christians and of tribal primitives" (p. 123). Life on any frontier, and the impulse of any pioneer, is portrayed as a necessity in that a pioneer is like a man pursued by a bear, willing to accept any sanctuary when surrounded by danger. The pioneer must be ruthless in pursuing ends, and since his environment is inhuman and hostile, he can worry little about implications or long-term consequences. Insofar as the pioneer is a person who acts out of necessity and pursues a fixed end with inflexible ruthlessness, any romantic portrayal of the pioneer having a heroic and limitless freedom is a myth.

Pioneer societies have a history of similar ruthlessness and inflexibility, attempting to exploit fellow humans just as they do natural resources. What evolves is a matter of the survival of the fittest—described with Turnerian echoes of the frontiersman stripped of his "garments of civilization, shouting the war cry and taking the scalp": "A reign of murder and robbery always comes first. This is always followed by a mass revolt against the exploitation and a period of mob rule or herd rule. This is essentially rule by violence and is always the government of men who have no capacity for balanced action. Vigilante movements, lynchings, shot-gun weddings, tar-and-feather parties now become the instruments of social action" (p. 129).

Following the writings of progressive journalist-editor Herbert Croly, who in *The Promise of American Life* (1909) and others of his writings similarly discusses the impact of the closing of the frontier, Fergusson sees the evolution of pioneer societies into agricultural societies followed by the formation of industrial societies and thus of "industrial pioneers." Fergusson, as his own kind of modern frontiersman, his own kind of self-reliant "man of purpose," finds himself between the worlds of "primary pioneering" known in his youth and of "agricultural/industrial pioneering" in his adulthood. He believes that the "heroism" found in the iron necessity of primary pioneers is lost. And although the ideal of the "man-of-purpose" still prevails in the industrial pioneer and in modern man generally, it is severely maladjusted. The "man-of-purpose," as modern man, is not much of an ideal; rather, he is a victim of change, incapable of using it to its best advantage. It is a portrait the man-of-purpose simultaneously rejects but nevertheless fears in its potential resemblance to himself.

Evidenced in such historical types, and in the fervor of his tone as well as his assertions, is a reflection of Fergusson's own family and personal history—and his compulsion to flee from the constricting demands of small-town, Old/New Town Albuquerque, and his inevitable escape to the larger, more anonymous, permissive cities.

Calling on his own experience as a timber cruiser, a citizen, and a writer, Fergusson offers several examples of what he considers to be the assumptions behind organic order in the world and what he terms "the ethic of balance." Nature and man are not opposed; Fergusson assumes that the principle of organicism is equally at work in living things, such as a Rocky Mountain forest, and in a city or a novel. When there is growth and action, there is never chaos, and for Fergusson growth and action are predicated on "balance." The life cycle of growth and decay and regrowth of forests is also applicable to the writing of novels.

In primitive and medieval societies, says Fergusson, emotional balance was maintained by extrinsic support in the form of taboos and compulsions. In contrast, the order of the modern world is based upon individual mobility—"the most distinctive character of the modern world" (p. 199). To illustrate this contention, he focuses in Turnerian fashion on the relationship between the frontier and the growth of cities. The city he chooses as an example is his own birthplace, Albuquerque. The causes which increased individual mobility over and above the migrations, invasions, and pilgrimages of earlier societies were the rise of cities and "the discovery of new worlds and the movement to frontiers" (p. 199). In Fergusson's account, both the movement to the frontiers over two centuries and the reverse movement during the "last century . . . from the peripheries toward the centers" were means of sorting the population. Whereas the move westward was primarily a movement of families, the move back to the cities is an individual movement. Such a conviction reflects the experience of three generations of his family: the movements of his grandfather Huning; his father, H. B. Fergusson; and he himself back and forth between the Southwest, the East, and the Far West of California. Throughout his discussion of cities, home, and individual mobility, his argument in favor of mobility for "footloose" wanderlust comes to take on the specific outlines of his own autobiographical "destiny," and destiny works as a central theme in much of his fiction.

Over a period of one generation, Fergusson reports that he watched Albuquerque grow from a village of a few thousand to a city of thirty-five thousand (in his later years he saw it grow to a metropolis of over two hundred thousand). Inherent in that change are all the forces of conformity and chaos, stability and imbalance—people arriving, people staying, people leaving. Using Darwinian assumptions and vocabulary, Fergusson allows for the "social forces" which permit a certain kind of local individual "who is genuinely adapted to the environment" to stay there, allows for the individual who leaves for the larger city but returns, and also allows for the person who arrives from rural communities and sees potential for growth even in a relatively larger town. Yet even while allowing for such forces and complexity, Fergusson values most the individual who strikes out in search of larger freedom and reward, the person who leaves the confining, stultifying town; and he identifies with the elite few who leave for larger horizons of personal growth—that is, Fergusson himself as he apprises it. It is a type nourished in the opening and closing of the frontier and found in numerous instances in his fiction. The dynamic of social forces in the changing city provides the kernel of conflict in several of Fergusson's novels, most notably *Hot Saturday* and *The Life of Riley* as autobiographical parables of Albuquerque's small-mindedness. In both instances he projects himself into characters, female and male respectively, who stay in Albuquerque but thumb their noses at its social strictures.

Much of what he says in his sketch of social and historical change in his hometown shares certain assumptions with the Darwinism of Turner's recurrent frontier thesis—but it is extended past the announced closing of the frontier in 1890. It underscores, on the one hand, his own wanderlust and, on the other hand, his need during the 1920s, especially, to return to his roots yearly. Fergusson, in both *Modern Man* and *People and Power*, sees modern society on a graded scale of interaction and flux in relation to the development and closing of the frontier. Relying on an analogy from physics, he compares the comprehension of matter to the understanding of society as a dynamic phenomenon: "Perhaps society will finally be understood as a pattern of ordered movement and ordered change rather than as a stable arrangement" (p. 205).

As important as Albuquerque was to Fergusson as a boyhood home, and as important as it and the geography and history of the surrounding region were for his fiction, "home" for him—and for his representative modern frontiersman—was, in the traditional sense, an anachronism. Any loss of a sense of roots is seen as a relative matter involving an exchange for greater freedom. His own life as a writer takes on clearer outline against such a perspective as this.

Modern Man represents an accessible integration of Fergusson's autobiography and his philosophy, as well as one of the theoretical springboards from which comes a better knowledge of Fergusson's literature and life. It is a book which is also something of an apologia for the direction his life had taken up to 1937, before middle age turned toward old age. As he grew older, it became even more obvious that he could not escape his frontier heritage. Such a book may also be read as a manifesto of the independence he gained through writing. Leaving the region of his birth and family roots was imperative for him—just as it was necessary to return time and again in his fictions and histories.

Unlike the ricos and their family system which so captured his imagination, Fergusson faced life as his own man, strengthened by an illustrious pioneer family heritage but destined to face society and make his own mark as a writer. Such a sentiment illustrates the double directions of the resourcefulness, the self-reliance, needed just as much by a modern frontiersman as by the mountain men and settlers on the other side of a fascinating line moving through time and space and known as the American frontier.

POWER AND PIONEERS

People and Power (1947) also clarifies some of the beliefs and assumptions in Fergusson's life and literature. It mirrors his attempt to face the world as he found it, in his mid-fifties, in the aftermath of World War II. In this book he struggles further with the roles and relationships of the individual and the group—relationships seen in the interactions of three cultures in the Southwest as well as in national politics, which he covered as a Washington reporter. His thesis is simple: "All power is organization and all organization is power" (p. 101). Advertisements for *People and Power* at the time of publication appealed to the reader's desire to restore his or her position in the organizational power structure of the world.[18] The changes brought about by the war heightened such a desire and are addressed by Fergusson throughout in his analyses of organizations. Linked to those analyses is his commentary on the causality of power in American life in relation to the pioneer and the opening and closing of the frontier. The urgency of the need to understand such forces is incorporated in the sales promotion of the book: "*People and Power* restores . . . a severely threatened balance: it analyzes the texture of American society from the point of view of the individual citizen."[19]

As with *Modern Man*, reviewers neglected to point out, if they realized it, either the autobiographical elements of the work or the author's interest in the American frontier. Among critics, Pilkington does not delve into autobiographical elements but does note Fergusson's insistence that the rugged individualists of the frontier era "were either incapable or unwilling to function as part of the social organization," and that ideas about the American dream and individual freedom, growing out of romanticized myths about wilderness and frontier, were ineffective in the twentieth century. Pilkington sees Fergusson's comments about the utopian promise of twentieth-century cities as being as wrong-headed and as mistaken as some of his prophecies about the future in *Modern Man*.[20]

Many of Fergusson's arguments and observations in *Power* are based on his experience and understanding of the American West and the frontier. In his chapter on individual liberty his thesis is that it was not so much the search for religious or political liberty which caused European emigration to America in the eighteenth century or the westering across the country in the nineteenth; rather, it was the lure of land, real estate (a reality he witnessed in his grandfather Huning and his father, and a theme he dramatizes in even his modern Westerns like *Riley*): "The whole western movement, from the first crossing of the Alleghenies to the last wave of dry-farm homesteaders, was a search for real property and for the right to own it and use it" (p. 18). Fergusson's "wave" metaphor is also Turner's—as is the belief that the key to American development was the "ever retreating frontier of free land." And Fergusson continues to parallel Turner in stating that the need for free land developed individualism and contributed to the growth of democracy. Fergusson cites Vernon Parrington and not Turner as a source; however, similarities with Turner's ideas about the significance of the frontier in explaining American history are just as frequent in *Power* as they are in *Modern Man*.

Fergusson argues in *People and Power* that just as the westering movement resulted from a search for private property, it was also motivated by the need for the individual to escape from the government—the Turnerian safety valve. Turner says much about the role of public domain and what translates into the "impulse of avoidance."

In his continuing review of American historical change from his mid-life vantage point (analogous to his own personal closing of the frontier of his childhood and youth), Fergusson returns again and again to assay the influences of the frontier. He goes beyond Turnerian speculation about the consequences of the closing of the frontier and of the "first period of American history," in attempting to account for how it affects him and all modern citizens. In his assessment, after the end of the frontier, population mobility ceased for a time until, in the early twentieth century, farm populations began pouring into cities. Then, during World War II mobility reached its high point, "when manpower was found to be almost as fluid as spilled milk, running all over the country in response to need and opportunity, requiring direction on a national scale" (p. 36). But Fergusson insists that while the closing of the frontier was significant, it was not the main factor causing the changes in twentieth-century American life. In this context, he joins, a half-century later, the controversy which followed in the wake of Turner's belief that the frontier was the single most important factor in the interpretation of American history, that "the true point of view in the history of the nation is not the Atlantic coast, it is the great West": "It has been said many times that the closing of the frontier is the main factor in the change which has come over American life. Change has also been ascribed to the fact that we are now a 'mature' society, which has stopped growing. This is hotly denied by others, who proclaim that we are on the verge of some great growth or expansion, of a kind never exactly specified. Both of these common arguments seems [*sic*] to be beside the point. The closing of the frontier is certainly a factor in change, but it is not in itself the main one" (p. 37).

In addition to the changes in American society caused by the desire for property and the rise of individualism—a phenomenon which increased with the opening of the frontier and lessened with its closing—another factor is important in Fergusson's own life history: the decline of the family. The decline of the family clearly weighs heavily on his mind as a major cause and effect in the process of change as discussed in both *Modern Man* and *Power*. He repeatedly illustrates his point with the instance of the decline of the "great houses" of the

Spanish ricos. The parallel with the rise and fall of the Huning-Fergusson "dynasty" at the turn of the century in Albuquerque is also apparent and contributed to Fergusson's own interest in the subject as a writer, especially as presented in the "epic" rise and fall of the Lucien Maxwell household in *Grant of Kingdom*.

Considerable proportions of *Power* deal with the respective mercantile and political successes and failures of Fergusson's grandfather, Franz Huning, and his father, H. B. Fergusson. Although Fergusson was glad to leave home, in the spirit of emancipation from family and small-town life, his family tragedies, the ends of their individual frontiers which were tinted with the darkness of depression and suicide, in addition to his two ill-fated marriages—all of these take on a tone of tough-skinned but poignant resolve to go on, highlighted against the universalized discussion of family change and dissolution discussed in *Power* and *Modern Man*. The decline of the traditional family and the individual male's separation from its security or suffocation, in addition to any resultant loss of inheritance, work as major themes throughout Fergusson's novels.

The private enterprise and entrepreneurship which enabled Franz Huning to build his castle is, Fergusson suggests, no longer possible. His analysis and assumptions are, again, cast in terms similar to Turner's: "The means of production then were free to every man. The earth and its fruits belonged to who could use them. Private enterprise was then truly both a right and an opportunity accessible to all. So a great tradition was founded. The tradition still lives but the condition had passed forever" (p. 50). But at the same time he says he holds few romantic misconceptions about the nature of rugged individualism on the frontier. His assessment of the frontier is characteristic of a man looking back at a past that excluded him from its opportunity. In his demythologized picture of the West, Fergusson portrays the American frontier as fostering comparative anarchy more than true individual freedom: "This negative character is perfectly illustrated in our pioneer tradition of personal freedom and rugged individualism. A whole mythical pioneer world has been invented to support it. All romantic and popular writing about pioneer days is full of references to its glorious freedom, based upon its lack of restraint.

But no one who has plodded through the documentary evidence of the character of pioneer life, as I have done in search of material for novels, can come away with the idea that it produced a genuine individual liberty" (p. 64). Thus, the frontier in Fergusson's extended expository arguments is regarded ambivalently, as involving destruction and death as well as continuation and hope. He looked back to it with a sense of loss and tragedy tempered by release and triumph; he was of the frontier and beyond it at the same time: "The westward movement of our own civilization could be dramatized as another example of [the] conflict [of machine versus nature]. Pioneering was truly a rape of the earth, destroying not only forests and wild life, but the soil itself. In fact, all pioneering is a kind of slow-burning warfare, in which men fight wild animals and the earth as well as each other. And yet behind the frontier came always men moved by a dream of order, men who built things and cultivated the earth with love and care, men who created the forms they imagined and added to life instead of destroying it" (p. 216).

Like the men of the frontier's end who "created the forms they imagined," what Fergusson lived he transformed into writing. The end of the frontier, the historical mutability it instanced, serves not just as a slogan for his philosophy, but as a metaphor helpful in explaining his life as a person and as a part of a family, a society, and a region in significant transition.

FRONTIER TRAGEDY

Any literary biography which attempts to gauge the real and imaginary significance of the frontier's ending on a writer's life and art must rely, at least in part, on Harold P. Simonson's *The Closed Frontier*.[21] Although Simonson is most directly concerned with Turner's thesis and the effects of the closed frontier on Emerson, Melville, Dickinson, Twain, Rölvaag, and Nathanael West, what he says has important implications for Fergusson as well. Simonson proposes that if the open frontier meant Edenic freedom and hope—that is, the American dream—then the closed frontier is equated with tragedy, experience, and the nation's coming of age: "The existentialism symbolized by a closed frontier replaces the idealism engendered on an open frontier. Instead of a limitless frontier there is a wall. The tension comes from the illusory prospect on the one hand and the certitude on the other. Existence in this tension is the heart of tragedy" (p. 6).

This is not to suggest that Fergusson is solely a tragic writer. In a sense he came of age before his birth, finding upon his arrival that the end had already come. In a sense he came of age in his denial of the romanticism he missed, as he was ushered into a realistic, technological, accelerating world—whether he wanted to move with it or not. In a sense he never came of age, always attempting to escape his heritage by wandering from city to city, and yet incapable of forgetting what the land and the legends of his birthright bequeathed him as a son and grandson of frontiersmen. He considered himself a realist and something of a hedonist, a fun-seeker who loved dancing and swimming, the outdoors, bright sun and fresh air, and pleasures of the body— sexual and athletic—as well as those of the mind—a self-styled "thinking man" with an ability and inclination to act. In his realism he accepted his present and was ready for whatever the future held, sought to meet it and shape it. Yet as a romantic he was continually drawn back into the past and into the transcendental transportations allowed by solitude and the wilderness.

His romanticism is often elegiac, bemoaning not just the days he lost but the days he never had, and has a strain of brooding disappointment, almost cynicism, which manifested itself in his tendency to satirize and question, to analyze and criticize his own idealism and that of the entire frontier mythos. And yet he was never truly disillusioned; he always maintained an exuberance to go on living, if for no other reason than to see what might turn up—"vamos a ver." Although Fergusson is not a fully tragic writer, all of these things do at least place him in a partially tragic vein associated with the closing of the frontier. Simonson points out that few readers of Turner's essay on the significance of the frontier see the "private agony" of Turner himself as a historian who sees the American dream change into something more violent and ugly than first envisioned—"the dream that to the West would always be a frontier where man could confront the new and raw environment and master it; and the fact that this geographic and psychological safety valve was shut tight" (p. 30).

Modern Man and *Power* demonstrate explicitly that Fergusson knew a similar private agony, the tension of which Simonson speaks. The more Fergusson experienced, as a remnant frontiersman become modern man, as a potential American Adam born too late into a fallen world but forced to accept a remodeled Eden; the more he pondered the tragedies of the closed frontier in his own transitional time; the more he struggled with his bit of history and attempted not so much to vault over its wall or reopen its closed door as to ride away from the process—the more he did this, the more he found himself writing right back into it in autobiography, in historical novel after historical novel, and in the novelistic history *Rio Grande*. All of his writings, although anchored in and often dramatizing twentieth-century urban life, always turned back, mournfully, satirically, and sometimes even tragically, to the older idealism of the frontier before its ending, before his own forced coming of age and a life described in his diaries as an "ordeal."

2

Huning Houses and Homes (1890–1906)

Franz Huning's life as a southwestern pioneer is surrounded by a legend colored by both fiction and fact, story and history. Huning's life figures so largely in regional history, and in Fergusson's own life and writings, that following Huning's life and the legend it has perpetuated is essential to an understanding of the ending of the frontier as Fergusson remembered it and tried to account for it in his life and fiction. Huning's world, his houses and homes, is the world into which Fergusson was born in 1890. It is a world at once in time and outside of time, a world Fergusson represented repeatedly in history and in story.

Aside from Fergusson's memories about Huning and his world, the extent of the Huning life history and its transcendence of pure history to legend and myth is most beautifully found today in Paul Horgan's short story "A Castle in New Spain"—a story which takes as its controlling image Huning's spectacular "castle," which he built over a period of three years in the early 1880s, and his earlier resi-

dence, an ancient and picturesque adobe hacienda known, appropriately enough, as "La Glorieta."[1]

Horgan moved to Albuquerque in 1915, ten years after Huning's
death. But Castle Huning still stood, and Horgan, in his close friendship with Francis Fergusson, Harvey's younger brother, associated
much of the civility which the Fergusson family represented with the
Huning legacy. For Horgan, "no more civilized family lived there
then or since."[2] Horgan's fictional counterpart for Franz Huning is
Anton Zahm, a characterization like all such composites of fact and
fantasy, which attempts to get at essences. Zahm's story is told in
roughly the same outline as Huning's own memoir,[3] from the time of
Zahm's arrival in New Mexico in the mid–nineteenth century as a
resourceful immigrant, until his death decades later, just into the
twentieth century—by which time he was recognized as one of the
area's most illustrious citizens. Albuquerque is portrayed as Los Al-
godones, a small river-valley town amidst the cottonwoods in the
upper Rio Grande Valley.

Zahm is characterized as a European exile determined to make his
name in New Mexico Territory. As a merchant, a husband, a father,
and a citizen, his personality and sensibility are those of a German
patriarch. His wife, Frieda—the endearing counterpart of Huning's
wife, Ernestine Franke Huning—loves Zahm deeply but resists what
she sees as his folly: building a castle in the style of those found in his
boyhood Germany. Once the patriarch decides on his dream house,
however, Frieda has little option but to follow his "law." Because of
her common sense and frugality, Anton's extravagance is tempered.
He constructs his ornate, strangely out-of-place castle. After his
death, Frieda, her two daughters, and her son manage to maintain an
impoverished gentility until the daughters are married and until the
son, Otto, decides to sell his father's land and estate for use as a new
airport.

Such a characterization of Zahm and his family only approximates the Huning family history. But essences are distilled; the legend
is nourished. The rise and fall of the Huning "kingdom" is dramatized simultaneously in broadly sweeping social-historical contexts
and in very personal, domestic husband-and-wife terms. Because of

this counterpoint, the changes in the town—especially those connected with the coming of the railroad—reflect the changes in the family, dramatized most obviously in the feudalistic attitudes of the father and the American, modern attitudes of the daughters and the son, Otto—who is a satirical counterpart to Huning's own son, Arno (1869–1936), who, upon inheriting the castle subdivided the Huning property for housing and commercial speculation, rather than for an airport.

Fergusson looked back at his youth and his grandfather's kingdom in romantic terms, that kingdom made all the more nostalgic and elegiac for the way it met its end. One of Fergusson's final fictions, a short story entitled "The Enchanted Meadow," reveals how, near the end of his life, he traveled back to his grandfather's kingdom and the spot where in an epiphany of landscape he decided he would become a writer. In Horgan's story, and in Fergusson's imagination and memory, Castle Huning was, in a phrase, a sight to behold. Huning, like his counterpart in Horgan's "Castle," had satisfied himself as an artist "who produced precisely the outward image of his inward conception."[4]

LIVING MUSEUMS

Franz Huning's life and times cast a long shadow over his grandson, Harvey Fergusson. Part of the extent of that influence is recorded in Fergusson's autobiography, *Home in the West: An Inquiry into My Origins* (1944).[5] Most literally, Fergusson's home was his grandfather's early home, La Glorieta, which he gave to Fergusson's father and mother shortly after the birth of their first child, Erna Mary Fergusson, in 1888. Erna was the only one of the four children of H. B. Fergusson and Clara Mary Huning who was born in Castle Huning. But Castle Huning also served as Fergusson's second home in his boyhood years. These two houses and homes blend together in memory and imagination as part of his encompassing home of Albuquerque, the West. After he grew older and left his western home for the East, Fergusson's early encounters with his real and legendary grandfather found their way into virtually all of his writings, fiction

Erna and Harvey Fergusson, ca. 1891. Courtesy of the Cobb Memorial
Collection, Special Collections Department, General Library, University of
New Mexico.

and history—writings which, in turn, continued to further the romantic legends associated with the Huning houses and homes.

Home, as book and as metaphor, is fundamental to any understanding of Fergusson's life—how he lived and wrote his life for
himself and for posterity. It too is a version of his life. Moreover, its
importance goes beyond any restricted interest in Fergusson alone.
Considered as autobiography, a genre with admittedly confused delin-

eations, *Home* is undeservedly neglected by commentators on the American experience and particularly on the westering experience as captured in autobiography and memoir.

Written past the halfway mark of his life (Fergusson was fifty-four when the book was published), *Home* came after a twenty-year career as a writer and after eight novels. At such a vantage point Fergusson can see, with the benefit of hindsight, and with skewed expectations for posterity, that his writings embody "a fable derived more or less directly from my own experience" (*Home*, p. 241).

He justifies establishing the boundaries of his autobiography at his first twenty-one years because his detachment in middle age from those years allows him a certain degree of objectivity and because that period of his life interests him for its process of rapid "change and growth." That "plastic" period coincided precisely with the first period of transition from the ending of the frontier into modern times. It is that period which shaped Fergusson more than any other period of his life and finds its way again and again, psychologically and thematically, into his writings, writings which are much more auto-biographical than he wants to allow.

In attempting to employ some kind of aesthetic form to supple-ment the distance which intervening years brought him, Fergusson in *Home* hits upon a synthesis of three autobiographies: his grand-father's, his father's, and his own. If, in his fiction, he did not always depend on "evidence," at least in his autobiography he attempts to stick to an outlined history of his family. To know him is to know his family's history. Whether or not this is a rationalization for his guarded refusal to delve into the intimacies of his grandfather's and father's lives is open to speculation. The fact that Fergusson is so objective in his "outline" that he neglects mentioning his younger brother, Francis Fergusson (1904–1986), and gives only the slightest nod to his sisters, Erna (1888–1964) and Lina (1895–1974); avoids any discussion of his father's suicide; cuts the story of his life short before the accidental death of his friend Frank Spitz and before his own two marriages—all this raises more questions than it answers about the "reliability" of his own "fabled" telling of his life. In relation to such concerns as sibling rivalry, divorce, accidental death,

death by illness, guilt, influences of forebears—in terms of all these, clearly he felt that his grandfather's and his father's westering was of the greatest importance.

Of greater importance are his own perceptions and developing self. Even in that regard, telling some things are forbidden, incapable of being put into words. He says about his rationale for dealing more subjectively with his own mind and emotions (and by implication his inability to speculate about the inner lives of his family—or to reveal the real traumas of his life): "When I came to myself I faced an entirely different challenge. Here the thing I had to describe was a process of becoming from the viewpoint of the subject. It seemed necessary to record what I had felt, for the impact of the forces that mold us is always emotional. Sometimes this was easy enough and sometimes it bordered upon the impossible. Especially when it came to describing my mystical experience and my early reactions to sex, the very words I needed seemed either lacking or forbidden" (pp. 246–47). So *Home* is an incomplete story, a mere impression of a consciousness and how it was determined. His fiction tells more of the story—but, again, not all.

Home had a curious reception among readers as autobiography. Many realized just how much the grandfather and father upstaged the grandson/son. Whose autobiography was this? Or was it really biography? Russell Maloney, writing for the *New Yorker*, said it best: "It's all there, except Fergusson."[6] James K. Folsom, in his pamphlet on Fergusson, gives *Home* more attention than any critic thus far. Engaging in a bit of psychologizing, Folsum sees Fergusson's portrayal of his grandfather Huning as "clearly an alter ego of Fergusson himself" insofar as he was "an intellectual, a lover of solitude and books, a man devoted to fact and logic, who, while taking active part in his own world, was never swallowed up by it." As for Fergusson's father, H. B. Fergusson, he is "the true opposite of the pioneer represented by Franz Huning," "a type of man often confused with [the pioneer]."[7] Folsom sees Fergusson's autobiography, then, as the story of his "gradual transferal of allegiance from that attitude toward the world represented by his father to that represented by Franz Huning": if the father represented allegiance to the past of the Old South, the grandfather represented belief in the future, and that essential "conflict between these two attitudes toward experience becomes a basic theme in most of Fergusson's fiction."[8] Folsom dichotomizes grandfather and father and their alliances a bit too drastically—or sees Fergusson as doing so—for both men were mixtures of their own special pasts and futures. But he is right in his insight into *Home* and into its thematic application to Fergusson's fiction. What Folsom fails to note, in the total scope of Fergusson's life, is that the final conflict was won by the past, especially during the last twenty years of Fergusson's life. The "autobiographies" he wrote at that time—especially *The Land of Lonely Women* and "The Enchanted Meadow"— lapse into sentimentality and nostalgia for adolescence in a much less controlled way than *Home*.

It is precisely in all the knotted motifs of *Home*—in Fergusson's attraction to the frontier times of his grandfather, in the attraction to his father's frontier experiences in White Oaks and Albuquerque but rebellion from his father's Old South ideals, in his escape from small-town social pressures to conform, and in his escape into nature and the outdoors so sublimely present in the Southwest—that the material for Fergusson's autobiography, for his historical novels, and for his history of northern New Mexico, *Rio Grande*, reside. Thus, the end of the frontier as it affected his life is a complex network of causality, tied to a definition of past, present, and future which is confused by the relativity of starting points. Furthermore, throughout his account of his own youthful sexuality and his shy avoidance of yet inevitable attraction to women are the clues and original contexts for the many loves, hates, and sexual "conquests" which serve as the plots for his fiction.

This is not to say that *Home* should be read exclusively as a handbook for locating autobiographical patterns and parallels with Fergusson's fictive characters and plots, or as the sole blueprint for a literary biography. He neglected (or avoided) telling the fullest possible story of his life, even within the twenty-one-year boundary he established. But in spite of its reticences and because of its revelations *Home* is successful on its own terms as the autobiography of a Westerner who also happened to become a modern American writer.

Certainly *Home* is focused on the beautiful and the bad aspects of Albuquerque as Fergusson's birthplace. He was deeply imprinted by the southwestern scene—the landscape, the sky, the mountains, mesas, and rivers. He opens his autobiography with the chapter "Home Is a Country" and paints an admiring picture of the view of Albuquerque and its surrounding landmarks as seen from the West Mesa, overlooking—from one of its sandhill bluffs—the Rio Grande. This spot, the spot from which he begins his autobiography and his perspective on it, is something of a shrine. It is a special spot in that Fergusson revisited it almost every year over a period of forty years. What that spot nurtures in him, he says, is the belief that the land endures and remains relatively changeless. At the time he was writing *Home* he lived in Berkeley, but his life had for many years taken on the pattern of leaving the West and returning to it—a rhythm of many years of going away and coming back, each East-West urge as mysterious in its way as the migrations of the waterfowl he loved to hunt.

So it was that during the time Fergusson lived in the East, homesickness and nostalgia were common emotions for him, as they are for many of the characters in his novels. Insofar as he identified with the Southwest, he can be regarded as a romantic with a disposition stamped forever by the region in which he was born. For Fergusson the East was equated with buildings, the atmosphere of the metropolis epitomized by New York. The West was essentially mountains as he knew them when he worked for the United States Forest Service. During his eight years as a journalist-novelist in New York, he traveled west to the mountains in the summer. Just how thoroughly the mountains of the Southwest were scored on his soul is seen in his inevitable return to them. He said he enjoyed the East and its cities and was determined to make and meet his future there as a clear-eyed realist; but the Southwest and its mountains always pulled him back, for they were at the core of his romanticism and were always waiting with their own kind of mystical and native greeting.

If mountains, space, and air all worked their way on Fergusson's soul and on his imagination and romantic sensibilities, so too did history and the longing for the pasts that were known to him by virtue of family legend. Franz Huning was his closest personal tie with the frontier, and Fergusson is quick to point out just how deep and lasting were his grandfather's influence and the remnants of the frontier which carried over into a boy's life:

New Mexico then was a wild country but it was also one with a long and picturesque history. It was littered with relics of its own past, living and dead. My grandfather's place abounded in decaying souvenirs of the days before the railroad. One of the old Murphy freight wagons that traveled the Santa Fe trail, with its six-foot wheels and heavy tongue, slowly fell to pieces in his yard. There were moth-eaten buffalo robes in his attic and guns he had carried against the Indians in the office at his mill. I lived in Old Town among people who belonged to the past—surviving families of the old Mexican aristocracy who still cherished their pretensions and their hand-hammered silver, and poor Mexicans of Indian blood who still believed in witchcraft and prayed for rain. I was born in a house which was a part of the town before the American conquest. My grandfather bought it soon after he came to Albuquerque and it was then said to be more than a century old. It was built of adobe with walls three feet thick, a flat earthen roof, bare rafters, and long wooden waterspouts. Originally it consisted only of two wings but my grandfather built two more, enclosing a courtyard in the Mexican fashion. An adjoining rectangle was surrounded by an adobe wall ten feet high with minor buildings inside it. They doubtless housed the peons in the old days. We used them to store coal, wood, and chicken feed. (pp. 8–9)

This house, these objects, and this scene of La Glorieta figure prominently in many of Fergusson's novels, especially *In Those Days* (1929). Both La Glorieta and Castle Huning, as houses and as homes, tend to fuse in this remembering, both becoming "my grandfather's place." It seems that even as a boy Fergusson regarded them as such, roaming often from La Glorieta—where he was born on January 28, 1890, and where he lived for the first eighteen years of his life—to Castle Huning, across the road to the south, where he explored the remnant frontier found in the attic, adventured into all the nooks and crannies of the romantic castle, sallied forth into the alfalfa fields, climbed the cottonwoods, and threaded through the Russian olives and willows along the river which served as a western boundary for the castle grounds. The flat roof of La Glorieta was a special place of

mystery, romance, and escape too, for it was there that he would seek
solitude, sit in the shade of the large cottonwood in the yard, read,
look at the mesa, the volcanoes, and the mountains, daydream, and
draw pictures.

In Fergusson's rememberings, his youth was that of an interloper,
part of but separate from the mixing of cultures which found the
"invading gringos" occupying "the shell of the dying Spanish culture" (p. 10). It is this clash of cultures which accounts for some of the
alienation sensed in his life and in the lives of many of his "gringo,"
vagabond protagonists. It is a logical consequence of his youth as a
member of the patriarchial gringo culture that his fiction dwells on the
ricos and the *pobres* of northern New Mexico. The Armijo family
which so dominated Old Town, people like the "wizened little Mexican" identified as Juan Gomez, who lived in the foothills of the Sandia
Mountains east of Albuquerque and whom Fergusson, as a boy, visited, represented even older frontiers. While the ricos and the Mexican aristocracy were in a waning stage of their culture by the end of the
nineteenth century, people like Fergusson's friend, "Gomez," were
changeless, enduring like the land. From *The Blood of the Conquerors*
(1921), his first novel, to *The Conquest of Don Pedro* (1954), his last
published novel, he immortalizes them under many an alias.

In addition to the Hispanic culture of Old Town, Fergusson
absorbed the ambiance of the Pueblo Indians and their dances and the
mystical brotherhood of the penitentes—and those cultures too per-
vade his writings. He explains his first-hand experience of frontier
history as a lingering but living history, essential to his outlook and the
formation of his personality: "The country as a whole was a living
museum of its own history. This, I am sure, gave me an impression of
time and change I would otherwise have lacked" (p. 12). That history,
that autobiographical legend and landscape, came by way of genealogical prologue in the form of Fergusson's grandfather, Franz Huning,
"curator" of more than one living museum.

FRANZ HUNING

The opening chapters of *Home* amount to a retelling of Franz Huning's life, interspersed with commentary about Fergusson's life as a

kind of inside-out image of his grandfather's life: two lives, past and present, old and young, juxtaposed. While he narrates Huning's life—relying on his grandfather's at that time unpublished memoir (later edited by Fergusson's sister, Lina Fergusson Browne, and published as *Trader on the Santa Fe Trail*) and relying on his own rememberings—Fergusson is struck by what he sees as similarities of blood, temperament, and calling between himself and his grandfather. As usual, time made a difference:

> *He and I were in boyhood about as similar as two so far apart in space and time could possibly be. It is even more striking how differently we were used by a changing world which seems to form and wield the individual as its instrument. He was carried West by a worldwide migration which infected a whole generation with its restless spirit. The backwash of that same great expansion took me to the cities. They were my only possible frontier. He did his necessary work as a pioneer but remained all his life an amateur student and writer. I have written millions of words and still go into the mountains with a gun, seeking some minor fulfillment for a half-thwarted impulse toward action and physical adventure. (p. 16)*

Fergusson portrays his grandfather as a writer-adventurer, a scholar who might have made a good anthropologist had he not sacrificed that capability to pioneering. Huning's fascination with the Spanish-Mexican cultures which he found as a stranger in the strange land of New Mexico and which so pervades his memoir as a special strain of exoticism is continued in Fergusson's writings. What Huning lived and "studied" in the Hispanic culture and language he found on his arrival in the Southwest, Fergusson grew up with and transferred by means of his own kind of scholarship into his historical novels. He suggests that Huning was not only a friend but something of a "colleague" of Adolph Bandelier in his studies (and, in turn, Bandelier, as well as other historic personages in Huning's background, including Kit Carson, make their appearances in Fergusson's fiction). Fergusson devoted much of his life as a writer to erecting a monument to his grandfather and his accomplishment as a prototypic pioneer trader—a monument made all the larger by its rising out of the truth of fiction.

Fergusson sees Huning as an "intellectual" pioneer both suited to and misplaced on the frontier. It is a portrait consonant with

Fergusson's own image of himself perpetuated by his own analogs of his fiction; and it is a portrait in keeping with the archetypal frontiersman, Daniel Boone, as explained by Smith and Slotkin. But that portrait is only half a figure. Fergusson dwells too on the businessman and entrepreneur in his grandfather. Huning's adventures on the frontier included building a large and prosperous mercantile business that reached out into other areas of enterprise (e.g., store, sawmill, flour mill, bridge construction, newspaper, etc.) in a growing town strategically located on the trails and rails of commerce. Heard in his descriptions of the rise of his grandfather's commercial kingdom are the notes of Fergusson's own delight and dismay at the coming and going of such fortunes made "in those days." All his life he maintained an interest in business and finance, motivated in part by a fear of poverty brought on by the financial straits in which his father eventually found himself and by the final dwindling away of the Huning estate—both part of his personal frontier's end.

Fergusson's diaries show notes on the stock market and on possible investments, and he banked enough of his pay as a Hollywood screenwriter in the mid-thirties and early forties to see him through his final twenty years. But he never had his grandfather's financial prosperity. Fergusson believed that the potential for wealth offered by the free enterprise of his grandfather's era was closed to him. The Huning family fortune, a fortune which at one time included ownership of much of the land which became downtown Albuquerque, never made its way as a legacy to Fergusson; and that lost fortune added to the tragedy he associated with the closing of the frontier and its potential. His destiny was to remember those days of prosperous enterprise, of "kingdoms" and fortunes made and lost, and to make that rise and fall, rendered in various degrees and kinds, one of the great themes of his novels, especially *Grant of Kingdom* (1950) and *The Conquest of Don Pedro* (1954). Fergusson views his grandfather as a man who, although he had the sensibilities of a writer, was still up to the challenge and opportunity of his time.

In keeping with his nature as a man of imagination and of action, Huning's grand desire to build Castle Huning was, in Fergusson's view, the effort of an artist giving shape to his memories, recreating the environment of his boyhood Germany. In its construction as the ideal made tangible, it not only satisfied the most heartfelt longings of a successful yet solitary old man, but it also provided an idyllic boyhood setting for Fergusson, offering all that a future writer of fictions might need. The castle and its "enchanted meadows" made for a microcosmic Eden, a wondrous place with its own savage and civilized, real and imaginary, stimulations.

The realization soon appears in Fergusson's accounts of Castle Huning and the castle grounds of just how Huning, in nourishing his own past, nourished his grandson's imagination and thus his destiny as a writer. With its indigenous forest of cottonwoods and its planted woods of poplars; its green and fragrant alfalfa fields; its Osage orange, catalpas, Japanese umbrella trees, Persian walnuts, fruit orchards of crabapple and cherry trees; its long canopies and trellises of vineyards; its aviary with a bizarre collection of birds; its bordering river with lazy currents to swim in and sandbars to rest on; its little stream, bridge, and pond with a flock of white geese (Horgan's story insists they were swans)—with such exotic abundance and variety, Fergusson never forgot the spectacle of the place and the man who imagined it, claimed it, and made it. If Castle Huning was Huning's frontier Xanadu, it was also his grandson's. In Fergusson's memory it was a virtual paradise, a sanctuary beyond his dreaming.

But what was Huning's and his grandson's glory soon deteriorated in the wake of the changes wrought by the railroad and the booming fortunes of New Town. Had Huning been able to outlive the ending of the frontier and capitalize on the business deals and wealth made possible by the growing metropolis, he probably would have become a multimillionaire. As it was, he became more withdrawn and reclusive in his final years, possessively patrolling his property and firing his shotgun into the air at fleeing trespassers. Huning's fortunes in New Town real estate, Castle Huning, and other investments were not bequeathed to Fergusson's branch of the family. Fergusson, however, had his legacy: an inheritance of the imagination, of memory, of romantic reverence for the outdoors and nature, of a comprehension of the vagaries of history, of a grandson's past which was his grandfather's future—both of them coinciding with the end of the frontier.

SANTA FE TRADER

In addition to *Home*, much has been written about the Huning legend. Regional historians, architects, and journalists have all added to what we know about Franz Huning, his life, and his era. Lina Fergusson Browne, just before her own death by a stroke in October 1974, saw through to publication the memoirs of her grandfather. *Trader on the Santa Fe Trail* is an invaluable resource—not merely for the specifics of chronology and event, but for what it reveals about Huning and his adventures as a Santa Fe trader on the southwestern frontier.[9] Huning's wife, Ernestine Franke Huning (1837–1923), and his daughter, Clara M. Huning Fergusson (1865–1950), Fergusson's mother, also felt compelled as "self-conscious" pioneers to record many of their memories. When all of these memoirs are considered in relation to Fergusson's *Home*, the influence of Huning and the two homes he made for his family take on even fuller force. Taken together, these memoirs, published and unpublished, are a treasure trove in the annals of American autobiography written in response to the ending of the American frontier in the Southwest.

Huning was one of four brothers who emigrated to the Southwest from Melle, Hanover, Germany, in the nineteenth century. Northern New Mexico and eastern Arizona came to be the places in which they chose to settle, and, as it turned out, prosper. (Only one of the four brothers, Charles, returned to Germany.) The stories of all the Huning brothers are interesting as frontier experiences; however, Franz recorded more of his experiences, and for present purposes, his is more relevant. Franz (1827–1905) and his younger brother, Charles (1832–94), were the first to come to the United States, arriving in 1848, the year of the ratification of the Treaty of Guadalupe Hidalgo. Relatively soon they and their cousin, E. B. Franz, had established mercantile businesses in both Albuquerque and Los Lunas, a smaller town some twenty miles south of Albuquerque. The next brother, Louis (1834–1901), arrived in the United States in the mid-1850s and worked his way across the prairies, reaching New Mexico territory in 1854; and after clerking for Franz and Charles Huning in Albuquerque, he joined the Los Lunas business of E. B. Franz as a partner in 1861. He

Lina Fergusson Browne. Courtesy of Francis and Peggy Fergusson.

later purchased the Los Lunas business in another partnership and after eight months bought full ownership. The youngest brother, Henry, born in 1838, was for a time a partner with Louis in the Los Lunas store. When they dissolved their partnership in 1888, their combined worth was valued at $750,000.[10] The story behind the end of that partnership is known only vaguely, but apparently Louis and Henry parted as enemies. The commercial frontier kingdoms built by Louis and Henry Huning epitomize the realization of the frontier promise of land and independence which Turner and Fergusson discuss. Franz Huning's kingdom was less sweeping, concentrated in what became the downtown and Highland sections of Albuquerque. Rather than extending into the control of future generations, like Louis Huning's mercantile business, Franz Huning's holdings took on a special quaintness, almost eccentricity, pointed paradoxically in the directions of the past and the future, as symbolized by his castle.

All of the Huning kingdoms influenced Fergusson, whether materially or mythologically. Fergusson had a special fondness for Louis's son, Fred D. Huning, and his grandson, Fred D. Huning, Jr., and their discussions about sheep ranching and business matters not only provided a contrasting role model to H. B. Fergusson, but also gave him much material and another character prototype for his writing. Louis Huning achieved his own special historical importance in Los Lunas and was clearly regarded as a "prominent pioneer . . . and a self-made man"—another builder and civilizer and representative of many such characters who made their way into Fergusson's novels. The successes of Henry Huning, also in the mercantile business, added further imaginative force to the saga of the Hunings, Henry's playing out of the American dream of acquisition on the frontier took place in Arizona—more remote to Fergusson and somewhat before his time.[11]

The frontier adventures of all the Huning brothers are magnified in that they came to the Southwest in the late 1800s and made their mark as brothers, joined together—at least initially—in a great family enterprise. But they all owed much to Franz as the eldest. The other brothers are more or less individually eclipsed by Franz, not so much because his rise and demise outstripped theirs in romantic and legendary style in the larger and faster-changing metropolis of Albuquerque as because his grandchildren did much in a public way through their writings to solidify his name and memory. There are, admittedly, different realms of publicity—and fame comes and goes regardless of words and books. But Franz Huning bothered to write his memoir, and his grandchildren—inclined as they were also to write—further immortalized that life.

Some of the details of Huning's memoir are necessary to know, and they are offered here by way of summary. They are interesting in and of themselves but, more important, they help us understand what shaped the mind and imagination of his grandson as a modern frontiersman, a writer-adventurer. For many years Huning's memoir existed only as a solidly bound daybook, its pages filled with the bold, heavily inked handwriting of an old man who had done much, had accomplished his dream, and had much to report. When Fergusson came to write the autobiography of his own youth, his grandfather's memoir existed mainly for the family. Fergusson was content merely to summarize and report in his own voice—although that often takes on the sound of Huning's voice—to retell his grandfather's remarkable if not "heroic" life story.

Huning was born and grew up as a farm boy in Dielingdorf near Melle in the principality of Bauerschaft, Germany. The sixth child of thirteen in his family, he worked hard, herded cows, and walked the woods by himself. He tells of reading travel books while stretched out under a tree, oblivious to the cows and his duties on the farm. Such a pastoral scene is reminiscent of the bosque along the Rio Grande which ran behind the grounds of Castle Huning, and of young Fergusson's time spent there and on the roof of La Glorieta in his own boyhood—a scene which replays itself in various wilderness scenes in Fergusson's fiction. It is clear, too, that Huning tried to replicate his own ancestral home in Melle in building Castle Huning. An untiring reader and a generally smart lad, Huning went to school at the age of nine and soon, he says, was at the top of his class. The outdoors and books were reconcilable—a combination which accounts for Fergusson's and his own versions of the archetypal intelligent frontiersmen. Throughout the account of his childhood, Huning stresses the importance of books and how that preoccupation even at times interfered with his attention to the lessons of the classroom. Again, the pattern matches Fergusson's dislike of school, especially military school, and his avowed tendency to daydream.

At the age of fourteen Huning left public school for a private school, where he was taught French and English. After two years at that school he decided that he would go into the mercantile business and was apprenticed for three years in a grocery, tobacco, and linen business. He describes himself as a bashful boy, not entirely suited to sales work and meeting the public. In 1847 he moved to Bremen and began thinking more seriously about an idea which he had first had during his apprenticeship: emigrating to the United States.

In 1848 he and his brother Charles left Germany for the *United States* with passage on the *Oneco*, an American sailing ship. Huning never saw his father or many other members of his family again. Even during the adventure of the sea voyage Huning felt the inclination to write an admiring verse about the ship's figurehead, an Indian warrior. He would soon meet flesh-and-blood Indians. The personality of the writer-adventurer which so imprinted Fergusson is dramatized again in such an anecdote. The *Oneco* docked in New Orleans, and the Huning brothers took a steamer up the Mississippi to St. Louis, arriving in January 1849. There they looked up some family acquaintances and were soon settled in jobs. Franz secured a position in the drygoods store of C. & F. Kunsemiller, and Charles found a job in a drugstore.

In September 1849 Franz Huning answered a call issued from the quartermaster of Fort Leavenworth for teamsters to drive mules to Santa Fe and on to California. He applied but wound up as a bullwhacker for a freight contractor hauling government stores to Santa Fe. It was an occupation much extolled in family lore. Ready to "see the elephant," as the metaphor for westering had it, Huning was determined to take the job, for it would take him across the plains— perhaps as far west as California. He signed on for thirty dollars a month and food. For ten days he practiced whacking and could soon use the ten-foot-long whips to some purpose.

On October 8, 1849, he set out across the plains from Fort

Leavenworth headed for Santa Fe along the Santa Fe Trail. Ten days out he arrived in Council Grove. In late November he reached Barclay's fort on the Mora River. Those were the two main settlements before Las Vegas, and Santa Fe, New Mexico.

Although he began as the stereotypical greenhorn, he soon learned how to yoke oxen, mend whips, make keys for the bows, and cuss like the trail veterans. He worked the night watch and enjoyed the less arduous tasks of a day herder. He endured the ribbing of the old hands, long stretches without water, lack of sleep and physical discomfort, and the worry of Indian harassment. At one point he carried a shotgun on night guard but realized afterwards that he had neglected to load it. He perpetuated the myth of his own inadequacy with the use of firearms because, he suggests, he was not a violent man. This scenario—archetypal in stories of westering—is utilized endless times by Fergusson: a greenhorn heads west and is transformed. He toughens up, sometimes regaining his health, changes in appearance, and is accepted by the naturals and older initiates. Robert Jayson and Leo Mendes are but two cases in point. Even in Fergusson's mountain men, Sam Lash and Jean Ballard, this transformation is noticeable and used to considerable effect in further romanticizing the West as a place of health and growth. Although violence is part of the scene, Fergusson's heroes are better suited to smart thinking than fast shooting.

By December 1849 the wagon train reached Las Vegas, a town of strange appearance to Huning. The houses were squat and all built alike of the same red adobe. In his words, the town "looked like a brick yard."[12] As his need to construct Castle Huning proved, Germanic architecture was much more to his liking than indigenous pueblo or Spanish territorial architecture.

Santa Fe was even more exotic than Las Vegas to the eyes of the young German. Huning entered the streets of that city on Christmas Day behind a partial team of three oxen. The local women commented on what a sorrowful sight the "muchachito pobrecito" made on his grand entry into the Royal City. For a man who would come to add much to the history of the region, in something of the same tradition of W. W. H. Davis's *El Gringo* and Josiah Gregg's *Commerce of the*

Franz Huning as a frontiersman. Courtesy of Li Caemmerer.

Prairies, his down-and-out arrival is subliminally reminiscent of Benjamin Franklin's arrival in Philadelphia. Huning had to be informed that Santa Fe was in New Mexico, not New Mexico in Santa Fe. Since winter prevented his continuing on to California, he stayed in Santa Fe and observed it with all the curiosity of a red-blooded youth in a strange land, an autobiographical archetype of arrival and initiation which remains as fresh in each telling as it is common in the annals of American literature.

Huning's description of his first days in Santa Fe is one of the most pleasurable and most significant portions of his autobiography. James Pattie, Gregg, Davis, and countless others have recorded their reactions to northern New Mexico. And to their accounts must be added Huning's first look, which augmented the accounts of other frontiersmen and provided imaginative source materials for Fergusson's narrated accounts of other arrivals. Huning's account affords a glimpse of just how remote yet vital a place like Santa Fe was in the middle of the nineteenth century. He had several companions on his foray, among them one friend named C. P. Cleaver and another named Louis Bartels. Like Huning, they were young men finding their niche in the promise of the frontier. Fergusson captures this "side-kick" theme of camaraderie in all of his frontier fiction. Huning's descriptions give considerable attention to regional architecture, to the houses, churches, and businesses, the streets and buildings he saw. All of this explains Fergusson's yearning for a home like Castle Huning and how he was able to use his grandfather's word pictures almost as if they were a photo album spread out in front of him as he wrote.

As Huning tells it, much of the energy in Santa Fe was directed toward gambling. Monte and faro attracted him for a short time—until he lost his first five-franc piece. He was frugal with his money and never gambled again. The colorful persons Huning met in Santa Fe represent a cross section of the frontiersmen frequenting the town at the time: Kit Carson, whose friendship continued into Huning's early Albuquerque years; the Canadian trapper sometimes down from Taos and famous at the monte table, Ceran St. Vrain; a mixture of military and business men, lawyers, politicians, and priests. One of the few women he mentions is Barcelo, also prominent in town gambling. Sensuality and sexual descriptions are missing, revealing as much about Huning's intended audience, perhaps, as about Huning.

In Santa Fe, Huning found employment in a store and soon—with the aid of his friend Louis Bartels, a Spanish grammar, a copy of *Don Quixote,* and the good will of his customers—was carrying out one business transaction after another entirely in Spanish. In addition to learning Spanish, Huning observed the dress and customs of the people who lived in and passed through Santa Fe. Fergusson gives this advantage of character adaptability rather extravagant emphasis in his novels, especially in *The Land of Lonely Women* and *The Adventures of Mark West,* two later, unpublished works. Facility with a new language and adaptability to native culture is a trait of many of Fergusson's fictive composites of his grandfather and himself, though there is little evidence that Fergusson himself was fluent in either speaking or writing Spanish.

Since Huning was essentially a trader-merchant and interested in the money to be made in the territory, he spends considerable time relating his adventures through the perspective of the "industry" of the territory at that time. When he arrived in Santa Fe, buffalo hunting was one of those primary industries, for all three races and cultures, and continued to be so until the railroads changed the traveling time and cultural conditions on the plains and lessened the need for dry buffalo meat and buffalo robes. In detail and overall attitude Huning is sympathetic to the buffalo trade and reveals that side of the frontiersman as a ravager of resources which Fergusson rises to criticize in his novels.

By far the most important fictional source for Fergusson in his grandfather's memoir is the trip Huning took to trade horses with Apaches in Arizona. Fergusson reworks this episode countless times in his novels. In the fall of 1851, Huning's former employer, Latz, returned to Santa Fe with the offer of a trading trip to Arizona Territory, a place Huning describes as "a complete wilderness" (p. 34). Huning accepted the invitation, ready for more adventure and strange sights/sites ever further into the "uncivilized" frontier.

The traders, starting in September and following Coronado's old route, reached Bernalillo, near Albuquerque, in a week. After a cou-

ple of false starts in September the expedition finally acquired enough
members and in October proceeded down the Rio Grande from Bernalillo to Corrales. As Huning tells it, the party consisted of "28
Mexicans, Mr. Latz and myself, with 18 or 20 horses, mules and
asses" (pp. 35–36). Huning is aware that this trip into the wilderness
of Arizona territory is much more dangerous and life-threatening than
his trip to Santa Fe from Leavenworth: "Here we were 29 or 30 men
all told, and all of them but poorly armed, and we were going right in
the midst of wild Apaches in the wildest kind of a country, where we
would be during the winter months" (pp. 36–37).

Huning reports that the group, working their way west over the
malpais toward the Gila, heading for the White Mountains, traveled
through a wondrous landscape with canyons and vistas which he can
only describe as "gorgeous." He resorts to this word frequently
which, in context, given his tendency to understate but still romanticize his experience, indicates how difficult it was for him to translate
into language—English, Spanish, or German—just how "gorgeous"
the sights were through which he traveled. The wildness and beauty of
it were beyond description; but he was seeing it as sublime landscape
and not relegating it to the picturesque or taking it for granted. He saw
it not merely as an adventurer but as a writer with something of the
artist's eye.[13]

The wonderment of the landscape is not quite matched by
Huning's descriptions of the Indians which he encountered. The
Coyoteros he describes as "a fine looking tribe of Indians, good riders
and had fine horses" (p. 43). Once the traders reached the Gila River,
they found the Apaches of that region preparing for raids into Sonora.
While they rested and traded on the Gila, Huning reports that he made
friends with several of the Indians and with some of the Mexican
captives living with them. He also made an enemy or two and once
came close to having an arrow plunged into him had not one of his
newly acquired Indian friends interceded.

After leaving the Gila the party traveled into the Pinal Mountains
looking for the Pinaleno Indians. They found a community of these
Indians, but the men were away, and Huning's group could not trade
with the remaining women and children. The traders continued on

toward the Tonto Basin in search of the Tontos. But the basin was too big to cross at that time of the year, and they turned back, trading and buying blankets, mules, and even a Mexican captive along the way. Soon after this the party decided to return to New Mexico Territory and headed again into the White Mountains attempting to retrace their original route back to Zuñi. The return trip was threatening and hazardous, and they were lost for over three weeks. The provisions ran out and horses and mules were killed for food. This did not bother Huning in and of itself, he matter-of-factly reports. What he missed was salt to flavor the meat. By the time Huning reached Zuñi he had animal skins for shoes; but cold weather and near starvation aside, he was in relatively good health. *In Those Days* includes Fergusson's dramatization of this entire episode, maintaining something of Huning's wry sense of humor, even amidst the romanticism, in his treatment of the initiation of a nimrod. In addition, the theme of man against the elements comes into play in a large way in *Wolf Song* and *Grant of Kingdom*.

After his adventure on the Arizona frontier, Huning returned to Santa Fe and nearby San Miguel in February of 1852. He studied Spanish and French for a few months; in the spring he went to Las Vegas, nursed his rheumatism in the mineral baths, and had a close call with some Utes who were harassing women at the baths when he stepped in to protect the women. Fergusson uses a version of this episode in Huning's life in the opening chapter of *Grant of Kingdom*, when Jean Ballard meets and falls in love with Consuelo Coronel.

In the early fall of 1852 Huning agreed to take a job with Joseph Hirsch, a Polish Jew and merchant in Santa Fe. While in Santa Fe Huning also met Gaspar Ortiz, a Mexican-American who made regular trading trips to Mexico (much in the way that Fergusson's Leo Mendes does in *Conquest*). Ortiz invited Huning to travel with him to Mexico. When Ortiz and Huning arrived in Albuquerque en route, however, Huning was offered a job by another Jewish merchant, Simon Rosenstein. In one of the most fateful decisions of his life, he accepted. William Jackson Parish profiles the early Jewish merchant in the Southwest as "cosmopolitan in his outlook, experienced in language, and not the least inhibited by the social restrictions of economic strata."[14] Huning and his brothers, although German Lutherans, shared many of these qualities which made pioneer Jewish merchants so essential to the settlement of the New Mexico frontier. Fergusson's tribute to his grandfather and the Jewish merchants for whom he worked is evidenced in *Conquest*.[15]

The Simon Rosenstein store was located in Old Town on the "south side of the plaza in the house of Manuel Romero" (*Trader*, p. 56). Albuquerque was a military garrison in the decade before the Civil War, and many of Huning's customers and friends were officers and soldiers. He describes the town as a "lively" place populated by "probably 6,000 men in Albuquerque—soldiers, quartermasters men, such as mechanics, clerks, teamsters and other laborers besides many gamblers and other camp followers" (pp. 55–56). Money was plentiful and so were fandangos and gambling, quarrels and killings— all the wild goings-on Huning had found a few years earlier in Santa Fe. Fergusson's fictional portraits of Albuquerque all tend to extend this idea of a frontier town.

After a few years with Rosenstein, Huning took a job in about 1857 with Judge Kirby Benedict as an interpreter and deputy clerk. He traveled with the judge to Tomé and Mesilla on the circuit south of Albuquerque and tells of the raucus conditions which surrounded frontier justice at the time. This trip represents Huning's third major journey in his memoir, which, in large measure, is a travel book cast as autobiography. (Fergusson incorporates Huning's experience with the judge in certain scenes of *In Those Days*.) During his employment with Judge Benedict, Huning took a room in a building west of the historic San Felipe de Neri Church on the Old Town plaza, in a building owned by Archbishop Jean Baptiste Lamy's helper in Christ, Joseph Priest Machebeuf. Some six years later, in 1863, Huning and his brother Charles purchased this property from Vicar Machebeuf and established the F. & C. Huning store in 1864. The real estate promissory note (dated June 24, 1863) pertaining to the sale of the lot on the "northwest corner of the public plaza," indicates that Huning and his brother paid the Reverend Joseph P. Machebeuf $2,217.00 on December 1, 1863.[16]

By the late 1850s and early 1860s Huning had come full circle as a trader on the Santa Fe trail. In 1849 he started across the plains to New Mexico as a bullwhacker. Eight years later he owned his own store and was hauling his own freight. By the time of the Civil War he was the owner of several teams of oxen, soon replaced by mules. In his trips back and forth across the plains between Missouri and New Mexico he had even more adventures.

In part it was the business generated by the war which helped him build his store in 1864. By the time of the war his business interests had expanded to Los Lunas and to Zuñi pueblo. He was joined in this expansion by his brother, Charles, and by E. D. Franz, whom he had first met on one of his trips across the plains. When the forces of the Confederate army made their attempt to march through New Mexico Territory under the command of Brigadier General Henry H. Sibley, supplies in Albuquerque were depleted, and Huning was in a strategic position to provide what was needed. His prosperity continued, and by 1863 he was able to purchase in St. Louis the necessary engines and machinery for a gristmill and sawmill and transport all this equipment back to Albuquerque. Moreover, that same year he traveled to Europe and visited London, Paris, and his old home in Germany. When he returned to the United States in July 1863, just a few days after the Battle of Gettysburg, he married Ernestine Franke in St. Louis and headed from Leavenworth once again across the Santa Fe trail to his home in Old Town.

Ernestine Franke Huning (1837–1923) was born in Muhlhausen, Germany, and traveled to St. Louis with friends. She met Huning there, and after their marriage they set out for the West. She kept her own fragmentary diary (translated from the German by her daughter Clara Huning Fergusson) of her two months' journey to the frontier. In her caring for her ten canaries and her interest in the beautiful landforms surrounding her on the trail, in her talk of Indians met—in all of her notes she seems more charmed than frightened by the frontier as it was opening before her. She viewed the Indians which she saw as either children or beggars, curiosities with painted faces, and did not seem fully to comprehend the violence and finality of Indian raids and killings which other Anglo travelers they met talked about. [17]

Just how hostile the Indians were on "the Santa Fe road" Huning and his new wife learned four years later, in 1867. That year he went to Dayton, Ohio, to escort his mother-in-law and her youngest son, Fritz, to Albuquerque. At that time, General Hancock's campaign against the Cheyenne and Kiowa had caused the Indians to seek revenge on white merchants and their wagon trains. But when Huning requested cavalry protection from the company stationed at Fort Zarah, Kansas, he was refused. As his wagons reached Plum Buttes, about fifteen miles west of Fort Zarah, they were attacked. In the ensuing melee the wagons were separated, and the one with Mrs. Franke and Fritz stalled in the sand—according to Huning's recollected version of the incident some twenty-seven years later in his memoir. In that dramatic retelling, the son was shot first and then the mother, after being mocked and ridiculed. But letters to Ernestine Franke Huning, home in Albuquerque, record that Fritz was wounded, lingered for a time and then died. His mother, in this epistolary account, then died of a heart attack brought on by shock and grief. Whichever version is correct, Huning was more distraught than at any time in his life and furious at the cavalry. Apparently Huning, using his Spencer rifle, did hit and wound one of the chiefs during the raid (*Trader*, pp. 88–96). Life as a Santa Fe trader also had its tragic, darker side.

RIO GRANDE HACIENDA

In his memoir Huning says very little about either La Glorieta or Castle Huning, the two houses which meant so much in his frontier history. The last few pages of *Trader* fade into random paragraphs summarizing what he did as a trader between 1867 and 1875, when he dissolved his partnership with Charles. Just why his brother decided to return to Germany is unknown. In any event, he died there in 1894.

If Charles grew homesick for Germany and therefore returned, Franz Huning did his best to bring Germany to New Mexico. In 1883, three years after the railroad came to Albuquerque and New Town was on its way, he built Castle Huning. He sold his inventory of goods in the Old Town store and went into the hardware business in New

Town. He also bought property in New Town to the east of the site of Castle Huning; and he rented out his gristmill, "Molino de la Glorieta" (the mill of the bower), for a time and then, after selling the hardware business, resumed operation of the mill, which was later destroyed in a fire. Through all of his dealings he made a considerable fortune, which, in his memoir, he laments could have been much greater had he been more of a businessman and less of a dreamer. In addition to monies earned, he also lost several thousand dollars on real estate south of Albuquerque and in misguided hotel and bridge ventures.[18]

The overall impression which Huning's memoir leaves is that he was very much a man of action, a man happier on the Santa Fe road to and from the United States than in his mercantile stores, or at his mill or even at home in La Glorieta or Castle Huning. Insofar as this is true, this side of the man is much the side which Fergusson idealizes in his fiction and identified with in his life as a modern frontiersman traveling back and forth between East and West. But there was also the other Huning, the domestic patriarch and the town businessman and esteemed personage who moved with the times from Old Town interests to New Town developments associated with the railroad, the illustrious owner of ancient La Glorieta and the builder of the romantic Castle Huning.

Precisely when Huning bought the old adobe hacienda on the Rio Grande known as La Glorieta is not known. Some of what is known about La Glorieta is reported in *Home* and, in fictional form, in *The Land of Lonely Women* and *In Those Days*. Numerous other commentators on local history have recognized its importance as one of the region's important residences.

The contrast between La Glorieta as an old Rio Grande hacienda and Castle Huning as an ornate refashioning of German architecture adapted to indigenous building materials could not be more striking— or symbolic. If Huning first lived in one of the oldest dwellings in the territory, he soon saw fit to build his own pleasure dome and live out his remembered conception of the German past of his youth amidst the pueblo-style dwellings which had first shocked him when he bullwhacked his way down the Santa Fe Trail. The fact that he constructed it exactly midway between Old Town and New Town adds to the symbolism of his effort.

The age of the old hacienda is submerged in myth. It is believed to be the oldest residence in Albuquerque. Journalist Howard Bryan says, "It was standing in 1803 and some believe it was built before the Pueblo Revolt in 1680."[19] Some accounts record that Huning and his brother purchased the house in the early 1850s from Catholic priests who were living there; others say it was purchased in 1861, along with 700 acres of land at the east end of the Old Town plaza.[20] Whatever the date of purchase, Huning took the house as a home in 1864, soon after the building of his mill, Molino de la Glorieta, and his marriage to Ernestine Franke. It was in La Glorieta that four children were born to Huning and his wife. The eldest child, Clara Mary Huning (1865–1950), was eventually to receive title to the property as a wedding gift ("in consideration of $1.00, love and affection") upon her marriage to H. B. Fergusson on April 14, 1887; they, in turn, raised their four children in La Glorieta. Besides Clara Mary Huning, Franz and Ernestine had three other children: a son, Arno (1869–1936), who inherited Castle Huning and lived there for thirty years after Franz's death in 1905; Lina (1872–94), the sister after whom Clara named her daughter, Lina Fergusson (Browne); and Elly (1874–80).

La Glorieta was located on Railroad Avenue (at what is now 1801 West Central), and on the east edge of Old Town, only two blocks west of and across the street from the spot where Huning built his castle (Fifteenth Street and Central, West), on the line between Old Town and New Town. The old hacienda was surrounded by 700 acres of fields and was crisscrossed by a network of *acequias* (irrigation ditches) leading from the *acequia madre* (mother ditch) to the east.[21] The fields and meadows were dotted by cottonwood trees. Huning planted or perhaps nourished an already-standing cottonwood tree in the yard of La Glorieta, an ancient, death-resisting tree which over the years grew to a circumference of nearly twenty feet. Part of the legend associated with this tree is that the blood of cattle slaughtered by Confederate soldiers during the Civil War fertilized it, bringing forth life out of death. Huning was a horticulturist of the first order, and Osage orange, crabapple, and various other kinds of trees and shrubbery added

La Glorieta. Courtesy of Francis and Peggy Fergusson.

to the "enchanted" atmosphere. Sylvester Baxter, writing for *Harper's* in 1885, found that Huning's La Glorieta and his Molino de la Glorieta lived up quite charmingly to their names. Baxter considered the mill one of the most picturesque of all the buildings in Old Town, "embowered in a grove of fine large trees planted by its prosperous owner, Mr. Franz Huning, one of the old residents, and a leading merchant and wine-grower."[22]

Huning is portrayed in family legend as either walking the ditches with hoe in hand, irrigating his property—or coming home and tossing on top of an old wardrobe the day's profits from his store, and planning the supervision of the farming with his loyal, long-serving (and stereotypical) servant, Juan.[23] Fergusson recreates semblances of these impressions in *In Those Days*, and, in the case of Juan, the Mexican servant, in "The Enchanted Meadow." All in all, Huning may be seen as living in a style not all that much removed from that of the ricos, the Spanish-Mexican aristocrats whose decline so preoccupies Fergusson in his novels and in *Rio Grande*.

La Glorieta originally had only two wings, north and east, arranged in an ell. Huning added two other sides to make the enclosed placita so picturesquely illustrated in *Harper's*. It consisted of a dozen rooms, large enough, with various adaptations over the years, to still serve into the 1980s as a private elementary school known as Manzano Day School. A fire in 1910 or 1911, just a few years prior to H. B. Fergusson's death in 1915 (during Francis Fergusson's youth at the house), gutted the southeast corner of the sitting room. That room had not been restored, perhaps because of lack of money, when H. B. Fergusson committed suicide. Fergusson avoids discussion of such a painful subject, in part because he ends his autobiography some years shy of his father's death. And even during the last decade of his life Fergusson chooses to remember—or at least writes about—La Glorieta with nostalgic romance and excitement rather than with trauma and morbidity.

Clara Huning's memoir allows more insight into the design and furnishing of the interior of the house in the years she lived there as a girl. As she remembers it, there were buffalo robes on the floor. In the parlor, the walls were whitewashed, with calico tacked to the walls about three feet from the floor to keep the whitewash from rubbing onto clothes. First a wood stove and then coal provided heat, while coal-oil lamps, supplemented by candles in the bedrooms and in going from room to room, were used for lighting. Only later were carpets brought from St. Louis to replace the buffalo robes. Until water pumps began to be used in the 1870s, water for use at La Glorieta was carried in barrels by wagon from the Rio Grande and then emptied into other barrels on the back porch near the kitchen.[24] Lina Fergusson Browne's memories are of a later era: "In the parlor the only picture I remember was a very large lithograph of a fearsome winter scene in Siberia, snow swirling around a sleigh with two or three terrified occupants being attacked by a pack of wolves. In the sitting room . . . hung a pleasing and, I believe, very competent portrait of our mother as a young woman which had been painted by her governess."[25] With such memories, such coldness and violence juxtaposed with memories of a loving face, the house had its good and bad ghosts.

La Glorieta almost miraculously has endured the destructive

powers of time and mutability. It has changed, generation by generation, assuredly, but it still stands. Clara Huning Fergusson's long residence there as a girl, then as a wife and mother, is quite unique even for her time. The house, made of the very earth out of which it rises, has outlived not just Clara but all of her children. Virginia F. Gillespie offered a sad account of the old house twenty years ago in 1967—still romantic but more sorrowful with its air of modern misappropriated electric wire corruptions, than Sylvester Baxter's pristine account a century earlier: "The hacienda stands today, much the same as in 1891 [when William Jennings Bryan visited H. B. Fergusson there]. The beams are still exposed, but electric wires thread through and around them. . . . Lilac bushes crowd the entrance walk, an old pear tree blossoms profusely each spring, bearing nubby fruit. . . . The old cottonwood is now but a giant with stubby limbs, putting forth only enough leaves to signify that it is still alive."[26]

The tree, the house, the family, exist primarily now in the world of legend. And a large part of the legend of La Glorieta belongs to H. B. Fergusson as well, for it was there that he literally met the end of his life and the "frontier" as he knew it. But H. B. Fergusson and the glory and tragedy of his life in the old Rio Grande hacienda merits a separate telling—another chapter in the consideration of the life and literature of his son. It is Castle Huning, more than La Glorieta, which must be seen as the predominant symbol for "grosspa" Huning.

FRONTIER XANADU

Fergusson prized both La Glorieta and Castle Huning probably more than the Old Town and the New Town which they can be seen as symbolizing. Like his grandfather Huning, Fergusson grew up infatuated with the acres of fields, meadows, and river bosque which surrounded both houses. These natural landforms more accurately represent his home as a boy. In the houses themselves a strange reversal of roles took place. His father, H. B. Fergusson, was the head of the household at La Glorieta—a new man in an old house. And his grandfather Huning was very much in charge of his castle—an old man in a new house. So the symbolism of Old Town and New Town is not exact. Probably Fergusson noticed the houses more in his adult consciousness than in his youthful subconsciousness. But both kinds of awareness about the places where he grew up were forever with him.

In the late 1870s Huning bought a tract of land consisting of 400 acres south of La Glorieta in hopes that he could sell it to the railroad. The acreage included all of the land between Tenth and San Pasquale Streets, from Central to the Rio Grande. When, in 1880, the railroad located roughly a mile east of Old Town and Huning's parcel of land, he kept it for his private estate. And, like Coleridge's Kubla Khan, Huning walled his domain with a protective fence, began to cultivate his trees, and built his "stately pleasure-dome." The road from Huning's acreage to the railroad depot became the main thoroughfare between Old Town and New Town, and Huning, if he did not have the railroad, at least had strategic properties on Railroad Avenue.[27]

The mansion itself consisted of fourteen rooms, with the estate in addition having several outlying service buildings, a garden and aviary, numerous running fountains and waterways, and a family cemetery.[28] If Huning Castle is envisioned in the Albuquerque of 1883, New Town consisted of only a few blocks of buildings extending westward from the railroad depot and tracks at First and Railroad Avenue. New Town land, however, extended to the eastern boundary of Huning's estate at about Tenth Street. The cultivated area of the estate, which fronted on Railroad Avenue and on which the castle itself was located, extended four blocks to Fourteenth Street, where a large acequia ran alongside a hedge of Osage orange trees planted by Huning.[29]

Inspired by his good luck and his good business, Huning began work on his castle in 1881. It was certain by 1880 that Albuquerque was to be an intersection for east-west and north-south railroad lines. The commercial advantages that would bring, complemented by the fine climate, high elevation, and clean mountain air, created a mood of expansion and progressivism. Huning was in the right place at the right time. When he started construction of his dream dwelling, he was fifty-four years old and had made a considerable fortune in the thirty-two years since he first arrived in Santa Fe. His grandson,

Franz Huning at the gate of Castle Huning. Courtesy of Li Caemmerer.

Harvey Fergusson, was nine years away from being on the scene, a scene he could not have better designed himself.

Huning was personally involved with the construction of his castle, serving as his own designer and contractor. The walls were made from over 250,000 terrones, or adobe-like bricks, cut by spade from his own property near the Rio Grande. Doors and other trim and hardware were imported from Chicago. The total cost of building the castle and of landscaping the grounds is difficult to determine. Terrones were about $2.50 per hundred, and masonry work cost about $11.00 per thousand brick. The trees were imported and planted over a number of years.[30]

A conceptualization of the interior of the castle depends on accounts of Erna Fergusson and of Arno Huning's daughters, who lived there for over twenty-five years after Franz Huning died. Those memories tell of a somewhat later decor than when the castle was first built and furnished. The double entrance door had frosted and etched glass panels. Niches on the side walls of the vestibule held statues of Goethe and Schiller. The long main hallway was panelled in beautiful wood which ran only part way up the full thirteen-foot ceiling. Just past the front door, a large newel post on the right supported a full-size statue of a knight in armor, said to be Boise de Guilbert.[31]

A small pipe organ occupied another wall recess—this one in the small hall leading from the main hall into the dining room. A Steinway grand piano was also positioned in the sitting room. One room's furnishings are representative: "Here [in the parlor] the wallpaper was gold to match the furniture, the carpet was yellow and gold. A light gray marble mantel stood on the south wall opposite the large double-hung windows to the front, with their glass curtains of Battenburg lace, and red velvet drapes falling in heavy folds to the floor."[32]

Such luxuriance contrasts sharply with Clara Huning Fergusson's description of the interior of La Glorieta in her girlhood. Perhaps Huning enjoyed the process of his rise to material success more than the actual prize. Perhaps this is why, in his final years, he withdrew deeper into himself and away from Albuquerque society. Fergusson too, as man and writer, much preferred the life and times of the frontier to that of parlors and fine furnishings.

Huning died in his castle at 11:45 A.M. on November 4, 1905. He was seventy-eight years old, and his obituary attributes his death to "a complication of diseases due to old age."[33] Clara Huning Fergusson records in her memoir that her father had a serious operation for gallstones which left him bedridden and from which he never really recovered.[34] His wishes for his funeral held out the hope that an Old Timer might rise and speak—presumably about the old days: "I direct that my remains be cremated, the ashes put into an urn and deposited alongside of my children, Lina and Elly. And I strictly forbid any and all religious nonsense. If any Old Timer should be handy, he may make a speech, but not mix up any cant with it."[35] Whether or not his grandson, Harvey Fergusson, at the age of fifteen was present at the bedside is not substantiated. In any case, Huning had made a lasting impression on the boy—just as he had on the entire community. Huning could never have anticipated that his grandson would later become that "handy Old Timer."

The end of Castle Huning is regarded now as a tragedy. Built as both a monument to Huning's past and to his new status in the New World, the castle should still be standing today, across the way from

La Glorieta. It is not. Arno Huning and his family lived there until the late 1930s, after which it became a private school known as Trudelle School, offering a quaintly Victorian education for aspiring middle-class parents interested in a refined alternative to the public schools in kindergarten and the lower elementary grades. But in the mid-fifties, when the castle was owned by attorney W. A. Keleher (who, as a boy, delivered telegrams to Huning in the doorway of the castle) and businessman A. R. Hibbinstreet, it fell victim to a system of values which long-time Albuquerque observer and journalist the late Irene Fisher, described as "a curious stage . . . in which everybody wanted something new; it's just a shame because they destroyed practically every historical building in Albuquerque."[36]

In 1954 the castle was condemned as unsafe for use as a school, but no alternative uses were planned, and it was allowed to sit vacant. Fisher, like many others, could not understand why there was no citywide outcry protesting such a shameful mistake. Erna Fergusson was, surprisingly, almost grateful for the final demolition when she compared that to the years of deterioration and neglect of the structure—as she noted in a letter to her brother, Francis: "And here goes our ancestral glory. It really seems a shame looking through the place and seeing the fine woodwork and hardware and all, that somebody should not have seen merit in keeping it as some sort of municipal center. But it won't be as hard to see the empty spot as to observe the ugly deterioration that has gone on for a long time with no care and vandals swarming through."[37]

Guy E. Hawkins of Jacksonville, Illinois, was hired to tear down the castle and did so in less than three months.[38] Marc Simmons offers an eloquent assessment of the magnitude of the mistake in his history of the town.[39] And professor of art Bainbridge Bunting wrote a plaintive and detailed "restorative" essay five years after the destruction of the castle. His essay is as close as posterity can come to sensing the ways in which the destruction of Castle Huning underscores the recurrent endings of the frontier. Castle Huning stood for nearly three-quarters of a century, a stately curiosity first on Railroad Avenue and then at 1508 Central West, a highway which served as the main street of a town, and then a city's segment on the nation's highway,

U.S. 66. For generations of travelers on this highway, both a regional and a national treasure fell to a wrecking crew. In Professor Bunting's words, "The loss of this handsome old mansion is irreparable and no amount of progress in the form of motel, filling station or supermarket built upon the vacated site can compensate for its destruction."[40]

A further twist of time's ironies is that thirty years after the destruction of Castle Huning, the land on which it was located is not a motel, not a filling station or a supermarket. It is a vacant, weed-strewn lot facing a string of Indian curio shops and fast-food eating places. Such conditions of twentieth-century urban pollution provide fateful contrast to the attempt at grandeur which Huning tried to create. In the 1880s, at a transitional spot between Old Town and New Town, between the frontier and the industrial West, the castle was an amazing showcase for Huning and his family, for Fergusson and his transitional times. Surrounded by hundreds of acres of varied kinds of civilized and savage lands—lagoons, irrigated fields, river bosque, desolate valley land extending to First Street and beyond the railroad tracks to Huning Highlands—Castle Huning was a kind of frontier Xanadu.

Although Huning's castle is now only a memory preserved in history and fiction, Huning established a legacy of name and legend as one of Albuquerque's prominent pioneers, and the Huning Highlands continues as an acknowledged historical district restored by caring citizens. And one of the downtown streets, Arno Street, remains as a further echo of the Huning name. But most of all, his legend and his legacy lived on in his grandson and in the books that Fergusson was inspired to write—in no small measure because of Franz Huning.

3 ▲▲▲▲▲▲▲

Rebel Sons (1848–1915)

Although Huning's total fortunes were dependent on the coming of
the railroad to Albuquerque and on the boom of New Town, his truest
self was allied with Old Town, his picturesque gristmill Molino de la
Glorieta, and his two homes, La Glorieta and Castle Huning. Huning
assuredly looked toward his future as a Santa Fe trader, but he most
truly represented the past era of the frontier—and "epitomized the
pioneer settler-merchant of the old era."[1] Beyond that, he represented, through the construction of his castle, the even older romantic
German past, which he attempted to reestablish on a line between the
past and the future, the frontier and the modern, in a changeless
landscape but a changing New Mexico territory. Huning's grandson,
Harvey Fergusson, was also pulled in both directions, in time and in
geographical space, but he was pulled most strongly by his grandfather's frontier past.

Yet Huning's influence on Fergusson was only one influence. If,
because of Huning, the establishment and the passing of the frontier
became an integral part of Fergusson's developing personality and

perception of history, the end of the frontier was also dramatized for him in his father, H. B. Fergusson. A frontier attorney, the son-in-law of Huning, an orator, territorial politician, and U.S. congressman, H. B. Fergusson was, on the one hand, a representative of the promise of the frontier and of its closing; yet, on the other hand, he represented the dying and already dead values of the Old South. While the frontier side of H.B.'s life appealed to his son, the son rebelled against the values associated with the Old South. In the biographies of his grandfather Huning, of his father, H.B., and of his paternal grandfather, Sampson Noland Ferguson, Harvey Fergusson saw two if not three pasts launched into their respective futures and ultimately repelled—archetypal beginning turned to archetypal endings.

If Huning's was the German past transported to the waning frontier of New Mexico territory at the end of the nineteenth century, H.B.'s past was that of the Southern aristocracy, the paternalistic values of plantation and slave owner and chivalric husband, applied to the changes entailed in a primitive southwestern territory on the road to becoming a state and attaining the relative civility associated with such status. In his experiencing of his father's life, Harvey Fergusson saw another version of the past played out in the life of a famous father who established himself in the frontier West and shaped the political future of the statehood era—a life that was full of ambition, forceful and forward-looking, and in the world's eyes, successful; but a life which ended in despondency and suicide. Harvey B. Fergusson, Jr., as Harvey Butler Fergusson's namesake and junior, faced a not uncommon fear of being like his father—and a fear of not being like him. As is common with fathers and sons, H. B. Fergusson rebelled against his father, Sampson Noland Ferguson, and left the South for the Southwest; but he took just enough of his Old South values with him to provide a basis for Harvey Fergusson to rebel against him. Both were, in their individual ways, rebel sons.

OLD SOUTH

In *Home in the West* Fergusson romantically identifies Huning as a Santa Fe trader heading for a life of adventure on the Santa Fe Trail and

H.B. as a southern gentleman who also goes west. That pattern of travel and emigration can be seen as well in the life of Fergusson's paternal grandfather, Sampson Noland Ferguson (H. B. Fergusson added the second *s* to the name for unknown reasons—perhaps in an extra flourish consistent with his overall style). His grandfather went to Alabama from South Carolina with money and with slaves. But in all likelihood he began, or so says his grandson, "as a pioneer clearing virgin pine forest, building his house of logs he cut, sprinkling the stump-lands with the white boles of his first crop" (*Home,* p. 50). In keeping with southern frontier values, he achieved the status of "aristocracy" as soon as he "owned enough blacks so that he could drop his hoe and ride his horse" (p. 50). As disagreeable and specious as Fergusson finds these values and the ascendency based on them, Fergusson makes it understood that his grandfather had an extra measure of legitimacy to his status as "aristocrat": he was also a physician and a Confederate officer, occupations as romantic in their way as Huning's dual role as a Santa Fe trader and Albuquerque entrepreneur. But if Fergusson accepts the occupations of his grandfather as distinguished, he rejects the values and culture which surrounded and nourished them. For a time during his youth and extending into his college days at Washington and Lee University in Lexington, Virginia, Harvey accepted H. B. Fergusson's indoctrinations of Old South attitudes; however, much before the time of his autobiography he came to reject them. His first three novels—*Blood of the Conquerors, Capitol Hill,* and *Women and Wives*—all reflect his rebellion from and satirical treatment of the Old and the New South. His rebellion seems absolute.

How H. B. Fergusson (1848–1915) became so wholly a product of the Old South and how he carried that identity with him into his new life on the southwestern frontier may be seen in outline by piecing together information from various family sources: letters from Sampson Noland Ferguson written during the Civil War; H.B.'s sister Sampie's handwritten memoir, intended mainly for her nieces and nephews; and the reminiscences of H.B.'s wife, Clara Huning Fergusson, about her life and marriage.

The origins of the Ferguson family in the South are traced in family records to a Scotch-Irishman named Ferguson who emigrated from Ireland to South Carolina just before the Revolutionary War and sided with the Tories in that struggle. One of the sons of this Scotch-Irish immigrant was General Patrick Ferguson, who led the British in the Battle of King's Mountain as an officer of Cornwallis and was killed there.[2] Another son, James H. Ferguson—brother of Patrick and father of Sampson Noland Ferguson—was born in Chester, South Carolina, in 1780. Little is known about this great-grandfather of Harvey Fergusson other than the fact that like his own father and brother, he was a staunch Tory and lived most of his life in Spring Hill, Alabama, earning his living as a farmer. Apparently James H. Ferguson had four sons and two daughters by a first marriage. He married his second wife, Elizabeth Noland, in the spring of 1817; she became Sampson Noland Ferguson's mother and Harvey Fergusson's great-grandmother.[3] In *Home* Fergusson speaks about the migrations and aspirations of his great-grandparents as early pioneers affected by their phase of the frontier: "When the great western cotton boom came along, these uplanders were quick to take the road with all their household goods in wagons and their blacks marching before them to the land where cotton was gold" (p. 53).

Sampson Noland Ferguson was born September 25, 1818, near Chester, South Carolina, and was, according to what record exists, fully grown when the family migrated to Alabama. He is described by his daughter, Sampie, as "six feet tall, well proportioned and very erect. He had dark hair, and brown eyes."[4] H.B. inherited this dark complexion and passed it along to his son Harvey.

Sampson Noland Ferguson first married in 1841. His first wife and their young son, Charles Washington Ferguson, both died within two years from unknown causes. Sampson married for a second time on December 17, 1844. He and his new wife, Mary De Liesseline Kennon Poyas, bore four children: Harvey Butler, Sampie, Ella, and Emma. Later, H. B. Fergusson and Clara Huning Fergusson were to name their last child Francis De Liesseline Poyas, in honor of H.B.'s mother.

According to Sampie, Sampson graduated from medical school in Nashville, Tennessee, some time prior to the Civil War and was a successful, practicing physician in Pickensville, Alabama, until the Civil War began.[5] A high-degree Mason who quoted Robert Burns and was known as "Squire," he served as a Confederate captain and doctor during the Civil War. Because of his war service he had to leave the management of his plantation to his fifteen-year-old son, H.B. The inference is easily made from Sampson's war letters instructing his son in how to conduct the family business and care for family members—especially Mary—that H.B. grew up as a good and dutiful son who made great efforts to maintain and further the welfare of the family. Sampson's stern expectations for responsibility, discipline, and self-improvement on the part of his young son make him seem demanding. One senses that H.B. had the same expectations for young Harvey. Sampson's "intensity," and parental fervor in this regard, especially after the death of Mary while he was at war, prompted Harvey's sister Erna to rebel from her grandfather's persona in his letters: "I would not have liked Grandpa. Wasn't that the most dispiriting letter he wrote his fifteen-year-old son after the mother's death, crying on the shoulder of the poor little kid! No, dear Grandpa would certainly have given me a pain in the neck."[6]

By the time of the war, Sampson and Mary had acquired a farm on the banks of the Tombigbee River, as many as 100 slaves, and a house in Pickensville. So there was much for H.B., age thirteen at the start of the war, to look after as a "conscientious, earnest little fellow," as Sampie describes him. Sampie's memoir makes the case that, far from being a "pain in the neck," Sampson was warmly regarded by his wife, his children, and friends: "He was a man of at least average education for the times, a loving and devoted husband and father, popular with his associates and superior officers—thoroughly good and kind. . . . He was often torn by the conflict between his sense of duty to his family on the one hand and to his struggling, bleeding country on the other."[7]

Sampson's sense of duty to his country won out. During the war he was captain of the Pickensville Blues, the first military company from the county to join the Confederate Army; and he joined the Fifth Alabama Infantry regiment and went immediately to Virginia, where he served the Confederacy in the first battle of Manassas. After 1861 he recruited and led a second company of troops as part of the Seventh Alabama Cavalry.[8]

Mary Ferguson died in March 1864, compounding the grief and obligations of young H.B. Just before his mother died, H.B., at the age of fifteen, promised to help raise his sisters, and, according to Sampie, kept that promise faithfully. In a letter dated April 20, 1864, and sent from Camp Powell, the boy's father advises him on his new responsibilities, on how to deal with the loss of his mother, and on how to shape his life on Christian principles: "Do you reflect and think that you had one of the best and most affectionate of mothers, who is gone forever and whose place no human being can fill, and that your only chance ever to see her again is to be a good boy, live a Christian, so that when you are called to die, you may go to Heaven, where . . . you know it was her greatest desire that you should be prepared to go. I want you to indulge frequently in a train of thought like this, and try to remember every word she ever said to you about doing, restraining your passions, avoiding bad words and bad company and bad habits."[9]

As Sampson's advice "to indulge frequently in a train of thought like this" indicates, H.B. was used to "indoctrination" from his father, and thus Harvey Fergusson does not use the word "indoctrinate" loosely in describing his own father's methods of child-rearing. Although he rebelled from those austere albeit well-intended Christian indoctrinations in his choice of becoming a journalist rather than a lawyer and in his indulgence rather than restraint of his "passions," Fergusson's portraits of his father, though often semisatirical, are never unkind.

Sampson constantly advised young H.B. to work on reading and writing—especially spelling. From earliest years H.B. took his education seriously, never rebelling from total application of his best effort. He attended boarding school in Mississippi for a time before the war and after the war attended Mr. William Taylor's school, which was located near the Poyas plantation, a half dozen miles outside Pickensville near Carrolltown. It was with Mr. Taylor that H.B. did his college preparatory studies. He entered Washington and Lee University in 1869 at the age of twenty-one, accepting little help from his father or anyone else. But he did accept General Robert E. Lee's offer to study in his office as a convenience, since Fergusson lived so far away from the university that he could not go back and forth to his room between classes. H.B. reportedly told many stories about General Lee as he knew him in and around Lexington. Two letters from Lee to H.B. are much mentioned in family memoirs but are not to be found. Nevertheless, General Lee apparently befriended H.B. and was a hero to him throughout his life, so much so that when it came time for his own son, Harvey Fergusson, to attend college, he saw to it that he returned to Washington and Lee.

In *Home* Fergusson portrays a lamentable end for Sampson, who placed all his assets in Confederate money and lost everything. In a sense, both of his grandfathers fell victim to old age and domesticity in a way somehow tragically at odds with their youthfulness and yen for adventure. This "tragedy" is mitigated somewhat by the fact that they lived full lives—always a prize consolation in Fergusson's novels.

He makes it clear that his maternal grandfather, Franz Huning, and his paternal grandfather, Sampson Noland Ferguson, were temperamentally and culturally different: Huning, a trader, frontier traveler, merchant, founder of a city, reader of books and builder of castles—a writer-adventurer; Ferguson, a physician, cotton planter, slave owner, soldier, sportsman, and "squire" who rode to hounds and could shoot a partridge. One embodied the values of Old Germany; one the values of the Old South. But they were both products of the frontier, both travelers and settlers who believed in the pride of family name. They faced the frontiers of the West and the South with a spirit of self-reliance and resourcefulness and were ready to face the risks involved in settling an unsettled region. They had their successes—but they also had their failures. Huning made a fortune only to have it dwindle in the hands of his descendants. Sampson Noland Ferguson, borrowing heavily to finance the purchases of slaves and land, was able to profit owing to the rising prices of cotton and manpower. He made a crucial, ill-advised mistake, however, in selling his holdings for Confederate money.

Always afraid of falling into penury, Harvey Fergusson sorely regretted that both of his pioneering grandfathers "missed easy

Franz Huning, H. B. Fergusson, and their families on the porch of Castle Huning, ca. 1900. *Standing (left to right):* Harvey Fergusson, Clara Huning Fergusson, Erna Fergusson; *seated (left to right):* H. B. Fergusson, Mrs. Huning, Franz Huning; *in front:* Lina Fergusson. Courtesy of Li Caemmerer.

chances to found a family fortune" which would have continued into his own generation (*Home*, p. 55). The frontier opened and closed for Sampson Noland Ferguson just as it did for Franz Huning. Both of them were made and undone by change, by their historical moment.

In Fergusson's perceptions, the end of the Old South for Sampson poses certain similarities to the end of Albuquerque's Old Town for Huning. A New South and a New Town awaited their grandson. But part of his new future ended also with his grandfathers' respective futures.

Something of Fergusson/Franz can be found in Jean Ballard in

Grant of Kingdom, and part of Fergusson/Sampson can be seen in the character of Major Blore in the same novel. As was so often the case in his art, these characters allowed their novelist-creator to open and relive again the closed frontiers of his grandfathers.

H. B. Fergusson extended the frontier spirit of his father and grandfather into the Southwest. He carried with him the values of his family, his upbringing, his region—the values of duty, chivalry, citizenship, and paternalism—into another frontier where Anglo-American intrusion had its ways with darker-skinned peoples; but this time there was an additional group known as "Mexicans" and "Spanish-Americans." H. B. Fergusson's roles as husband, father, lawyer, and politician all reflect his identity as a southern gentleman transposed to the Southwest. Harvey Fergusson describes his father's own personal myth as totally romantic. And although none have seen it in quite this way, it was H. B. Fergusson's romanticism which made him such a kindred spirit of Franz Huning. They were friends as fellow adventurers nostalgically promoting and building upon their respective pasts. H.B.'s personal myth was the myth his son was indoctrinated to believe as a boy but rebelled from as a man. Fergusson recreates something of the Old South in his screenplay *Stand Up and Fight* (MGM, 1939) but has his hero rebel from it, sell his slaves, and head west to a new life. But the Old South gets relatively little attention in Fergusson's fiction, and when it does, as in *Women and Wives,* it is treated satirically.

Samuel Noland Ferguson's hope, one that was part of what it meant to raise a son to be a southern gentleman, was that his son take a special interest in words, both written and spoken. His letters to his young son during the Civil War are filled with high-sounding advice about clean living and with fastidious admonitions to pay more attention to spelling and grammar in his letters. H.B. took these admonitions seriously, as he did anything dealing with the "political" power associated with language. His inclination to oration was evidenced early. When Lee surrendered, H.B., then only in his teens, "climbed upon a cotton bale and made a speech to the assembled slaves" (*Home,* p. 58). In keeping with his allegiance to the traditions involved in the making of a southern gentleman as they resurfaced after the war, H.B.

entered Washington and Lee University (then known as Washington College) in 1869. General Lee had just become president of the school.

While at Washington College, H.B. studied Latin, Greek, French, mathematics, and political and military history. He graduated with both a master of arts and a law degree in 1873 and 1874, respectively. For his M.A. degree he delivered a prestigious speech known as the "Cincinnati Oration," and he studied law with John Randolph Tucker. Although Harvey Fergusson believed that both his father's and his own college educations were the wrong ones to adequately prepare them for the new eras they successively faced, he does concede that at Washington College his father was able to nourish his interest in words.

It is no small part of the family legend that H.B. wrote a novel melodramatically entitled *The Rebel's Son*. Whatever its content, the title, and the implied theme, afford ironic insights into Fergusson's own shaping as a writer. If Franz Huning, the writer-adventurer, influenced Fergusson's becoming a novelist, so did H. B. Fergusson. Perhaps *Stand Up and Fight* is Fergusson's version of his father's melodramatic first novel. If not, the symbolic application to father and son as "rebel sons" is appropriate. He was proud of his father's literary efforts and viewed himself as taking up where his father left off.

H.B. taught at a school for girls, the Shenandoah Valley Academy, in Winchester, Virginia, for two years after his graduation, all the while helping to educate his sisters as promised. In 1876 he began the practice of law which would be his destiny on the southwest frontier. His first affiliation as an attorney was in Wheeling, West Virginia, where he gained the experience that partially prepared him for his relocation to New Mexico Territory in 1881. An illustrious future awaited him, both in the mining town of White Oaks in Billy the Kid's notorious Lincoln County in southeastern New Mexico—and in Albuquerque. It was in Albuquerque that he settled permanently, married, and raised a family; Albuquerque provided the political base from which the territory and then the fledgling state sent him to Washington, D.C.—first as a delegate in the Fifty-fifth Congress (1896–98), then as an elected congressman to the Sixty-second Congress in 1911, on the eve of New Mexico's admission to statehood, and once again to the Sixty-third Congress.

FRONTIER ATTORNEY

In 1881 the young lawyer was sent by his Wheeling, West Virginia, law firm to what is now the ghost town but was then the mining boom town of White Oaks, New Mexico, to look after the mining interests of their clients, the heirs of "Uncle Jack" Winters, who were involved in litigation concerning the ownership of the Homestake mine. Lincoln County had been predominantly a cattle-ranching region until gold was discovered in the late 1870s; it turned overnight into New Mexico's answer to Virginia City and Cripple Creek. One of many outlaws, George Wilson, found the North Homestake lode in 1879 and sold it to Jack Winters for a horse, a bottle of whiskey, and $40.[10] The North Homestake, one of the biggest strikes in the area, gave up an estimated half million dollars in gold—part of a combined yield of over three million dollars if other mines around White Oaks are included.

H. B. Fergusson arrived at the peak of the boom time and saw the best and the worst of the promise and the failure of frontier profiteering and waste. All of Lincoln County was a hotbed of frontier settlement where violence and lawlessness were everyday occurrences. It was an appropriate place for a southern lawyer with chivalric ideals to set up shop. The population of White Oaks peaked at about four thousand frontier personalities. Some notorious outlaws—including William Bonney, Toppy Johnson, and Jim Greathouse—came to town now and then. Billy the Kid's path almost crossed H. B. Fergusson's. And Harvey Fergusson, in his essay for H. L. Mencken's *American Mercury* on Billy the Kid (1925), and in his chapters on southeastern New Mexico outlaws in *The Life of Riley* (1937), puts some of his father's White Oaks ambiance into narrative form.[11] Billy the Kid's end (July 14, 1881) came in the town of Lincoln within months of H.B.'s arrival in White Oaks. But there was still plenty of frontier excitement, warranting the decision of the newly arrived attorney to carry a six-shooter in a pocket holster (*Home*, p. 64).

But if White Oaks was a place of violence, it was also a place of promise. William A. Keleher, among others, in his study of the "fabulous" frontier indicates that H.B. arrived in White Oaks at the height of the flurry of prosperity and instant fortune associated with those gold-rush days. Reputations, as well as wealth, were being made there, and the young attorney's routine business trip was so propitious that as soon as he recognized the potential of the time and place in which he found himself, he decided to stay and stake his "claim."[12]

H.B.'s involvement with the Winters litigation and the Homestake mine is the stuff of frontier romance. In 1879 Wilson and Winters struck it rich on their Homestake claim. Sustained work and relentless celebration soon found "Uncle Jack" Winters dead and buried a mile south of town. After his death, two principal suits grew out of the dispute of the Homestake partnership: one of them involved the validity of the claim of ownership by the Baxter Gold Mining Company, and the other case—the one in which the Winters heirs were represented by H.B.—became regionally famous as "Brunswick v. Winters' Heirs." When the litigation ended, the nod went to the heirs, and H.B. was launched on his way to success as a frontier attorney, a "rebel's son" worthy of recognition and the friendship of several local citizens who were destined for inclusion in the pages of frontier history.

Some of that friendship and camaraderie came by way of three other bachelors all of whom teamed up with H.B. to share a cabin for their living quarters: William C. MacDonald, Emerson Hough, and Albert B. Fall. MacDonald later became the governor of New Mexico; Hough, who was one of the attorneys in the Baxter case, left the law and attained literary fame as a writer of Westerns; Fall, after many years of legal prominence and political popularity in New Mexico, entered national politics as secretary of the interior in the administration of his friend President Warren G. Harding. Fall's name became synonymous with corruption, bribery, and the Teapot Dome scandal.[13]

The Winters case was only the beginning of H. B. Fergusson's establishment as a southerner in the Southwest. While waiting for the case to come to trial, he reportedly played checkers regularly in the post office and in this way became acquainted with "all comers," and in the process made many useful political contacts.[14] Just how much money he made as a lawyer in White Oaks is not easy to determine. But in a certain sense, he made much of his fortune there—if a monetary value can be placed on a reputation as a frontiersman. In White Oaks he made a name for himself, one that would be further enhanced upon his marriage into the Huning family in Albuquerque. But he also had the good fortune to actually strike gold and prove the claim of the frontier as a place of opportunity.

In White Oaks, the excitement of the Homestake strike was matched only by the gold of the Old Abe mine. Keleher and others report that "considerable money was spent in developing it into a property and it paid fabulous dividends to its owners for many years."[15] H. B. Fergusson became one of the Old Abe's three owners after the original claim was lost. Old Abe was first established in November 1879 and turned out to be a much bigger find than the Homestake. Its original owners—J. M. Allen, O. D. Kelly, and A. P. Livingston—worked on the assessment of the new mine for three years but lost their title in 1883 because they stopped working the mine.[16] In 1883 the title was open again for relocation. In January 1884 H.B., in a partnership with John Y. Hewitt and William Watson, located two new claims, both of which were on the property formerly known as the "Abraham Lincoln." These claims were the "Robert E. Lee," probably a name chosen by H.B., and the "White Oaks." In spite of the renaming, however, the mine continued to be called the Old Abe. By this time H.B. had moved north to Albuquerque because of the even greater promise it held for him as an attorney with a growing interest in politics. As an attorney, he knew that the original owners of the Old Abe had ignored the legal requirements of ownership, and along with his partners he was eager to satisfy the demands of claim and gamble on a vein already discovered. The claim was successful and its recovery better than anything White Oaks had known.

H.B. was at the height of his fortune and career as a lawyer in 1890. The Old Abe continued to put money in his pockets for many years. Harvey Fergusson remembered those glory days only in outline—the reality merged with legend: "My father told me afterward that during this period he felt sure he was going to be a rich man. I remember it vaguely at the height of the family prosperity, when we had a Negro cook and a Mexican gardener and gave many lavish entertainments, designed to promote my father's political fortunes" (*Home,* pp. 76–77).

Fergusson states in his autobiography that his father never really became a westerner in the same sense that his grandfather Huning did—never learned to speak Spanish, never took to the wilderness as a hunter, never developed a fascination with "the natives," because, he speculates, his father was too deeply rooted in the outlook of the Old South (*Home,* p. 65). But surely H.B. lived the life of a western frontiersman for a brief time in White Oaks, just as the frontier itself was closing.

White Oaks itself was destined to die and become a picturesque ghost town featured in colorful tourist brochures. The railroad sealed its death in bypassing the town and running instead from El Paso to the town of Capitan. The rest of H. B. Fergusson's life in the Southwest would be in another railroad town to the north. It was there that he would mix his fortunes and future with the past of Franz Huning.

NORTH TO CLARA AND MARRIAGE

The future of Albuquerque in 1883 was much brighter than the future of White Oaks. Veins of ore would run out, but the railroad ran to Albuquerque and assured its place on the economic map. H.B. headed north to that curious place with its two towns, old and new. It was New Town that interested him. It was a smart move for a forward-looking young frontier attorney. Seventeen years later he took his ten-year-old son back to White Oaks. Fergusson's memories confirm that his father had read the signs right: "I remember [White Oaks] very clearly as a quiet little place where graying men talked about great days that were over" (*Home,* p. 66). In 1883 the "great days" were just beginning for H.B. and for Clara Mary Huning, soon to be his wife.

In Albuquerque's New Town H.B. established a law partnership with N. B. Childers and began to practice law—and politics. As a frontier Democrat, he ran for district attorney in 1885 and won the election. From that time on—for a period of thirty years—his legal practice and his political career complemented each other. Only near the end of his life did the expense of keeping two careers, Washington congressman and Albuquerque attorney, prove the two efforts ultimately antagonistic.

In addition to his abilities as an attorney and a politician, another factor worked to H.B.'s advantage in winning acceptance in New and Old Town: he married the daughter of Franz Huning. Clara Huning Fergusson was a pioneer in her own right. She lived a long, full life and represented the Huning/Fergusson names with her own special toughness and gentility. She survived her husband by some forty-five years and never remarried after his death. In her later years she lived with and was looked after by her first-born child, Erna. Family letters and newsclippings indicate that she was an ironic combination of geniality, civic participation, and reclusiveness. Clara died September 3, 1950, at the age of eighty-five.

Born January 8, 1865, in Huning's La Glorieta, she prided herself on being the first Anglo, blue-eyed baby born in Albuquerque, and she promoted the family legend that area "Mexicans" came from near and far to catch a glimpse of her as a local curiosity because of her white skin and blue eyes. La Glorieta was filled with memories for her—as a girl growing up, as a wife and mother who raised her family there, and as an anguished woman who lived through the ordeal of the events which led up to and followed her husband's suicide in the very house where she was born, where Harvey Fergusson, her second child, was also born. Fergusson loved his mother very much and bases many of his female characters on his memory of her life in old and new Albuquerque. Her recognizable fictional counterpart appears most nostalgically in *The Life of Riley* as Mary Chase Morgan Riley, the mother of Morgan Riley. But all of Fergusson's ideal, "saintly" female characters have something of his mother in them, for she figured into his overall attitude toward women.

Clara's memoir deals more with the life she spent as a young woman growing up on the southwestern frontier, and with her husband's career, than with her children. She devotes only a brief paragraph to her son Harvey. Even so, her story is also her son's story. The

Clara Huning Fergusson. Courtesy of Francis and Peggy Fergusson.

frontier strongly affected her life—the forming of her personality. And her memoir, general as it is, shows just how much her history is intertwined with the pioneer history of New Mexico. Born at the end of the Civil War in Old Town, over her long life she grew up with Albuquerque's New Town. Spanish and German were the first languages she learned. She did not learn to speak English until she was six years old.[17]

When Clara was nine, her father took her to Santa Fe to the Loretto Convent, where she attended school for a year.[18] That experi-

ence is described as a nightmare in her memoir. She had never been
away from home before and was put in a large dormitory room with a
bare floor and a stove at one end. The regimen was as strict as the
setting was austere. She was perpetually chilled. She would awaken at
six-thirty in the morning and cross an open courtyard to another
room, where she washed out of a basin filled by a dipper from a tub. A
Loretto sister was always there to see that the children washed in spite
of the cold. Clara and the other children were then marched to a
chapel for mass and then given breakfast, described by her as a "poor
meal."

As a result of her year in Our Lady of Light, Clara could not bear
even the name "Santa Fe" for many years, and the experience made
her fervently loyal to Albuquerque. She had a governess for the next
three years, and then at the age of thirteen, she was taken to another
boarding school—this one, the Kirkwood Seminary in Kirkwood,
Missouri, near St. Louis, where her father regularly obtained most of
the merchandise for his mercantile business in Old Town as well as
materials for his various building projects.

In 1881, when Clara was sixteen, she went to Germany with Mrs.
A. Staab from Santa Fe, whose family lived in Wiesbaden. There she
spent two years in a Lutheran school run by a Madame Brandeis and
her daughter. Clearly, Huning's German roots ran deep, for while he
sent his daughter back to his Hanover homeland for crucial years of
schooling, he was planning the building of a bit of Germany in
Old/New Town.

When Clara returned, Albuquerque was a transformed town.
When she left in 1881, only the railroad station existed in New Town.
Now, in 1883, frame buildings of all shapes and sizes were being built
around the depot; and a streetcar, pulled by a mule, ran between Old
Town and New Town, thanks to the enterprise of her father, his
investments in "the Albuquerque Street Railroad," and his efforts in
establishing the thoroughfare of Railroad Avenue.[19] Socially, Albuquerque was still a small town where everybody knew everybody else;
there were church festivals, small dances, card parties and a multitude
of other social functions. Clara also returned to find her father's
"castle" almost ready for the family to move into. She was able to

enjoy, within months of her return, a gala open-house festivity on New Year's Day 1884.

With Clara's return to booming New Town and her father's Castle Huning, another momentous event soon took place and a new era in her life began. She does not give any details about how she met H. B. Fergusson other than to say that soon after her return from Germany and his move to Albuquerque in 1883 they met. However, very soon after H.B. had established his law practice in Albuquerque, Franz Huning struck up a friendship with the new attorney. This naturally led to convenient socializing with the Huning family and with Clara.

H.B. and Clara were married on April 14, 1887, at 8:30 P.M. in St. John's Episcopal Church. The *Albuquerque Democrat* of the next day wished them *bon voyage* on their honeymoon and on their "road through life." H.B. was thirty-nine; Clara was twenty-two. For the first year of their marriage they lived in Castle Huning, and their first child, Erna, was born there January 10, 1888, nine months later. As a present commemorating that event and for the token sum of a dollar, Huning gave Clara and his new son-in-law La Glorieta as their new home, and they moved there shortly after, in 1888.

SOUTHWESTERN POLITICIAN

H.B.'s career as a politician was one of the glorious phases of Clara's life and left a deep impression on all four of their children. Harvey's destiny was especially shaped by his father's political career and his years in Washington, for H.B. took his son with him and allowed him to see some of his heights of glory. He was at the height of his political career during the years he persuaded Harvey to attend his *alma mater*, Washington and Lee University. And it was during H. B. Fergusson's years as a congressman that Harvey decided to give up a career in law and, rather than continue in his father's footsteps as H.B. had hoped, become a journalist. Being the son of a congressman in the nation's capitol worked to his advantage and became a crucial part of his destiny.

Politics meant more to H.B. than even he, and in the end probably Clara, wanted to admit. He sacrificed both time and money for his political career and when the end of that career came, he was unable to shake the depression which accompanied the loss of an election, illness, and his return to Albuquerque. In keeping with life's ironies, territorial politics made him and statehood politics broke him.

Harvey Fergusson attributes much of his father's success as a politician not only to his complete dedication to the Democratic party and its causes but also to his skill as a rhetorician in the tradition of oratory which flourished in the Old South. Upon analysis, H.B.'s speeches reveal a flair for adapting the principles of classical rhetoric both in the structure of his arguments and in the methods of his appeals. There is much flamboyance and hyperbole, but there is also substance in content and in strategy; more ability than the son allows his father. Insofar as H.B.'s style as an orator brought him success with his constituency and his colleagues, the same overstated manner also dramatizes some of the differences between the father's and the son's attitudes toward words and the world.

The son, as a modern frontiersman, rebelled from his father's style, as a speaker and as a man, in favor of simplicity. As a boy of twelve listening to H.B.'s speeches about freedom and democracy, young Fergusson squirmed uncomfortably in his seat. The end effect of his father's "sound and fury" was that Fergusson, although the product of a liberal arts education not all that unlike his father's, avoided such flamboyancy in his own writing, and although he tried making a few speeches early in his career as a journalist, soon renounced speech making altogether. When it came to using words as a speaker or writer Fergusson tried his best not to be his father's son.

It is yet another irony of his making as a writer that he chose to rebel from H.B.'s desire that he follow in his chosen profession and become a lawyer. Rather than study law and return to Albuquerque to join the family firm, he decided to become a journalist. That apprenticeship in Washington was still partially carried out in the shadow of his father's position and prerogatives as a congressman. If his father was confident of the rightness of his world view and confident in the ways he expressed it, Fergusson was better suited to the questions and qualified certainties of a newsman in a new generation, facing a new age, albeit as a hereditary pioneer.

Fergusson rises to his own best eloquence in his account in *Home in the West* of how his father helped build the Democratic party and established his political base in New Mexico Territory. Part of H.B.'s constituency was built from the "dry farmers" who settled in eastern New Mexico in the late nineteenth century; another part included the predominately Republican Spanish Americans, who regarded him, says his son, as a patron in the tradition of the old days of the ricos. The influx of the dry farmers is described in terms consistent with Turnerian assumptions, vocabulary, and metaphor concerning the ending of the frontier: "Tall, angular men driving wagons loaded with household goods, tow-headed children and poultry, they were the last wave of the Western movement, seekers of free land after all the good land was gone, hereditary pioneers with no frontier before them" (*Home*, p. 71). There is something of Fergusson himself (and Turner) in such a description and something of Fergusson's father too in his identification with such a constituency and cause. Whatever the dynamics of the changes taking place on the frontier, H.B. cultivated these old Democrats in new times, and his attentions paid off. The Democrats sent him to Washington.

H. B. Fergusson's way to Washington was relatively hard and long. He was first nominated as a delegate to Congress at the territorial Democratic convention of 1892. His major supporters were his old White Oaks friend Albert B. Fall, and Jack Fleming from Silver City.[20] H.B. was defeated, however, by Antonio Joseph, an opponent who would block his nomination as a territorial delegate to Congress again at the 1894 convention. With Joseph's defeat in the ensuing election, H.B. became a party favorite for the nomination in the next convention in 1896. He sided with another friend, William Jennings Bryan, and his views on free silver and the agrarian revolt.[21] In so doing, H.B. spoke in opposition to President Grover Cleveland and New Mexico's territorial governor Thorton. H.B. lost the nomination this third and last time by three votes. But with the continued support of A. B. Fall and William Jennings Bryan, Fergusson was the natural choice for the Democratic nomination when L. Bradford Prince, the official nominee, proved an ineffective campaigner and his nomination was withdrawn.

H. B. Fergusson as a congressman. Courtesy of Li Caemmerer.

The state election of 1896 saw H.B. pitted against Republican Thomas B. Catron. When the votes were counted, H.B. had won by just short of a thousand votes. Had Bryan defeated William McKinley, considerable patronage for H.B. and for New Mexico would have been a certainty. But with McKinley's victory in 1896 H.B. was part of the minority in Congress.[22] He was nevertheless successful in his first term as territorial delegate to Congress. He introduced two statehood bills and saw to it that legislation was passed which named Santa Fe as the permanent capital of the territory.[23] Moreover, during this first two-year term he was successful in the proposing and passage of the Fergusson Act. Most would agree that this act was his greatest accomplishment, and the one for which he is best known. Marc Simmons goes so far as to say it "earned him such plaudits at home that he became, unquestionably, Albuquerque's most illustrious son."[24] Calvin A. Roberts comments that although H.B. had numerous accomplishments in his various roles as partisan, orator, reformer, and public servant, his sponsoring of the Fergusson Act was his most important role.[25] He introduced his bill on February 16, 1898; it passed both houses of Congress and became law on June 21, 1898.[26] By virtue of the Fergusson Act, New Mexico was allocated approximately four million acres of land for public education and other institutional purposes.[27]

Although he won renomination at the end of his term, he was unable to defeat the Republican candidate, Pedro Perea, in the fall election of 1898. H.B. lost by 1,100 votes, presumably owing to Perea's enthusiasm for the Spanish-American War and to the division of voters on ethnic lines—an ironic development, given H.B.'s championship of New Mexico's Hispanics, which sorely disappointed him.[28] He was defeated in the next election (1903–4) by Bernard Rodey.

Until 1911, when he won election to the House of Representatives as a Democrat, Fergusson occupied himself with his law practice—including some notorious trials like the murder trial of Jim Gilliland and Oliver Lee, which found H.B. and Albert B. Fall the winning counsels for the defense, and long-standing Republican adversaries Thomas B. Catron and Richmond P. Barnes losing for the prosecution. In 1910 H.B. participated in the constitutional convention as the territory began its transition into statehood. Ironically, given the fact that he did favor statehood, he could not support the constitution as proposed by the Republican majority at the convention. The Republicans advocated, for one thing, the partisan election of judges, and H.B. felt this was an invitation to the growth of Republican power generally. He thus gave speeches, wrote innumerable letters, and led a group of Democrats in voting against the new state constitution on November 21, 1910.[29]

All in all, H. B. Fergusson's stand as a territorial politician was to advocate the utilitarian principles of the greatest good for the greatest number. Although he lost the battle of the state constitution, he had positioned himself for reelection as representative from New Mexico in 1911. This time he went to Washington from a state and not a territory, New Mexico having attained statehood on January 6, 1912. He served in Washington for a year and then for another term, continuing his high-style Democratic rhetoric—always a tireless advocate of progressive philosophy and policies, always proud of how he went to Washington and the hard-working, honest way he got there. When he was refused one more term as a congressman, he was more reluctant to leave and return home than anyone could have guessed. He faced what his son Francis many years later characterized as a "dreary end."

DREARY END

H. B. Fergusson's death certificate, signed by P. G. Cornish, M.D., on June 10, 1915, reads, "To the best of my knowledge and belief, the cause of his death was as herewith written: suicide by hanging."[30] The legalistic wording of the Certificate and Record of Death offers a final irony to the life of one of frontier New Mexico's most illustrious politicians and attorneys. Few people at the time of H.B.'s death knew that he killed himself. The press reported the cause of death as apoplexy.[31] Moreover, subsequent commentators on H.B.'s life and accomplishments were either unaware of his suicide or preferred to avoid mentioning it. Harvey Fergusson in *Home* says nothing about suicide in talking about his father's death. More recently, others have attributed H.B.'s death to a stroke. But in the rememberings of H.B.'s youngest son, Francis, a child at the time, his father slit his own throat.

There were many causes for H.B.'s belief that he was a failure, and many reasons for his final act to end his life. He was in financial straits; he was ill with a flu-like malady that had hospitalized him, and emotionally he showed signs of neurosis; his marriage was not the happiest, due to incompatabilities enhanced over the years by the difference in age between him and Clara and by certain extravagances of living; moreover, William Jennings Bryan, for whom he served as secretary very briefly in 1915, resigned as secretary of state and, in effect, ended both his and H.B.'s political careers.

There are many causes and many effects surrounding H.B.'s suicide. But all add up to this: he killed himself and caused great personal sorrow, especially his young son Francis, age eleven at his father's death. Clara Huning Fergusson had her reasons for seeing to it that the public knew nothing about the circumstances of her husband's death. Perhaps she felt that suicide was a disgrace which diminished his name and hers. But H. B. Fergusson's accomplishments are not diminished by his suicide, and Clara noted those accomplishments with pride in her memoir. His fall from a position of comparative glory may be viewed as an ending that underscored the effect of the end of the frontier not only on an illustrious congressman but also on his children and on how one of them developed as a novelist.

One contributing cause of H.B.'s suicide was money—or lack of it. The vein of Old Abe gold had run out and been spent on quality living. An investment in California real estate never brought a profit. The line of succession to the Huning fortune went more directly to Huning's son, Arno, than to Clara, who had already inherited La Glorieta. Living the life of a congressman, keeping up two households (in Washington and in Albuquerque), educating four children, travel involved with his family and for the Democratic party and politics— all of these were expensive.

Records show that campaign expenses were always especially significant in H.B.'s attentions. Each campaign depleted more of his funds. He was a "poor" Democrat and ever soliciting financial help. He appealed with characteristic Old South eloquence to William Jennings Bryan, among others, for campaign support in 1911, saying: "None of us is rich, many of have seriously impaired our resources in fighting [the Republican 'gang'] in the past. We must have help from

Democrats outside of our borders, or stand by in grief inexpressible
and see the greatest of opportunities pass by us, helpless to avail
ourselves to it."[32] Even after winning the 1911 election, H.B.—with
money matters still very much on his mind—wrote to H. H. Pierce, a
friend at the Census Bureau in Washington, in an attempt to receive,
as soon as possible, what he hoped was his accumulated salary, saying:
"I wish you would make some inquiries for me touching the matter of
when my pay as a member of Congress begins. . . . I want you to
make the inquiry for me, of some long time member, or other officer,
because a party here has asserted that even though I am not sworn in
until December 4, 1911, my salary, as a member and all perquisites,
attaches from the beginning of this 62nd Congress, or March 4,
1911."[33]

His expenses at home were not so much the upkeep of La Glorieta, for that was in poor repair and rented out for the three or so years
the family lived in Washington. Clara and young Francis, who had
been born in 1904, were his most immediate family responsibilities.
Lina was enrolled in boarding school in Los Angeles until she moved
east with the family and attended design school in New York. Erna
was at least partially self-sufficient, since she had finished her master's
degree in 1913 at Columbia and was teaching in the Albuquerque
public schools prior to H.B.'s final term in Congress—although she
joined the family in Washington as well. By 1913 Harvey was with his
father in Washington, after having graduated from Washington and
Lee in 1911 and then trying his hand at a job with the U.S. Forest
Service. Law school gave way to newspaper work, and by the summer
of that year Harvey was close to being on his own. H.B. wrote home to
Clara with some good news in July, saying their son was, after a
fashion, now salaried and with a byline: "I enclose . . . a clipping
from the paper on which he works [*Washington Herald*]. His managing
editor told him to write a feature story on a book lately issued by the
Agriculture Department. The fly catcher article is its result. He has
been given more important work lately; and seems encouraged by
remarks of other attaches of the paper on his efforts. I think he will
soon be on a self-supporting basis. He is receiving now the magnifi-
cent salary of six dollars per week."[34]

The clipping is long lost, but H.B.'s pride, and good-humored relief, in his son's first successes as a journalist is obvious in the letter. Elsewhere in the same letter H.B. speculates about the consequences of the upcoming November election. If he is reelected, he plans to continue to send Lina to school in Los Angeles and to move Clara, Erna, and Francis to Washington with him and Harvey. But if he is not reelected, matters will be different. Money will be scarce and, he suggests, poverty near: "It is difficult to decide as long as my reelection is uncertain. If I am not elected, I shall be very weak financially and besides, my life in Washington will end on March 4 next."[35] Reelection did come and the family was moved to Washington and resided in a home on Q Street near Connecticut Avenue; however, the weak financial position about which he was worried was only postponed.

After he lost the 1914 election and completed his last duties in the spring of 1915, he went to work for a time as the personal secretary of William Jennings Bryan. He took the oath of that office on March 5, 1915. It is natural to speculate that the position was a sinecure. In late March, Bryan attempted to have H.B. appointed ambassador to Mexico. That did not materialize. After only a month or two, H.B. quit as Bryan's secretary. He then contracted an unidentified illness and returned to Albuquerque in late April or early May to recuperate and was hospitalized briefly. Clara and Francis returned to New Mexico with him.

Bryan was having his troubles as well. World War I and President Wilson's reaction to the sinking of the *Lusitania* altered Bryan's political career in an unexpected way. Bryan followed a line of strict neutrality toward Germany, and, in part because he thought President Wilson too belligerent in his response to Germany after the *Lusitania*'s sinking, he resigned on June 8, 1915. H.B. committed suicide two days later. Although Bryan did not die until 1925, a few days after the infamous Scopes trial, in which he helped prosecute John Scopes and faced the rigorous cross-examinations of Clarence Darrow, his political career more or less ended with his resignation as secretary of state. That decision must have added to H.B.'s anxiety about his own future. Bryan's telegram of condolence to Clara, while not exactly perfunctory, is still more formal than one might hope, and reflects some of his sense of the ending of his own career: "I am distressed to learn of the death of your husband; for twenty years we have been in cordial and sympathetic cooperation in the field of politics; I counted him among the most useful men of our party as well as among my personal friends; it was a great pleasure to have him with me as private secretary."[36]

It is generally reported that the strains of office during Fergusson's last term were too great for him and that, returning to Albuquerque, he "suffered a nervous breakdown, followed on 10 June 1915 by a fatal stroke."[37] Clara in her memoir, like Harvey in *Home*, is quiet on the subject. If one judges from Clara's memoir, her marriage was happy, and her husband died of natural causes. But a different version of H.B.'s "dreary end" is told by his youngest son, Francis, who recounts with painful honesty his father's final months.

Francis was only eleven at the time of his father's death. Born late in his parents' lives—H.B. was fifty-five, and Clara was thirty-nine—Francis, almost from his earliest memories, pictures his father as "shaky, worried, and silent," and generally "in pretty bad shape."[38] H.B. was so worried over a five-year period near the end of his life that he neglected to include Francis in his will, which had been drawn up before Francis's birth. Only in 1922, when Francis was eighteen, did his mother as "statutory guardian" arrange with probate court for Francis to inherit an "undivided $3/32$ of the property of [his father]."[39]

Francis remembers that at the age of seven he would go to meet his father as he returned from his Washington office. He recalls seeing H.B. get off the trolley which ran from the Capitol, and even at that time he was shaky and infirm. The general impression Francis kept of his father is that he was not in good health during the entire period he knew him.[40]

When H.B., Clara, and Francis returned to Albuquerque in what Francis remembers to be April of 1915, they moved back into La Glorieta. The damages of the fire which the house sustained earlier had not been repaired. After H.B. returned from his hospitalization, he and Clara lived in different parts of the house; their marriage had not been good for some time—at least as long as Francis could remem-

Francis Fergusson, ca. 1915. Courtesy of Francis and Peggy Fergusson.

ber. Francis guesses that they were probably "killing each other off" in their resistance to each other, not so much over money but because of incompatability. Their marriage puzzled Erna as well. The year Clara died, Erna wrote to Francis recounting some of her bafflement about her mother: "How a girl with such a background came out with so agonizing a sense of inferiority that she actually made herself as dull and inconspicuous as she could, refused to dress well, covered up her lovely neck and shoulders, ran from people, declined the position a superior husband made for her? This baffles me."[41] Whatever the reasons, Clara and H.B. were miserable as husband and wife at the time of his suicide. As for H.B., Francis remembers: "He was pretty awfully lost; and his health was not very good. My memory of him was . . . seeing him walking up and down the irrigation ditch, wearing a bathrobe, city shoes and socks, and carrying a shotgun over his shoulder for self-protection, and he would be walking along the ditch, a favorite walk of his. He still got along all right with me. I was probably his only connection with humanity. His friends didn't come to see him. He had nobody to talk to but mother and she was so filled with blame over the mess they were in financially, and worried about what was going to happen next."[42]

It is rather curious that in this account of H.B.'s final days, there is an echo of the behavior of Franz Huning, who also allegedly patrolled the ditches with his shotgun. Perhaps the two accounts merged, somehow surfacing as the same behavior in different men and misremembered somehow by either Francis or Harvey. In any event, what happened next for H.B. was tragic for all concerned. Francis recounts it with special pathos:

When I woke up one morning I realized that something was wrong. I didn't know what it was. There was no sound, nothing. I stuck my head out into the placita. And I saw my mother who had just come [back] across. . . . I asked her what it was. She told me my father had died. I said, "Were there any wounds?" She said yes, that he must have cut his own throat. But she was a really self-controlled woman, and very strong. Her strength was to come out later . . . ; but she was absolutely sunk by the events. She couldn't do much except in monosyllables. She said that she could see

him—I think it was on the way back to his room—and she followed him I
guess and there she found him with his throat cut and gone or about to go.⁴³

According to Francis, Clara called the mortician, Mr. Strong, who said he could fix H.B.'s throat so the slice could be concealed, as well as the fact that the death was a suicide. She also called her brother, Arno, then living in Castle Huning, and "they put together the necessary details."⁴⁴ Although Francis remembers nothing about the physician who filled out the death certificate verifying that H.B.'s suicide was by hanging and not a slit throat, perhaps Dr. Cornish went along with the fabricated "details." Either that, or Clara was confused about the means of death. That family and professionals would hush up the truth of H.B.'s death shows how persuasive Clara was—and how sacrosanct was H.B.'s past reputation. Erna and Lina returned from Washington immediately. Harvey "begged off," wanting "to stay out of any possible family troubles." Apparently, many of H.B.'s friends had been frightened away by his wild and paranoid behavior in his final month. Few even came to his funeral. His body was cremated, and Clara had his ashes strewn on the mesa.

So it was that the territorial attorney, who had made his way from the frontier to Washington, returned to La Glorieta as an old and broken man—a disappointed and distraught man, consumed with his own sense of failure, defeated by the thwarted hopes he held in common with his friend William Jennings Bryan. Like Franz Huning, the promise of the frontier waned along with his own life's living. In each individual instance was the reenactment of the more universal instance of youth's hope dwindling with the despair of old age—of approaching or arriving at endings.

Harvey Fergusson says something along these lines in his account of his father's end; perhaps all "reflective" men see any given life as essentially a deteriorating proposition. It is in the very nature and cycle of change—beginnings and endings, ascents and descents: "I think a man who reflects upon a rich and varied experience can hardly fail to understand that the individual destiny is normally both an ordeal and a defeat, even though it has incidental triumphs" (*Home*, p. 77). This elegiac attitude is the one Fergusson also had toward his own life. If *destiny* is a common word for him, so is *ordeal* in his diaries and his novels. His overall view of life thus seems somehow partially cynical, partially pessimistic, partially tragic. H. B. Fergusson and his son were both prone to making reflective resolutions and then attempting to live up to them. Harvey Fergusson almost yearly in his diaries made long "retrospective" entries to see how he measured up. H.B. resolved when he was a student at Washington and Lee College, "That so far as there is life in me I will be a man!"[45]

H.B. and Harvey Fergusson both shared that resolve; and both father and son, if rebels, were reflective ones. In a larger context, their destinies reveal the way they attempted to achieve their resolve to be men in the face of the ordeal of change which took shape for them in large ways as the passing of the frontier. With the end of his father's and his grandfather's world, Fergusson looked out on his own new world, and for him that meant backtracking to the East. He perhaps even viewed it as a sanctuary which he dared not leave at the time of his father's death, not even to attend his funeral. For some reason, as he reached his majority and his father met his death, he felt that in Washington he could see more clearly the newness of the old East and the oldness of the new West. From that perspective he wrote his first novel about the West—while in the East. After a try or two at writing novels set in the East, he realized that the West was his grand subject. As he says in *Home* (p. 79), he saw himself amidst all the changes in his life, and at this particular moment in history, as a man facing life "in the hard cold light of a morning after"—after the end of the great pioneering adventure.

The morning after H.B.'s death found his son even more on his own, materially, than before Huning's death. Whatever the light of the new day, however, it was magnified by the brightness of previous frontier days when pioneers found their world, a great and sublime emptiness, all before them—just as the light of the morning after was dimmed by the twilight in which Fergusson lived his youth as the grandson of a Santa Fe trader and the son of an Alabama rebel.

4

Morning After (1897–1923)

Whether considered as part of the passages of an individual life or of historical change more generally, the ending of one frontier usually implies the beginning of another one. Thus Harvey Fergusson, born in the year which was said to mark the end of the frontier, saw himself as a hereditary pioneer, part of a new generation of the West which "faced life in the hard cold light of a morning after." His morning after, not unexpectedly, brought both the light of new beginnings and regrets. His destiny was to backtrack to the newer industrial urban frontiers of twentieth-century America. It was a backtracking which allowed him to redefine his own youth in the West and the frontier times of his grandfather and father through the prism of the East.

Fergusson's position in literary history is now that of a writer of the American West. He is regarded as holding a representative but minor position in the tradition of realism which developed in America in the late nineteenth and early twentieth centuries, a tradition associated largely with midwestern novelists who saw anew American small towns and big cities. The romantic strain in the development of the myth of the West and the popular frontier and Western novel is usually not seen in Fergusson's writings. Nevertheless, Fergusson's romanticism cannot be denied. He was, paradoxically, a romantic realist trying to see his own life and historical moment in the hard light of the morning after, but nostalgically lamenting the end of the frontier and ever attempting to reperceive and recreate it.

First as a practitioner of journalism, he honed his skills as a writer of the satirical novel of manners and of the historical novel with an eye toward the simplicity and precision required of a newspaperman. Regardless of novelistic form or style, however, Fergusson infused his fiction with his own autobiography and with the biographies of his family. That in itself was not uncommon—nor were the themes with which he dealt: westering; the East and West defining each other; the battle of the sexes; small-town and big-city manners and mores; the development and alienation of the writer; nature versus industrialism; primitivism in conflict with civilization; the assimilation of diverse racial and cultural values; the rise and fall of great men and moments; and the spirit of place.

Fergusson's writings assuredly verify Turner's frontier thesis, but they also give evidence to the belief that the frontier, albeit a major force in the shaping of American history, was only one of many formative influences. One of the most prominent of American literary historians, Robert E. Spiller, accepted Turner's thesis thirty years ago but added this qualification: "[Turner] claimed to be telling the whole story when he was telling only part of it."[1] In this view, the processes of expansion in the nineteenth-century American West were counterbalanced by industrialization, especially typified by the railroad and that special time and place when at Promontory Point, Utah, in 1869 a golden spike marked the completion of the first transcontinental railroad. That action, of course, contributed to the end of the frontier in a much more dramatic way than the proclamation of the Census Bureau. Fergusson realized this. New Town was a product of the coming of the railroad that was almost simultaneous with his birth; and his portrayal of the West in his historical novels plays up this fact—what Leo Marx documents in his analysis of literary texts throughout nineteenth-century American literature as the consequences of the appearance of "the machine in the garden."

The world into which Fergusson was born may thus be seen as a special southwestern version of a larger national process which since the beginning of American national identity and the exploration of the West—whether by Lewis and Clark, Boone, or others—fascinated, indeed preoccupied, American writers. In Fergusson's world these larger national themes of cyclical change were painted on a canvas which, although highlighting the late-nineteenth and early-twentieth-century Southwest, filled in the larger backgrounds of Hispanic ricos and penitentes, as well as the urban East.

In the themes and settings which make up Fergusson's books, the frontier endings of his grandfathers and father, his mother and sisters, and the pioneer legacy which his entire family inherited were but the beginnings of a second frontier, a second stage of American history, for Fergusson and for the nation and larger world of which he was a part. His name thus belongs in lists which include Twain, Howells, Norris, London, Lardner, Lewis, and Anderson—those writers who represent the American literary realism and naturalism that came in the wake of the closing of the promise offered by the frontier.

Satire and skepticism were part of Fergusson's inheritance, but so was the romantic promise of the open West which he could not forget. Try as he might to shape himself as a realist, to demythologize the West of his forefathers, he was drawn repeatedly to mythologizing the West and westering. If not the anxiety of the modern era then certainly the ambivalences of his times were reflected in his renderings of both the early and late frontier, a line which by definition kept moving, recurring, looking forward and backward even when it reached the West's farthest boundary, the Pacific.

LONE RIDER

As a boy growing up in Albuquerque, Fergusson knew both the old and the new frontiers, the pastoral and industrial, the waning romantic pioneer era and the dawning of the era of realism. The Southwest he was born into was a place of cultural and historical laminations, owing in large part to the lingering influences of Hispanic and native American cultures as the Anglo-European and Anglo-American influence continued its ascendancy. In *Home* he describes his youth as divided between two civilizations. He lived in Albuquerque's Old Town but went to school in New Town and spent his early years connecting between those two worlds, "liking neither of them very much, lured from the first by the unpopulated freedom beyond the picket fence" (*Home*, p. 80). Albuquerque had a population of approximately 10,000 at the turn of the century, and literally out of his front door was the wildness of the river and the mesas.

Just how far the ambivalences of growing up in such a locale affected his life is affirmed once again in his 1967 preface to the Apollo edition of *Rio Grande*. In this essay, which amounts to a return to Albuquerque and a look at the changes in the city and its surroundings over a seventy-year period, Fergusson observes that even amidst the many changes and the growing population, one thing is constant: "I know of no other place where the wilderness is so close to the city, or where the primitive survives so close to civilization."[2] Fergusson found such a strange mixture of primitive and civilized congenial, and in one way or another he revisited Albuquerque in book after book throughout his career.

Such ambivalences of place shaped not only his personality but also his themes. He grew up an observer, iconoclastic and rebellious when it came to small-town conformity and gossip, choosing to see society through the critical eyes of a skeptic and a satirist, pretending to be unable to accept fully the romanticism of the old West but nevertheless saddened into disillusionment by the old lost world and his newly inherited one. His double sense of loss was at once ironic and compensatory, for he found both solace and discomfort in the spirit of place he knew as a youth. Insofar as there was constancy to his memory and perceptions, it focused on the landscape: his lonesome love of the river, the mesas, and the mountains.

The extent of Fergusson's need to identify with the frontier aspects of his youth is apparent in nearly all of the publicity which took shape as "author's profiles" behind the actual personae of this

Albuquerque in the 1890s, looking north along Second from the corner of Second and Silver. Courtesy of the Cobb Memorial Collection, Special Collections Department, General Library, University of New Mexico.

fiction. His earliest memories in such statements go back to the period between 1895 and 1901 and the wildness of the town and its environs: "Gambling was wide-open and cow-punchers and sheep men crowded the saloons on Saturday nights. The surrounding country still was wild and it was the first thing that caught my interest. I had a horse and a gun by the time I was eleven and spent nearly all my time hunting and riding, mostly alone."[3]

Such publicity, although romanticized wish-making to a degree, formulated for the purposes of advertising, tends to promote Fergusson's personal myth as a macho Western author. Nevertheless, it contains a big portion of autobiographical truth. There is reason to believe that Fergusson, as a youth and later as a man, was indeed a lone rider, in the tradition of the lonesome cowboy, roaming the mesas and mountains of his native state on his horse, with his own gun, shooting ducks, quail, and deer, and, not entirely in his imagination, riding the range with cowpunchers and sheepmen. Just how much he was responsible for the creation and continuation of this image of a "lonesome-cowboy" youth is also witnessed in a letter written when he was sixty-one, to Texas writer J. Frank Dobie. In a nostalgic aside filled with his own kind of authentic ethos as a man of the waning West, Fergusson remarks: "I guess the wild horses are about gone now. When I was a kid in Albuquerque there was still a little bunch on the mesa West of town. . . . They were unmistakably wild animals and it always gave me a thrill to see them."[4]

Real horses and guns, not toys, were a major interest of Fergusson's childhood. Horses in particular obsessed him as early as the age of five; and aside from the fascination they hold for most youths, especially those influenced by the mystique of the West, Fergusson conjectures that he saw them as a means of escape from boredom and restraint (*Home*, p. 84). His serialized novel, *Proud Rider* (1935–36), illustrates the fascination with horses, and the life of escape and freedom, which continued throughout his life and made itself known in his many travels. Moreover, the vagabond life becomes a prominent theme in his fiction of the 1920s and in the portrayal of a majority of his fictional heroes and counterparts.

Not only in his childhood, but also in his many pack trips into the northern New Mexico mountains, in his job as a timber cruiser with the U.S. Forest Service in the Carson National Forest as a young man, and in his various fishing and hunting trips throughout his life, Fergusson experienced first-hand the solitary life of a lone rider, adventurer, and hunter—the type of character he repeatedly portrays in his novels. His image of himself as a solitary man, a hunter, was deepseated and essential to his self-concept: "The lone hunter is the most individualistic of human figures, as far back into the past as you can trace him, and I was apparently by birth an extreme individualist in an exact sense of the word. I was profoundly averse to moving except on my own impulse and I was even more profoundly averse to any interference with my spontaneous movement" (*Home*, pp. 89–90). Fergusson's initial ten years as a lone rider, from about the age of seven—when his father first lifted him onto the back of a pony—until the age of sixteen, when he left Albuquerque to attend school at New Mexico Military Institute, allowed him to soak up the kind of feelings and perceptions of a latter-day mountain man which colored not only his fiction of the frontier West but that of the second frontier of the

Harvey Fergusson, 1895. Courtesy of the Cobb Memorial Collection, Special Collections Department, General Library, University of New Mexico.

individual confronting the city. It was a role which would entail the loneliness of the writer, first as a tough and individualistic journalist and then as a struggling novelist.

Implicit in his own musings about how he came to be the kind of rebellious, individualistic loner that he did is the fact that the solitary life of a lone writer (a hunter after truth and beauty, accuracy and art) was well suited to a lone rider. Through words, memory, imagination, and history, he could write/ride away and escape: "It seems to me now I mounted a horse when I was a boy and rode away, and that I have spent most of the rest of my life trying to return without ever wholly succeeding" (*Home*, p. 100). The means of that attempted return were initially as a cadet at military school, then as a college student, and then as a writer.

CADET AND COLLEGE

Perhaps because of his individualistic make-up, Fergusson's public statements about his formal schooling all reflect a similar kind of dissatisfaction and rebellion. Whether in the public schools of Albuquerque, at New Mexico Military Institute in Roswell, or at Washington and Lee University, he felt that he learned relatively little. An attempt at night sessions of law school after graduation from Washington and Lee lasted only a few weeks. Certainly formal schooling (including two semesters at the University of New Mexico in 1907–8)[5] made him knowledgeable and informed, but what is significant is his insistence that school in whatever form grated against every instinct and attitude of his personality and was a general waste of time: "I was bored by school and read very few books before I was twenty, but I liked to draw pictures. One year I went to school in Washington, D.C., where my father was a delegate to Congress from the territory of New Mexico, and one year I went to the New Mexico Military Institute in Roswell, where I was drilled so thoroughly that I know the manual of arms and still jump when I hear reveille in the morning. At Roswell I acquired a greatly improved carriage and a lasting aversion to military discipline. At the age of eighteen I went to Washington and Lee University, in Virginia, for the somewhat irrelevant reason that my father had gone there in 1870 when General Lee was president. I there acquired a B.A. degree and a profound distaste for academic instruction."[6]

At the age of sixteen Fergusson was sent to New Mexico Military Institute in an attempt by his father to lessen his son's awkward social ways and general shyness. Fergusson concedes that he was slightly round-shouldered and cared littled about his appearance (*Home*, p. 187). His year at NMMI was an attempt to correct these "inadequacies." H. B. Fergusson was held in considerable esteem by

Harvey Fergusson (standing, second from the right) and other cadets at the New Mexico Military Institute. New Mexico Military Institute photograph.

NMMI, if for no other reason than that the school had received 50,000 acres as a result of the passage of the Fergusson Act,[7] and he had been honored with the request to deliver the school's first commencement speech. Although NMMI has a fine record of achievement and boasts of a virtual who's who in New Mexico and the Southwest among its graduates, for Fergusson his time there was a nightmare of hazing and fighting and general torment. As he describes it, "To a shy boy raised on solitude and freedom all this was just as delightful as a term in penitentiary" (*Home*, p. 189).

After two semesters in the "college" department of the University of New Mexico, from fall 1907 to spring 1908, Fergusson enrolled in Washington and Lee University. Fergusson's account of his four years at Washington and Lee, from 1908 through 1911, is told almost as harshly as his account of his year at NMMI. Just as he compliments the overall curriculum and campus of NMMI as it developed in later years, so he concedes that Washington and Lee evolved into a better school than the small college and town he knew, both of which for him were "truly relics of the past and . . . dominated by the old and by their memories" (*Home*, p. 191). To his mind the college and Lexington represented traditions of the Old South and the "Lost Cause" and all the atrophied viewpoints and values they implied. What Fergusson found was dignified and endorsed snobbery and a condescending fraternity system.

His college career amounted to a time of dual allegiances, in that Fergusson was promptly initiated into a fraternity because of Sampson Noland Ferguson's Civil War service and H.B.'s membership in the fraternity system. Conformity, deference, pride, faith in the cult of woman-worship, fellowship, and racial prejudice in one form or another—these were the traits which he found success at college demanded (*Home*, pp. 192–93). While Fergusson later came close to an outright denial of the value system which he found in effect at Washington and Lee, the situation was not intolerable for him at the time he experienced it. His understanding of what he experienced was cumulative. Much of his account of life as a cadet and at college deals with what might, in old-fashioned terms, be called "wenching." His account of interracial sexual behavior is offensive to today's sensibilities even though the mores of the time and place are presented honestly. Fergusson was no racist, but in the 1980s his anecdotes about white and black sexual encounters are embarrassing. It is to Fergusson's credit that he was not up to the "requirements of this phase of college life," but he protests too much about the evils of "exotic black girls" and "boys who went nigger hunting" (*Home*, p. 196).

Fergusson followed a course of studies which included Latin, Spanish, economics, commerce, German, oral debate, two years each of history, geology, and biology, and three years of English.[8] In spite of such studies and the discovery of Lafcadio Hearn and Tolstoy as favorite authors, Fergusson later regarded his college years as "a period of gloom and stagnation, relieved by some moments of drunken delight, of furtive escape and rebellion" (*Home*, p. 197).[9]

His course of study at the University of New Mexico (which included French, Greek, and Latin) and at Washington and Lee was that of a liberal arts education. In his own accounts, he is not explicit about what he studied. His account of his education stresses values

Harvey Fergusson on his graduation from Washington and Lee, 1911.
Courtesy of Quail Hawkins.

more than subject matter. As far as he was concerned those values were provincial, middle-class, capitalistic, and patriotic—filled with acceptance of America and with optimism regarding the future. He reports in his autobiography that it never occurred to him to doubt those values until many years later. Portraying his formal education as more or less narrow-minded social conditioning rather than "education," Fergusson attributed his real education to the reading of H. L. Mencken, Van Wyck Brooks, and Randolph Bourne—the "prophets of a new day." Deeply imprinted by the substance and tone of skeptics and satirists such as these, Fergusson saw his formal education as something to be repudiated and his mood of rebellion and individualism is given as the reason for such a judgment.

Thus his institutional education represents an episode in his life which he held up to denial. As such, it allowed for the confirmation of his solitary and individualistic temperament and contributed to the formulation of a subject matter in his books which closely paralleled in characterization and setting his own backtracking to the East, allowing him some degree of liberation in the consoling thought that the American frontier, before the coming of machines, and the alleged corruption of America by big business and technology, could be held out as a pastoral ideal. In his early novels, at least those about Washington life, he embraced the iconoclastic view of modern American life. In his middle and later phases, at least in his novels about the first American frontier, he indulged the other side of his ambivalent view of America in a restructured, romanticized view about the frontier and its closing. Whatever its transmutations, he was able to take the common story of his own times—that of the American dream—and serve it up in numeorus satirical versions applied to both men and women. In one novel after another he takes the basic plot of the "success" story and turns it inside out by presenting a hero or heroine who wants little to do with money and status—or by opening them up to satirical treatment if they do. In part, his escape from the West and his aspirations to become a journalist and later a novelist were reactions to the restraints he associated with the small town. Even so, he worked hard at his own form of success as a writer. He too had his bosses—whether Haskin, Mencken, Knopf, or others. He knew, if he did not believe it, that total independence and nonconformity for a writer who wanted to publish was another myth.

MOUNTAIN MAN

Recognizing that the traditions if not the myths of his pioneer grand-fathers and the Old South and New Mexico territorial frontier of his father were in the past, Fergusson, upon graduating from Washington and Lee in 1911, returned to Albuquerque to face his own future. Freed by what he regarded somewhat ironically as his failure—that is, his failure to conform to small-town Albuquerque society and to the *status quo*—he took recourse in the abiding solace of his youth as a lone rider: he took to the mountains in search of further freedom. If his education had been a series of failures, those failures set him free "from the mold of class, from the reverence for authority, from the fear of convention"; the social tradition he inherited was not for him insofar as it was of one world and he faced another one. He would be his own kind of "mountain man." It was a complex decision which would eventually prepare him to write *Wolf Song*, one of the best mountain-man novels ever written.

His first move away from the theoretical world of formal educa-tion into the practical world of work came with his employment in the U.S. Forest Service. It too presented an interesting mixture of inde-pendence and bureaucracy. On the surface it allowed him a way back into the wild. He could revel in the majesty of the Sangre de Cristo range in northern New Mexico, observe deer and elk, turkeys and trout, breathe fresh air and see distances which stretched into obliv-ion. Perhaps more than any other endeavor, his time spent in the forest bridged the worlds of conformity and independence. It was merely a temporary escape from the cities he felt he had to confront. But it was an escape into the wild which would impress him strongly and provide him with much material for fiction and his spirit.

Fergusson spent at least one season—summer into fall—in the employment of the U.S. Forest Service. His autobiographical account places that time as the summer of 1911—after graduation from college and before his father's 1912 term in Washington (*Home*, pp. 226–31).

It is likely that H.B.'s political influence helped secure the job for his son. At that time Fergusson was twenty-one. Despite Fergusson's own account, there is some official uncertainty about just when he worked for the Forest Service. Warfel states that "during and after his college years [he] spent several summers working for the United States Forest Service."[10] Forest Service records list him as one of ten assistants working "reconnaissance" under the supervision of H. G. Calkins in the Pecos National Forest in the July Field Program for 1910. Fergusson's name does not appear in any other program for the July 1910 through April 1913 period.[11]

At that time the Forest Service was in its infancy and undergoing administrative reorganization in an attempt to upgrade personnel from amateur to professional status. Partly because of this pressure, Fergusson, after completing his summer doing reconnaissance in District Three (the Southwest district), and more specifically in the Pecos National Forest, took the ranger's examination recently instituted for appointment as a forest ranger. Had his father not intervened and convinced him that a job in Washington and the study of law were more desirable, Fergusson would more than likely have served under the supervision of pioneer conservationist Aldo Leopold, who was, from 1912 to 1914, one of the supervisors in the Carson National Forest.[12]

Fergusson worked as a timber cruiser and mapmaker in the Carson National Forest, which, along with the Jemez and the Santa Fe forests, constituted the Pecos National Forest. Part of the vast range of the Sangre de Cristo Mountains in northern New Mexico, the Carson alone contained over 966,000 acres, extending to Taos and including all that portion of the Jemez Mountains north of the Chama River.[13] Fergusson describes his work as "cruising timber [with] a crew which moved by pack train and wagon across a great wilderness of yellow pine in the northern part of the state" (*Home*, p. 226). The job of a timber cruiser on reconnaissance was to obtain a rough estimate of the stand of green and dead timber, by species, in any particular division of the forest.[14] In the words of long-time Southwest forest ranger Ed C. Groesbeck, "A timber cruiser goes through the forest and estimates the volume of timber in board feet or cubic feet, on each forty-acre tract or section of 640 acres." Groesbeck's colleague Lou Liedman explains that a timber cruiser estimates a log at 16 feet and then figures how many logs a tree will yield and how many board feet, depending on estimates of the tree's diameter. A tally sheet records this information for each species.[15]

On Sundays Fergusson began to spend more of his leisure time writing. His mountain surroundings provided the inspiration and the subject matter for his first attempts at fiction. One of his earliest stories, soon destroyed and never published, was inspired by a mountain lion he observed while on reconnaissance—an animal which came to occupy his imagination in his daily treks through the remote canyons of the forest named after the heroic frontier scout and acquaintance of Franz Huning's, Kit Carson.

In a sense, Fergusson's compulsion to write was symbolized by the pursuit of the lion for its prey. His developing preoccupation with words and writing in the midst of the silences of the Sangre de Cristos and the whispering of the pines eventually took him to the nation's capital, to Baltimore, New York, Texas, Louisiana, Mexico, Panama, and the West Indies, back to the Southwest and on to the further wests of Utah and California—always observing, always on the special kind of reconnaissance known to the hunter's awareness, the cruiser's estimates, the writer's eye. Even in the crowds of the metropolis and in exotic southern locales, those lonely but inspiring days of discovery in the Carson forest stayed with him and influenced, in repeated scenes, much of what he included in his novels. The lesson learned as a U.S. Forest timber cruiser, a modern mountain man, was stamped into his spirit forever.

WASHINGTON

When Fergusson returned to Washington, D.C., at his father's urging in 1912, it was to enter law school and presumably follow his father's profession—perhaps in politics, but more likely as an attorney in Albuquerque. His father was in Washington once again as a congressman. It was a doubly significant year, since it was the year of New Mexico's statehood. H.B. soon knew that his son would not finish a

law degree. In the time it would take Fergusson to become a lawyer—
three years hence—H.B. would return to New Mexico and, failing to
reestablish his own practice or regain his health and recoup financial
losses incurred while in politics, would end his life by his own hand. It
is doubtful that had Fergusson become a lawyer and returned to
Albuquerque, his father's despondency would have lessened.

Fergusson stayed in Washington, and after a decade as a journalist
for numerous newspapers, he wrote his first novel, *Blood of Conquerors*
(1921), about another young lawyer, Ramon Delcasar, who, although
a Spanish-American, represents an intriguing composite of what his
author-creator was and might have been. Two other novels, *Capitol
Hill* (1923) and *Women and Wives* (1924), soon followed. They similarly incorporated aspects of Fergusson's life, including his first marriage and the accidental death of his closest friend, all colored by the
extrapolations of fiction. Closer to classification as satirical novels of
manners about the aspirations of young writers in the political and
bureaucratic spin of Washington middle-class society than identification as historical novels about the Southwest on the verge of the
twentieth century—as is the case with *Blood of the Conquerors*—these
two Washington novels nevertheless confirm that if Fergusson had
anything to say as a novelist, it came directly from the experiences of
his life history in confluence with his heritage and the larger history of
his times. Try as he might to escape it, his future as a man and as a
writer in Washington was also his past in the Southwest.

He had attended school for one year in Washington before, during his father's first term as a congressman. But this second time, in
1912, his father utilized the same kind of influence that had helped
land Fergusson his summer job with the Forest Service, and obtained
for him a job in the House Office Building folding mail. It was a boring
job for a former timber cruiser and a budding author who wanted to
write his own ideas on paper rather than stuff envelopes with the
bombast of Washington politicians. After a few weeks of work in the
House Office Building by day and law school by night, Fergusson
wandered into the city room of the Washington *Herald,* one of the
lesser papers in the capital. Almost before he knew what he was
saying, he asked the managing editor for a job.

His first assignments, without pay, were such things as flower shows and church suppers. He traveled by streetcar to numerous similar social events, observing, listening to speeches, copying down names and addresses—work similar to that of some of his fictional Washington characters. He would then return to the newspaper office, write out a short account in pencil and then type it awkwardly with one finger. When the edited versions of his news accounts finally appeared, albeit hidden on the back page, he felt a new kind of exuberance which confirmed in him the belief that he was suited to newspaper work as he had been to timber cruising. The power of observation, first realized as a hunter and then on reconnaissance in the mountains, now found an outlet in the city, another kind of wilderness.

He came to think philosophically about the process in somewhat naturalistic terms which were later applied to his method of writing fiction. After countless articles about minor aspects of Washington church and club life, Fergusson was assigned to cover a rifle competition. As a result of this article, in which he was able to emphathize with America as a nation of riflemen, endorsing the frontiersman's right to bear arms, he was offered a full-time job at $8.00 per week.

Besides the Washington *Herald*, he worked on several other dailies, and in many capacities, in the East and the South, during the next ten years: reporter for the *Herald*, for the Savannah *Morning News*, and from 1912 to 1913 for the Richmond *Times-Dispatch;* reporter with the Washington bureau of the Chicago *Record-Herald* in 1913–14; and editor for the Frederick J. Haskin newspaper syndicate from 1915 to 1922.[16] During this last period, in 1918, Fergusson's close friend from Albuquerque, Frank M. Spitz, who had traveled to Washington to work with Fergusson, was drowned in a canoeing accident. Thus, two years after his father's suicide, Fergusson experienced a second major tragedy in his life, one for which he assumed considerable guilt. A year later, in 1919, Fergusson married for the first time, and that ill-fated union sorrowfully affected the next several years, through prolonged separation and eventual divorce.

By 1923 he was ready to strike out even further on his own as a freelancer, placing short fiction in popular magazines and many articles in the Baltimore *Evening Sun,* and trying to devote most of his time to writing novels. The decade from 1912 to 1922 provided him with crucial emotional and aesthetic experiences for his first three novels, for even though *Capitol Hill* and *Women and Wives* were not published until 1923 and 1924, respectively, they owed their existence to Fergusson's time in Washington. The death of his friend, his first marriage and divorce, the people he met, worked with, and observed, were reshaped in his fiction. Certainly his father was a major influence during this Washington period. But so was Haskin, and perhaps most important of all was his fortuitous friendship with Henry L. Mencken and, as a result, his affiliation with Alfred A. Knopf, who became his publisher.

Just about all of Fergusson's newspaper work focused on Capitol Hill. As a correspondent for the Chicago *Record-Herald* he sat in the Washington press gallery, where his chief duty was to keep in touch with the Illinois delegation in Congress. It was an experience treated satirically in his Washington novels. During his seven years with the Haskin Syndicate he was, in effect, the *Haskin Letter*—both writing and editing it. As a result, he followed many kinds of political and economic data closely and wrote scores of articles about the government, traveling as well to the West Indies, Panama, and Canada on assignment.

HASKIN, MENCKEN, AND KNOPF

Fergusson took one of the most important jobs in his career as a journalist in 1915. Frederick J. Haskin needed an assistant for his syndicated newsletter. It was a demanding job in that Haskin intended to turn much of the writing of the column over to his new employee. Fergusson needed a job and took it on first offer. Haskin had spent many years as a correspondent for such important midwestern papers as the St. Louis *Globe-Democrat* and the Kansas City *Star.* He was known for a notable series of articles on the Klondike and on the Spanish-American War and was known as a reputable foreign correspondent who had published interviews with the emperor and empress of Japan and Pope Pius X. After such accomplishments he settled in Washington. There, he started the Haskin Information Service and wrote a syndicated "Answers to Questions" column which made him one of the nation's best-known columnists. His daily letter on government dealt with explanations of what various departments were doing and how they were constituted. His bureau became "the largest free information service in existence, supplying factual information on a great variety of subjects." He employed a large staff of research assistants but based much of his service on his personal background as a journalist with experience all over the world.[17] For Fergusson the job promised a variety of assignments which included considerable travel opportunity. It would also provide material for his Washington novels.

Employment by Haskin led to two major events for Fergusson: he convinced his Albuquerque friend, Frank M. Spitz, to move to Washington and work with him for Haskin; and he met H. L. Mencken as part of what seemed to be a routine assignment. In 1916, a year after Fergusson began his employment for Haskin, he sent for Spitz. Two years later, in the spring of 1918, Spitz was dead. Aside from his father's suicide in 1915, Spitz's death was the most tragic event experienced by Fergusson during his Washington years. It intruded in veiled ways into his fiction of the period every time Fergusson wrote about camaraderie.

Spitz was born in Albuquerque in 1894, four years after Fergusson. They grew up together and were best friends for more than a decade; both their pasts and their futures seemed to run in similar tracks. There were decided differences in the heritage of these two individuals, but in rough outline they were almost like brothers. Spitz, like Fergusson, came from a pioneer merchant family that had helped settle Santa Fe and Albuquerque at the turn of the century. Edward Spitz, Frank's father, emigrated to America from Bohemia (Czechoslovakia) and worked in the general merchandise and delicatessen business before joining the Ilfeld-Vanderwart Wool Company as secretary in 1909. In 1913 he became secretary-treasurer of the Ilfeld Indian Trading Company and by 1923 was vice-president of the Louis Ilfeld Company, one of the Southwest's largest merchandisers and wool businesses.[18] Edward Spitz was not as renowned an Albuquerque merchant pioneer as Franz Huning, but the Spitz family was one of the more prominent immigrant families to settle Albuquerque.[19]

Frank Spitz worked for a time as a clerk for the Louis Ilfeld Company, but after graduation from the University of New Mexico and graduate study at Columbia, and upon the urging of Fergusson, he moved to Washington. At the time of his death, on Friday, March 22, 1918, Spitz was twenty-four years old and living at the YMCA in Washington, a detail Fergusson makes imaginative use of in his portrayal of Ralph Dolan's friendship with Henry Lambert in *Capitol Hill*. As Spitz's elder, Fergusson had generally introduced him to the Washington scene and served as friend and advisor. But he was unable to save him from drowning.

Spitz was the first drowning victim of the spring in the dangerous waters of the Potomac below Chain Bridge—a stretch of the river which claimed many lives to drowning. Fergusson and Spitz had taken a canoe into the river intending a Friday afternoon of pleasure. The pair left Moore's boat house and paddled up the river on the District of Columbia side, and according to the news accounts of the accident, when they were about one-quarter of a mile past Chain Bridge, they decided to cross to a stone quarry on the Virginia shore. The current was stronger than they realized, and the canoe overturned in midstream and threw them into the water.

They were both good swimmers, but they first grabbed the canoe. When it got away from them, Fergusson swam to the shore—about 100 feet away—but Spitz turned back thinking he could again reach the canoe. He miscalculated his strength and, too weak to make it to the boat or the shore, sank beneath the surface. Fergusson reported that he estimated Spitz was 200 or so yards away from him at the moment he went under. He was hopelessly out of reach. The body could not be found, and Fergusson could only wire his own mother in Albuquerque and tell her of the accident and that Spitz was dead.[20]

Fergusson kept many of Spitz's unpublished poems and filed them among his more personal remembrances. He attached the following note to those poems: "He was my best friend . . . I still regard him as the most intelligent and gifted person I ever knew intimately."[21] Spitz's death affected Fergusson for the rest of his life, not just because it was Spitz, although that was sorrowful enough. But the time of Spitz's death was crucial, for Fergusson traced the real beginning of his career as a writer to that period. Whatever the true nature of the guilt and no matter how he attempted to expiate it, Fergusson carried it with him for the rest of his life. That guilt was compounded by the death of his second wife, Rebecca McCann, ten years later. The death of his friend, and then his wife, became linked in his mind with his struggle as a writer: "Every writer has a dominant experience which colors all his work. Mine was ultimately one of fulfillment and growth, after the age of 38. It started in 1917–1929, about. It was accompanied by feelings of guilt, acts of self-punishment, by blunders, misfortunes, and by two tragic experiences that left a permanent scar on my psyche."[22]

It was Haskin who led Fergusson to Mencken in one of the luckiest assignments of Fergusson's tenure with what turned out to be his longest and last full-time employment as a journalist. As two rivals who had shared drinks and damnations of the politicians responsible for the inconvenience of attempting to ban their beer, Haskin asked Mencken for permission to do an article on the book Mencken was writing on the American language. Permission was granted, and Haskin gave the assignment to Fergusson. In terms of his future as a novelist it was one of the most important meetings Fergusson ever had; and, ironically, it led indirectly to Haskin's firing Fergusson, insofar as he did not want to employ a part-time novelist.

In the first of what would be many reciprocated visits throughout the 1920s and into the 1930s, Fergusson called on Mencken one afternoon at his long-time family residence on Hollins Street in Baltimore. The exact date of this visit is difficult to ascertain. Odds are that it occurred in August 1919, since Mencken wrote a note of thanks about the article to Fergusson on August 20, 1919.[23]

As Fergusson tells it, Mencken met him at the door and escorted him upstairs to the paper-strewn study where he wrote. The first item on the agenda was a drink of Mencken's home brew. Mencken gave Fergusson the information he needed for the "Haskin Letter" and then turned the tables and asked him if he did any kind of writing other than for Haskin—and if he had anything in progress. What was perhaps merely a polite expression of interest, by a noted literary impressario always on the lookout for new writers, hit paydirt. Fergusson swallowed hard and said, "Yes, at the present time I am writing a novel." Mencken responded with a career-making invitation: "When you finish it, send it to me. I have a kind of stand-in [i.e. George Jean Nathan] at the office of Alfred A. Knopf and he might be interested in your work."[24]

In fact, Fergusson had already completed *Blood of the Conquerors* after working on it for over a year while in Haskin's employment and during a past summer "vacation" back in New Mexico. Perhaps Fergusson had bargained for a bit more time when he told Mencken that he was "working" on a novel actually already finished. Perhaps he was as intimidated as he was excited and honored. One thing is certain: Fergusson knew Mencken's reputation as a literary critic, author, and discoverer of new talent. His fate as a writer was in the hands of a good man to have in his corner if only Mencken liked his work: "There were many opinions of Mencken, but there was no doubt that he had become the most powerful literary critic of his day. He had been called a literary dictator. I was painfully aware that he was very much more the arbiter of my literary destiny than any other one man."[25] Whether Mencken's nod (or Nathan's or Knopf's) would be favorable or not, Fergusson knew opportunity when he saw it. And when he knocked on Mencken's door the next Saturday for dinner with Mencken's celebrated club of literary luminaries, the manuscript of *Conquerors* was in hand. Mencken promised to read it that very night and to write Fergusson his appraisal soon thereafter.

Needless to say, he liked it and became an advocate and mentor for Fergusson. Not only would Mencken put in a good word with Knopf; he reviewed Fergusson's novels favorably, all the while furthering his own vested interest in the whole endeavor. Thirty years later Fergusson said of Mencken, "He is famous as a critic who achieved a unique leadership in America literature at a crucial period in its history, but I think only the many writers he helped, giving his time and energy and hospitality, know how personal and human his conception of that leadership was."[26]

Fergusson wisely cultivated Mencken's friendship. His letters to Mencken from 1920 to 1934 are not especially obsequious. But they are respectful of a man ten years his senior and indicate that Fergusson sought not only approval but advice. They are also evidence, at least by implication, that Mencken remained convinced, during the early years of Fergusson's career, that Fergusson was a writer who proved the potential of his first novel, and a literary find—a friend he enjoyed seeing. Although Mencken lived until 1956, after Fergusson's first three novels, Mencken had little to say about him. Mencken encouraged Fergusson's contributions to the *Mercury* well into the 1930s, but Fergusson felt that by the time of *Hot Saturday* (1926) Mencken's critical help was largely gone.

Even so, Mencken's influence on Fergusson and the help he extended to him when he was a beginning novelist is much greater than anyone has ever traced. In significant ways it was Mencken who influenced Fergusson if not actually to write *Capitol Hill* and *Women and Wives*, then to write them in the way that he did. Mencken was more at home with the politics of such city novels than he was with Fergusson's novels about the nineteenth- and twentieth-century Southwest, even though Mencken turned his attention to the Southwest in *The American Language* (1919) and noted the changes in the American vernacular which were accelerated by the movement of much of the population into that region. And he defended Fergusson's western themes on their own terms even to the extent of serializing *Rio Grande* in the *Mercury* against editorial opposition, as well as running articles by Fergusson on the West and its developing history. Fergusson represented at once a typical and a unique manifestation of the kind of writer Mencken and his kind of cranky critics welcomed. Mencken's background as a skeptical newsman and an advocate of realistic-naturalistic fiction and social commentary in the aftermath of World War I and the gaudy 1920s coincided with Fergusson's developing world-view—both when he read Mencken and the *Smart Set* in college and later as a young writer when he attempted to free himself from romantic nostalgia for the frontier and its closing.

Fergusson accomplished a notable thing for a young writer from the hinterlands of the American Southwest. He did not just read the

H. L. Mencken. Courtesy of the Enoch Pratt Free Library. Reprinted by
permission.

critics who were shaping American literature and national literary
taste; he met these men and absorbed them while still keeping his own
regional character. Just as he embarked on his career as a journalist
and then novelist, a new turn in American literary history was beginning. Fergusson read Mencken's diatribes in the *Smart Set,* in which
he denounced the " 'Yiddo-Presbyterian culture' as a travesty on
civilization"; read his scoffing jibes at "boobus Americanus" and that
species' uncomplicated belief in "simple slogans, good business and a
kindly god."[27] Fergusson read and was led by Mencken, Brooks,
Bourne, and all the other "bright young prophets." But if Fergusson
followed, he also helped direct those attitudes and values of the changing 1920s by his own expression of what a "hereditary pioneer"
confronted as he backtracked to the East in his own particular "morning after." Much of Fergusson's rebellion took the form of reaction to
conservative, repressive "Puritan" sexual values, but the rebellion
was grounded in intellect as well as in emotion. To understand how he

found himself in tune with the social and intellectual mood after World War I, one has only to look at his relationship with Mencken—and with Knopf.

Mencken, like Waldo Frank and other "literary radicals" of the twenties, was very much in sympathy with the attacks of Sinclair Lewis on "main street" and "Babbittry" and with Theodore Dreiser's brand of naturalism. In short, he was sympathetic with any approach to literature and politics which was satirical in tone and radical in program.[28] Mencken's heyday as an arbiter of national literary taste soon declined in the aftermath of the Depression because of his anti–New Deal position. As David Remley says, "Mencken's satirical wit came to seem irrelevant or downright nasty to people who had lost their bank accounts and could not find work after 1929."[29] In his capacity as critic and editor he championed other newcomers besides Fergusson, most of whom attained greater recognition as major American authors: Dreiser, Sinclair Lewis, Upton Sinclair, Sherwood Anderson, F. Scott Fitzgerald, Ruth Suckow, and Eugene O'Neill, for example.

Mencken's attacks were leveled at a cultural cross section of evils: evangelical religion, censorship, superpatriotism, prohibition, Rotarianism, and the American bourgeoisie, which he referred to as "booboisie."[30] Just about everything he disliked was subsumed under what he called "Puritanism," as practiced by "one who, because of physical cowardice, lack of imagination or religious superstition, is unable to get any joy out of the satisfaction of his natural appetites."[31] Such an attitude and its implicit antithesis of liberalism and hedonism is reflected throughout Fergusson's writings, including his diaries. Ironically, Mencken ended up much more the reactionary than the liberal; and Fergusson followed much the same fate. But when Fergusson was writing his first novels, Mencken represented the epitome of antiestablishment criticism. Both this vision and his glib, irreverent style left considerable imprint on Fergusson.

Much of what Mencken looked for in a novelist became apparent in his reaction to Dreiser's *Sister Carrie* (1900) and *Jennie Gerhardt* (1911). Mencken held *Carrie* in reverence as "a novel of magnitude" and took every opportunity in his *Smart Set* reviews to "ram the idea that [it] must be read."[32] When Dreiser sent Mencken the manuscript of *Gerhardt*, Mencken responded with approval that it met his criterion of a good novel: "An accurate picture of life and a searching criticism."[33] Much more than a reviewer of such fiction, Mencken was a partisan advocate. Dreiser and Mencken and, in turn, Fergusson, were in league against "Puritanism" as Mencken defined it. That Dreiser was something of a sexual libertine, determined to hop into bed with almost every woman he met, and that he projected such longings onto his characters in such works as *The Genius* (1915) only increased Mencken's resolve to devote his energies to "Combatting Puritanism."[34] Mencken's criteria for good fiction, then, follow the standard represented by *Carrie*. Mencken thought it a good novel because of its realism, its plot built on probability, characters who acted "as if they moved in real life," and action which although tragic or even dreary was nevertheless plausible.[35]

All of these preferences—or as he called them in his successful series of books, his "prejudices"—were long in place, thanks to Dreiser and *Carrie*, and help explain Mencken's reception of Fergusson when he came on the scene as a new novelist in the 1920s. Since its opening chapter—which finds the male protagonist on a train eyeing a good-looking woman—parallels the opening of *Carrie*, it is not surprising that *Blood of the Conquerors* struck Mencken's fancy as a worthy novel.

Little magazines and radical literary critics aided in this receptivity for a new novelist like Fergusson. Mencken and Nathan edited the *Smart Set* from 1914 to 1923. Also, the *American Mercury* was founded with Nathan in 1924—with support from Knopf, who had become Mencken's publisher with *The American Language* in 1919.[36] Not only would Fergusson publish several essays and chapters of *Rio Grande* in the *Mercury*, but in addition, Mencken's friend and publisher, Knopf, became Fergusson's publisher.

Knopf was one of the new publishers of the 1920s who helped create the postwar audience. Knopf worked first for Doubleday and then other publishers before starting his own business in 1915, aided by his wife, Blanche, who took an active part in publishing decisions. He first met Mencken in 1914, when he traveled to Baltimore to meet

Alfred A. Knopf. Photograph by Fabian Bachrach.

what could only be described as a phenomenon among literary critics and columnists. Just one year into his new publishing venture, Knopf enlisted both Mencken and Nathan as Knopf authors.[37]

He became a publisher known for quality books—both in content and in appearance. He was also courageous and published what he believed in, resolved to back his authors in the midst of controversy.

Moreover, Knopf gained a reputation for being honest, fair, and efficient in payments of money to his authors, although in later years Fergusson and Knopf had a falling out over Knopf's reluctance to publish *Modern Man*, which Knopf felt would not repay his investment. When Mencken came up with the idea for the *Mercury* in 1921, he wanted Nathan to serve as a full partner. Knopf would be the publisher, and with Knopf's wife and business partner, Blanche, the four of them organized the *Mercury* in 1923. Knopf took a two-thirds interest; Mencken and Nathan were partners, sharing the other third.

Fergusson's timing for stumbling into the midst of such a powerful and respected triad was more than auspicious. By the time the *Mercury* began, Fergusson was an old friend. Mencken wrote to Fergusson and personally invited him to submit something: "Knopf, Nathan, and I are at work on plans to set up a new monthly review—a genuine humdinger, I fondly hope and pray. . . . I needn't say that I hope to have you in it. Have you any ideas? If so let me hear them. I assume that you'll want to get some relief from the novel now and then. What we want primarily is new and sound information, and secondarily good writing. You are elected."[38] Fergusson's meeting with Mencken, a presumably routine interview, placed the young Washington journalist squarely at the top of the nation's literary and publishing "hill."

FIRST NOVEL

Fergusson worked on *Blood of the Conquerors* (1921) for more than a year. It was finished by the time he interviewed Mencken, but it was the labor of stolen moments and of his first thirty years of living. It represents the central interest of his writing, which, although not voluminous, was prolific and varied—including fiction, history, philosophy, autobiography, and essay. First novels are always revealing and usually extend in one way or another into all subsequent work. Insofar as it is true that all novelists write one novel over and over again, then Fergusson was never free of *Conquerors*. In it he made the first of repeated attempts as a novelist and a historian to deal with the themes of mutability and the end of the American frontier.

In autobiographical terms, the novel's protagonist, Ramon Delcasar, although Hispanic, represents the lawyer Fergusson might have become, returning to the past of his bloodline and resigning himself to his small-town past rather than facing a second, newer frontier of the big city. In this sense, Delcasar is both Fergusson's potential self and his denied self. In such a context—and in his later novels—Fergusson's fascination with the fall of the Spanish American ricos, those second- and third-generation heirs of the conquistadors who settled the Southwest, is not all that dissimilar from the rise and fall of his own grandfathers and, in turn, his father, whose personal and family fortunes yielded to the more universal demands of success and failure, life and death.

Certainly the novels of Fergusson's early Washington phase, while he was working as a journalist but becoming more preoccupied with writing fiction full-time, evidence elements which may readily be viewed as autobiographical. It is a process which extends through his novels with a contemporary setting, wherein the author becomes an even more recognizable likeness of himself, his own hero in his various characters and narrators. In the novels set in the more distant past, the autobiographical aspects which inform the fictions of the plot become those of his family—more particularly his maternal grandfather and his father. Fergusson's purer historical narratives, although they have many novelistic techniques, provide a more obvious synthesis of past and present, of verifiable places, events, and personages beyond his family history. Taken as a whole, then, all of Fergusson's writings reflect his own "biography."

Conquerors is an important first instance.[39] Erna Fergusson insisted that the young protagonist of the novel, Delcasar, was a schoolmate of her brother's, easily recognized by all who read the novel as both an individual and a type.[40] But surely the character found most prominently in Delcasar is Fergusson himself. It is Delcasar who, as the center of consciousness and the narrator's attention, struggles with many of the cultural questions which interested Fergusson in his own early adulthood. Delcasar is twenty-four when the reader first meets him. The timespan of the novel is not long—a year or two. Fergusson wrote the novel at the age of thirty but was thinking about it many

years prior to that. The time of the novel is during the first quarter
of the twentieth century—the time of Fergusson's twenties as well.
Thus, Fergusson as author is contemporary with his own main character.

Delcasar is a Spanish American with the "blood of conquerors"
(the conquistadors) in his veins, and like Fergusson he lives in two
worlds (historical and cultural, and geographical). More of a transitional man than a marginal man, Delcasar must get his bearing on just
who he is, was, and will be in relation to many societal and historical
polarities: the modern Spanish-American in relation to the traditions
of his genealogical and cultural past; the Spanish American in relation
to the Anglo-American; the primitive and the civilized; the rural and
agrarian tradition in relation to the urban; the West versus the East;
the future as hope turned despair; the glories of the past turned to
disillusionment; and so forth. These polarities are not just contrivance
for the sake of the story. They are conflicts which Fergusson himself
faced in his own life—and chose to work through again in artistic ways
in novel form.

Insofar as he is his own main character, why did Fergusson choose
to make Delcasar a Spanish American and representative of the
younger generation of that culture? For one thing, it allowed Fergusson a needed degree of aesthetic distance through which he could
dramatize in a greater way the struggle with transition and marginality
which, although it faced privileged Anglo-Americans like Fergusson,
was even more intense in its pressures on the minority culture, dominated as it was by the Yankee influx into the Southwest in the nineteenth and twentieth centuries. Fergusson's own grandfathers and
father had met with their financial reversals, and their worlds had
eroded in their later years even though their names and positions
remained in good standing. Fergusson, in his way, faced similar reversals in inheritance of land and money to those Delcasar faces in the
days of fading glory for his race. His conflict, symbolized by possession of an Anglo-American woman, is an effort to reestablish those
glories. Delcasar allows Fergusson a distance which might be seen as
mitigating his sorrow at the demise of his own family. This empathy
across racial and cultural boundaries partially explains Fergusson's

sustained interest in the dispossession of the great landed families of Spanish Americans in the early twentieth century as he witnessed it in the Southwest.

In the course of *Conquerors*, Delcasar returns to his home in New Mexico after finishing a law degree at a Catholic law school in St. Louis. In transit on the train and on his arrival on home ground, he encounters Julia Roth, who as a tourist to exotic southwestern landscapes and cultures and a nurse for her tubercular brother, Gordon, in effect conquers the conqueror. Like the historical Yankee conquerors who dispossessed the Spanish after they in turn dispossessed the American Indian, the Spanish, and Mexican-American, she returns to her eastern home, and Delcasar must in turn backtrack once again, this time all the way to New York. As a kind of fictive parable of the recurrent frontiers of settlement that Turner proposed, Fergusson strikes upon a theme and a plot structure which serves him well in recomposing his own life experiences.

Much of Fergusson's rendering of Delcasar's character depends on the lure which the West holds for him and his enjoyment of the independent ways of the lone rider and vagabond. Such a life of freedom from social and marital restraints is a trait that Fergusson knew in the keenest of ways all his life, and a trait which he projected into nearly all of his fictional analogs. Fergusson suggests that such a closeness to the land is a peculiarly Spanish-American trait. But given his own youth as a free spirit, it is clear that he identifies strongly with such an attitude. However, as an Anglo-American, steeped in his own ethnocentric alliances, he also feels compelled to dissociate himself from the Spanish-American viewpoint and portray it as "primitive." Explain it as he might, as a self-proclaimed and modern frontiersman he could not escape from the lingering attractions of primitivism. If Ramon loves the earth and the sheep camps of his ancestors, Fergusson liked the same things and talked about sheep herding often with his cousin Fred Huning, Jr.[41]

Even at the beginning of the novel only one thing can compete with Ramon's fascination with Julia. That is the land of his birth. As he looks out of the train window on the way home from St. Louis, he forgets about the beautiful passenger who has so captivated him and looks long at the landscape passing before him." It was the one thing in the world that he loved, and the only thing that had ever given him pleasure without tincture of bitterness" (p. 13). It is this feeling for the land of his birth that drew Fergusson back time and again not only to write about that country and its history but to actually spend as much time there as possible, particularly during summers, and either write about his Washington or New York experiences or store up more ambiance and inspiration to write about when he returned to the East. As his first novel proves, if the East gave him a new perspective on the West, the West allowed him to put both regions into words and finally get them on paper.

To no small degree, Fergusson's subsequent novels are present in seedling form in *Conquerors: Capitol Hill* and *Women and Wives* begin where Julia Roth's New York leaves off; *Wolf Song, Hot Saturday,* and *Footloose McGarnigal* pick up the themes of the vagabond life of male freedom, in past and contemporary settings; *Grant of Kingdom* and *The Conquest of Don Pedro* return again to Hispanic land rights and cultural conflict with the encroaching Anglo culture; *The Land of Lonely Women* and "The Enchanted Meadow" return him again to his youth as a lone rider.

Fergusson dramatizes all of this in terms of the battle of the sexes and the conflicts arising out of East-West regional values. He structures Delcasar's conflict with marginality around his wish to win the love of the refined (but silly) New Yorker, Julia. To do this he feels he must have the inheritance which he feels his uncle, Don Diego Delcasar, owes him in his own position as the living male heir to the many thousand acres of land granted generations past to the family by the Spanish monarchy when the Conquistadors claimed New Spain.

The significance of the title and the theme of conquest take on yet another of many ironic meanings in the convolutions of a plot of love as well as of hatred, murder, and betrayal. An added irony is that Fergusson returned to this theme of his first novel in his last published novel, where the idea of conquest again surfaces in the title: *The Conquest of Don Pedro.* Ramon's love for Julia and his infatuation with her "civilized" but vapid society life in the East are counterbalanced by his lust for Archulera's sensuous earth-mother daughter, Catalina.

These two types of women, white and brown, civilized and primitive, reoccur in Fergusson's other novels.

Another aspect of his character and motivation and of the two worlds in which he lives, is that Delcasar frequently changes into his oldest clothes, picks up his gun, saddles a convenient horse, and rides off to Archulera's to hunt, enjoy the beauties of nature, and sleep with Catalina. That Fergusson infuses his love of the out-of-doors and women into Delcasar's character is obvious. As with the other polarities in the novel, Fergusson is more than sympathetic with Delcasar's atavism in such instances, for he suggests satirically that there is considerable sterility and meaninglessness in the Anglo world of Julia, her priggish and sickly brother Gordon, her snobbish mother, and, indeed, most of the other Anglos who congregate around her, both in the Southwest and in New York.

It is often observed that Fergusson satirized the folly of his first marriage in his third novel, *Women and Wives*. It might also be observed that Julia Roth seems a likely analog for Fergusson's first wife, for the breakup of his first marriage was close to the time he wrote *Conquerors*. The satirical edge and the ironies of plot, character, and theme cut both ways and add another level of ambivalence, localized with the narrator and behind him Fergusson, as he points out the follies of both sets of characters, male and female, Spanish Americans and Anglo-Americans. But Fergusson as implied author stops short of becoming misanthropic in the values he implicitly holds up, for his standards are those of common sense and decency.

The plot is tightly wrought for a first novel and much closer to Fergusson's forte than *Capitol Hill*—but somewhat melodramatic and formulaic. Archulera, it is presumed, although he is never explicitly identified or brought to justice, does assassinate Diego, and Ramon inherits all of his uncle's lands and does pay Archulera the blood money he has promised him. What Ramon must now do is prevent the acquisitve lawyer, MacDougall, from gaining all of the Delcasar land in the northern part of the state. This locale, prominent in Huning's trading trips and memoir, becomes a familiar setting in *Wolf Song* and *Grant of Kingdom*. This northern New Mexico land is at a premium because the railroad wants the right of way.

Progress and fortune come to the new West, at once opening and closing the frontier. Delcasar thus wages a campaign to foil Mac-Dougall. To conquer MacDougall and—he believes—to thereby conquer Julia, he devises the plan to renew his ancestral ties with the penitente land holders and solidify his influence over all real estate deals with the native land owners. With the aid of Antonio Cortez, who serves as his advisor and representative, Delcasar joins the penitente brotherhood—an ancient fraternity of flagellation, blood, and crucifixion which reenacts Christ's passion. The penitente brotherhood, like the rico culture, provided Fergusson with some of the most exotic and romantic material for future novels as well. Delcasar convinces the penitente leader, Salomon Alfego, that he is indeed sincere in his desire for brotherhood in the blood of the conquerors, the inheritors of the religion, and government of the Conquistadors.

In some of the most dramatic scenes in the novel—scenes which are written from Fergusson's own experience at witnessing a penitente ritual when a youth and from his own fascinated researches into an organization and cultural forces which he both understood and disapproved—Delcasar is initiated by means of agonizing whipping and bloodletting. He is a conqueror for a time. But Julia's family, long opposed to Ramon's growing involvement with her, whisks her away to the state capital. In this struggle of prejudice and power, the Anglos seem again to be the real conquerors.

All of the activities and places are replicas of actual Albuquerque places and goings-on which Fergusson knew first-hand and describes in various ways in subsequent novels, especially *Hot Saturday* and *McGarnigal*, and in his autobiography, *Home in the West*. Delcasar's spiraling demise picks up momentum when he takes up with a local waitress, Dora McArdle, in the Eldorado lunchroom. Like Catalina, Dora is a foil to Julia, though not as much the earth mother as Delcasar's Mexican-American sexual partner, and is prototypic of Fergusson's many erotic women who enter easily into sexual involvements: "She was coarse and commonplace, but she was also shapely, ripe-breasted, good natured, full of the appeal of a healthy animalism" (p. 215).

Fergusson felt his greatest successes as a novelist were with his portrayal of women characters and mentions this proudly in his diaries. From his earliest work, the complexities of sexuality become an integral part of his plotting. For him the sexual impulse was one of the most important impulses in both his life and his art—and he saw a strong correlation between his creative urge and his urge to wander: "This sexual impulse is a thing so deeply rooted . . . that every individual is really at the mercy of it, those who deny it not a bit less than those who indulge it. . . . [A man] seeks to rationalize this nightly stream of impulse and instinct, but he has petty success. Sex is only the most obvious and turbulent part of it. The wandering impulse and the creative impulse are of the same massive and uncontrollable character."[42] The matter of the "sexual impulse" is beyond a doubt the most dominant subject of inquiry in Fergusson's diaries, from early entries in 1910 to later entries in his last diaries in 1967 which attempt to trace the history of sexuality in America.

Given Fergusson's preoccupation with sexuality, none of the portrayals of women in *Conquerors* is entirely favorable. The portrayals dramatize Fergusson's social conditioning as much as his psychology in the apparent belief that there are basically two kinds of women: the high-class and the low-class, the good and the bad, the saint and the whore. Even so, the "high-class," refined Julia is the worst of the three women characters in *Conquest*. It is her stupid conformity and lack of resolve which contributes to Delcasar's ruination. However, Fergusson is also clearly saying that Delcasar is his own worst enemy in his blind devotion to such a silly woman. In his satirical treatment of Julia and in his impatiently sympathetic treatment of Ramon, Fergusson ultimately denies the values of both. Similarly, although there is an abiding attraction in the earthiness of Catalina and Dora, they represent relative degrees of stagnation and degeneracy. Fergusson faced the dilemma, in his fiction and in his life, of needing both kinds of women but remained restless in the satisfactions gained from either kind.

Ramon has his failings. Julia's actions, however, are unforgivable in Fergusson's scheme of male-female relationships. Hers is a failure of will: "She could hold out forever against pleas which involved an effort of the will on her part" (p. 246). She is at once a mindless automaton, at the mercy of her family's wishes and her own social conditioning, and a heartless "tease," unwilling to ever follow through to any real allegiance to Ramon. This idea, perhaps a result of Fergusson's experiences with his first wife, Polly Pretty, is relentlessly developed in both *Capitol Hill* and *Women and Wives*, as well as in others of Fergusson's "novels of manners" such as *Hot Saturday, Footloose McGarnigal,* and *The Life of Riley.*

Ramon enjoys Julia sexually, and in a sense loves her, but he is paradoxically "conquered" by her own lack of will which compels her to stay in New York with her husband. Delcasar, as a hereditary "conqueror," has been "conquered" in true naturalistic fashion—or by what he believes to be his destiny. Fergusson editorializes about Ramon as he does about Ralph Dolan, John Strome, Alec McGarnigal, Morgan Riley, and others of his heroes (including, to a point, himself in his diaries): "Like all men of a primitive type he had a strong tendency to believe in fortune as a deliberate force in the affairs of men. It seemed clear to him now, in his depressed and exhausted condition, that bad luck had marked him for its prey" (pp. 252–53). After all of his struggles to cross over into Julia's Anglo, Eastern world, Ramon ends where he started—just as she does. The implication is that his longings are, if understandable, nevertheless misplaced and futile.

Like all of Fergusson's novels, *Conquerors* is bound by auto-biography and is beyond it. Fergusson said: "In all my novels, I never think of the hero as myself. He is truly a creation."[43] Delcasar is a creation but is his author as well. There are striking similarities between the novel's opening chapter and the opening of *Carrie,* and many of Dreiser's naturalistic assumptions radiate throughout not only Fergusson's first novel but his second and third. Julia Roth drifts her way to success and a satisfied life every bit as much as Carrie does; and Ramon goes to criminal lengths similar to Hurstwood's tactics in the pursuit of his obsession. Since Mencken liked *Carrie* so much, the similarities must have impressed him, just as he saw similarities between Sinclair Lewis's novels and *Capitol Hill.* Fergusson was obviously imprinted by Dreiser and Lewis, and thus Mencken's support is not surprising. What Fergusson added to Dreiser's and Lewis's works went beyond the collision of small-town Midwesterners with big cities like Chicago and New York, for his was a decidedly southwestern setting and atmosphere, which meant the added complications of multiracial interrelationships.

CAPITOL HILL

It was partly as a result of Dreiser's influence that Mencken saw Fergusson as one of the important "new men" in his reviews for Knopf's list for the fall of 1921. At the end of that year Fergusson wrote to Mencken in appreciation of his support. He was disappointed by the book's sales, but thanked Mencken for all he had done: "Your rating me as the most promising of the recent debutantes would give me the big-head if I were at all subject so such swellings. I hope some of your readers will take heed and buy the book. At last report it had not sold more than enough to buy me an overcoat."[44]

Along with a new overcoat and a sheaf of favorable reviews,[45] Fergusson also had a second manuscript to discuss with Mencken. He had worked on his first Washington novel for many months in his spare time from duties with Haskin. As early as the summer of 1920 he indicated to Mencken in a letter from New Mexico that a first draft was under way on a novel so different from his first one that he did not quite know how to judge it and needed Mencken's advice."[46] The revision of the first draft took longer than expected. Fergusson wanted to go to Europe to finish writing it and had projected a scene to take place in Paris and thus wanted "to lay a couple of chapters there"; but lack of money made him abandon his long-desired European trip and return in the summer to New Mexico, where at least he knew he could always find the inspiration to do such writing. Haskin fired him in the fall of 1922, after the publication of *Conquerors*, saying "You have found your wings, now you can fly," and Fergusson was more dependent than ever on Mencken's favor—for advice about his novel and for future work as a journalist.

General belief has it that Mencken responded to Fergusson's "Washington" novel only after it was published. But the truth of the matter is that Fergusson was seeking Mencken's advice on both legal

Harvey Fergusson, 1921. Courtesy The Bancroft Library.

and artistic matters very early on. He was also asking Mencken during the summer of 1922, while in New Mexico, to help him find work on the Baltimore *Evening Sun*. While Mencken put in a good word for Fergusson both at the *Sun* and with editor Norman Hapgood, Mencken also suggested that Fergusson call his second novel simply *The Hill*, and offered advice on other matters. By June 1922 Mencken had read the manuscript of Fergusson's second novel and thought it looked "very good, indeed." In addition to thinking that the central character, Ralph Dolan, was realistic and that the picture of Washington was accurate, Mencken advised Fergusson not to mention the Willard Hotel explicitly; to tone down some of the scenes "of fornication"; to let the story go in length and not try to hold it down; to disguise the Illinois senators recognizable as "Lewis and Sherman"; to play up the "horrible life of department clerks" and the "newspaper-press-agent alliance"; in short, he recommended to Fergusson to "Let her go!"[47] Fergusson wrote Mencken at least twice during July 1922, confirming that he liked Mencken's idea for a title: " 'The Hill' does the work very well. 'Capitol Hill' would be even more unmistakable."[48]

Mencken was serving as Fergusson's editor as well as his advisor in contract negotiations with Knopf over royalties on both American and foreign editions. During his consultations with Mencken, Haskin was growing more and more impatient with Fergusson's part-time novel writing; and Fergusson left the Haskin Syndicate in the late fall of 1922, shortly after an operation to have his tonsils removed and the septum of his nose straightened. He did free-lance journalism, outlined several stories for popular magazines such as *Redbook* and *Mc-Calls*, worked out of the *Sun* office, thanks to Mencken's efforts, and generally awaited the appearance of his second novel, *Capitol Hill*, a novel meeting Mencken's criteria for a good novel even more than did *Conquerors*.

In this "Novel of Washington Life," Fergusson projects himself most directly into the character of Ralph Dolan. Here and in his next Washington novel, *Women and Wives*, the plot centers on the aspirations of a writer, which Fergusson was in the process of becoming, rather than on the ambitions of a lawyer like Delcasar—the profession

Fergusson rejected in order to become a journalist and a novelist.
Particularly at this formative stage of his life as a writer, Fergusson
resorted to one of the most common plots and its supporting means of
characterization: the portrait of the writer as a young man. Again
Fergusson succeeds, however, in distancing himself from all of the
characters, and particularly from Dolan through a kind of naturalistic
observation edged with satire.

The episodes of Dolan's life which make up the novel begin in
1912 and extend over a five-year period, beginning just prior to World
War I and ending after the war. As the novel opens, Dolan is twenty-
five, and at its close he is thirty. Thus, the time span is roughly
identical with Fergusson's own early Washington years, from the time
of his graduation from Washington and Lee University in 1911
through his years as a Washington journalist into his time with the
Haskin Syndicate. Unlike Fergusson, however, Dolan is to become an
important and powerful politician. Fergusson makes it clear that as
Dolan's shadow self, the author refuses to take Dolan as seriously as
he takes himself.

Through the course of his climb up the social and economic
ladder in Washington, Dolan moves from one job to another and from
one woman to another—always with considerable self-confidence and
ruthlessness. He has a knack for improving his condition by means of
knowing and working the system of patronage; and he does so with
few ideals to compromise. Like his fictional predecessor, Delcasar,
Dolan is motivated in part by primitive, animal instincts, by a need to
satisfy his creature comforts, and by his own self-interests. Dolan is
not so much likeable or dislikeable as he is presented for what he is,
usually foolish, at times shrewd, always self-interested, ultimately
more a naturalistic specimen than a convincing person. On the simplest level, these numerous episodes deal with his rise to better jobs
and a better class of women. It is through these episodes that Dolan
and the reader see "Capitol Hill."

Prone to assuming the persona of a writer on the outskirts of
bourgeois respectability, and preoccupied with the sexual impulse,
Dolan himself is first encountered in a Washington hotel waking up
after a tryst with a Washington hooker charmingly named Emma. He

is new to town, and as a result of his sexual indulgence and Emma's fee, he is short $293.[49]

Using certain lingering similarities to both Dreiser's *Carrie* and to Henry Adams' *Democracy*, Fergusson portrays Dolan as a resourceful and determined man—just the kind of personality that Washington needs. There is no heading home for him, as there was for Delcasar. Somewhat the masher salesman, like Dreiser's Charles Drouet, Dolan prides himself on being an accomplished ladies' man. But he is more naive than he realizes, and Emma—like Washington itself—is only the first of many disillusionments for Dolan. He remains resilient in the face of his setbacks, however. A drifter and man of experience, Dolan left college after one year. Prior to landing in Washington he had been in most of the major cities in the United States, and as an early fictive version of Franz Huning and an anticipation of Robert Jayson and Leo Mendes, Dolan developed his talents as a salesman—of himself and of products like the one he now peddles: college fraternity jewelry. Like Fergusson, Dolan is a fraternity man and is able to parlay that membership into money. He is a gambler, quick with cards, and a teller of "Rabelaisian stories" in the mold of numerous Fergusson heroes.

Dirty stories notwithstanding, he is in his way an artist: "In the fabricating and telling of these tales he was an artist without knowing it" (p. 7). Facility with words, however, is complemented by a will to action. Unlike Jim Royce, Fergusson's counterpart and the writer figure in *Women and Wives*, Dolan's will to success is much more of the world and not of the ivory tower. Like the all-prized, self-made American male which Mencken and Fergusson satirized even while becoming, Dolan's American dream at the age of twenty-five is one that would take him all the way to the top of the "hill": "A desire to get away from his easy half-vagabond habits, to thrust himself in among the mighty, to accumulate the goods of life which had hitherto flowed easily through his fingers, and so to body forth his power in the visible splendour of possession—this had become his dream" (p. 8).

It is no surprise that Fergusson's first three novels are so thematically overburdened with the notion of ambition and success. In his aspiration as a writer of novels, Fergusson was attempting something of the same thing that his characters, his projections of himself, were trying to do. Delcasar and Dolan are outsiders who long to be on the inside—and even though Fergusson derides such ambitions, he shares them. He looks satirically at some of the shallow values of his young heroes and heroines, but he does not fault their energy and drive, and he dramatizes the link between the sexual impulse to seduce and conquer and the conquests of vocation.

Dolan is not alone in his ambition. As Dreiser dramatizes it in *Carrie,* the city has long been a magnet for the young. And Dolan, once graduating from a rooming house on Pennsylvania Avenue to a room at the YMCA on G Street, soon begins to meet other young men with dreams of success. Another Fergusson characteristic enters—the portrayal of the man's world of friendship. Dolan's lackluster quarters at the Y (where Frank Spitz also lived in Washington and where Fergusson liked to play handball, swim, and take Turkish baths) match his first job: busboy at the Circle Lunch, one of the city's lower-class lunchrooms. He works from seven in the evening until seven in the morning for eight dollars a week (Fergusson's early salary as a newsman). Dolan's good nature and ability to tell a story and play craps make him well liked by his fellow employees.

Ralph introduces himself to the secretary of the Y as a future law student and a member of the First Congregational Church of Muncie, Indiana, and hypocritically agrees to the "Puritanical" rules and motto of the place. In the least expensive arrangement possible, Dolan rooms with two other "upstanding" Christian men, Henry Lambert and William Cooley. His relationship with these two frames the novel and gives it much of its coherence, for throughout Dolan's five-year climb he compares his progress with that of his two friends.

Cooley initially works as a clerk in the Interior Department. Here Fergusson builds on Mencken's advice to play up the dismal life of the government clerk. Cooley, however, is able to work his way up. He studies osteopathy and by the end of the novel is an established, wealthy doctor. His interests, in keeping with Fergusson's interest in tracing the sexual revolution after the end of the frontier and the beginning of what he viewed as the new frontier of a sexual impulse and "new morality" of the 1920s, are revealed in Cooley's books: *Sex*

Problems in Work and Worry and *Will Power and How to Cultivate It* (p. 22). Lambert begins as a reporter on the local afternoon newspaper and is another one of Fergusson's writer figures, a kind of first attempt at Jim Royce in *Women and Wives*. He is a thorough-going literary type, aspiring to be a playwright, is the highbrow of the trio of friends, and is in love with a woman in Baltimore. By the end of the novel he decides to write a novel about Dolan and Washington, allowing Fergusson a "play within the play" structure for his *Künstlerroman* plot. Both as friends and as foils to Dolan, these two characters, it is suggested, face similar struggles to Dolan's on their way to whatever good life Washington can provide. All three characters reflect certain composite aspects of Fergusson's own identity.

To be in Washington is to become involved in the politics of government as well as the politics of sex. Fergusson links Dolan's drifting into politics to two factors familiar in his own biography: (1) Ralph's historical moment and genealogy as a hereditary pioneer in the wake of the ending of the frontier, and (2) the system of patronage and nepotism by which the capital functions. He finds himself in a new urban frontier where the skills of the hunter are still needed: "It was to him a jungle where he would hunt, and where the hunting promised to be good" (p. 43). So Dolan goes through a number of political jobs for various Washington politicians: among others, the Honorable Charles A. Rickert of Indiana and the Honorable Henry C. Murkle of Colorado, who arranges for Dolan to work in the folding room of the House Office Building—the same job Fergusson himself held for his father. It is the lowest of government jobs as Fergusson describes it. Dolan's co-workers are described with the same disapproval and disdain seen in a later essay on the subject of Washington jobholders Fergusson sketched out for Mencken and the *Mercury*.[50]

Only Jim Duval, a man from Colorado who "claimed to have Indian blood in his veins," is spared Fergusson's disdain. Duval is a westerner, a former cowpuncher. Lured to Washington by Murkle and the promise of a seventy-five-dollar-a-month government job, Duval left the good life in Colorado and longs to return, homesick for the West and a true man's life. Duval is one of the novel's countless minor characters, but Fergusson uses him to great effectiveness to dramatize his common theme that the climate and landscape of the West are associated with health and that the East, its climate, and its institutions are somehow corrupted and promote illness of body and mind. Duval catches one cold after another, develops pneumonia, and dies. Fergusson uses Duval's death, along with call girl Helen Hobart's murder, to reinforce the naturalistic assumptions of the work that life is an ordeal and only the luckiest of the fittest survive.

Ralph's next job is that of secretary to the Honorable James Buchanan Randall from Texas—another westerner. Congressman Randall is fashioned after Fergusson's father. He too is a southerner and "belonged for many years to the class of ornamental politicians . . . bred in the traditions of . . . high public service, flowery eloquence, and chivalrous quixotic courage" (p. 55). Like H. B. Fergusson, Randall is a Democrat involved in sponsoring homestead legislation before the Committee on Public lands. Randall too has neglected his law practice and "grown poor and grey" in the service of the Democratic party in the West, where he migrated after the Civil War. At the age of sixty, his whole life is wrapped up in the passage of his land bill—parallel to the Fergusson Act. Randall prepares to make his fight "with the weary, dogged hopefulness of an aging dreamer," and Ralph answers mail and helps write letters and the one crucial speech to be made on the floor of the House of Representatives when the homestead bill comes before it. Randall is portrayed as an old fool but a likable one; and his fate and that of his daughters is roughly that of H. B. Fergusson and his daughters, Erna and Lina, who took pride in their father's political career but suffered some economic and emotional hardships from it too.

Only a few years removed from his father's suicide. Fergusson renders his father's fictional counterpart satirically and without sentimentality. Randall's wife and daughters live in an ordinary middle-class home, all too aware of the sobering fact that—as H. B. Fergusson and his wife discovered—"a congressman as such enjoys no real advantage in Washington society" (p. 64). It is as an escort to Alda (a name similar to Erna and Lina, Fergusson's sisters), one of Randall's daughters, that Dolan finally meets the president—another disillusionment, for he is merely a "huge, weary perspiring fat man" (p. 66).

This presumably is William Howard Taft; no doubt, William Jennings Bryan would have been treated more favorably, as a family friend, had he—in his third attempt at the presidency—defeated Taft. Although Fergusson softens his satirical treatment of the Randall family, his dissatisfaction with family life generally shows through.

With the inauguration of the next president, "a thin eager man" promising a new freedom for the people (presumably Woodrow Wilson), Dolan gets a publicity job for Representative Frank H. Rauschuld, a Republican from a large western city. Rauschuld is a man of wealth and considerably more promise than Randall. In correspondence with Mencken, Fergusson, much worried about the liabilities involved in a *roman à clef* such as *Capitol Hill,* identified the politican who served as the real-life model for this western senator: "Rauschuld is a composite portrait of forty-nine bounders, but is based on Fred A. Britten more than on any other one man. I do not think the resemblance is close enough to cause trouble. Do you?"[51] In any event, it is Rauschuld-Britten who is Dolan's main employer through the middle portions of the novel and the main means to Dolan's becoming an important man in his own right.

Furthering the pattern of Dolan's passage from woman to woman, his next lover is Rauschuld's stenographer, Ethel Conner. Ralph and Rauschuld both become enamored with Ethel, and she enjoys the attentions of both men for a time. Although Rauschuld is married, Ethel consents to lunches and dinners, but lets him proceed in his seductions to no more than one forceful kiss. Ralph begins his courtship by taking her canoeing on the Potomac up to Georgetown and eventually convinces her to visit his apartment. Such activities become a habit. Their canoe rides are not without danger, for every year "a good many couples upset their frail craft and every year a few were drowned" (pp. 121–22). Fergusson avoids the pain of fictionalizing his accident with his good friend Frank Spitz, both here and in *Women and Wives,* and turns it instead into occasions for romance and adventure.

Rauschuld's jealousy causes him to fire Dolan when he finds Ethel embracing Dolan one day in the office. Ethel then leaves for a job in South America, and Dolan, fearing the prison of marriage, lets her go. He believes that his political fortunes are ruined. His way with words, however, and his potential as a writer are his salvation. Lambert, now a reporter on the Washington *Sun,* tells Dolan the paper needs a new reporter. So Ralph starts over—this time at ten dollars a week. His position on the *Sun* is for all practical purposes the same as Fergusson's first reporting job on the Washington *Herald.* His assignments are the same as Fergusson's: flower shows, rifle shoots, town meetings.

Ready for yet another stage in his climb up the ladder of Washington success, Ralph is convinced that only through patronage will he truly ascend once again. There is little doubt through the course of the novel, even when Dolan is fired by Rauschuld, that great success will come his way. Fergusson, too, survived Haskin's firing, but on a different set of principles, by which he was true to his need to write. In this respect Dolan represents Fergusson's antiself and displays a kind of conformity similar to that of Julia Roth in *Conquerors.*

Another break comes for Dolan when he is signed on as a correspondent for the *"Herald-Enquirer,* an important midwestern daily" (p. 137). This episode seems to be based on Fergusson's experience in the same capacity for the Chicago *Record-Herald.* Dolan's duty is to keep in touch with the state's congressional delegation and visit the White House and the various national departments for news of interest to his particular state. The two Illinois senators Ralph contacts regularly are Senator Thomas Jefferson Wells, a Westerner and liked by Dolan, and Senator Shadwell, who is satirized as partly deaf and a parody of Abraham Lincoln. Mencken identified them readily as Senators Lewis and Sherman.

It is in his capacity as Washington correspondent for the *Herald-Enquirer* that Dolan meets the most important woman in his string of liaisons, Jane Belden. He meets her at a gathering of the Federal Association of Woman Suffrage, a setting that allows Fergusson to deal more directly with the subject of women and women's rights, the subject which would move even more to center stage in his next and third novel, *Women and Wives.* Fergusson covered meetings of the National Women's party and women's rights lobbies in the capital and interviewed Alice Paul, the vice-president of the National Women's party and one of its most prominent workers. In his news accounts, Fergusson is far from scoffing at the demands of the "radical feminist point of view" as expressed by Miss Paul, especially in regard to divorce, alimony, and the overall "mediaeval" treatment of women in Maryland.[52] Fergusson's portrayal of Belden is doubly important—as Dolan's love and as the character and thematic strand which Fergusson felt he must develop even more fully in another book. Her real-life counterpart is more than likely a composite of types like Alice Paul and an early love whom he almost married after college. Although Fergusson was especially secretive about actually naming the many women with whom he became romantically involved, he discusses in *Home* his real-life involvement with a woman like Jane Belden whom he calls "Alice." She is described as a "suffragette," "engaged in the struggle to win the vote for women" (*Home*, p. 216). They meet, talk, and tussle in much the same way as Dolan and Belden.

Dolan's work and women are never of any real duration on his way to the top. When the *Herald-Enquirer* drifts toward insolvency, Dolan looks toward the Philadelphia *Star* as another stepping stone. Always on the make, Dolan fits the first of the two types of men Fergusson sees in the newspaper business: either the "ambitious young adventurer" (Dolan) or the frustrated novelist or playwright (like Lambert). At the last minute the *Herald-Enquirer* is given a stay of execution in the form of a new bureau chief and a change in policy. But the new chief is a fanatical hero worshipper of Teddy Roosevelt (who continued to oppose Wilson's reluctance to enter the European war) and is unreasonable in his political and personal demands on Dolan, so the Philadelphia *Star* becomes Dolan's next position just as America is on the verge of entering the war.

As Dolan's career picks up steam, Jane inherits some family money, indulges her high-brow tastes in reading and art, takes a magazine job in New York, and drops Ralph for her new, more sophisticated editor. Another woman has passed out of Dolan's life, and with Jane gone, Dolan is on his own in lining up new social contacts. Again Fergusson depends on the West and the frontier as a means of characterization and of furthering his theme. Dolan meets Henry Balzell in a Turkish bath, drops a few names, and comes up with an invitation to visit Balzell. Balzell is involved in Washington high society, thanks to the inheritance left by his frontiersman father, a man of great toughness and energy. Like all of Fergusson's frontier types, Balzell's father is portrayed heroically; his son, Henry, represents the kind of neuresthenia and emotional and physical disintegration that came with the end of the frontier and his widowed mother's resulting move to Washington. The elder Balzell's good life and name on the frontier allow the younger Balzell to suffer through the social demands of his family position in Washington. He is, however, but a flicker of the flame that was his father: "In his thin and sickly body dwelt some spark of the resolute spirit that had made his father a menace to savages, a conqueror of the wilderness. A grave and silent man, with no more joy of revelry in him than an owl he had none-the-less conscientiously devoted his life to entertainment" (p. 208). Through this characterization of Balzell, as with Duvall languishing away in the bowels of Washington's clerkdom, and later, the old Indian fighter, General Bledsoe, Fergusson comments on his nostalgia for the West and the frontier before its demise.

It is through Balzell's introductions during their joint visits to the various debuts of the season that Dolan, at one of the most fashionable apartment houses in the capital, meets his next woman: Gwendolyn Shorts, the daughter of wealthy Mrs. James B. Shorts. Gwendolyn is quiet and cow-like but strangely attractive to Dolan and conducive to Fergusson's satire: "She was as restful to look upon as a blue-grass pasture on a summer evening when the cattle chew their cuds and long shadows lie down to sleep under the trees" (p. 214). Fergusson has more fun with Gwendolyn than with any of Dolan's other women— "she had the build and the blubber of a seal; a chunk of tallow"—but his satire is affectionate even so.

Throughout the novel Fergusson keeps the war and its major issues much in the background, emphasizing manners and adding to the sense of the relative triviality of Washington society. Dolan follows his seemingly endless sequence of jobs, shifts his work as a publicist and becomes a lobbyist. While keeping his connections with the *Star* and his access to the White House press gallery, he begins work as a lobbyist for Colonel Melvane, a rather sinister and mysterious manufacturer, strikebreaker, and profiteer who is involved with the National Commercial Association. Dolan's job as a lobbyist is a step higher on the ladder of success. Ironically, he "arrives" during the tragedy of world war.

Dolan's pragmatic credo becomes ironically apparent in relation to Mrs. Shorts and Gwendolyn. He knows that his way to success depends on being officious. While seeing Gwendolyn and serving as her escort, his next sexual involvement is with another socialite, Mrs. Richard P. Bledsoe, the wife of General Bledsoe, an old Indian fighter and cavalryman who, as his own kind of famous frontiersman, had distinguished himself in the Indian wars against the Sioux and the Comanches. Such a reputation does not prevent his becoming a cuckold. Caught in a June-December marriage of convenience, Mrs. Bledsoe hires Ralph to lobby secretly for the appointment of the general as ambassador to Denmark. The general's appointment is assured, but Dolan takes credit for it anyway, and his payoff is not just money but the sexual favors of Mrs. Bledsoe. Dolan's escapades by this point are so fantastic as to be funny, unintentional as this kind of humor seems on Fergusson's part. As an unscrupulous rake and opportunist, Dolan is by this point utterly beyond credibility.

What saves Fergusson's overburdened episodic string of work and women which make up Dolan's climb is his sense of the craziness and, behind that, the darkness of it all. His strongest satire—at odds with the kind of light satire he uses in describing personages like Gwendolyn—is his account of the effects of the war on Washington and the victims left in the path of the destructive forces at work in the capital and the world. With the coming of the war, civilization and savagery are locked in struggle. Capitol Hill, the ostensible ideal, is corrupted. By this point in the novel Dolan has come full circle. The dull Washington which he first saw when he hit town is now charged with energy. Ralph's role now becomes to work for the Red Cross as a lobbyist for Col. James Randolph Bleason, recently appointed to an executive position with the Red Cross in Washington. Ralph uses his position to line up wealthy fathers who want their sons exempted from military service. Dolan finds excitement in such dealing, and although Bleason's alcoholism and philandering are burdensome for Dolan, he perseveres because of his six-thousand-dollar-a-year salary and his own exemption from service overseas.

Once married to Gwendolyn, Dolan's dream of success comes true. With the war over, he becomes head of the National Commercial Association and has a house on Massachusetts Avenue, three servants, three cars, all the material comforts. After all, "What was Washington but a great crowd of men and women struggling for love and money and security. Most of them were weak and stupid and did not get much. He was strong and clever and got a great deal" (p. 295). Always Dolan's foil, Lambert still suffers from his idealism and his longing for freedom. Finally, he is engaged in just what Fergusson has spent three hundred pages doing in *Capitol Hill:* he is writing a novel of "Washington life" with Dolan as the central character. In this respect, in a more truly autobiographical sense, Lambert—although less developed than Dolan—is an important character and represents the writer mirroring his own struggle with some of the same conflicts. That writer appears again in what might be considered a sequel to *Capitol Hill*—Fergusson's next novel, *Women and Wives.*

But it must be remembered that the hero of Lambert's (and Fergusson's) book is Dolan; and he, too, is a writer. Thus, both of these characters represent two sides of the writer: the journalist and the novelist that Fergusson himself was during those years on Capitol Hill. If Dolan promises to be a great man in a rather ridiculous, undeserving way at the end of the novel, in that perception is also the glimmer of Fergusson's own expectations and ambitions. *Capitol Hill* is an important book because in it we find a box within a box, an author writing about two characters who are composites of himself, selves and antiselves, an author incorporating his own biography in the biographies of his characters.

Capitol Hill met with encouraging success, at least initially. As Fergusson's second novel, it attempted a much broader scope in setting and plot than *Conquerors.* This scope is at once its strength and its weakness, and although it probably enabled him later on to write chronicle novels like *In Those Days* and *Grant of Kingdom, Capitol Hill* confirmed that Fergusson had much to say, and that his real forte was the historical novel over and above the novel of manners or what he called the "journalistic novel." *Conquerors*, as things turned out, was much more characteristic of the kind of novel that Fergusson was destined to write best. And he would return to it in *Hot Saturday*.

The first edition of Fergusson's second novel sold out within a month's time and was much talked about in Washington and Baltimore. Mencken praised it over and above *Conquerors*. That novel he had found to be of "extraordinary depth and beam, and of many merits in detail."[53] And when it came time to review Fergusson's novel of Washington life, Mencken was unqualified in his praise, saying that if *Conquerors* showed "certain doubts and hesitations" of a first novelist, Fergusson was now writing "directly and with assurance." In many respects, Mencken saw Fergusson's work as better "stuff" than Sinclair Lewis's *Babbitt* or *Main Street* and insisted that Fergusson knew Washington better than Lewis knew small-town America: "The result is a picture that lacks some of the charming quality of Lewis' brilliant sketches, but it is a picture . . . that is a great deal more searching and profound." Mencken described the point of the novel as proving that decency is bound to fail in Washington—"that the man who gets on down there is the man who keeps his eye upon number one, and is not incommoded by unfamiliar and perhaps dangerous ideals."[54] Mencken saw Dolan, "a scoundrel from snout to heels," as the key to the novel, as did Fergusson.

Fergusson spent considerable time in his diaries theorizing about Dolan. He felt that as far as novels go, "the central character is the making or breaking of the book," and that Dolan—although partially autobiographical—was based more on observations of a man he knew for a few months and representative of a type of character who was soundly integrated with his environment and by that fact created his supporting characters: "In Ralph Dolan, by luck rather than design, I hit upon a central figure who had this typical and indigenous character, and the novel owes most of the strength it had to this fact."[55] Seeing his own success with Dolan as belonging more to the tradition of Sherwood Anderson's conception of "man as an animal with a vision of beauty, tied to a life that is always incomprehensible and often ugly," than to Sinclair Lewis's novels, Fergusson expected much critical stir and lasting sales for *Capitol Hill*.[56] The brisk sale of the first edition, the talk (some of which was heartening because it was "indignant"), and Mencken's review in the *Sun*—all of these were encouraging. Mencken, for some months after *Conquerors*, had been telling people that "this Fergusson will be heard of later on."[57] And in a letter to Sinclair Lewis, Mencken singled out Fergusson, Dos Passos, and Ruth Suckow as "youngsters who show great promise."[58] Three years after its publication, Mencken was still enthusiastic about Fergusson's second novel: "I can recall, indeed, but one American political novel of any value whatever as a study of character, and that is Harvey Fergusson's story of Washington, 'Capitol Hill'—a series of casual sketches, but all of them vivid and true."[59]

Fergusson soon reconsidered just what *Capitol Hill* meant for him as an artist and found himself floundering between ideas for novels which were at the same time "realistic, poetic, mystical, symbolic." But there was not one single idea which he could seize upon with any real confidence. What he began to settle on was the belief that *Capitol Hill* represented for him a misguided direction: "I doubt whether the journalistic novel carefully worked up seeking to set forth a whole community, city, epic, or other institution, the novel as per Zola, Lewis, George is my forte. I tried it in *Capitol Hill*. All my efforts to make it inclusive were a strain and all its strength lay in flashes of insight."[60] Twenty years after publication, Mencken observed to James T. Farrell that *Capitol Hill* "was not bad, but it never made much of an impression."[61]

Notwithstanding such hedging on the eventual impact of *Capitol Hill*, Mencken was impressed with Fergusson at the time of the novel's appearance. Mencken was an illustrious critic, Fergusson a hot new property, and they enjoyed an amiable relationship. Mencken published several of Fergusson's shorter pieces in the *Mercury* in the first decade of its existence. In their profile of the ideal reader for their new magazine, Mencken and Nathan were seemingly also describing Fergusson and the vantage point he occupied as a new writer: "The reader [Mencken and Nathan] have in their eye, whose prejudices they share and whose woes they hope to soothe, is that William Graham Sumner called the Forgotten Man—that is the normal, educated, well-disposed, unfrenzied, enlightened citizen of the middle majority." Their commitment as editors was nothing less than "to keep common sense as fast as they can, to belabor sham as agreeably as possible, to give a civilized entertainment."[62] In keeping with such an editorial policy, and in support of Fergusson's free-lancing, Mencken accepted and ran two essays and one short story by Fergusson in the first three years of the *Mercury:* "American Portraits: The Washington Job-Holder" (1924), and "Billy the Kid" (1925), and the short story "The New Englander" (1926). In 1930 Mencken ran a travel essay, "Seen and Heard in Mexico," followed in 1931 by several chapters of Fergusson's comprehensive history of the Southwest, *Rio Grande*.[63]

Most of Fergusson's contributions to the *Mercury* reflect the themes of the novels he wrote in Washington and New York (and in New Mexico during summer visits) during the 1920s and 1930s. His correspondence with Mencken makes clear that the *Mercury* pieces were journalistic fillers written to help support himself both between jobs as a journalist in Washington and after he decided to move to New York as a full-time free-lancer; and they were efforts to keep the social channels of communication open with Mencken. Secluded in New Mexico for a summer to work on his next novel, *Women and Wives,* and with the appearance of the first issue of the *Mercury* just months away, Fergusson responded to Mencken's announcment and invitation to submit something, offering congratulations and asking for Mencken's help as well: "All luck and glory to the new review. There is certainly a wide field for it. I will be glad to work for it in any way I can. As soon as I finish this book I expect to go to New York, and I will then be both prepared and compelled to devote myself to journalism for some time. A chance to do honest work would be most welcome."[64] The first issue of *Mercury* appeared in January 1924, and Fergusson had his certificate as a founding subscriber, and an article ready for the spring issue of the first volume, shortly after he arrived in New York at the end of October 1923.

Before he could face the promise and disappointment of the writer's life in New York, however, he had to finish *Women and Wives,* his second Washington novel and one which he later believed his least successful. If New York was his destination in the next phase of his life as a writer, Washington was still his subject and New Mexico still his inspiration. All three places found their way into *Women and Wives*, as did his first marriage and divorce. As in *Conquerors* and *Capitol Hill* he was still very much his own story.

WOMEN AND WIVES

In *Women and Wives* (1923), Fergusson's third novel, he tried his hand again at rendering into fiction his Lexington, Virginia, college and his Washington, D.C., newspaper experiences. Although female psychology and sexuality and the institutions of marriage provide central themes, Fergusson again structures his events around the *Künstlerroman* plot—the development of the writer. The major conflict in the novel revolves around the tendency of marriage to stifle the growth of the artist. The politics of marriage and art rather than the politics of journalism, lobbyists, and government take center stage. The changes taking place in Fergusson's own life serve as a backdrop for the characterizations and happenings in the novel—especially his attempts to establish himself as a professional novelist in New York while still needing to bring in money as a free-lance journalist in Washington, and the breakup of his marriage to Polly Pretty.

Fergusson conceded to Mencken that the theme of the story was a "bromide," but he believed that the characters were realistic creations and insisted that they were the whole book, just as he had believed in the case of his previous two novels.[65] From the beginning he had problems matching the overall design of the novel with its characters, in a way not unlike his worries over the "journalistic" aspects of *Capitol Hill:* "The problem is one of form; to make a continuous novel is really a clumsy device, especially the frigid woman; possible central figure a man who is an artist in love, a lady killer; a woman for [the] central figure; her desperate pursuit of a man; great stuff here only a design lacking."[66] Fergusson felt he never solved this problem of form and bemoaned the fact as much as five years after the novel was published: "In *Women and Wives* I took a . . . pattern and did a hasty piece of work. This and not the choice of subject was the mistake."[67] If one sees the novel as merely about a marriage and a divorce, then it does read like a bromide, and neither the pattern nor the characters are particularly redeeming.

Some readers might go so far as to say that the characters are as commonplace as the theme. The frigid woman and the artist in love are types in a typical situation: a wife and a husband and their friends, some married, some not, serve as influences and alternatives to the norms and aberrations of the central couple's marriage. The age-old design of the lovers' triangle enters in, but with complexity in that more than one man and more than one woman affect the husband and the wife and alter their respective perceptions of each other and of themselves.

What prevents the novel from being quite the bromide Fergusson suggests is that it is the woman who frees herself from the restraints of an inhibiting marriage and the husband who falls into the captivity of a second marriage and thus into the second major mistake in his life. It is a mistake which is especially serious insofar as it prevents him from becoming the writer he wants to become, a mistake that prevents him from realizing the freedom he has always sought in order to become a real writer. If the first wife, Catherine Royce, is meant to be a counterpart of Fergusson's wife, Polly Pretty, and the husband, Jim Royce, is meant to be Fergusson's analog, then the design is especially ironic. Insofar as Royce enters into a second disastrous, stifling marriage of complacency, the entire novel might be read as a commentary on Fergusson's overall aversion to marriage and his reluctance to remarry—this time to Rebecca McCann, his second wife, whom he was seeing while he was awaiting final word about his divorce from Polly.

Although the details of Fergusson's first marriage and the true temperament and personality of his wife are difficult to establish, their involvement with each other, as far as can be determined from Fergusson's diaries, lasted over a period of approximately five years, from 1919 to the summer of 1924. The speculation that Catherine Royce is a counterpart of Polly is given credence by Fergusson's notations that he was not the one to end the marriage. In 1922, while Fergusson was still working on the novel, he recorded this note: "It seems to me I should be able to put Polly out of my mind for keeps. That all the worry about her has been absurd. She broke up the marriage and her conduct certainly to a great extent absolved me from my obligations; but it would be more obviously disastrous for me to either live with her or support her. . . . From now on I decline to carry her on my mind."[68]

She remained very much on his mind, however, particularly as related to his quandary about whether or not to move to New York or stay in Washington and his worries as to whether or not Polly would hit him with a demand for exorbitant alimony. Fergusson was intimately involved with at least three women at that time: Polly, Jeanette Mirsky, and Rebecca McCann. They all lived in New York and threatened to sidetrack his concentration if he moved to New York before his divorce was final. Rebecca wanted him to come to New York in September 1922; however, as Fergusson wound up his 1922 summer in New Mexico, he weighed the pros and cons of such a move in relation to whether or not he wanted to get a job there, what he could show to editors, and most important of all, the matter of the New York adultery law: "All this makes it look like a sound idea to stay in Washington and push the divorce and try to go to New York next winter a free man."[69] As late as June 1924, Fergusson was still worried about Polly and the divorce and what disasters might result to his pocketbook and his reputation if a reporter who was "on the trail of my divorce" dug up anything. Moreover, "if a lawyer gets Polly's permission to move, he can hold me up for everything I own and hurt me in the market too."[70] Indications are that the divorce became final that July. Whatever the exact details, Fergusson experienced considerable anguish over the matter of his first marriage—and even more over his second. In view of these facts, *Woman and Wives*, at least autobiographically, should not be dismissed too readily as an insignificant novel.

In tracing the fictional history of the marriage of his typical wife and husband facing Washington and New York society in the 1920s, Fergusson begins with the college courtship of Catherine Larue and Jim Royce. After their marriage, they enjoy a few short years of what they believe is wedded bliss. In that time they establish a home and Jim secures a government job, but then the arc turns downward: their marriage starts to deteriorate as a result of almost inevitable forces and through no one particular cause; they both become involved in adulterous affairs; they separate and are divorced. Catherine realizes the potential of the artist which has, ironically, been in her all along; and Jim—in a cross-pattern—gives up on the artist which is potentially inside him but is thwarted by his government job of bureaucratic drudgery. Because of his job, his marriage, and his general refusal to actually write, his artistic inclination and much-talked-about talent never manifests itself. It is Catherine Larue Royce who replaces Ralph Dolan as the successful character and the "artist" and Jim Royce who recedes into conformity and sterility. Royce is not literally killed off, like so many "victimized" characters in *Capitol Hill*, but he nevertheless dies a kind of spiritual death through alcoholism and a second marriage to a woman who is considerably inferior to Catherine in social class, artistic sensibility, and intelligence. In returning to his old office fling, Fanny Miller, Royce assures himself a life of even greater obscurity.

Fergusson, through his narrator and Jim Royce's consciousness, observes that the complex web of reasons for the ruination of Catherine and Jim's marriage is partly due to their times, to a kind of frontier's ending. It is an explanation very much in keeping with Fergusson's theories about his life as a hereditary pioneer facing the "morning after." If there is promise in such an explanation, it sounds almost like a rationalization: "They had never made a real marriage in the sense that their parents and grandparents had made marriages. . . . They had come to maturity in a time of restlessness and change, when youth was instinctively rebelling against restraint, seeking a new ethic of life and love."[71]

The tragedy of Royce's life is his failure to act on his aspirations, to carry out his hopes to write a great narrative of quest and adventure, to live his life fully. Such inactivity is always the basis for regret if not outright condemnation in Fergusson's scheme of values. His heroes always live life to the fullest. And Fergusson himself no doubt saw Royce as his own antithesis. Whatever Dolan's failings, he acts on his ambitions. Like Ramon Delcasar, Royce lapses into domestic complacency. His agony is that his adventure narrative is wholly imagined, never lived, never journeyed, never written. He is clearly the antithesis of the heroic frontiersman—Huning, Sampson Noland Ferguson, even H. B. Fergusson—as well as of more modern men of action admired by Fergusson, like Mencken, Knopf, and Haskin, or men of poetic sensibility like his friend Frank Spitz.

After Catherine informs Royce that she wants a divorce and will stay in New York and work her way up as a fashion designer, Royce vows that he too will do what he most deeply wants to do: write a long book, "a brilliant, daring book that would startle the public" (p. 296). The story, and in some respects the motive, are recognizable as the kind of book Fergusson himself wanted to write and eventually did write in *Grant of Kingdom*. If Henry Lambert in *Capitol Hill* would write the projected equivalent of Fergusson's *Capitol Hill*, the very novel which gives Lambert life as a character, then Royce will write the equivalent of Fergusson's later trilogy, *Followers of the Sun* (1936). Royce wants to call his novel *In Search of the Sun*. Fergusson thus envisions one of his own future creations, one which came into being many years later. Royce sees the scenes and the plot in his mind's eye: "The story concerned a man who had led a humdrum life for years, and who suddenly, under the urge of a mysterious inspiration, turned his back upon all his familiar occupations and duties, and struck out across country roaming southward. 'In Search of the Sun,' he thought he would call it" (pp. 296–97).

By implication, part of the reason for Royce's failure is his excessively romantic idea of just what the writer should write, where his hero should travel, and how he should live. Fergusson's own choice of subject was the Southwest, the old and the new frontiers of that region; and even though it is an exotic place filled with encounters with sublime landscapes and dark-skinned peoples, it is not the same as the tropics of Kipling and Conrad which imprint Royce. Fergusson obviously would prefer to temper Royce's flamboyant visions and high romanticism by means of which he would narrate his hero's adventures: "From much reading of Conrad and Kipling and other great artists who had written of the tropics, he had in his mind a complete and lovely picture of the Southern lands and oceans where his hero would go" (p. 297). Royce never writes the great romantic roaming novel, never becomes his own hero. It is no small coincidence that at the very time Fergusson was writing *Capitol Hill* and *Women and Wives* he was deciding to move to New York and write novels full time—to act out his own dream. Royce only dreams of doing what Fergusson did, was doing in the creation of Royce, and of what Catherine does, in effect, by finding a new life of self-sufficiency, of freedom to dare life as an artist.

Although there is something of Fergusson in Jim Royce, there is perhaps an even more recognizable semblance of him in Catherine's long-time suitor, John Strome. As his name suggests, he is a strong man and the one man whom she could have loved, and eventually does, in preference to Jim. Something of a romantic stereotype of the ladies' man, Strome acts on his desires in a much more "masculine" way than Royce does. Even at college (which is clearly a fictional counterpart of Washington and Lee) Strome is more decisive than Jim. Nothing like Royce or his fraternity brother and friend Arthur Aspinwall, Strome waits for Catherine outside her window one night and by his good looks and animal presence lures her outside. He tells her that he loves her and that she is beautiful, the ideal of womanhood represented by his mother. He kisses her and leaves saying they will never meet again. But they do—in Washington and in New York.

Strome reappears almost too coincidentally at crucial times in the story. The memory of Strome's kiss and his indescribable appeal work subconsciously on Catherine in lessening Jim in her estimation after she marries him. She first reencounters Strome after she and Jim move to Washington for Jim to take a job as a government publicist for James E. Carnavon (who is modelled after Haskin). Jim's friend Arthur Aspinwall, like Frank Spitz, also moves to Washington to accept a patronage job as assistant to the executive secretary of the American Association for the Improvement of Public Morals. At Aspinwall's housewarming party Catherine meets Strome again, and they subsequently begin meeting at Ravells, a place frequented mostly by the new woman. Strome has retained his idealized philosophy about women and shares some of his thoughts with Caroline, reinforcing in her the belief that the clothes she has designed, made, and wears are works of art. Even so, Fergusson's attitudes toward women as expressed in Strome's relationship with Catherine amount to male dominance. Although Strome idealizes women, he is placed in a superior position by the narrator, who says some blatantly sexist things which hardly seem intended ironically. For example, as Catherine drifts further into her adulterous affair with Strome, the narrator observes, "It was just being overwhelmed by his superior logic and facility and his amazing fund of information that she did enjoy, for the minds of women crave to be fertilized no less than their bodies" (p. 140).

Because Strome is an old college friend now working at the Smithsonian, he is thrown into opportune meetings not just with Catherine but with Royce and Aspinwall at their club. And like them, he is a writer—but of a different sort. Where Jim writes insipid, bureaucratic prose and only dreams of writing an exotic adventure novel, and where Arthur has a screenplay he wants to show to D. W. Griffith, Strome is involved in writing for the sake of writing—about the Southwest, the subject of Fergusson's own most heartfelt books. Strome's writing, although romantic to a degree, is considerably more realistic and actually finds its way to paper. With some irony, given the clandestine meetings between him and Catherine, he explains his writing and his book to Jim. Like Fergusson behind him, he links the sexual impulse and the creative artistic impulse: "We are a nation of thwarted authors and jilted lovers. . . . I cheerfully plead guilty to both counts. . . . The only woman I ever loved married another man, and I am even now engaged in writing a book, which will probably never be published. It's going to be called 'The Seven Golden Cities' and it's based on a report I made for the Smithsonian on the seven cities of Cibola" (pp. 158–59).

Women and Wives, then, reflects not just the individual quests of Catherine Larue, Jim Royce, and John Strome for freedom—in their lives, loves, and artistry—but Fergusson's own struggle for independence and identity as a writer. *Conquerors, Capitol Hill*, and *Women and Wives* all deal with characters who both fail and succeed in their own respective attempts to do what they want to do—to exercise their freedom of choice to act or not to act, on their own terms. Like his characters Ramon, Ralph, Catherine, and Jim—characters Fergusson felt were both real and of a type—Fergusson found that the interrelationships of heredity and environment, of gender and culture, and especially of time and place were much more complex than either fiction or autobiography could explain.

In the strangest and yet in the most apparent of ways, Fergusson's past—his boyhood in the Southwest, as the grandson of a pioneer Santa Fe trader and the son of an illustrious territorial representative to Congress, and his early adulthood as a journalist in the nation's capital who one day just happened to interview H. L. Mencken—helped determine that he would be a writer of novels and in those books reinvent again his memories of the past and his dreams of the present as they converged in a time he thought of as a "morning after."

5.

Novelist East and West (1923–1931)

Fergusson was very much a novelist aware not only of the historical past and present but also aware of his geographical past and present, as represented by New York and New Mexico, East and West. He made a habit of returning to New Mexico after time spent in the East. He did so after graduating from college and continued this pattern into the 1920s. He could not live in New Mexico, and he could not live away from it. By the spring of 1923, at the age of thirty-three, he decided to leave Washington, spend the summer writing in Albuquerque and in Santa Fe, and then return east—but this time he would live in New York.

The 1920s were a particularly difficult time for him—but a productive one nevertheless. He had his three passions—writing, women, and the out-of-doors—and at least the first two of these were giving him pleasure and causing him trouble. On his thirty-third birthday he observed: "My chief kick on life is that it seems to move away so swiftly. . . . Am also troubled by the complications at once ridiculous and painful, of my love affairs. I now have three women, and am bound to disappoint two of them."[1] His mood alternated from happiness to despair. He knew he wanted to write novels, but the poor sales of his first three attempts proved to him that he had to do what he considered hackwork to make a living. He had to find the right environment in which to write, and he had to decide about his growing involvement with Rebecca McCann—about his own divorce and hers.

In the summer of 1923, then in Taos, Fergusson thought Washington might still be his best base of operations: "My best bet is a flat in Washington with a set seaside place to work. In summer a short trip; south in winter and this [New Mexico] and Europe for change and stimulus. My problem is to find a way of making a living without a job. Next time I make a trip to New Mexico I'll come here first, then Santa Fe, and finally Albuquerque where I'll do whatever I can in writing. . . . New Mexico will never be a place to live for me unless I had someone like R. [Rebecca McCann] to live with. Hate to leave here. Feel I have not mastered the place but the way to get the work done and get in shape is to leave. I'm falling behind. Getting thin here. Tackle it again another time."[2] But Washington was second choice to New York, considered mainly because of the difference in divorce laws. That same summer, in New Mexico, he set his sights on New York: "It seems increasingly clear to me that I belong in New York. My dream of escape into a more primitive environment is a vestige of infancy. Really, I enjoy such an escape only for a short time. I crave ideas, books, interesting and civilized people. I am going to go to New York with all my belongings and bet my stake on an effort to establish myself there. . . . Locate a place on Long Island where I can live on a hundred a month and so write a book if I have four or five hundred ahead."[3]

All of the summers during the 1920s were important ones for him, for they reconfirmed that the West was to be the major setting of his novels, and his next four novels—*Hot Saturday* (1926), *Wolf Song* (1927), *In Those Days* (1929), and *Footloose McGarnigal* (1930)—all revolved around that setting. The first draft of *Women and Wives* (first called "Two in a Flat") also had been written in New Mexico.

The summer of 1923, like most of his summers in New Mexico during this period, was not all work. He typically swam daily in the

Rio Grande, took long hikes along the river and in the mountains, took numerous short trips in his car, socialized with artists and intellectuals in Taos, Santa Fe, and Albuquerque, dated many women, was captivated by young Alice Henderson and entertained by Mabel Dodge Luhan, met Mary Austin and Harriet Monroe, and grew to enjoy Witter Bynner and his "performances" at his showcase house in Santa Fe. More importantly, he tried to straighten out in his own heart just how he felt about Rebecca McCann. In his continued vacillations between the wilderness and socializing, between obligation to Rebecca and promiscuity, he reenacted his divided allegiance to the East and the West, responsibility and freedom.

One of his automobile trips that summer took him through southern Colorado and the Navajo country. Writing from his mother's home on Orchard Place in Albuquerque, he told Mencken that it was fine country to work in, "if you can dispense with . . . society."[4] He agonized about the life of a novelist, not always sure that novel writing was worth the time and work it demanded—especially in light of the disappointing sales of his novels—and he expressed that doubt to Mencken, wondering out loud, "whether it is really intelligent to stick to such an exhausting and unprofitable job."[5]

If, however, Fergusson was doubtful about working hard for himself and a limited readership, he was certain that New Mexico was an essential part of the process in which he was caught up: "I get lots more work done that I ever do in the East. It's a healthy country and no distractions. I recommend it to you the next time you tackle a major work."[6] He faced the realization that his novels would never bring in much money and in letters to Mencken in August and September of 1923 proposed articles about Washington which Mencken might use in the *Mercury*, chatted about his experiences in Albuquerque (which included attending a Ku Klux Klan meeting, and told Mencken about the local roadhouses and entertainments, which took on fuller fictional detail in *Hot Saturday* and *Footloose McGarnigal*.[7]

Their correspondence indicates that Fergusson took every opportunity to ask Mencken for his help in lining up work. Mencken recommended Fergusson for such positions as an editor for the National Magazine Corporation in Baltimore, for which he received a

Harvey Fergusson (*right*) and Witter Bynner in Santa Fe, 1922. Courtesy of Paul Horgan.

tentative offer of a hundred dollars a week—better than he could do as a freelancer in New York. Fergusson left New Mexico on October 24 and arrived in Washington three days later, talked with the management of the National Magazine Corporation, and then proceeded to New York City, where he checked into the Hotel Yorker at the end of the month to await a firm offer from Baltimore and to continue work on *Women and Wives.*

By November 15, 1923, he had moved to the Royalton Hotel, turned over the manuscript to the typist, and submitted the essay "The Washington Job-Holder" to the *Mercury,* which Mencken accepted and published in the spring of 1924. Since the job in Baltimore never materialized, Fergusson was left with his choice of living and writing in New York City. His separation from Polly Pretty and his developing romance with Rebecca McCann notwithstanding, he was finally in America's mecca for artists.

During the winter and spring of 1924 Fergusson reworked some autobiographical fiction (probably "Clouds of Glory," a manuscript of 220 pages, never offered to a publisher, in which, significantly, he calls himself Andrew Jackson Hardy, Jr.) and started a new novel which he did not identify in his letters to Mencken, but which was presumably *Hot Saturday.* Fergusson was at work on this novel, which he first called *Saturday Night,* as early as 1923 and found it painfully "autobiographical," as he recorded in the spring of 1925: "My state of mind with regard to 'Saturday Night' is one of doubt and agony. I cannot feel sure [it is] either a good novel or a comprehensible one. The writing of it is going to yield the full measure of pain that comes of probing one's complexes and my feeling is now that I can do no better than go ahead and write it, keeping fully before me the fact that it is likely to be a failure. It has pushed at my mind almost two years. If I turn away from it then I definitely renounce the strongest instinctive prompting as a guide."[8]

But most of the spring of 1924 found him writing short fiction and doing freelance work. The summer of 1924 took him, along with Rebecca McCann, once again to New Mexico, where he resided in Santa Fe and considered the possibility of making it a permanent residence.

Fergusson's involvement with Rebecca McCann had started much earlier than the summer of 1924—and it culminated in their marriage in 1927 and her death that same year. The one or two accounts of McCann's and Fergusson's marriage do not reveal the storminess of their long courtship and brief marriage. Fergusson saw other women while he was seeing Becky—and he was at the point of exasperation because of her outbursts of temper. His diaries reveal that they fought constantly and that she threatened to commit suicide more than once in what he viewed as attempts to control him. Yet out of all the contention one senses that Fergusson loved her as much as he could love any woman. His dedication of *Wolf Song* to her helps confirm this.

As Fergusson's divorce from Polly was about to become final, he invited Rebecca to join him in Santa Fe. He was apprehensive about what his mother and others would think about such a summer liaison, in that both were still married (Rebecca's divorce from her second husband was not yet final); but Fergusson relied on his sister's advice in handling such a delicate situation. Residence in Santa Fe rather than Albuquerque made it less of a provocation to his hometown's sense of morality. This pressure no doubt found its way into the sexual complications of *Hot Saturday*.

He met McCann in Albuquerque in mid-June and took her up to Santa Fe for the remainder of the summer, until September 5. The day of her departure he recorded one of many such notes of doubt about their relationship and his hesitation about being tied down again in marriage: "The question that still agitates me is whether I am capable of devotion to B[ecky]. If not to her then certainly to no one. I felt her as a drag socially, unable to move among others freely because of my obligation to her. It is a conflict I can't resolve. Let destiny resolve it. If she wants to stick I will too and take what comes."[9]

Fergusson's correspondence with Mencken during the summer makes clear that Fergusson was not fully committed to any project, but as the serendipitous nature of the material-gathering and writing process proved, he was collecting material which would be of great value in both *Hot Saturday* and *McGarnigal*—and later in *Rio Grande* and *Grant of Kingdom*. But more significantly, out of what seemed an

Rebecca McCann, 1927. Courtesy of The Bancroft Library.

unproductive and personally traumatic summer, the conception of his "mountain man" novel, *Wolf Song*, was taking place. Once *Hot Saturday* was finished, *Wolf Song* would prove the most powerful and sustained burst of creative energy of his life. The preparations for that experience were gathering energy in his Santa Fe summer with Rebecca McCann, what he regarded as one of the worst summers of his life. Assuredly it was a formative one.

As he looked at the projected plan of work for the summer and then at the amount of work realized, an air of disappointment pervades his letters to Mencken, as evidenced in comments made in midsummer: "I was a bit up in the air about my work and do not know for sure what I will do next. I had intended writing a short novel and several short stories this summer, but Knopf advised against the short novel and suggested I write a book about New Mexico for the tourist trade. I started this in the hope of selling some of the stuff to the mags, but I am discouraged by the fact that two other magazine writers are out here ahead of me working in the same field."[10]

By the first week in August he was still preoccupied with writing an autobiographical novel which was having a hard time taking off, and with the theme of New Mexico as a "racial frontier," notably the Anglo-Mexican conflict he was observing in a new light that summer. Much of his inability to concentrate was due to the attention he gave Rebecca. His diary for this summer reveals the disturbance that that relationship caused in his life. Rebecca returned to the East by September 5 and must have left in something of a rush, since she had no residence established in New York. By October, at the end of his seasonal stay in New Mexico and just before his own departure for New York, Fergusson had only a few articles and a short story or two in rough form as evidence of what he hoped would have been a productive stay in the Southwest. The worry, distraction, and time he put into dealing with "Becky" and in "bumming around in search of material," plus an "intestinal infection which took all the pep out of [him]," prompted him to forget writing and marital worries for a time and go bear hunting. In a humorous "mountain man" parody which Mencken could enjoy, Fergusson confessed: "I have not caught up with any bear thus far, and do not expect to, but the hard exercise is getting me back into shape."[11] His bear hunt, like many of the other experiences of that summer, eventually turned up in fictional form in *McGarnigal*. His "bumming around" and socializing were utilized, in part, in *Hot Saturday*. After Rebecca left, his spirits soared into "genuine joy" to be rid of her. Ironically, he demonstrates some of the same lack of initiative and tendency to drift that fictional characters like Julia Roth and Jim Royce do: "No doubt that I want to remain free and I have no courage to claim freedom unless she offers it."[12]

ALBUQUERQUE SATURDAY NIGHT

In *Hot Saturday* Fergusson carried over some of the themes, situations, and characters of his first three novels. The essence of the continuity is his own autobiography—how he incorporated, again, his own life into his fiction. He may have said he expected his fourth novel to be a failure, but it is not. Eventually he sold it to the movies; but the higher the stakes for success, the more of a disappointment the novel was for him. It shocked his hometown and caused him some damaged local reputation. He discussed the possibility of dramatizing the novel with his brother, Francis; however, they could not agree on the right approach. But it remains a more enjoyable novel than *Women and Wives*. It represents one extreme of his fiction—his most condensed novel—and allowed him, by contrast, a better grasp of the "chronicle" novel which in *Grant of Kingdom* would be his greatest accomplishment.

By using the "day-in-the-life," or more correctly a "night-in-the-life," structure common to other novels of the time, in focusing on one young and sexually ambitious woman, and in moving his locale to the Southwest, Fergusson came up with a simpler and more satisfying plot than his previous "journalistic" novels. This new plot is still episodic, still deals with the motivation to "succeed" as portrayed in his first three novels, but it is considerably more unified. Set in a small town on the Rio Grande during the jazzy 1920s, the book develops Fergusson's persistent East/West, frontier/modern themes in conjunction with the idea and imagery of the "heat" of passion and place, sexual conquest and the loss of innocence—in this case the virginity of a twenty-year-old hometown girl with an inclination to move in the fast lane, Ruth Bruck. She is a composite of many of the women Fergusson knew at the time, East and West, and her aspirations to escape are not unlike his own.

Ruth's hometown is also Fergusson's. The Albuquerque of the novel, like Ruth herself, is a place of contradictions, caught in the transitions of the end of the frontier. Ruth is a kind of new "pioneer"—a zesty, red-headed flapper with a look and reputation as a "red-hot mamma" which is not totally deserved. She is another transposition of the flappers who populate Washington and New York in *Capitol Hill* and *Women and Wives*, taken from the hot lights of the big city to the hot desert climate of New Mexico. It is her struggle against the gossipy small-mindedness of her family, her high-school romancers, and the town itself that causes her to set her heart on a young chemist and heir to a half-million-dollar family fortune in New York, Wilbur Fadden.

The year of this particular "night in the life" is, for all practical purposes, contemporary with the publication date, 1926. Albuquerque has a population of 55,000 which has increased from 30,000 in just two years. Fadden, in town like other pulmonary patients for his health, finds himself awkwardly susceptible to Ruth's seductions. The lover's triangle which Fergusson favors so much in his plotting enters again. Fadden's foil is a darker, more worldly vagabond with a name which, perhaps a bit too obviously, fits his character: John Romer. Another recasting of John Strome in *Women and Wives*, and of the "lone rider" side of Fergusson, Romer—as a more socially unacceptable suitor, but ironically the appropriate one in Fergusson's and thus the novel's scheme of things—takes Ruth sexually before Fadden comes to his senses and decides to disregard the rumors of Ruth's sexual looseness, a "looseness" which Romer has just helped confirm. Ruth, however, is successful in her materialistic goals in spite of herself; she both consummates her passion for Romer and obtains a marriage proposal from the cuckolded Fadden. What seems at one point to be a "Hot Saturday" which consumes her with passion and sexually "ruins" her, actually allows her, Phoenix-like, to rise from the ashes of her love and lust to escape the confining pettiness of her hometown into wealth and wedded bliss in the East with Fadden. Ruth, too, is reminiscent of Dreiser's Carrie.

In addition to all of Fergusson's rather heavy-handed use of sun and heat imagery to advance his plot and establish characters and setting, he structures the novel around the small and large trips which make up Ruth's fateful Saturday. Ruth has the use of the family car and likes to drive it (even realizes a certain erotic pleasure in doing so); and it is this motorized freedom which enables her to work her will with men. The automobile, as much as the train, is essential to Fergusson's theory of the new morality which he witnessed in the 1920s in the aftermath of the frontier. He uses the car in *Hot Saturday* as a symbol not just of the machine in the Garden, but of Eve as driver-engineer. She is another rendering of the new, liberated woman—but she is also the eternal temptress and tease, a type so often portrayed by Fergusson. In his staging of an Albuquerque Saturday night he creates a setting for an ageless "battle of the sexes," played out against a frontier versus modern counterpoint.

Ruth begins her Saturday at the beauty parlor readying herself for her well-planned campaign, an erotic assault that is ostensibly a picnic in the mountains that afternoon with young Fadden. The night with Romer and Fadden's proposal will be the outcome. But against such an anticipatory opening Fergusson satirically introduces his cast of characters based, seemingly, on his own family and friends—all types which reappear in *McGarnigal* and later in *Riley*. In a combination of the techniques of the *roman à clef* with the historical novel, recognizable "portraits" appear and reappear. It is no wonder that the novel created a stir in Albuquerque and that Fergusson, after publication, recorded in his diary, "I am . . . worried about how much bad feeling I have stirred in Albuquerque."[13]

But if the conformity of a small southwestern town is satirized in Ruth's longing to escape, the object of her desire, Wilbur Fadden and his eastern home, is equally the brunt of Fergusson's barbs; for Wilbur as an easterner is no match for the westernized Romer. Ruth, for all her bravado and identification with Fadden and the fads of the day, is still naive and untried, caught up in the dreams of youth and ambition. As she drives away from the beauty parlor, (an institution used to even greater effect in *Riley*), seeking only the fresh air and freedom allowed by her car, and with her thoughts and designs dreamily concentrating on Fadden, she fantasizes about her marriage and her escape to the wonderous East: "[New York] was all the elements of her ideal of beauty piled together in shining abundance. . . . It was everything she lacked and longed for—money, light, speed, clothes, people—innumerable, astonishing people she had never met before, moving gracefully through an intricate, endless round of pleasure."[14] For Ruth it will be the ideal of East or West as opulence and leisure— not the dusty frontier past which she associates with her town and especially with her friends, Judge Budlong and his daughter Alma. The judge is a living anachronism and takes on the outlines of Fergusson's own father, H.B., the lawyer and congressman. His daughter, Alma, is recognizable in name, visage, and demeanor as Fergusson's sister Erna.

Alma with her elderly father lives on Seventh Street, in Old Town—the same area of the city where Fergusson's grandfather Huning settled and built his castle and where Fergusson grew up as a boy in La Glorieta. Significantly, Old Town is west Albuquerque, and New Town is east Albuquerque, "historically" inverted and respectively associated with past (West) and future (East). The Budlong house, somewhat like a scaled-down combination of Castle Huning and its orchards and La Glorieta and its timelessness, is a legacy of the 1880s, one of the oldest houses in the area, representative of a once forward-looking dwelling now lost to disrepair and the past: "It was a tall square frame . . . with dormer windows thrusting through an old slate roof, and a wide pillared porch, shedding in flakes the last of many coats of blue paint. Its sagging corner and failing picket fence, its ancient wood lilac bushes and dying apple trees told the world that something in this town had been dignified and respectable long enough to get rotten" (p. 24). The frontier of the 1880s is long past, and even nostalgia for the strength and fervor of those days—of Budlong the pride of the family—is a dead end, alluring as it once was. The judge was quite the politician and orator in his day, speaking on all kinds of topics from the fall of Rome to the Constitution and the founding fathers. It was the judge who introduced William Jennings Bryan when he came to town (as was the case with H. B. Fergusson, who remained Bryan's protégé) and it was the judge who ran for nearly every political office. Like H.B. he ended broke and in debt: "He didn't have a dollar now, they said. Alma kept him going on her salary as librarian. It was lucky for him she hadn't married" (p. 26).

Romer is the typical masculine ideal in Fergusson's fiction—a recasting of Ralph Dolan in *Capitol Hill* and John Strome in *Women and Wives*, and an anticipation of Sam Lash in *Wolf Song*, and of McGarnigal, Riley, and others of Fergusson's own autobiographical analogs. Where Ruth, a materialist, drives her powerful automobile and identifies with the city and its future as machine and technology, Romer, a philosophical idealist of transcendental cast, walks and identifies with the outdoors, with nature, the river, and the sun. As opposites they attract and complement each other. The sunshine and the slower-paced side of the town have cured him, and he respects them as a consequence. He is described as "a new man in a new world" (p. 38), but much of his psychology sides with the older world;

and the world which he does inhabit is all a matter of his perceptions. He is a kind of Emersonian "eye" giving meaning to all he sees in nature. The West for him is a kind of Eden, and he accepts it and is joyous in its bounty. His special spot on the river is described as "a bit of earth as it fell from the hand of God" (p. 52). His transcendentalism and freedom of spirit, gained by having nearly died and come through, make Ruth's idealized longings for escape to the "heaven" of New York—at least up to a point—seem sophomoric.

While Ruth's first ride of the day takes her to Hairpin Hill and reveries of escape to the East and marriage to Wilbur, Romer's walk takes him from the sanitarium down the Center Street (Central Avenue) of New Town with all of its noise, bustle, and color. He "roams" into the respectable residential section of Old Town, through the slums of "shack, hovel and dump" toward the park where he meets Ruth, and then to the river for a solitary swim. His stroll is like a walk back through history. And his need for solitude on the one hand, and for Ruth's vivacious companionship on the other, seems to parallel Fergusson's own dilemma while weighing his need for Rebecca McCann.

Romer's transport through town is much slower and more significant in its portrayal of the panoramic historical forces at work changing the town than Ruth's exasperated attempt to pass the jitneys of migrant Okies and impulsively fly away inside the expensive New York touring cars. Romer sees the old and new frontiers of the town, and if he cannot exactly reconcile them, he nevertheless accepts both for what they are.

To accommodate Romer's perceptions and alliance with the vitalistic forces of historical change, and by implication, with the life force, Fergusson uses the metaphor of a weed—"a hardy weed that could grow anywhere and choke out any other growth" (p. 40). Like Dolan, Lash, and others of Fergusson's heroes, Romer is an enduring bit of protoplasm. The implicit naturalistic suggestion in the growth of the town (and in Romer's character) is that life comes from death. The town as organism had choked out the Mexican village in the transitional days of Spanish conquest and absorbed the Mexicans; similarly, it had choked out the frontier town "of wasteful enterprise and violent revel," and that pattern of change which ended the frontier intrigued him: "Old men could still describe it to him. Dancehalls, saloons and gambling-joints flared red and yellow along a single street. Cowboys, buffalo-hunters, prospectors, played and fought, threw away life, money and energy. But the town needed that these things be used, not wasted. Pioneers did their job and gave way to money-makers in stiff collars and stiff respectabilities, cautious and over-disciplined as the pioneers had been wild and daring" (p. 41). The Turnerian germ-wave theory of history seems the basis for such historiography.

Romer is regarded by these stiff-collared moneymakers, especially Gus Bruck, Ruth's well-heeled, stodgy father, as a loafer and a lunger. Drifter that he is, Romer perceives the town and its history without engaging it. As a roamer, he desires to settle neither in business nor in marriage; he desires to make neither money or children in the town, but merely to experience it, observe it, pass through it. The mood matches Fergusson's, particularly that part of his personality which wanted freedom from the entrapments of Rebecca and any other woman whose idea of adventure was to "have babies." In this context, one of Fergusson's "honest" appraisals of Rebecca after her death attempted to justify their relationship as almost predestined: "The truth is, she wanted and needed change, an adventure, marriage; travel first and babies later was the only adventure she could plan or imagine. Almost any clean or respectable man with a little money would do. In a word, with all her strength . . . she had neither sensibility nor imagination."[15]

Using the same structures of clandestine meetings with a socially disengaged and rebellious outsider first used with Strome in *Women and Wives*, Fergusson balances the novel with an opening and a closing rendezvous between Ruth and Romer on the "hottest day of summer," in the first meeting of the pair in the morning—when Ruth, on her way to the picnic with Fadden, sees Romer alone in the park, stops, and rekindles the sexual magnetism which has developed between them—their passion is thwarted, leaving it to build for the rest of the day. But in their final rendezvous at night, Ruth comes to him in his rat's-nest room , and they love freely and fully, without promises and future commitment. Fergusson's diaries are full of allusions to such free and passionate encounters, even in the days after Rebecca leaves for the East after their 1924 summer in New Mexico.

Like Sam Lash, Alec McGarnigal, Morgan Riley, and other such types, Romer is an outsider who considers marriage and sees some of its benefits—but only to a point. It is an ambivalence which weighs heavily on the spirit of all Fergusson's strong male characters and which he seemed to experience even more dramatically than his most freedom-loving bachelors. Like Fergusson, Romer's whole character poses the question of where he belongs and should be—East or West, single or married, on the move or settled: "A part of him was content to do this ['wander and look at things . . . , savouring a thousand lives but never devouring one'], took pride in the sense of a special destiny. But another part of him longed for something warmer and more comforting—wanted to marry a plump, strong, ignorant girl with no nerves and no ideas, wanted to love her, quarrel with her, get babies out of her, build a little wooden house to keep them in" (p. 47). The conflict Fergusson was having with Rebecca is reflected in such a passage. It is a conflict that faces all of Fergusson's major male characters.

As an extension of Fergusson, Romer is an important character. He is the fourth love of Ruth's life, and the first from the larger world outside her home. He is part of the influx of "nuts" and "exotics" (as Fergusson put it) who immigrated to the art colonies of Taos and Santa Fe in the 1920s and to the tuberculosis sanitariums in Albuquerque. Although Romer hails from a small town in Indiana and is to a point identical with Dolan, although he is a man with a government pension from his army enlistment and more a soldier than a writer, he nevertheless is interested in ideas. In keeping with his intellectualism, it is at one of Alma's teas that Ruth first meets him.

Fadden's perceptions of the West are not so profound or romantic as Romer's—in part because the West has not literally given him a second chance to live, as it has Romer. Fadden is more practical, with not much room for the nonsense and clichés often spouted about the West and its wide-open spaces. His view of the West occupies a middle ground between the Utopia which on one level it is for Romer and the desolate, godforsaken hell which it is for Ruth.

Fergusson uses Ruth as the fulcrum on which he weighs these respective views of the frontier and modern West. As she drives Alma Budlong and the garrulous old coot Doc Jaggers out to the end of canyon road (through Tijeras Canyon, in the Sandias east of town) for their picnic, she tries to enter into the usual small talk with Fadden about the relative merits of the West and East. In keeping with his interest in people over places, Fadden reduces the majestic Sandias, which in frontier times had been sublime obstacles representative of the terror and the beauty against which pioneers had to measure their resolve, to small talk. In the end both the clichés and their refutation are left with some credence—again showing Fergusson's ambivalence. But the mountains seem to have the last word.

Since mountains were so important to Fergusson as a stabilizer in his nineteenth/twentieth-century marginality, his description of how history has confronted geology, civilization intruded upon wilderness, is dramatized by the serious past approaches to the mountain and the present frivolous one: "Mountains that had been a mystery and danger to one generation were a toy to the next. Pioneers had approached mountains with prayer, tightening their belts for want and effort, and their children flew up them, spooned and feasted on their austere heights, found nothing there to harden body or spirit" (p. 147). The sense of loss is apparent, and yet the loss is not felt to be complete. The mountains still hold their dignity.

After the group arrives on the crest of the mountains and starts to eat, talk, and enjoy the geniality of the moment, shades of a more primitive, savage world find them out. Out of nowhere a large, lean, and craven wolflike dog appears. With starved ribs showing through his ragged coat, he sits ten feet away watching them eat. Fergusson romantically describes him as "a spectre of savage want at their banquet" (p. 161). Ruth is the only one who does not attempt to scare the cur away. Certain that what ails the dog is hunger and not hydrophobia, she first offers it a sandwich and then feeds it a plate of scraps by hand: "Slowly she transformed starving resentment and fear into warm wriggling eagerness. Finally she held the ugly head in her lap, completely subjugated" (p. 163). Woman not man has tamed the wilderness—just as she tames Fadden and, to a point, Romer.

The climactic episode in this confrontation of civilization with savagery occurs when Ruth and Fadden leave the group and climb a trail even higher on the crest. A thunder and rain storm catches them, and they give in to their instincts and emotions in a passionate kiss. The front of Ruth's blouse is so soaked that she is, in effect, naked before him, in a primeval state: "It stripped her to the waist before him, so that her bold and pointed young breasts leapt out at him like a challenge" (p. 174). On their way back down from their climb, after their kisses, they see a "great grey deer with wide antlers in the velvet," and they marvel at the sight as if it were the very spirit of the mountain. Nature is finally made supernatural again, perfect in its romance, beauty, and wonder.

Ruth's nakedness conquers Fadden. Her nickname, Lion Tamer, proves true, and Fergusson accedes to the superiority of the sexual impulse and of man's inevitable need for woman. Thus Fergusson uses an innocent enough but contrived picnic to dramatize the antipathy he still senses as a modern man and hereditary pioneer, between wilderness and civilization, mountains and people, male and female, East and West.

When Fergusson sat down to begin serious work on *Hot Saturday*, he recorded this entry in his diary: "About to start 'Saturday Night,' and full of doubt and agony. For one thing I cannot feel faith in the form. For another, I am full of the neurotic fear which arises from writing about any real place. Yet this is the thing I can write if I can write anything, and there is nothing to do but either go ahead or else admit defeat as an artist."[16] His refusal to shy away from his own life experiences and the challenge to give them fictional form assured that he would not know defeat as an artist. *Hot Saturday* proved that as, for its time, a courageous erotic novel. Reviewers in the national press were more favorable than many readers in Albuquerque, who saw the whole thing as scandalous, in part, no doubt, because of its honesty.[17] *Wolf Song*, however, was the one to wait for—for the writer and for the

readers. In that novel Fergusson went west in high fashion and secured his reputation.

LOVE SONG

As might be expected with such an artistically successful novel as *Wolf
Song* (1927), several important experiences surrounded its writing. In
some ways it seems clear just how and why the novel came to be. Its
greatness can be attributed to Fergusson's zeroing in on the themes
which were always part of his heritage, always embedded in his autobiography, always around the edges of his earlier fiction. But just what
catalyst brought about the alignment of form and subject so recogniza-
bly superior as to account for Fergusson's first triumphant aesthetic
success? A first answer, but only a partially satisfying one, is that
Fergusson left contemporary autobiographical fiction behind and
found his true subject in the nineteenth-century American West—in
distant rather than modern historical fiction. *Wolf Song*, nevertheless,
does reflect Fergusson's autobiography. Insofar as the answer lies in
the complex web of circumstances and motive which were Fergusson's
life at the time he wrote his mountain-man novel, one clue resides in
the dedication—"For Rebecca"—two heartfelt, significant words
made all the more forceful by the dedication's simple prominence and
by the story behind it.

   Wolf Song and Rebecca McCann were both special to Fergusson,
and the novel reflects the joy and the anguish that love for his second
wife meant for him. The whole story of their love is lost in a tangle of
diary notes and other accounts which are biased to the point of making
a myth of an ideal marriage out of one which was anything but that,
and of confusing the facts of Rebecca's death and Fergusson's role in
it. The outlines of their relationship are clear, and they point to
Fergusson's writing *Wolf Song* as a love song for Rebecca and for the
mountain man—and as a lament.

   After their 1924 summer in Santa Fe, Fergusson followed Rebecca back to New York, where he again tried to live the writer's life.
He found "a cheap place to live and a good place to work . . . way

uptown by the river" and took a flat there in the spring of 1925.[18] The mountain-man novel began to take shape in his mind that summer, although he had considered the topic the previous summer. He began outlining *Wolf Song*, after a month of research and note-taking in the spring of 1925, and began writing it in earnest during the next summer (1926), burying himself alive on Washington Heights, as he told Mencken, "writing a book about pioneer days in New Mexico": "It is a little longer than *Hot Saturday* but contains, for better or worse, the most spontaneous writing I have done."[19] Knopf had a copy of the first draft of the manuscript in his office by September, and in October Fergusson sent another copy to Mencken for his reaction. Cather's *Death Comes for the Archbishop* was also due to be published the following year, and Mencken liked them both, seeing the Southwest as enjoying a banner year. The next year, 1927, was also an important year for Fergusson: he married Rebecca McCann, *Wolf Song* was published, and by December Rebecca was dead. Less than a year after their marriage, Fergusson faced not only the regrets of his first marriage but the guilt of not having done more to prevent his second wife's death. The guilt was compounded by the pained joy that he was free from a marriage he never really wanted in the first place.

A bit more is known about Rebecca McCann than about Polly Pretty. Fergusson wrote many entries about Becky in his diaries and almost nothing about Polly. For all practical purposes Polly does not exist in his diaries. Becky, on the other hand, made a major difference in his life. She was an artist in her own right and very much a professional who looked forward to a long career which she seemed convinced would complement her marriage. She was born in Quincy, Illinois, in 1897, she thought of Illinois as home, and her ashes were sprinkled over a lake in a Chicago park thirty years later.

Fergusson met Becky through her work for Haskin as an interviewer and illustrator.[20] She became best known for her syndicated verses with pictures which ran as the feature "The Cheerful Cherub." She wrote to her friend Mary Graham Bonner that her purpose was to capture the human nature of things: "I'm not trying to reform the world or to make every one smile. . . . I'm trying to make my little verses human; they're cynical too, and I like to make them about all

Harvey Fergusson and his bride, Rebecca McCann, 1927. Courtesy of
the Erna Fergusson Collection, Special Collections Department, General
Library, University of New Mexico.

subjects—including the frailties of the readers—for their author understands frailties too!"[21] Rebecca's first marriage was to an aviator,
Harold Watson, during World War I. He was killed in the war, and she
then married an officer in the naval Medical Corps, but that marriage
ended in divorce. Her third marriage, to Fergusson, took place in
Galveston, Texas, according to Bonner, or in Salt Lake City, according
to news accounts (Fergusson's diaries confirm neither spot).

Bonner's version of their marriage is much more idyllic than what
is recorded in Fergusson's diaries. According to Bonner's account,
Rebecca "married Harvey Fergusson, the novelist, in Galveston,
Texas, and together they went to Salt Lake City. Harvey was working
over a book with a southwestern setting and Becky's work could be
done on mountain tops, hotel rooms, or sitting on a rock in a country
field. Here they climbed mountains, swam, worked and mapped out
their future with all the confidence that would have been realized had
she lived, for they were supremely congenial and happy."[22] In Fergusson's version Becky was not such a cheerful cherub; rather, he
portrays her as neurotic and subject to frequent outbursts of rage.

Fergusson's diaries do record moments of congeniality and happiness, but there are some vast discrepancies with Bonner's angelic account.

On January 26, 1927, Fergusson left New York alone and headed for New Orleans and Galveston for warm weather and further work on *Wolf Song* and other freelance possibilities. In a retrospective entry written four days after leaving New Orleans, he described his last night with Becky as "disturbed, sad and yet gay too." He said good-bye to other friends, including other lovers, feeling that he was leaving a good life but compelled to do so. The whole journey reads like nothing less than an escape. On the train and for a week in New Orleans he forgot his troubles (presumably Becky's desire to get married and worries over work and money). Always in need of women, he records that he "walked with two girls" and "necked one despite her objections at first." And on his way to Galveston, he recorded a telling appraisal of his involvement with Becky: "I not only do not want to marry her, I do not even want to see her. Yet there is no escape but an act of violence and bad faith of which I am incapable. . . . Let me not fool myself. There is a fundamental incompatibility. She wants far more of me than I can give or than I want of her. I will have to fight for every bit of freedom I have."[23]

If Becky joined him in Galveston, his diaries or letters to Mencken do not record it. By mid-February Fergusson was settled in Galveston and wrote to Mencken about the place—how he enjoyed it, and possible Texas topics he could turn into essay form. In April he headed on to San Antonio and then to Albuquerque. By May 3 he was in Albuquerque for two weeks and took a trip to Santa Fe with his sister and the Ilfelds. His diaries record flirtations with, among others, Alice Corbin Henderson's daughter, Alice. Still no mention of Becky being with him. By May 14, he had traveled on to Salt Lake City and been there for two weeks, playing handball, swimming, and roaming the Wasatch Mountains. According to his diaries, Becky did not join him in Salt Lake until May 29, 1927. If we rely on Fergusson's diaries, he and Rebecca must have been married at some time after this date.

They settled down, "after a nervous spat," to lovemaking and work. Fergusson was pleased with the way his book was proceeding and yet apprehensive too: "It seems too slow moving, lacking high music and spontaneous outbursts." When he could concentrate, the book almost wrote itself and was "alive": "I see clearly that what enables me to write is the complete absorption in the task and the outburst of spontaneous power which gives at least a momentary conviction that the thing is good and alive. It is the unforseen image that leaps out shining and complete which gives the convincing sense of creation. This has given many small outbursts but no great one. . . . I seem to unroll a scroll which is already complete inside of me."[24]

Becky had her monthly tantrums but seemed "less absorbed in them"; Fergusson continued steadily at work writing his "well-knit and alive prose";[25] they fished and hiked and sunned in the mountains, along the Provo River. By August 14, 1927, *Wolf Song* was published to good reviews, and Fergusson summarized things this way: "good work, good hikes, good days with B."[26]

Fergusson and Becky remained in Salt Lake for the remainder of the fall. He found it a good place to work and might have stayed longer. But his "destiny" was otherwise. In December they made plans to go to Albuquerque for Christmas. Accounts differ on the details of what happened next—but not on the result. Bonner says that they left Salt Lake separately, Fergusson driving alone in a snowstorm, "feeling it unwise for [Becky] to take such an arduous trip." According to Bonner, Becky went first to San Francisco to buy some clothes and then met Fergusson in Albuquerque: "But a slight cold turned into a heavy one as feverishly she gaily danced at a fancy dress party. She was ill only a few days. And then for the last time she went to Chicago."[27] Other accounts record that they drove down to Albuquerque together and that during the drive Becky caught pneumonia and died soon after reaching Albuquerque.[28] The latter account would seem to be more consistent with the guilt which Fergusson felt at her death. But he had other things about which to feel guilty besides her catching pneumonia.

If *Wolf Song*, as a lament for the passing and passed glory days of the mountain men, may also be read as an allegory of Fergusson's own desire for freedom and his resignation to keep his promise and try again to reconcile the life of a lone writer with the responsibilities of a husband, then the pathos of his remorse for a lost wife and lost opportunities to make things somehow different rings through diary entries like this one: "The pain most impossible to resolve is bound up with the memory of what small differences in my action would have saved her. That I did not see her plight was desperation, that I neither stayed closer to her, nor rescued her from it—that is permanent regret. . . . By understanding I could have very much avoided it. There would always have been danger to her, as there is to others of this type, but it could have been greatly reduced. I do not believe she ever wanted to die less than then."[29]

For better or for worse, Fergusson's love for and reluctant marriage to Rebecca McCann may also be sensed in the joy and sadness of the improbable, but inevitable union of Sam Lash and Lola Salazar.

SAM LASH AND LOLA SALAZAR

Wolf Song is, by consensus, one of the best fictional accounts of mountain men ever written. Delbert E. Wylder resists ranking it among the top three mountain-men novels as John R. Milton does, but he does list it among the best fictional treatments of mountain men.[30] David Stouck sees *Wolf Song* and Howard O'Hagan's *Tay John* as two of the earliest examples of the genre and among the best seven or so such novels.[31] *Wolf Song*, in addition to being a mountain-man novel, is also a love story, and ironically so, given the stereotype of the mountain man as a confirmed bachelor; and in terms of the book's title and pervasive lyricism, it may be regarded as a love song reflecting Fergusson's love for Rebecca, for the vanished frontier, and for wildness. In this sense, the taming of the novel's main character and center of consciousness, the mountain man Sam Lash, parallels the taming, marriage, and domestication of Fergusson as a lone rider, writer, and modern-day mountain man.

Rebecca McCann was no Lola Salazar, and there is no real need to push to the breaking point similarities of the book's themes and characterizations to Fergusson's life. But Becky did share with Lola a temper which flared under the right circumstances. Lola's anger is sufficient to tame Sam and his sidekicks, and Fergusson uses that trait to great dramatic effect in the novel. Much of the book's power seems to reside not only in the fact that Fergusson poured so much of his own struggles with women and his assumptions about them and about marriage into *Wolf Song*, but in just how he did it, how he synthesized his autobiography and his family's biography with the architectonics of the novel. Once again he worked out some of his ideas about mutability, endings and beginnings of the various kinds of frontiers represented by the coming and the going, the appearance and disappearance, of the fascinating figure of the mountain man in the American West—a figure destined to transcend history and myth into the "truths" of Fergusson's fictions.

Stouck sees *Wolf Song* written in the manner of an impressionist novel, "comprised of carefully selected, suggestive scenes which do not attempt to tell the whole story."[32] But there is much more of Lash's story and of the era than one first realizes. Structurally, *Wolf Song* works on at least two levels: it offers us a panoramic, historical, at times journalistic account of the who, what, why, where, and when of mountain men; and it tells the more personal story of one particular mountain man, Lash, and his sidekicks, Rube Thatcher and Guillon, and how their temporary need for contact with civilization by means of trading in Taos, leads to Sam's falling in love with Lola Salazar, the beautiful daughter of a Mexican patriarch of the town, Don Solomon Salazar. A third level, if one chooses to think of it in this way, is the glimpse which *Wolf Song* affords into the waning civilization of those Spanish Americans known as *ricos*. Fergusson's departure from the conventions of the mountain-man novel in pairing Lash off with a true lady of aristocratic background rather than with a stereotypical squaw offers further insight into the influences of Rebecca during the writing of the novel.

Fergusson's pattern is to introduce Sam and his companions, begin and continue the motives and complications of their story in the novel's time framework, and then juxtapose this with larger contexts, larger forces, and shifts of history. Thus, he is able to capture the times and the types and personalize them so that the entire narrative reads like an epic, with individuals who are recognizable in their own right but who also represent larger abstractions as cultural and historical symbols inside and outside of time—larger than life. Much of the authentic texture of the novel is achieved by his masterful use of dialect (influenced by George Frederick Ruxton), which adds the realism of regionalism and local color, and by certain naturalistic assumptions about the smallness and yet the ironic greatness of man's spirit. It is partly because of Fergusson's "scope" that noted Western novelist Frank Waters ranks Fergusson as one of the best southwestern writers: "Fergusson knew New Mexico intimately, and his historical research was profound. He embraced the whole period of the Mountain Men, the weakening Spanish domination as the Anglos came in. Spanish life and customs he knew intimately. This is rare nowadays. All this gives a great scope in time, culture, and events to his books."[33]

Lash's importance as a character is that he is able in the course of his life—through circumstance, good luck, and, needless to say, Fergusson's contrivance—to span two historical epochs: the epoch of free-spirited adventurers and that of the settlers and builders. His life is thus supremely individualistic and self-reliant, and yet devoted to the values of community. Fergusson's own reluctant marriage is reflected in these conflicting urges. Lash loses but he also gains; for his loss there is compensation, and therein lies the sad/happy ending of the novel.

Taos is the nodality for much of the novel and thus of pivotal importance in *Wolf Song*. In Taos the old and the new meet and merge in dramatic and exotic ways, ways that Fergusson experienced first-hand in his many summer visits there in the 1920s. Lash makes three visits to Taos, each of which progressively marks and clarifies his destiny. *Wolf Song* opens with a stirring chapter written in a style which, as William T. Pilkington observes, is within the tradition of the Anglo-Saxon heroic epic.[34] Lash heads for Taos, *in medias res*, for the second time in this opening, hell-bent for a spree but also with some small motive of revenge, for on his first visit he was, although a member of a "conquering" race of Anglos, outshone by the "greasers."

On his first trip to Taos, Sam was younger and alone, a mountain man in his own right, but not as surely one of the initiates as he is when the novel opens and he lopes over the ridge of the Rockies direct from the South Platte with six beaver-laden pack mules and in the company of old Rube Thatcher, the veteran of the bunch and Sam's mentor, and Guillon, a hot-tempered, rough-and-ready ex-convict and trapper ready to fight the "greasers"—or Sam, or anyone else—at the least provocation. Guillon is—humorously, as Fergusson works things— no match, however, for the equal anger of one "greaser": Lola.

On Sam's first trip Taos meant "white liquor and brown women, fat eating and store fixings."[35] On his second he meets Lola, falls in love, and boldly abducts her in a wild elopement forced on him by the disapproval of the Salazar family. On his final visit to Taos he is reconciled with the Salazars and ends his life as a mountain man, a compromise in exchange for an inheritance of part of the land, wealth, and portion of the rico heritage. He is helped along in his decision by the realization that the way of life for mountain men is dying; rather than die with it, he "adjusts." His marriage to a Salazar is a union that will allow strength to come from two ways of life which separately are all but rubbed out. Lash's realized inheritance seems much like the inheritance Fergusson himself might have had from his grandfather and from his father had not debt and H.B.'s suicide dictated other- wise.

Lash's philosophy, like that of all mountain men, as Fergusson stresses it by means of leitmotif, is that a person must continue until "rubbed out." His heroism comes from his almost existential resolu- tion to persist to the end. Lash's motive is not unlike Fergusson's own resolve to persevere through the ordeal of life—a notion that runs through his diaries as well. The West brings Lash success and life, and he meets it more than halfway, reconciling idealism with pragmatism so as to survive and, presumably, prosper.

Combining the life and times of his grandfather Huning with the legends of Daniel Boone and Davy Crockett, Fergusson sketches a childhood for Lash which destined him for a life as an explorer of the majestic West. Fergusson's own love of the outdoors also does duty in the portrait of Lash. Lash's birth in Kentucky and his Old South ancestry in plantation aristocracy parallels H. B. Fergusson's origins. As part of the exposition on Lash's childhood has it, "He remembered arms of his mother holding him a little while and her voice telling him

about a white house in Virginia and niggers and tobacco fields—
telling him sadly he was gentlefolks, half way at least" (pp. 16–17).
That frontier had ended and in typical Turnerian fashion turned into
the frontier of Lash's parents: "[He] grew up in a log house in western
Kentucky, where his father was among the first to build and plow"
(p. 16). As a boy, Lash knew the frontier of "puncheon floor, straw
tick and copper kettle, hoe cake and hominy and wild game for meat,"
and he always knew that "brown skin was to shoot at and Indian hair
to lift" (p. 16).

To grow up then was to head west—to freedom, to excitement, to
wonderment. H.B. knew something of the same south-to-southwest
spirit of westering. And Fergusson's description of Lash's destiny in
the West follows Turner's theory of recurrent frontiers, sequence by
sequence, frame by frame. Conestoga wagons, St. Louis as the gate-
way to it all, Hawken rifles, buffalo herds, saloons with liquor, gambling, women, dancing and hell-raising—Sam experiences it all. No
settler suited for a plow and a house, Sam heads for the further West—
the wild, still-to-be-tamed West. Finding his place is not so much a
matter of East or West as of being free, on the trail, on the move and
unencumbered: "Hurrah for the meat! Ho boy, hurrah for the mountain doins!" Fergusson's own compulsion to travel back and forth
between New York and New Mexico and to take countless smaller
trips throughout his life explains why he identified so closely with a
character like Lash and why marriage was such a threat to his liberty.
His 1927 trip from Louisiana to Texas and then on to New Mexico and
finally to Utah seems to be reechoed in Lash's peregrinations.

At the time Lash rides into Taos for the first time, at the auspicious age of twenty-one, he meets the priest who will help him [later]
in his troubles and in his peace-making with the rankled Salazars; he
learns the Spanish language and ways of loving; he sees that rico
women are for the time being out of his reach; and he takes a job as a
wrangler of stock and mules for an expedition headed into Mexican
territory through the San Juan and Inscription Rock country in north-
western New Mexico, on to the White Mountains and the Gila in
Arizona, and, in a second leg, on to California and Los Angeles. It is

essentially the same trip which young Franz Huning took after his arrival in Santa Fe. It is also the same trip that Robert Jayson takes and which Fergusson so painstakingly details in *In Those Days*. In both the real and the imagined versions, the episode serves as a rite of initiation. Lash learns to live off the land, to survive in the face of hostile, life-threatening forces. He becomes a special kind of man—a fighter, a mountain man.

What Lash learns during the trials and hardships of such an extended tour of the West—like the Spanish conquerors before him and like Lewis and Clark, Josiah Gregg, James Pattie, Franz Huning, and countless other historical counterparts—is that the West, as place, idea, way of life, and especially as mountains, is in his blood. Fergusson felt the same thing as a result of his early years as a lone rider, his hunting and pack trips, and his experience in the Kit Carson Forest as a timber cruiser. He offers his homage to mountains in *Hot Saturday* and he does it again in *Wolf Song:* "Mountains had laid their spell on him as they did on all of his ilk. Mountains were his work and his passion" (p. 38). Mountains are so much a part of his identity and his conception of the West that they are inseparable from his plots, where key settings are called for to allow key things to happen—either a recognition or an exhilaration of spirit, either romance or adventure. In *Wolf Song* it is no happenstance that Sam's do-or-die fight with Black Wolf takes place in the mountains—an environment suitable for high deeds and passions of either love (as in *Hot Saturday*) or death (as in *Wolf Song*).

In the second half of the novel, after Sam has taken Lola away from her family in Taos, there are two fight scenes which dramatically balance each other. Both of them prove Sam's manliness and his abilities as a fighter of men; and yet both of them underscore just how powerful Lola's hold on him is, how strong her love is in controlling him. Sam and Lola are involved in a larger kind of struggle, the battle of the sexes which Fergusson was living and anguishing over daily in his relationship with Becky. Like Fergusson and Becky, Sam and Lola cannot live with or without each other. Both of the novel's fight scenes take place, appropriately enough, in the mountains; one fight is in the company of friends, Sam's sidekicks and Lola; the other takes place with an enemy, Black Wolf. Both, however, end in Sam's reunion with Lola.

The first fight is a "ruction" or "hugging" with Guillon, who, as tradition has it, gets drunk on the first day out. It is a rough enough fight, with its own dangers, but it is not life-threatening and ends in farce. In most ways it is drawn as comic relief to (or anticipation of) Sam's life-or-death combat with Black Wolf some few days later. Sam is portrayed as a wolflike fighter, and Guillon is described as a bulldog, adding to the overall portrayal of Sam as a lone wolf who, in his battle for his life with another loner, Black Wolf, will meet a kind of reverse, American Indian double of himself. Lola, in a burst of anger, interrupts Sam's fight with Guillon by slipping a hot coal down Guillon's pants. Lola has tamed both men.

The second fight also occurs in the mountains but further into the wilderness where two solitary men challenge each other and engage in a combat which only one survives. Lola is present at this fight only in spirit, but decidedly so. Sam initially thinks he can leave her safely at Bent's Fort and sally out once again to trap in the western mountains with his friends. It is Sam's preoccupation with Lola, however, and his memory of her that makes him careless enough to be tracked by Black Wolf. She has been his reason for escape and almost his undoing, paradoxically, as his obsession. Black Wolf's purpose is to steal enough horses to impress the father of his love, Ameertschee. He is a southern Cheyenne, ready for battle and alone. As he rides, he sings "the wolf songs which are always sung by lone warriors" (p. 161). The ironies are many. Motivations of love force both men into combat; again hatred is somehow mixed with love. Is the implication that both warriors would be better off without their respective women? In a certain sense, Black Wolf and Sam Lash may be regarded as extensions of Fergusson, who in the writing of the novel and dedicating it to Rebecca McCann was singing his own kind of wolf song out of the frustrations and beauty of love.

After five days away from Lola and the fort, Sam arrives at the valley of the Cimarron. Black Wolf also converges on this special mountain crossroad, and their own fates mirror the topography. There is, ironically, another element in the convergence: it is also the Cimarron valley where the Salazar family has its land grant, the mountain area which Sam will be asked to help develop and tame after he himself yields and is tamed by Lola, her priest, and her father.

Fergusson's mastery at handling the potential in such a situation is further developed in the relationship between Lash and Black Wolf. Their eventual confrontation affords another kind of "marriage." Moreover, Sam's life as a lone wolf will be brought to just as final a death in his capitulation to Lola and the Salazars. Implicitly, it would seem, Fergusson is describing his own figurative demise, his longing yet reluctance in his own marriage, as he describes Black Wolf's and Sam's "embrace" in their knife fight: "It [the knife] buried almost to the hilt in the brown naked belly of his foe, and the Indian pitched down upon him, his hands closing in a hard spasm on Sam's throat" (p. 189). Black Wolf dies chanting his death song, a song that has some of the same melodies and intonations as his love song.

The novel ends with Lash thinking of Lola's white, round breasts and saying (with much help from the narrator/author): "Go where he will a man comes back to a woman. She pulls him down, she holds him down. . . . She sucks out of him power and longing to go" (p. 202). Fergusson confessed to his diaries much the same sentiment about his love for Becky. The dedication, and the book, have a greater tinge of love-song/death-song irony than usually suspected.

In his own life Becky's death freed him—to a point. He was still saddled with guilt about his responsibilities for the condition of her death and about his failure to somehow treat her differently while she was living. With other choices and conclusions—about the Christmas trip to Albuquerque, about the fever, about the medical attention— Becky might have lived. But then what? In an important sense Fergusson relived his marriages and the issues of male and female will in all his fiction, including those novels after *Hot Saturday* and *Wolf Song*. For Fergusson, marriage reflected the institutional transitions resulting from the ending of the frontier and somehow seemed to symbolize the wilderness tamed. The love song of *Wolf Song* carries its own melodious lament into *In Those Days*, a story of happier times, of his grandfather's times, when marriages seemed to last.

After Becky's death, Fergusson returned to New York and his writing. By March 1928 he wrote to Mencken from a new address, 64 East 108th Street, saying he planned to stay in New York indefinitely. He had no plans to leave until the summer, when he would again return to New Mexico and to his next novel, which was already under way.[36] His major concentration was the finishing of *In Those Days* (1929), the novel that most fully transformed his grandfather Huning's life into fiction and was a continuation of *Wolf Song* in Fergusson's attempt to chronicle the opening of the frontier in the Southwest from the time of the mountain men in Taos through the settlement of Albuquerque by storekeepers and merchants, from the days of the Santa Fe Trail to the coming of the railroad. Whether he realized the whole pattern or not, he was in the middle of what would become his *Followers of the Sun* trilogy. As was the case in the writing of others of his novels of the 1920s, the East gave him a heightened perspective on the West and on his heritage as the bona fide Western writer he was fast becoming.

If *Wolf Song* is dependent on Taos for its account of the personality and place of the Southwest, *In Those Days*, like *Hot Saturday*, is a story about Albuquerque. But its "scope" (to use Waters's word) is not one day in the life of an Albuquerquean like Ruth Bruck. Rather, it is the story of Albuquerque, old and new, from the mid-nineteenth century to the coming of the railroad at the end of that century and the coming of the automobile in the beginning of the twentieth. The same narrative structures that Fergusson relied on in previous novels are also at work in *In Those Days:* namely, the placing of an individual and the changes in that individual's life against the background of his or her times, thus affording both a historical and an individual "biographical" account of change. The wilder topographical aspects of the West such as mountains and mesas, rivers and plains, are again set in contrast to the magnetism of the city and its attraction of settlement and growth. In *Hot Saturday*, Fergusson utilized the metaphor of city as weed, spreading like an unstoppable organism to cover everything in its path. That particular organic metaphor is not sustained in *In Those Days*, but the idea is similar: the rapid influx of population triggers the growth of a relatively dormant frontier city. The coming of the railroad assures that growth and reflects the population shifts under way. That growth and change is little more than the theme of the winning of the West by the "civilizing" forces of money and marriage; of dramatizing the East's seemingly deliberate attempt to end the frontier or at least push it further west. *In Those Days*, because of its extended scope and time span, is Fergusson's largest-scale novelistic adaptation of the Turnerian thesis of recurrent frontiers.

The individual life which Fergusson sets against the changes affecting the West and particularly Albuquerque is that of Robert Jayson, a man who in his growth from youth to old age during the course of the narrative is himself an instrument of the changes which establish the city as a major railroad and merchandising center. Jayson's story is the story of the city. In his arrival, building of friendships and his own business; in his loves, engagements, and eventual marriage; in his rise to the status of founding father and eminent citizen— in all of these is the combined story of Fergusson's grandfather and father and the men they typify. The result is to set in perspective the relative particularity and generality of events common to the curious polarities of historical fiction.

The chronicle of *In Those Days* is reflected in the simplicity yet comprehensiveness of the table of contents: Wagons, Indians, Railroad, and Gas. Jayson knows all these "historical" stages—and thrives, for they represent the West as physical health and opportunity. The words "in those days" become code words, often reiterated throughout the novel, to trigger the historical perspective Fergusson is taking. But the motif is more than mere connotation. Huning's memoir frequently uses the same expression—"in those days"—and no doubt influenced Fergusson's narrative choices and point of view.

Fergusson does not tell a retrospective story from Jayson's memories or nostalgic yearnings for youth; rather, the narrator assumes the omniscience of a present-day historian and Westerner—a voyager much like Fergusson himself—who knows "those days" almost as if he were there and seems to wish himself back there to those good times. Through his narrator, Fergusson is back there, on that frontier, in those days. The persona of *In Those Days* is not all that distinguishable from the persona of Fergusson's autobiography, *Home in the West,* or from the persona, and, behind that, the personal anecdotes, of *Rio Grande.*

Jayson arrives in Santa Fe as an innocent. He is assuredly not a rough-and-ready mountain man like Sam Lash, although Lash also undergoes his initiations as a blond giant in a world of brown-skinned peoples. Nevertheless, Jayson is like Lash insofar as he is "sufficient to his fate," an "atom of unconquerable life" (*Wolf Song,* p. 190). Jayson is caught up in the powerful wave of settlement heading west. Fergusson sets the historical stage, capturing the strivings of each of the four stages of settlement which Jayson faces, before he focuses on Jayson as individual amidst the swarm. Through Fergusson's own feeling for westering, the reader, like Jayson, is caught up in the excitement.

In Those Days, like *Wolf Song,* offers some of the most passionate writing about the exuberance of settling the West to reach the pages of historical fiction. In Fergusson's descriptions of Jayson's times, of what he faced, of the stirring of his bodily juices—in all these things his overall joy of life pulsates in every sentence. Given his plan, Fergusson's modulations from the widely historical to the narrowly personal retains the same exuberance. His description of the West and the westering spirit which lured Jayson and his historical inspiration, Huning, which, in turn, moved an entire continent and served as a safety valve for a nation's discontent, and which was Fergusson's own birthright, is illustrative of the point: "Men who had killed and stolen went West if they got away. Men who had failed went West with their assets and left their liabilities behind. Men of imagination were struck by an idea of the West as by disease. Western fever was as real as smallpox and sent men chasing dreams across a continent. The sting of a woman's no sent many a man West and many another went to lose a woman he couldn't stand."[37]

It is important to see, too, how Fergusson in *In Those Days,* completed in the aftermath of Rebecca's death, blends his guilt and sorrow over his wife's death into the diary account of Huning's own experience with death and guilt; important to see how in the writing out and imaginative reliving of his grandfather's westering Fergusson attempts to exorcise his own personal remorse over the irretrievable loss of his wife.

Jayson's motive in heading west is typical of the historical motives Fergusson catalogs. Jayson leaves his sweetheart, Elizabeth, in the East and joins a wagon train headed for Santa Fe. His longing for the idealized Elizabeth—another expression of Fergusson's dichotomy of woman as saint and sinner—is similar to Lash's longing for Lola and his inability to leave her, if only temporarily, at Bent's Fort and at Taos. It also can be viewed as representing Fergusson's sense of destiny working out his ambivalent attachment to Rebecca.

After Jayson establishes himself in business in Albuquerque, he returns East, to the demarcation point of St. Louis, picks up Elizabeth and heads west again to take her to join him in his new life in Albuquerque. They never make it. Jayson's party is attacked by Indians, Elizabeth's wagon is separated from the rest, and she is captured and taken away. Her fate is unknown, and the uncertainty makes Jayson all the more anguished. She is never found, although a rescue attempt is made, and she is presumed dead at the hands of her captors. The journey, which ends in such tragedy, is drawn generally from captivity myth and directly from Huning's journey from St. Louis with his wife's mother and brother—a trip which also ended in tragic death and left Huning with a lingering sense of responsibility and guilt. Insofar as *In Those Days* retells two tragic deaths in Fergusson's past and their psychic scarring, it is, autobiographically, one of Fergusson's most cathartic novels.

On Jayson's first trip west across the prairies, he is both surprised and disgusted at how inadequate he is—at how much he is a stranger in a strange world. As his novelistic destiny will have it, he—like his historical counterpart, Franz Huning—grows to accept the landscape between Santa Fe and St. Louis with its exotic beauty and takes many trips back and forth along the Santa Fe Trail as a trader and owner of the wagons used to carry goods to his store. What is only a potential future of success, of making a place and a name for himself "out there," out West, does become his reality. It is this potential in Jayson's westering which, alluding also to Jim Royce's adventure romance, provides the title for the trilogy *Followers of the Sun* which

Blood of the Conquerors, Wolf Song, and *In Those Days* would later become: "And he, trudging westward alone, was hardly a person anymore, but only a bit of dust and blood following the sun" (p. 12).

After his arrival in "a little adobe town beside the Rio Grande south of Santa Fe"—that is, after his arrival in Albuquerque—most of the first section of the novel deals with Jayson's acceptance by the Anglo, Spanish American, and Mexican-American population: how he gets a job, learns Spanish, forms what turns out to be lifelong friendships with an Anglo, Tom Foote, and a rico, Diego Aragon, and is sexually attracted first to an ostensibly lower-class Mexican-American woman named Maria and then to a rica, Doña Nina. The characters who hold forth in a store owned by Abel Doxey, where Jayson first works as a clerk and bookkeeper, are taken almost to the last detail from Huning's memoir. The plaza which Doxey's store faces is a fictionalized image of Old Town, itself the result of a succession of frontiers. When Jayson first arrives, the town is in a dormant stage, built around a plaza dominated by its old adobe, twin-towered church (e.g., San Felipe de Neri) and Don Aragon's great house (an echo of La Glorieta and Castle Huning as family emblems). The permanence is only a look; change is about to accelerate.

Doxey's store is a visible manifestation of change in the face of the changelessness represented by the church and Aragon's great house. The village, clustered around the plaza, is an idyllic and picturesque locale, reminiscent of Huning's La Glorieta and Molino de la Glorieta as portrayed by the travel writer for *Harper's* in the nineteenth century, Sylvester Baxter, or by Huning's more austere accounts of his first impressions of Santa Fe as recorded in his memoir: "Little brown houses with blue doors and windows sat under cottonwood trees. Each had a bit of orchard, patchy fields of grain, clover and chili, and a long stretch of wet alkaline pasture reaching to the cottonwood bosky by the river. Redwing blackbirds and meadow larks were many and vocal and almost every cotton wood tree contained the soft voice of a dove" (p. 16). Fergusson gave *In Those Days* the subtitle *An Impression of Change,* and he aptly established the stasis before the frenzy—both in the town and in Jayson's life.

One of the digressive but important stories young Jayson hears in

Tolliver's saloon is a horrifying captivity story, in a much darker vein than most of Fergusson's interpolated stories, which foreshadows the captivity of Elizabeth and implies certain parallels with Fergusson's guilt about Rebecca McCann's death. The old drifter, Skillman, tells the story. He has been a trapper, a mountain man some thirty years past, has lived on the periphery of civilization and beyond it, and brings back strange and startling stories to the ears of naive newcomers to the West like Jayson. While Judge Turnbull, in the high style for which he is renowned, stumps for the railroad, Skillman tells Jayson a story of torture and savagery out of the past; it is no fiction, although the years have colored its telling, and it works as both a myth and a prophecy. The saloon and everyone in it, for the duration of the story, occupy a transitional present, hovering between two times, two truths, two worlds. Jayson's own, then unforeseen, loss of Elizabeth to another captivity will prove it so.

Skillman is himself a remnant of a past frontier—with long white hair worn after the fashion of the mountain men; he is akin to an aged Sam Lash, but one who refused to outlive his dying era, a man with a guilt to expiate, a man with an almost demonic burden which seeks release in a timely utterance: "His eyes showed something inside him burning its way out like coals in a banked fire" (p. 24). His narrative is a muddled tale of his love for and marriage to a Mexican girl named Consuelo Alarid in a river town south of Albuquerque. In an incident similar to Lash's leaving Lola and roughly similar to Fergusson's leaving Becky for Texas and Utah, he left her and went on a trapping expedition into the Gila. When he returned, he found the town sacked by Apaches and Consuelo gone. What he found when he located the Apache camp was burned into his soul forever: "They found two of the captive women dead and one of them, Skillman's girl, hanging naked by her thumbs over a slow fire, roasting to death as a sacrifice to Apache Gods who had sent the scourge of smallpox" (p. 26).

Skillman's alcoholism, guilt, and gruesome tale reinforce the idea that the West for Jayson could become a fearsome place as threatening as it is promising. He will face something of the same guilt which Skillman does in an era that still has its degree of savagery, its own primitive frontier. Skillman's tale is highly melodramatic and the stuff of dime novels—up to a point. It is an effectively frightening story, not the least because of Skillman's psychological trauma in and behind the telling. He seems an all too painful and convincing surrogate for Fergusson's own tragic tale of marriage, death, and remorse.

Skillman's tale of terror begins to fulfill its own telling and take on personal shape for Jayson. After he becomes a merchant-trader in partnership with his friend and traveling companion, Foote, historical and individual forces converge. By the time business builds to allow Jayson to return east for Elizabeth, prairie and mountain Indians strike back at the encroaching Yankees. The end of the frontier and the end of Indian cultures coincide, and in the process an upsurge of racial violence victimizes Jayson and his bride. That phase of the end of the frontier was especially costly. Human beings paid the price, but so did gods and an entire culture.

Using the epic technique which is so effective in the opening pages of *Wolf Song*, Fergusson, in his second portion of the novel, "Indians," begins again *in medias res* with Elizabeth riding in a light spring wagon along the Arkansas somewhere between Walnut Creek and Pawnee Rock (a special place in Huning's personal myth and in Fergusson's fictional settings). Jayson rides beside the wagon on a powerful saddle mule. He is not worried about Indians, for he has traveled the same route five times before without incident. The Comanche chief, White Buffalo, has become something of a friend and has accepted gifts of food and clothing in the past. Elizabeth is nervous—and rightfully so. The West for her, during her travel from St. Louis to this point on the Arkansas, is a place for fear if not outright panic. On the trip east Jayson had met a big expedition of cavalry heading north to look for Sioux and led by a handsome young officer "with long yellow hair and yellow whiskers." In this veiled characterization of Custer and the soon-to-be catastrophe of Little Big Horn, Fergusson attempts to place what happens to Jayson and Elizabeth in a wider historical context, compounding in the process the sense of ironic naivete in both the young officer's and Jayson's obliviousness to the tragedies which await them.

Pawnee Rock, ironically, had itself been responsible for Jayson's own change in attitude about the prairie. When he first camped there, it worked a wondrous change in his perceptions, bringing him peace in a way that, as Fergusson describes it, amounted to a kind of satisfaction in the face of uncertainty—the trait Keats called "negative capability": "That night he had discovered, as though by revelation, that he loved the wilderness" (p. 106).

It is a familiar idyllic scene in Fergusson's novels, going back to his own solitary experiences as a lone rider and hunter and as a timber cruiser—and beyond that, to Franz Huning's love of that very same spot on the Arkansas and of the forests of his homeland. Ramon Delcasar, John Strome, John Romer, Sam Lash, Robert Jayson, Alec McGarnigal—Fergusson infuses all of these fictional counterparts of himself with a similar sense of contentment and revelation while alone in the wild. True to the theme as it appears in his fiction, man cannot live alone as a solitary wanderer and primitive in worship of nature and the land. Man's need for woman, the sexual impulse, prevails—and so does sexual union, either in or out of marriage. In Jayson's case, Elizabeth is a past he knows he cannot escape, dare not escape for the damage it might cause her. He hopes he can accommodate her into his new life and the changes wrought on him by the West and its new freedoms: "Through her he would bring the past into the present and bridge the gulf that sundered him from home and older self" (p. 109). It is a situation and a sentiment Fergusson indicates that he also felt in relation to Rebecca.

Such an adjustment, however, is not to be for Jayson. He loses Elizabeth to the Indian raid and is left with the guilt and, strangely, the freedom which her tragic fate and the uncanny conclusion and application of Skillman's history/story allows him. As the attempted rescue becomes more and more futile, he has two hallucinations which trouble him waking and sleeping. In both dreams the story of Skillman's Consuelo Alarid takes on special mutations: "In one of them he saw a slim white body pegged to the ground and writhing. . . . In the other he chased an Indian and caught him and pulled his head off as one might pull the head off a chicken. . . . He felt all the time that he had killed her" (p. 117).

Huning's Indian encounter which serves as the basis for Fergusson's fictional account was no hallucination and no fiction. Huning met White Buffalo, the Comanche chief, in a St. Louis saloon. Otherwise, the attack on Huning's wagon train is followed in outline by Fergusson. In his memoir Huning does include a reference to a meeting with General Custer in the summer of 1867, then on a campaign against the Cheyennes and Kiowas. His grandfather did love to camp at the foot of Pawnee Rock and on at least one trip climbed the rock, after a supper of buffalo hump, and surveyed the surrounding vastness—as does Jayson.

There are, however, some significant differences between Huning's account and Fergusson's fictional rendering of it: Huning was escorting his mother-in-law and her youngest son, Fritz, from Junction City, Kansas, to Albuquerque. He had requested a military escort but was refused. His letters reveal he was indignant about that refusal and was apprehensive about Indian attack and about traveling alone in such a small train of only five wagons. He was attacked by a party of about one hundred Cheyenne and Kiowa warriors. As circumstances developed, including the separation of his mother-in-law's wagon from the rest of the train and the jamming of his Spencer rifle, he had to stand by in horror. The boy was killed at the first onslaught, and his mother was shot with a pistol soon after, causing Huning the greatest trauma of his life. At least this is the version of the affair in his memoir, written nearly thirty years later.

Fergusson's fictionalized version turns a mother-in-law into a wife. His own autobiography and desired but regretted marriage seems to supply the answer as to why he altered his family history into family fiction.

Elizabeth represents the female emotional center of the novel. Her transport across the plains, the camp at Pawnee Rock, the Indian conflict, and her captivity and murder all represent Jayson's past in the East intruding upon his future in the West. There are other emotional centers in the West, however, and both of them involve other women, other adventures. One occurs relatively early in the novel, soon after Jayson's arrival in Albuquerque, serves as part of his initiation, and focuses on the rico tradition; the other takes place late in the novel, after Jayson is established, when, with the coming of the railroad, his wealth increases and, after an engagement which misfires, he settles into a happy marriage.

The rico connection is essential to understanding Fergusson's conception of the frontier—and of sexuality and marriage in those times. After a flirtation with Doña Nina, prior to her marriage, and after a seduction by the warm and caring earth mother Maria, Jayson gives up the comforts of civilization as he has come to know them and faces the hazards of the wilderness and the older frontier which Skillman has described to him. If Fergusson's unpublished autobiographical fiction, such as *The Land of Lonely Women,* is to be believed, he experienced his first sexual intercourse with a Mexican-American woman very much like Maria, who worked as a cook and maid in his parents' home. Because of Maria and Doña Nina and their sexual favors, Jayson fast approaches manhood in the macho tradition of the West. Another experience, however, is also necessary—and this is a journey of archetypal proportions whereby he proves up to the place and his potential in it.

He accompanies his good friend and future partner, Tom Foote, on a horse-trading expedition with the Apaches at their great camp somewhere in the Gila in the White Mountains and encounters the descendants of the Apaches who had ravaged and tortured Skillman's Consuelo—in presumbaly the very same place, or nearby. It is a trip which initiates Jayson into a new manhood in the West and is essentially the same trip, with the same purpose, as Huning's horse-trading trip. Fergusson had also used this trip in *Wolf Song* as an initiation journey for Sam Lash; and it represents, symbolically, not just westering, but Fergusson's essential need, part of his heritage and identity as a modern frontiersman, to spend his life traveling.

Once into Arizona, Jayson and Foote meet Cochise and succeed in making a good trade for horses. But on the return trip they are hit by what they feared even more than unfriendly Apaches: a snowstorm. They lose their way, and men, horses, and mules face starvation as a result. After nearly three weeks of nothing to eat but boiled horse, Jayson proves the savior. He climbs a tree and is the one who sees the direction to follow out of the wasteland which they thought would kill them. They work their way back to the Rio Grande Valley and arrive home in December, after three months on the trail. Jayson is an older and a wiser man, and now eligible for even more recognition by the ricos and especially by Doña Nina. His new look and demeanor, gained on the trail, reflect a similar transformation experienced by Huning after his trip into the Arizona wilderness. When Jayson looks into the mirror, "he felt with a shock that he looked at another" (p. 86). His "look"—the beard, his "brick-red face," his eyes, "bright with health"—allow him to enjoy, deservedly, he feels, the seductions of Doña Nina, who, although married, finds it within the value system of her culture to "reward" the gringo as a woman "traded and used, watched and guarded, taking sweet revenge on all her masters" (p. 91). The assumptions behind such dramatized behavior, if historical, are also ethnocentric.

Fergusson, as a reporter and as a reader-researcher, was familiar with theories of Nordic superiority and with anthropologists like Franz Boas who took a critical attitude toward the theory. The extent to which Fergusson himself subscribed to such a theory whereby darker-skinned native American, Mexican-American, or even Spanish American women (hardly brown-skinned) preferred blond, Anglo men is problematic. One can make inferences, given the sex appeal of Lash and Jayson—both blonds—since Fergusson has Mexican-American and rico women automatically swooning at their feet and regarding them as superior to men of their own race. Fergusson, a Nordic type, grew up amidst the darker-skinned peoples of his home state, and emotionally he no doubt aligned himself more with Anglo culture. That is mitigated by his strong attraction to the earth and the people closer to it, stereotyped in his fiction as Hispanic women, Hispanic gardeners and servants of one kind or another, and "primitive" American Indians.

Intellectually, he could advance the points of argument in both the thesis and antithesis of the theory, which took on special national importance during the 1920s because of immigration legislation. Fergusson was no malicious racist. Although he saw the controversy about Nordic superiority, swirling in Washington while he was a journalist in the 1920s, as "highly debatable," he nevertheless suggests in his mountain-man fiction what both sides of the argument seemed misguidedly to agree upon in the mid-twenties: "that in the greater part of Europe and America the Nordic man is an animal out of his natural climatic range and tending to die out for that reason."[38]

Change in the form of the railroad ends the wilderness frontier for Jayson and establishes a more urban, civilized one. The approach of the Santa Fe railroad through southern Colorado, to Trinidad and on through Raton Pass in northern New Mexico retraces not only Huning's trips when he took his daughter to that railhead for the ride to school in St. Louis but also the route of many recurrent frontiers, as suggested in Turner's theory: "It followed the trail the Indians had made, the trail conquistadores in iron armor had followed, and after them the mountain men—the trail wagons and coaches had widened into a road. Rails crept down the Rio Grande, prodded sleepy 'dobe towns into sudden frantic life. . . . Once more the good old days were gone" (pp. 134–35).

Fergusson, like Huning in his memoir, spends much time describing the celebrations involved the day the first train left for the East. Jayson is by this time a prominent citizen. He has a German housekeeper, Mrs. Latz, a fine carriage and team of bays, good clothes, "a hundred-dollar solid gold watch in his pocket," and a house which is more than respectable. He has paid for the education of Mrs. Latz's daughter, Annie, who is home from school in St. Louis (like Fergusson's own mother, Clara Mary Huning). He owns a sawmill and a one-quarter interest in a silver mine in Socorro (a composite of Huning's mill and H.B.'s Old Abe mine). He plans to marry a cultured woman named Emily Robinson, not for love, but because she is part of the new life in New Town, part of the surge of progress associated with the railroad. Jayson now thinks, not about the picturesque and sublime beauty of the West, but about the gains to be made by plundering the environment. He has changed again with the times and is now greedy, acquisitive—as much the type as the individual.

His friend and former partner, Tom Foote, corners the saloon and liquor business. And his rico friend, Diego Aragon, becomes sheriff, making New and Old Town alike adhere to his tough-fisted enforcement of the law. In all such characterizations and settings are the silhouettes of Franz Huning, H. B. Fergusson, Elfego Baca, and numerous other luminaries of early Albuquerque and Socorro. There is enough of Huning in Jayson for him to be saved, in the plotting of the novel, from a loveless marriage to Emily. Annie Latz, who seems a fictional embodiment of Ernestine Franke Huning and her daughter Clara Mary, proves too ripe and alluring, and her kiss of gratitude and passion awakens Jayson to the obvious realization that despite their difference in age, he loves her. Insofar as his grandparents' and, to a degree, his parents' marriages were long and happy, Fergusson arranges a similar fictional marriage for Jayson and Annie—as if only in the nineteenth century were such marriages possible.

The railroad is soon matched by other modes of transportation as the industrial revolution continues into the Southwest. The fourth section of the novel, "Gas," portrays the times after the invention of the automobile. By this time Jayson is something of a relic, passed over by history. He is known as Old Man Jayson by all the boys. His sawmill, silver mine, and store are only memories: "The world he had lived in was dying all around him and it became his duty to bury the dead" (p. 233). Foote's glory days are also over, as are Diego Aragon's and all the ricos whose influence he represented. Jayson even outlives Annie and must thus bury his wife, as he had their son, who died prematurely. Jayson's almost incredibly long life seems sustained by the scope and purpose of the novel. He has outlived his own history for the purposes of the novel; and both his character and the novel suffer for it. Out of necessity, Fergusson skims the surface of Jayson's final years with one flashback after another, one memory and then the next. Jayson suffers from a failing heart, but at least he has lived a full life and is not afraid to die.

Perhaps Fergusson attempts too much. Admittedly the chronology of the novel is too long and the scope too great—and as a result the unity suffers. *In Those Days* represents a return—but a further refinement—of the journalistic novel Fergusson first tried in *Capitol Hill* and was finally to perfect in *Kingdom*. If Fergusson is allowed the benefit of his design, within it he succeeds admirably. And if the novel is seen as a catharsis for Fergusson's own guilts associated with Rebecca McCann's death—a catharsis achieved primarily through Skillman's interpolated captivity story and, in turn, the captivity and death of Jayson's first wife, Elizabeth—the novel and its design become even more intriguing and substantive. In this one novel are the lives of three generations of Fergusson's family, including his own.

Fergusson tried, in *Hot Saturday* especially, to get away from the journalistic or chronicle novel and felt he had made some headway in modifying his method to changing needs and times. But as *In Those Days* proves, the chronicle novel was deeply ingrained in him from his first experiences as a journalist and as a novelist. Although in his next novel he returned to the twentieth-century setting, there remains much in it out of his past and out of what he thought for a time was a methodology he had discarded as a writer. One of his strengths which he saw developing in the 1920s was the poetic summary of a personality in its history. *McGarnigal* is such a book.

WORSHIP OF THE PRIMITIVE

If Robert Jayson seems most wholly drawn from the life and times of Franz Huning and other family histories, Alec McGarnigal, the hero of Fergusson's next novel, *Footloose McGarnigal* (1930), seems most wholly modeled on Fergusson himself. After Rebecca's death Fergusson returned to New York, and then took a trip to Cuba and Mexico during the late part of 1928 and early part of 1929. He returned from Mexico in February and took up residence at 64 East 108th Street. By that time he had written most of *McGarnigal*, but in correspondence with Mencken he indicated that the manuscript would not be ready until May or June of 1929.[39] At least two trips seem to serve as a basis for the journey structure of *McGarnigal:* the Mexico trip and Fergusson's swing through New Orleans, Galveston, San Antonio, Albuquerque, Santa Fe, and Salt Lake City in 1927. Fergusson's notes on New Orleans with "some references to prohibition," and on "the conversion of the French quarter into a Greenwich Village and a bandey town," were notes he planned to work into a 2,000-word article for Mencken as well as into an article called "Texas Heroes or Hero Worship in Texas."[40] Many of the observations of the Louisiana and Texas trip made their way into *McGarnigal*, which was published in January 1930; and the Mexican article, "Seen and Heard in Mexico," which dealt with Fergusson's experiences in and reactions to Cuernavaca and Mexico City, ran in the *Mercury* in June of that year.[41] Fergusson had no real urge to turn into a writer of travelogues for dailies or magazines; rather, he turned his journeys into picaresque fictions.

Always fond of the journey as either a controlling or an incidental structure in his novels, Fergusson makes the route of his 1927 trip the basis for Alec McGarnigal's grand tour of the South and the Southwest. As a variation on older patterns, *McGarnigal* also allows Fergusson to recreate and update the more southerly route west of his own father and to transpose Franz Huning into the characterization of Alec's dead uncle, for whom Alec was named and who, in his bequest of $500 and in his own ingrained wanderlust, serves as both a model and a means for his nephew. Fergusson's/Alec's wanderings through the South and the Southwest are homages to family traits and bloodlines, so that what might be regarded as the "chip-off-the-old-block" motif dominates.

In both *McGarnigal* and "Seen and Heard in Mexico," Fergusson is preoccupied with primitivism. In correspondence with Mencken, Fergusson observed, "I have written the greater part of a novel, which will run to seventy thousand but might be cut. It has little serial value in the usual magazine sense but some journalistic value as it consists in part of a sort of satire on the contemporary worship of the primitive."[42] Insofar as *McGarnigal* is such a satire, it poses the question of whether the primitive or the civilized is the more desirable way of life and whether or not a choice between the two is still available to modern man. For Fergusson, the Mexican and the Indian were one and the same: primitives.[43]

Throughout the 1920s, but especially during the summers between 1922 and 1924, Fergusson records that his interest in the primitive was not so much in the Pueblo Indians and their ceremonials as it was in the contact of primitivisim with civilization: "I am not really much interested in primitive people. Albuquerque interests me far more than any Indian pueblo. Wild country interests me for its own sake; but I am more interested in the reaction of a civilized man to it than in the adjustment of primitive man."[44] Such an attitude explains the motive for his satirical treatment of Taos artists and other Easterners in *McGarnigal*, who move to the Southwest, adopt "primitive" dress, and pattern their lives around attending Indian ceremonials and Mexican-American fiestas—completely caught up in the mystique of Pueblo Indian and Mexican-American cultures.

Even so, Fergusson's satirical perspective was based in his own yearnings, established in "infancy" as he described it, for wilderness and things "primitive." He may have intended *McGarnigal* as a satire on "the contemporary worship of the primitive," and although his hero escapes to a primitive landscape and culture and is almost taken over by them, in the end he gives up the solitude and exoticism of the West—including the lure of "primitive" women—to return to New York. Even with the satirical edge to such happenings, the protagonist and the reader do not become totally convinced that the primitive life is not the best life. In *McGarnigal* we see Fergusson's own personal struggles at accommodating the East-West forces and tensions in his life.

Written in Fergusson's characteristic anecdotal style, *McGarnigal* has little real plot. What plot there is involves the maturation and quest for identity of Alec McGarnigal. Just a year out of college he grows weary of his job in New York and, thanks to an inheritance of $500 and some Texas property from his great uncle, Alec quits, heads for Texas to see his "ranch," and vaguely plans to go on to California and visit his aunt. His travels take him to New Orleans, San Antonio, Santa Fe and Taos, and the mountains of northern New Mexico. On his way, and upon arrival in each locale, he meets interesting people from diverse walks of life, makes a good friend or two, and inevitably falls in love and carries on both brief and extended affairs with the various kinds of women he meets. The one woman he chooses at the end of the string of affairs is very much like the prototypic sophisticated, "emergent" Eastern woman who turns up in all of Fergusson's fiction. Again, this character, an artist named Amaryllis Oldfield, seems a composite of Polly Pretty, Rebecca McCann, and other self-willed modern women who attracted Fergusson.

Alec's uncle and his uncle's stories of his life as a free spirit out West, plus McGarnigal's own birth and early childhood in Texas, point him west again as a young man with an urge to rediscover his roots. How the West came to be in Alec's longing and part of his more mysterious spitirual inheritance sounds similar to what the West meant to Fergusson as a child riding free on his horse and listening to stories of the exploits of his grandfather, his cousins and uncles in Los Lunas, and his father. For all practical purposes, Alec's Texas is Fergusson's New Mexico: "Alec had been born in Texas himself, yet his conception of it and of the West in general was derived almost wholly from his uncle's lore. . . . He [young Alec] had ridden a pony and played at being a cowboy, and it was always wide, windy country and galloping horses he thought of when his restlessness was in him."[45]

Uncle Alec is much more of an influence on young Alec than his own father, who is portrayed, only in passing, as "gray and bitter," literally beaten to death by "endless disappointments" (p. 15). (Again, H.B. enters into his son's fictions.) Alec's identity as a westerner is indicated by his nickname, Tex, given to him in college because of his "little drawl" and his constant retelling of his Uncle Alec's stories of the frontier and the good old days. This nickname identity must be tested in his adulthood by encounters with real and imitation westerners. The story takes on the proportions of perhaps the most favorite of all stories of the West: the initiation of the greenhorn.

In the process of his initiation, Alec finds his uncle's Old West recognizable but very much changed. It is changed in silly ways which are subject to ridicule, but also in regrettable ways. The frontier of Uncle Alec's telling, like Uncle Alec himself, is dead. McGarnigal— and over his shoulder, Fergusson—does his best to revive it as authentically as he can. Ultimately, however, he decides to turn his back on the tragedy of its demise and dismiss with a laugh its leftover codes of chivalric male pride and macho honor. The Indians, the Mexican-Americans, to some extent the forest rangers, and, especially, the eccentric artists and intellectuals he meets in Taos all seem replicas of the original, too stylized for him—only parodies of truer selves and more meaningful conflicts.

The mountains, the landscape, the place itself, captivates him and reaffirms the greatness of the Old West more than anything. Yet the magnitude, wildness, and remoteness of the mountains must ultimately be rejected for society and the amenities and challenges of the East, eastern women, and the metropolis. The tensions of the novel, such as they are, are created by McGarnigal's trying to decide whether the West he remembers, has heard about, and idealizes is the West in which he can live. The whole search for the "reality," past and present, of the West is complicated by the irony that Alec begins his trip west on a train headed across the Midwest. It is another characteristic Fergusson opening, traceable to *Conquerors*. In this opening, seemingly patterned on Delcasar's train ride, Fergusson places his hero again in the company of a woman. Satire and comedy of manners provide the mood and mode; and the woman's talking drives Alec away from romance and into a conversation with a fellow traveler of his own sex and age, a fellow named Carruthers from Iowa. In *McGarnigal* the male world and the world of solitude and imposed celibacy is given much free rein. Carruthers suggests that Alec head for the Texas oil-boom country with him. Since Alec has a degree in engineering it would be a natural, suitable destination. Alec is determined, however, to go on to San Antonio and find his ranch. After a few hours together during a stop in New Orleans, Alec and Carruthers leave by different trains for different fates. Carruthers is merely the first of such foils for Alec. In this instance he is the means for acting out middle-class "Puritan" values and assumptions which Alec does not share.

When Alec arrives in Texas, he visits some of the old haunts of his uncle and attempts to recapture some of the romance of the cowboy life instilled in him through Uncle Alec's tale-telling. The landscape which he crosses on the way to San Antonio conjures up the overwhelming feeling of home and kin: "He looked upon this country of his origin and his forebearers with a bewildered eagerness, hardly knowing what he hoped or wanted of it, yet yearning toward it with a desire that ran in his blood and pounded in his heart" (p. 30). Fergusson's diaries reveal several prose-pictures in which he describes the rich color and vast spaciousness of the country between Galveston and San Antonio, and the transfer of these notes to the novel is effective.

Once in San Antonio, Alec meets Texans who are stereotypically tall and congenial. The old San Antonio is very much eclipsed by the new. San Antonio—although exotic because of palm trees and Mexicans from across the border—reminds Alec of an imitation New York, but with laughing, oil-rich people playing with a bright new city as if it were a toy bought by the oil which never seemed to stop flowing from the earth around them. He learns from his uncle's agent that his uncle's ranch is heavily mortgaged and has nothing on it but brush and an old house built in the 1850s once used to fight off Comanche attacks—no oil. He walks through the city and comes across the ruins of another kind of building, the Alamo.

The Alamo, in Fergusson's scheme of things, is part of the same all-but-vanished frontier of word and legend as Uncle Alec's stories. Representative of this, young Alec comes across a movie entitled *The Alamo*. It promises to be an inferior film, but it is one he nevertheless wants to see, if for nothing else than the inevitable fights and galloping horses. Before he leaves San Antonio, he does see the film with a woman who represents her own kind of fall, her own kind of illusory "history," which reflects the new/old Texas. If the Alamo is reducible to a grade B film, the new Texas woman is similarly not all that she might appear to be, or that her pioneer counterpart was.

Edna, the married woman Alec has picked up in San Antonio, is much like Emma and Helen, Ralph Dolan's first conquests in *Capitol Hill*. In fact, much of *McGarnigal* reads like the chapters of *Capitol Hill* and *Women and Wives* which portray Dolan and Royce with their male friends out to "meet the Janes." Taken in series, Fergusson's ever-present descriptions of wenching grow tedious. Still, the accounts were true to Fergusson's own involvements with women and his interests in eroticism in fiction. In his own classification of types of men and artists, Fergusson believed that the "erotic" novelist was superior to either celibate or homosexual writers, saying, "Most good novelists are erotics. Women continually drag them back to reality."[46] In Fergusson's view, authors like Stendhal, George Moore, and Maupassant were representative of erotic writers. Such men, thought Fergusson, devoted themselves to women and solitude and were always at odds with the world. Moreover, he considered himself such a man and such a novelist—and *McGarnigal* a representative erotic novel.

Reviewers found nothing particularly shocking in *McGarnigal*, noting that although the plot was light, the descriptions of the landscape and many of the characterizations were charming and underscored the obvious: the second half of the novel, once McGarnigal reaches New Mexico, is by far the more interesting.[47] What reviewers did not understand is that *McGarnigal* is less a novel than a retelling of Fergusson's 1927 summer trip and of modern man's legacy of the westering spirit. Autobiography especially determines this novel; otherwise, there is no really successful aesthetic reason for the opening scenes. But in the major portion of the novel, which takes place in New Mexico, both aesthetic and autobiographical aspects pick up momentum.

Because of Alec's friendly ways, he meets a fellow fraternity brother in San Antonio, Robert Syme, who sets him up with a job in New Mexico with the U.S. Forest Service. This job gives him an excuse to move on, with no romantic commitments or entanglements, and gives him a destination and the kind of out-of-doors job he feels he needs, consistent with being in the West. Insofar as possible he is reliving his uncle's footloose life. Fergusson takes every opportunity to satirize Alec's innocence along the way. Alec learns, however, what many of the people he meets never learn—that the frontier can never be fully resurrected. Even so, Alec is hard-pressed to lose his idealized vision.

Once Alec is in New Mexico two kinds of West are diametrically drawn: the remote mountains and forests of the northern part of the state, and the historic town of Taos. This time Taos is an artists' colony rather than a rendezvous point for mountain men, as it was in *Wolf Song*. Fergusson's concern with place is again presented in terms of the convergence of indigenous inhabitants, tourists, and transplanted artists from the East. Social comedy and satire enter into Fergusson's account of both native and tourist culture and the newcomers' "worship of the primitive." As successful as such satirical treatments are, any success the novel has ultimately depends on the scenes of solitude and wilderness.

McGarnigal's summer job as a timber cruiser with the U.S. Forest Service amounts to a personal essay on Fergusson's own experiences in the same capacity when he too was just out of college. Fergusson begins again in the middle of things with Alec high in the mountains on his first day alone, new to such places and very much the tenderfoot. That day he is amazed at the beauty and magnitude of his surroundings. No longer does he compare himself to the "swarm of cockroaches" which he likens to New York crowds. Instead, looking down on thousands of square miles of forest, he is more like the last man on earth—or the first. His task is simple enough, demanding only clear perception and concentration. His friend, Syme, teaches him the requirements of timber cruising: use of a compass, a barometer, the map-making, and the recording of estimated board feet.

He makes a few more turns on the mountain, and then as dusk approaches he realizes something else—he is lost. Significantly, he does not know whether to turn east or west; he is literally (and figuratively) somewhere between both crucial directions, both implications. Nature is not less picturesque, or more terrifying and sublime: "He was not scared but neither was he happy. He was conscious of this grand country now as a large cold hostile blackness piling up all around him and of himself as a small helpless emptiness with nothing to fill it" (pp. 67–68).

Primitive thoughts and images now overtake him; and although he is convinced that he is not really afraid, a certain primordial terror of "beasts that long ago lurked by water holes and leapt from trees" is brought to consciousness by "the dark forest" (p. 69). This seems a retelling of a mountain lion story which so haunted Fergusson when he was a cruiser. Fergusson continues to project his own remembered fears and feelings into Alec. With the setting of the sun Alec does the instinctive thing: he builds a fire. During the night's darkness his thoughts jump from the amenities of New York living to his uncle's old stories about mountain men and hunters facing adversity and starvation in the wilderness. Alec realizes that in a certain sense he is only playing at being lost, and, by extension, that he has "only played at living." In comparison to the real adversities faced by earlier mountain men in the days of the frontier, his situation is not dangerous. But he does come to a new awareness about what frontiersmen faced. Huning's experiences enter in again as Fergusson explains Alec's new realization: "He understood how men could eat their shoes, their horses and even each other. Maybe only men who had starved and had fought for their lives knew what life was. Comfortable people only played at living" (p. 71).

Fergusson stresses the basic theme of the novel through Alec's recognition of the real and illusory wilderness. It is a motif usually associated in American literature with Emerson and Thoreau: solitude in nature often means deeper insight into what is authentic and what is false, into what is original and what is derivative, into both individual and social truths. In that disparity lies the basis for philosophy but also for satire. Fergusson illustrates this point humorously when Alec returns to camp the next morning, devours a breakfast of ham and eggs, and takes some good-natured ribbing. He talks tough like a real Texan should talk and hides the fact that his only real wandering (and wondering) up until the day before has been in the Bronx. The mountain wilderness has brought him face to face with himself; but he does not reveal his true self to his companions.

In this first mountain incident, then, Fergusson juxtaposes again the illusory and the real, confirming that the wild and woolly West of Uncle Alec is now mostly a residue of memory and exaggeration, impossible to simulate—too far gone.

Extending the contrast of Alec's lost night, alone in the mountains, with his return to a comfortable breakfast next morning is his initially wonderous but soon taken-for-granted perception of the wilderness landscape as he gets more experience as a cruiser and, when he is not cruising, in his ribald story-telling about women and carnality. Alec plans a trip to Taos in August to take the ranger exam and to socialize. His fellow rangers are a friendly enough bunch, all of them from diverse backgrounds but similarly motivated by a love of the out-of-doors and adventure. Like all men alone—or so suggests Fergusson—they are prone to a limited range of conversation and are preoccupied with tall tales, off-color jokes, and lusty conjectures about women. All of these narratives lead to the conclusion that it is futile for men to try to live alone without women.

Throughout these narratives, in a pattern which becomes the basic structure of *Lonely Women*, Fergusson takes the opportunity to level a blast at the "conventional repressions of American life" and light-handedly argues for free sexual involvement. Both Uncle Alec and his nephew are examples of the kind of promiscuity Fergusson, through McGarnigal, advocates. Given the lasciviousness of the fireside stories, Fergusson's conclusion about the value of the strictly male camaraderie found by Alec during his summer with the forest crew seems primitive enough—true men banded together in adventure against the unknown.

From the relatively lowbrow, macho world of the campfire, Alec moves to the effeminate, highbrow artist colony of Taos. This world, wherein intellectuals identify with either cowboys or the local Pueblo Indians, confirms even further the discrepancies between reality and illusion which Alec experiences in the mountains and allows Fergusson considerably more leeway for satire. Alec first hears what Taos is really like and what he can expect there from his friend Syme. Syme tells such exaggerated stories about both the artists and Indians that Alec, on the eve of his departure from the mountains for Taos, feels "as though he were about to explore some mythical region where even the laws of nature were not obeyed" (p. 92). Syme typifies the artists as "the most amazing collection of nuts in the world" and claims that the Indians at the pueblo are pagan phallic worshippers who keep a fifteen-foot-long snake and feed it a live baby each spring.

The reality of Taos is something short of the mythical region Alec constructs in his mind on the basis of Syme's and his uncle's stories. But it is nevertheless an odd enough spot, an exotic convergence of past and present, the frontier and the modern, the real and the replica. Mexicans puff cigarettes in shady doorways; Indians in blankets walk through the plaza; horses stand tied to hitching posts; high-powered cars with "smart silky girls" in them rumble through the narrow streets; and painters dress like circus cowboys, accompanied by costumed Indians as models: "It seemed to be a place where past and present had violently collided, upsetting the orderly processes of time and change" (pp. 110–11). Alice Mayer, one of the most eccentric persons Alec meets (he regards her as a harmless lunatic), tells him what he has already intuited—but in considerably more mystical terms: "What you feel here is the human richness of a place which is one of the spiritual centers of the universe—a place where men come without knowing why and stay because they must" (pp. 131–32). Fergusson directs strong satire on the town of Taos. He works in, in fictionalized form, many of the personalities and "eccentricities" he had observed first-hand: Mabel Dodge Luhan and her Indian husband, Tony; Witter Bynner, the noted poet, usually attired in Indian garb; and Mary Austin, the writer and expert on "Amerind" literature, whom he first met at the home of Alice Corbin Henderson. Such real-life personages are easily recognizable, respectively, in characterizations of Mrs. Whitehorse and her Indian husband, in Rynder, and in Alice Mayer. Alec's main Taos contact, recommended by Syme, is an artist named Harms, a man who typifies the strange contradictions of illusory past and real present, for he is an individual so highly stylized as to be an imitation of the frontier West that was once Taos. When Alec first sees Harms, he thinks Harms is the ghost of Uncle Alec—or some semblance of him—riding out of the past to greet him. The reality of Harms soon establishes itself, however, for on closer look, Alec sees that he wears an incongruous pair of spectacles with "heavy celluloid rims," too gaudy and theatrical for a true man of the frontier. Harms, like his friends, is cosmopolitan, has lived in London and Paris, but came to Taos "to soak . . . in a primitive life—a life of elemental realities" (p. 105). He represents the pattern behind Fergusson's satire: he is unable to get to know the Indian culture, soon becomes disillusioned with the primitive life, and now paints nothing but landscapes, mountains, and solid rock.

The whole assembly is first depicted at Rynder's great museum of a house. Rynder is an obvious fictional counterpart of Bynner—a man with a "shinny bald pate, heavy-rimmed spectacles and three or four silver Navajo bracelets on each arm," decked out in a richly embroidered Chinese robe (p. 118). Fergusson visited Bynner in Santa Fe more than once during the 1920s and recorded in his diaries his reactions to Bynner, and others he met, at least once in 1922 and again in 1924: "At night Witter Bynner: he holding all by his truly marvelous capacity for giving himself to others: he sang, he played; he showed his collection of Indian art; he read letters from Henry James and O'Henry. Whatever his reaction to life he is no abberant. He's a man adjusted, singularly looking out, singularly capable of all kinds of human contact. He won me completely."[48] Much of the detail of those visits as "social orgies" is carried over to the pages of *McGarnigal*. Mrs. Whitehorse, a rich, squat, middle-aged lady with an "imperious" and "worried" expression, and her Taos Indian husband ("bunchy in the middle, dressed in riding trousers, puttees and a purple silk shirt with a pink scarf about his neck") are Fergusson's caricaturized versions of Mabel Dodge Luhan and her husband, Tony. Fergusson called on Mrs. Luhan, for example, in July 1924, and enjoyed her hospitality: "Everybody cordial and interested."[49] His satire is lightly done, for as he also recorded in his diary, in Taos he was in a "society of similars" which attracted him at the same time that he tried to distance himself from it.

Alec's main romantic involvement in Taos in Amaryllis Oldfield, a sculptress from Boston with a studio in Santa Fe, who has come west in search of "primitive" truths. Her "bobbed blond hair" and "bouncing breasts" catch Alec's eye first thing, and he begins his attempts at seduction. Amaryllis is about the only person he meets among the Taos crowd who does not strike him as "strange as animals in a zoo" (p. 123). Portrayed as more highbrow and intellectual than Alec, all of the Taos crowd is set in opposition to Alec and Amaryllis, who seek action over intellectualism and imitation. Amaryllis, for her part, tells McGarnigal that she wants to know a true man of the country, a true westerner, for she is sick and tired of artists: "I want a man that can look at me without thinking of paint" (p. 127).

It is Amaryllis who suggests that Alec accompany her to the Santa Domingo corn dance. Fergusson records his reactions to his own attendance at that Pueblo dance in August of 1924 and utilizes those memories in *McGarnigal*. The occasion of the corn dance points out again how the "primitive" rituals of the Pueblos, although lasting into the 1920s, are only echoes of past dances. Alec senses that he is one of the Anglo intruders who are as much a spectacle for observation as the primitive dancers.

Alec is less interested in the ceremonial dances and in philosophical speculation about Indian-white relations than he is finding Amaryllis and trying to make love to her—another "primitive" urge.

When he does find her, she offers him more disillusioning talk. To her, Taos and Santa Fe are no different than Greenwich Village, which she sees as encouraging more talk about art than actual work. She feels she can escape no further into primitivism, solitude, and work and thus will return to the East and try to settle into more work the second time around. But their physical attraction to each other, at the moment, prevails. They leave talk about art aside and escape to the fiesta at the edge of the pueblo. It is dominated by Mexicans, and the color and dignity of the celebration soon have them joining in another kind of dance. Their sheer pleasure is interrupted, ironically, by rain—as if the Indians and their harvest dance had struck a responsive chord in their gods. Alec, too, releases his passionate, pent-up emotional energy and kisses Amaryllis in the rain.

Before Alec can accept that he is falling in love with Amaryllis and that he is as much an easterner and a city man as a westerner, he must go into the mountains again—this time with no companions—at least for a few weeks, as a fireguard. In this section of the novel he is presented even more dramatically as a man between two worlds, east and west, civilized and primitive. He rides a horse out of Santa Fe, as another of Fergusson's "proud riders." Something of a prototype of Edward Abbey's later "brave cowboy," Alec is a living anachronism: "[He] felt like a relic of some remote past everyone else had forgotten. He was tempted to turn the gray loose and beg a ride in a machine" (p. 158).

Fergusson eventually stages a dramatic chase, on horseback, of a locomotive which resolves this vitalistic-merchanistic ambivalence in Alec. Before Alec can return to the world of machines, however, he must play out a final episode at the Bullard ranch. There he meets Jim Bullard and carries on an affair with Bullard's silent, olive-skinned, black-haired "cousin," Lucretia Bullard, who ushers him into a sequence of events and a sexual relationship which take him back in time to an even more exaggerated simulation of the Old West than the previous timber-cruiser and Taos-artist sections of the novel.

After much talk with Bullard about horses, Alec obtains a fine mare named Fox. On this red bay, with its black stockings and a white blazed face, Alec rides proudly, like a time traveler, further into the wilderness. There he meets Lynch, the ranger he is to replace as a fireguard. In leaving all traces of civilization, Alec is aware that his journey from New York has taken him farther and farther into his encounter with the primitive; farther away from city, to town, to the forest, and now to the very "heart of solitude" (p. 175).

After a bear story or two, in mountain-man tradition, Lynch leaves Alec to his own resources in facing up to the job and the loneliness of "complete and silent desolation" (p. 189). As was the case earlier in the summer when he was a timber cruiser, Alec's thoughts now turn again to women. Fergusson's own philosophy about the end of the frontier, about sex, and about society shine through Alec's lonely musings about the universality of the impulse he is experiencing: "Would any man [even the old-timers who traveled thousands of miles alone] ever come home except to a woman? Maybe such dreams were needed to tie men down, to make them work and breed" (p. 199).

Even the primitive life—riding horses in the mountains and loving an "earth mother" like Lucretia Bullard, who rides out to visit him—has its complications. The memory of Amaryllis and her refinement enters Alec's life again. Fergusson too could not remain in Taos and Santa Fe or in the wilderness "hunting bear" at the end of his 1924 summer with Becky. She left for New York and called him there in the fall. So it is with Amaryllis and McGarnigal. Amaryllis writes and wants to see him again when he returns to New York. With Amaryllis on his conscience, McGarnigal nevertheless indulges his animal passions for Lucretia. In yet another of Fergusson's stock sex scenes, they physically fight, she resists, then she gives herself to him. McGarnigal and Amaryllis had fought and then loved in her Santa Fe home. But in contrast to his night with Amaryllis, Lucretia and Alec experience the primitive freedom and animal innocence of intercourse on a grassy mountain ridge surrounded by the forest.

Two events occur which free Alec from his job on the mountain. Bullard confronts him in a classic, but satirized, Old West "showdown"; and Lynch returns dissatisfied with McGarnigal's inattentive work. Alec takes these reversals as somehow funny, and during his farewell to Lucretia, they both break into laughter. Any attempt to rescue her from Bullard's clutches, in formulaic melodramatic fashion, is presented as anticlimactic. Fergusson levels his satire at the conventions of the Western itself here—but almost in spite of himself, for he has given himself over perhaps too far to parody them.

Alec does not ride off alone into the sunset. Soon the man on horseback merges with and is replaced by the Freudian image of the iron horse. Alec's escape route out of the mountains leads him directly to first the sound and then the sight of a transcontinental passenger train pointing the way, "like a long black arrow, tipped and spotted with light," back east to civilization—and to Amaryllis. The scene is an important one, in its ambivalences of east versus west, and in its imagistic and metaphorical vividness.

McGarnigal's relinquishment of the West for the East takes him full circle. And when he does arrive in New York, the reader can only guess that Alec's mind and heart will be back in the West, back among the primitives. *McGarnigal*, then, in its "satire on the contemporary worship of the primitive," represents Fergusson's own struggle to reconcile the lure of the West and of the East, the solitary and the social life. By the time it was published in 1930, he had already made up his mind to head west for good, but to the Far West.

For over a decade, and especially between 1924 and 1930, Fergusson was what he called "a commuter between New Mexico and New York." Like his fictional extension of himself, Alec McGarnigal, he too opted for the city. But once in the city, and after his two Washington novels, he spent his time as a writer dealing with the frontier, with the West. Soon the excitement and stimulus of New York was not enough, and scriptwriting for motion pictures took him first to Los Angeles and Hollywood and then allowed him to settle comfortably in Berkeley. To that extent, East was reconciled with West in the next important phase of Fergusson's life. At the age of forty he found a place where he could, for all practical purposes, settle down and think again about how change affected his own life against the larger sweep of history.

This time he was on the farthermost shore of where the frontier had stopped, where he could look back into the distances of space and time with a somewhat different, but continuing, perspective.

Far West (1930–1971)

The decade of the 1930s saw a major change in Fergusson's life. He moved from New York to California and reenacted the destiny of his family and their counterparts in his fiction: he too became a "follower of the sun." His sister Lina, as a result of her marriage to Spencer Browne, the great-grandson of California pioneer and writer J. Ross Browne, lived in Berkeley. It would be this family connection, plus his general preference for northern California, which eventually determined his taking up permanent residence in Berkeley. During the 1930s he was first lured to Hollywood for the work and money earned from writing film treatments and scripts for the movies. During this period he continued his summers in New Mexico when work for films allowed it, utilizing that special place for what he considered his serious writing as well as for inspiration and source work for films. Although the writing of screenplays allowed him to prepare financially for his old age, his priority was still the writing of southwestern frontier history, both as fiction and as "faction."

RIO GRANDE HISTORIAN

After finishing *McGarnigal* in the spring of 1929, Fergusson settled again for a time in New York and continued his association with Mencken and the *Mercury*. Fergusson's essay on his Mexican trip, "Seen and Heard in Mexico," ran in the June 1930 issue. He had approached Mencken even before *McGarnigal* about the possibility of publishing an article on New Mexico in the *Mercury*, which was running a series on various states. As early as 1925 Mencken had published one of Fergusson's New Mexico pieces, "Billy the Kid." An early short story, "The New Englander," was published by Mencken in the *Mercury* in 1926.[1] In his work for the *Mercury*, the *Nation*, *Scribner's Magazine*, and other "little" periodicals, Fergusson's nonfiction expressions of his interest in northern New Mexico, and particularly the *rio arriba* portion of the Rio Grande, were gaining momentum. What had provided a historical background for his fiction was now emerging into the foreground.

Fergusson's hope that Mencken would run an essay on New Mexico became part of the impetus for what turned into an entire history, built of separate, identifiable essays. By the spring of 1930 he was hard at work on just such a book and was submitting chapters as he wrote them both to Mencken and to Knopf. The summer found Fergusson back in New Mexico writing his history of his beloved state. As might be expected, given his developing talents as a novelist, his "history" turned out to be a narrative, *Rio Grande*, which reflects considerable use of autobiographical anecdotes and novelistic technique laced with his journalistic-chronicle style, and in which the river became the controlling metaphor for the place, the people, and the events discussed.

In June, Fergusson wrote to Mencken thanking him for arranging an advance and for serial publication of *Rio Grande* in the *Mercury*, in addition to book publication by Knopf. The exposure and the money were most welcome: "I will send you another chapter of the Rio Grande book soon. It is needless to say how much I appreciate your making the arrangement you did as it enables me to go ahead and finish the book with assurance of making a living while I work on it. I will also be delighted to see the stuff in the *Mercury*."² The terms of the arrangement were a contract with Knopf by which Knopf was to pay Fergusson three thousand dollars in ten monthly payments, half of it to be an advance on the book and the rest to pay for the portions used in the *Mercury*.³

In the early fall of 1930, and more or less in the middle of writing *Rio Grande*, Fergusson took his first job as a scriptwriter in Hollywood. It was a short stint of only a few weeks, but he found the work easy and was successful at it. Thus began a phase of balancing writing for the movies with trying to write what he really cared about, his Rio Grande history. Now, at midlife, he was at least in the West—albeit the Far West and not the Southwest, which continued to dominate his writing. He was able to work a few of his Hollywood experiences into his next novel, *The Life of Riley* (1937); however, the Southwest overshadowed all else—with the exception of his two philosophical treatises on modern man and power.

Knopf had planned to publish *Rio Grande* in book form in the early summer of 1931, but in December 1930 Fergusson asked Mencken to try to postpone that date until late August or September until the economy improved. He was well along but not finished, and in addition to the chapters Mencken already had, Fergusson had finished a chapter on General Armijo and almost finished one on Padre Martinez, the priest whom Archbishop Lamy excommunicated. In January, he planned to leave for San Francisco and finish the book there. He hoped to send Mencken two more chapters in January, two in February, and the last one in March. How difficult it was to balance movie work with the *Rio Grande* chapters (complicated by the aftermath of the Depression) is clear in his explanation to Mencken. He still had his bosses even with the independence: "I landed here in October on a five week movie contract. Somewhat to my surprise I wrote with great ease and speed what the supervisor pronounced to be a good script. They made a verbal agreement with me to do a couple of adaptations, and then ran out on the deal because of hard times and orders from New York. I was about to depart when the bank here in which I had deposited my dishonest gains closed its doors and I am now waiting around to see what I can get out of it and when. Meanwhile I am at work on the book. On the strength of my investigations to date I nominate this town the arsehole of the universe. When I get back to civilization I cannot say for sure."[4]

That Fergusson considered Los Angeles more of an inhospitable "frontier" town than others he had known is made even clearer in his reaction to San Francisco when he did arrive there in January 1931. As he gravitated across the bay to Berkeley and began exploring the Berkeley hills and the university beneath them, he found conditions more than suitable for the writing he really wanted to do. He started the new year writing two to three pages a day and doing some editing. Partly because of Berkeley, he was able to finish two more chapters of *Rio Grande* in relatively short order and was in good spirits even though short on funds when he informed Mencken that he liked where he now was: "Here is the piece on Armijo [Chapter 9 out of a total of twelve in the book version] and I will send the one on Padre Martinez within the month. My financial catastrophes worry me very little as I have never been used to having much money anyway. I think I'll stick here at least until I finish the book. It seems to be a very pleasant and civilized spot. It is hard to believe that it is in the same state with Los Angeles."[5] He liked the Bay area, and adding to what he regarded as the "civilized" aspects of Berkeley, he liked the low cost of living: "Out here prices are toppling and I can eat dinner for less than I ever have since 1914."[6]

In addition to his writing, between January and March he visited his sisters and took long daily walks. Lina, who was married to Spencer C. Browne, Jr., became a major factor in Fergusson's eventual move to Berkeley, since she lived first in Piedmont and then in Berkeley at One Eagle Hill, a house once owned by J. Robert Oppenheimer. Erna lived in Albuquerque with her mother, but stayed with Lina in California from time to time. During the winter and spring Fergusson began exploring California. He drove to Palo Alto with his brother-in-law, visited the Oakland and Berkeley libraries with mild curiosity, played handball, and rode over the San Marcos Pass and up the mountain valley, where he lunched in a small tavern and talked casually with an old man about California.[7]

Fergusson was unable to finish *Rio Grande* in Berkeley as he had hoped. But by the end of January 1931 he had completed the chapter on Padre Martinez and sent it to Mencken. Feeling that the book was already too long, he dropped his idea for doing a chapter on the sheep business. On March 6 he sent Mencken the next-to-the-last chapter and took off on an extended trip down the California coast from San Francisco, stopping to consider Carmel as a possible residence and, in Santa Barbara, to play polo and move in "very swager society." He then went down to the Mexican border and east to the Rio Grande and up the river to Albuquerque. The weather in Berkeley was near-perfect, he told Mencken, but he could not work in it for some undisclosed reason, probably because going back to the Southwest during the summer had been his habit for so many years. He was back in New Mexico for the spring and summer of 1931 and worked there on the final chapter, establishing his "headquarters" at his mother's and sister's 1021 Orchard Place residence. He promised to have the final work to Mencken in late May or June.[8] By early June, Fergusson was pretty much finished with the book and was now actually living what he had written about, down in the Rio Grande Box, hiking to the bottom with hip boots and fishing tackle.[9]

At Fergusson's request, Knopf had suspended payment on *Rio Grande* when Fergusson was in Hollywood. By that second arrangement, the $1,500 paid up to that time (October 1930) was to serve as the advance, and Mencken would pay for the serial rights as he used them. As Fergusson left for this trip back to Albuquerque to finish *Rio Grande,* he requested the resumption of payments in May, still worried about getting his movie money out of the closed Bank of Hollywood. With meager remuneration for *Rio Grande,* as for all of his books, the money offered by further scriptwriting plus the pleasantries of Berkeley insured his return to California in the spring of 1932—after another side trip back to New York during the fall and winter of 1931 and some visits there with his brother, Francis. By then he had a new book and further credentials as a Rio Grande historian.

The first serialized installment of *Rio Grande* appeared in the May 1931 issue of the *Mercury.* Entitled "Rio Grande: The River, the Valley, and the People," it was the lead essay and was much promoted

Harvey Fergusson fishing. Courtesy of The Bancroft Library.

by Mencken, against considerable opposition in the *Mercury* editorial office. Mencken's editorial assistant, Charles Angoff, opposed running any chapters of *Rio Grande* on the grounds that they were dull and did not reflect the tempestuous changes taking place in the country after the stock market crash of 1929. Mencken listened to Angoff's objections, then simply said: "We'll use the Fergusson. After all, the responsibility is mine."[10] The argument over the suitability of *Rio Grande* for *Mercury* serialization led to a widening rift between Mencken and Angoff, for Mencken planned to use a half-dozen installments of Fergusson's book: the first four in May, June, July, and August, respectively, and two more in subsequent issues, pending Fergusson's completion of them.

Mencken, in addition to positioning the first installment as a lead essay, also featured the series in full-page subscription solicitations, complete with a portrait of Fergusson looking manly and debonair. Mencken had promised his readers a "prize package" of a new work of American history—book and magazine—and Fergusson wrote to him as early as March thanking him for his promotion efforts, and saying: "I am very much pleased with the way you are playing the stuff up. I doubt whether you will succeed in drumming up much trade with the prize package offer, but I appreciate the compliment."[11] In the editorial notes accompanying the first installment, Fergusson commented on some of the aspects of the frontier which he saw as a boy growing up in the Rio Grande Valley and related those anecdotal experiences to his motive, method, and ethos behind the writing of *Rio Grande*. As a "historian," he saw the things he wrote about: "I must have seen something of all the types and actions of pioneer society, and doubtless those early impressions, many of them long lost to conscious memory, are what furnish my imagination now."[12]

Knopf published the full book in August 1933. It was well received by reviewers, although sales were not spectacular. Reviewers latched on to Fergusson's credentials as a native New Mexican of pioneer ancestry who reached his own majority the same year New Mexico became a state. He was touted as the proverbial native son with "the feel of and for the land and its people."[13] An especially long and favorable review by Maxwell Anderson in the *Nation* called it a fascinating book, "exciting both to lovers of romance and American history. . . . Here, in little, is an epitome of history." Anderson put his finger on certain Turnerian assumptions behind the "epitome of history" Fergusson had succeeded in writing: "An ancient order, laboriously built upon blood and conquest, settles down to a brief period of flower. The rabble of another race overruns it and sets up another system of living."[14]

Fergusson's long-time friend and colleague Paul Horgan—another novelist-historian, who would some twenty years later write his own history of the "great river"—in his commentary for the *Yale Review*, saw to the heart of Fergusson's history as that written as only a native son and novelist could write, about historical change and mutability across the face of the sublime southwestern landscape. Horgan saw *Rio Grande* as a synthesis of everything Fergusson had written to that point and in that respect a kind of epitome. The subject he saw as essentially the same as that of Fergusson's fiction—but treated in even wider "scope" than in the novels, with more universal application, in its chronology of the region "from the early Indians to the latest A.T. & S.F. Country Club occupation."[15] In Horgan's view, Fergusson's "maturity as an important American writer" allowed him to set in order nicely the history of the area where he was born and grew up. It was an upbringing which not only qualified Fergusson to become a Rio Grande historian but helped assure that he would be one.

Rio Grande is a reshaping in the form of history of much of the subject matter and patterns of the historical fiction which Fergusson used in most of his prior novels. Moreover, his subsequent novels after *Rio Grande* build on this work as well. As such, it represents a special cumulative showcase for his materials and methods as a writer of history—history as fiction and as "faction."

As Horgan suggests, and as any reader familiar with its serialization knows, *Rio Grande* might well be regarded as a series of a dozen separate essays about northern New Mexico. The fact that half of the essays were serialized in the *Mercury* and that Fergusson projected other chapters that were never finished underscores the fragmented nature of the book. It achieves its unity, however, by its chronological arrangement, by its concentration on the events and people which came to and settled the *rio arriba* portion of the great river, and through the idea that the character of a land determines the character of its people. Aside from the opening essay chapter, "Country," events and landscape are of secondary importance in Fergusson's history-story, giving way to people—both as types and as individuals—whose lives were influenced by the country and in turn influenced it. The constancy of the river, the mountains, and the mesas, the topography of the land, its flora and fauna and overall ecology, provide the backdrop of permanence, or at least of much slower change, for the human history acted out over the relatively tiny span of the three or four centuries of Fergusson's account.

All of Fergusson's Western novels—and the Western elements of his eastern novels and certainly his *Followers of the Sun* trilogy—read like companion volumes to *Rio Grande*. Much of Fergusson's autobiography is embedded in this history just as it is in his novels. There is a fine line between ohistory and fiction as he writes the two forms, and between the importance of biography in his writing of his historical novels and his novelistic history. Both in his introduction and in his comments on bibliography which frame *Rio Grande* Fergusson attempts to justify his motive and his method, his brand of historiography, and of personalized, popularized, narrative and dramatic history over quantitative, "scientific" history, by pointing out that he is more than aware of the story in history: "A good realistic novel, it has been said, is history that might have happened, and the same is very largely true of a good history."[16]

That Fergusson is interested in the theme of mutability, that he is interested in how the frontier and associated frontiers appear and disappear recurrently, is obvious in his introduction. The Rio Grande basin was a particularly interesting region of historical study for Fergusson in that it was a place where journeys and migrations started and ended, where battles were fought, and where destinies of whole races of people were changed if not decided. But such endings, although known in the Rio Grande basin, are known as remnants of the past as seen in what Fergusson terms "human actuality." His fascination with the possibility of seeing such endings prolonged justifies both what he writes about and why he writes about it. "Human actuality"—that is, "biography"—in the face of the forces of change is dramatized here no less than in his novels.

The concluding chapter, dealing with Albuquerque "Old and New," confirms that *Rio Grande* is written in homage to Fergusson's youth and the family history which evolved in the way it did to make Albuquerque his birthplace and the Southwest his "destiny." As the book went through its various editions, Fergusson's introductions underscored how the original "present" of the 1931 edition soon became merged with the earlier version, romantic and realistic, of the frontier past. His "Preface to the Apollo Edition," written in 1967, is a case in point.

There, he points out that in 1930, when he completed *Rio Grande*, the population of the "new/old" town of Albuquerque was approximately 30,000. By the time he took a retrospective look, nearly forty years later, at his original retrospective history of the Rio Grande, the population was nearly 300,000 and growing.[17] Expressing his continuing love for his hometown in his 1967 preface, he explained again that his attraction for the place was founded in its antithetical primitive and civilized nature. What he still liked about it was the meeting of one world, one frontier, with another. That idea of "frontier," almost by definition, is seen in his identification of the central theme of *Rio Grande*—that the character of the land is the character of its people. It is a theme which interested him in his previous novel, *McGarnigal*, as well as in "The Cult of the Indian" essay, also written in 1930.

Albuquerque, as originally portrayed in the "Old Town and New" chapter is still another, earlier remembering of Fergusson's, one closer to his childhood and the ending of the frontier—situations, causes, and results—which his family and he himself first experienced. The Albuquerque of his middle age (1930) represented the fusing of past and future in a present which had accommodated the old (premachine) and new (postmachine) frontiers. The theme of the entire chapter is that of forced synthesis of two antithetical forces— how Old Town was expected to merge with or be surrounded by New Town.

His design of the frontier towns which provide the nexus of his novels is reflected always by what happened in Albuquerque—sleepy village of the past confronting boom town of the future. What he experienced as a boy and saw continue into the future in Albuquerque was a universalized process of frontier.

As he catalogs the various types of "money masters," the merchants who rose with such a boom town out of the romantic, more heroic, and less pragmatic West, one sees not only the inspiration and prototype of Franz Huning and H. B. Fergusson, but Harvey Fergusson too. These "men of destiny," these practical moneymakers—the representative Italian and Jewish merchants—people Fergusson's fiction from first to last. In *Rio Grande*, in skeletal form, weighing on Fergusson's mind and imagination thirty years before it reached its most successfully realized novelistic form, is a version of the plot, grounded in biography and history, of *The Conquest of Don Pedro*. *Rio Grande* serves as both a synthesis and a preview of Fergusson's grand frontier theme, in faction and in fiction.

Other examples of how *Rio Grande* embodies Fergusson's grand theme are plentiful. Fergusson marks the creation of New Town with the coming of the railroad in 1881. By 1890, the time of his birth, it was relatively civilized and peaceful, but with wilderness and primitivism in close proximity: "By 1910 it was almost a model of what a small American town should be" (p. 282). As such, it is the kind of town which Fergusson, as a young writer, sought to satirize. But unlike many frontier towns—most notably for him, the towns of Santa Fe and Taos—New Town boomed because of the railroad. Progress came and yet the Southwest retained its ability to thwart dreams of riches, the promises associated with the myths of the Southwest. The legend of Cibola and the Seven Golden Cities—the wealth which Coronado and numerous others after him never attained—is a theme worked out by Fergusson in his fiction as early as *Women and Wives*.

This precise confrontation of the land and its people with change, and the simultaneous acceptance and resistance of it, is what defines the frontier history of the Southwest for him. Among all the regions of the United States, the Southwest is where the great American dream of change, progress, and success most strikingly failed to come true, according to his perceptions. In his view, "primitive stocks and folk-ways" resisted social change, or the forces of frontier, just as ada-mantly as "rock and sun have resisted the plow." The result, accord-ing to Fergusson, is a kind of parody or stylization which he attempted to satirize in *McGarnigal*.

What Fergusson attempts, and realizes, in *Rio Grande*, then, is not so much to get at the color and atmosphere of New Mexico (though he does that) or its exoticism (though he does this as well), as to sketch out in chronicle terms the substantive links whereby the cultural and geographical history of the Rio Grande Valley and its outlying mesas and mountains fit into the larger patterns and forces of the rest of American experience. The then-current influx of painters and writers to Santa Fe and Taos which he documents in *Rio Grande* and fictionalizes in *McGarnigal* Fergusson poses as another "fron-tier," another "new spurt of life, just as the coming of the beaver trappers and the wagon traders" (p. 287).

In 1930 he could anticipate nothing of the ironies of Los Alamos, Trinity Site, and the military bases; space-related technologies and laser research; defense, microchip, and computer industries; geother-mal explorations—all existing alongside native American cultures. Nor could he envision any of these environmental and cultural adapta-tions in his introductory revisitation in the 1950s.

The significance of *Rio Grande* is multifold in relation to Fer-gusson's life and in the overall canon of his works. It is significant on its own terms as a panoramic look at the relationship between a landscape and the peoples of three cultures in the oldest region of exploration and settlement of the United States. It is significant as an influential book in the literary history of the Southwest, adding to a tradition of American river books which reaches back to Thoreau and extends to the twentieth-century works of such narrative historians as Bernard DeVoto, Paul Horgan, and Jonathan Rabin. And it is signifi-cant as a condensed account of the history of the country which inspired and gave direction and purpose to Fergusson's life and thus to his writing.

It is thus worthy of note that Fergusson chooses to begin *Rio Grande* with an essay on the Country and offers his descriptions and feelings about it from the point of view and persona of a naturalist and modern mountain man. To illustrate the chronicle perspective which he chooses, Fergusson tells of climbing to the top of one of the Sangre de Cristo's highest points, Wheeler Peak, which at an elevation of over 13,000 feet allows him a view of almost the entire Rio Grande Valley and beyond.

It is an effective narrative convention, but one which demands some suspension of disbelief, for he "sees" and relates more than he could physically really see. But Fergusson's descriptions provide the figurative as well as the literal vantage point for his ensuing historical and autobiographical narrative. The first day he walks up Taos Canyon toward Blue Lake, the legendary lake of the inhabitants of Taos Pueblo, alluded to in *McGarnigal*. He passes through the numerous life zones found in New Mexico, from desert to arctic, a progression which has the same effect as if he "had gone from North Carolina to Hudson Bay." He climbs past the timber line into the arctic zone, a special place for Fergusson, as evidenced in one of his few published poems, "Timber Line," a poem indicative of the essence of his spirit and one he wanted read at his funeral.[18]

On top of Wheeler Peak he peers to the west and the south, into deserts, between the river and the mountain range, where the "Jornado del Muerto" lies, the "journey of death" which the Spaniards knew and named and which figures in the real journeys of Huning and the imagined journeys of characters like Leo Mendes, the peddler-merchant in *Conquest*. Suddenly Fergusson is transported in fancy to the valley itself—the riverbed with its sometimes flooded and now empty channels. He describes the divisions and zones of the river which historically were so important in the system of Spanish land grants (so important to *Kingdom*): the arable land, the marshy meadows, the bosques where wood could be cut. The cottonwood trees which in large measure make up the bosque and so characterize the upper Rio Grande Valley are described in emotionally charged detail.

In his climb up Wheeler Peak and his look at the country of his very being, Fergusson also indirectly illustrates just how the character of a country determines not only the destiny of its people but also the shape its literature takes. His constant attraction to and use of rivers and mountains, deserts and rains in his writing, the very mappings of the destinations and journeys of his settings, plots, and characters come from the deeply felt belief that the Rio Grande and the Southwest were determiners of what Fergusson wrote and of how proudly he wrote it and why.

Rio Grande represents a transitional point in Fergusson's life and writing. Its publication marked the beginning of his far western residence in California (though he did return to New York during the fall and winter of 1931) and marked his new job as a Hollywood writer and the beginning of his later middle age. For him the 1930s became an important decade of taking stock, of attempting new forms of writing: screenplays, serial fiction, and, extending from his Rio Grande history, other nonfiction in the form of his philosophical treatise, *Modern Man*. In addition, he wrote another autobiographical novel, *The Life of Riley*, again in the mode of the picaresque. Serial fiction interested him in somewhat the same way that writing for the picture business did: he needed the money. And he was drawn again to the novel in the continuation of his major interest over three decades—attempting to understand, then recreate himself in fiction. The decade continued to have its ups and downs, the tough going of what he referred to in his diaries as the "ordeal" of life.

PICTURE OF BUSINESS

During the roughly ten years Fergusson wrote for the movies, he established his home base in Berkeley. Film assignments kept him in Los Angeles for weeks and months at a time, and he kept a temporary residence there. But he always returned to Berkeley. He liked it well enough to live the rest of his life there.

Only in a special sense is it appropriate to think that Fergusson's work in the picture business was the main focus of his life during the 1930s. Judging from his diaries and correspondence, although he did not like the "arsehole" of Los Angeles and Hollywood, he did like the money which scriptwriting allowed him—the security it gave him when he did work, and what it promised for his later years. The picture business did interfere with his serious writing, but it was something of a trade-off. Writing for films allowed him a livelihood that his books and other freelancing did not; and it gave him time for his serious writing, for travel, and for friendships, including a romantic relationship which retains the anonymity of initials in his diaries. But as his many retrospective diary entries toward the end of the decade illustrate, the picture business was good to him, socially and, to a point, artistically, for he was able to adapt some of his fictional conceptions to his film work. Although he felt to a certain extent that he really did not earn the money he made—at least, not in proportion to the amount of loneliness, sweat, and hard work that went into his fiction—he did feel that his far west move and his work in Hollywood allowed him to get ahead: "The picture business has given me more feeling of security than I ever had before, and also more feeling of being a part of the social whole. It almost abolished a longing for flight and retreat. . . . It has stimulated me to fully living."[19]

To anyone interested in Fergusson specifically, and in film history more generally, a detailed accounting of what occupied him from the time he began in films with his five-week stint in December 1930 until the time he ended his "picture business" in 1942 provides a somewhat typical window on the life of a Hollywood film writer in the 1930s. He left little record of his time and work in Hollywood. Much of his work was in the realm of "treatments" and in team projects which left him little room for recognition.[20] The exact circumstances of what took him to Hollywood are not all that clear. Ostensibly a Hollywood agent read his novels and recognized some potential for screenwriting. One source pinpoints this in 1931.[21] In any event, by 1932, Fergusson was in the picture business. He wrote to Horgan sometime after Knopf had agreed to postpone the publication of *Rio Grande* until the "next summer" of 1933. At the time of his letter to Horgan, Fergusson had worked for about thirty-seven weeks for three studios and had had nothing appear on the screen. He shared his experiences with his friend and fellow writer, saying, "Somewhat to my own surprise I have generally been able to produce something that suited my immediate supervisor, but it has always been laid on the shelf or kicked in the pants by someone higher up. There is an elaborate hierarchy and all of them now are scared to death. Also, they tend to send for a writer of my sort only if they have a book or an idea they do not know how to handle themselves. The easy assignments all fall to the old-line movie hacks. It would be a maddening world if you took it seriously but if you keep your fingers crossed and your tongue in your cheek, it is worth something as an experience. It is also the only place in the world where they are passing out any money now and authors must eat."[22]

Fergusson left other hints as to just how much of his time was devoted to the movie industry. As he looked back at the decade of the 1930s in a 1940 retrospective, he tallied his published books as three: *Rio Grande, Modern Man,* and *The Life of Riley.* The three books sold no more than a total of 15,000 copies, brought him some limited fame but no commercial reputation, and had no cumulative effect. Throughout a nine-year period (1931–40) he had about 125 weeks of movie work: "I did not give more than 1/4 of my energy to pictures," he wrote in his diary.[23] By the spring of 1940 he expected no more than twenty-five or thirty more weeks of picture work, "all told."

Such a tally indicates that Fergusson worked twice as much on the writing of books as he did in the picture business. A full three-fourths of his time was free for serious writing, travel, relaxation—or recuperation. He seemed to establish a pattern of work which he charted over the weeks and months which amounted to a spurt of energy that lasted about six months, followed by a minor slump, and then a slight recovery. After that he would not accomplish much. As a result, he resolved to devote the first and the last of his burst of energy to the writing of books and tried to save the remainder of his recovery time for picture work.

As 1942 ended, the end of another one of his personal frontiers, this one as a script writer, he assessed not only how he budgeted his writing time but how his life had divided itself into phases and how much money he had earned. On Christmas Eve 1942, at the age of fifty-two, he saw his destiny as amounting to small trips and a life without women. The picture business was over, and the profits counted: "Decade 1932–1942 illustrates the mystery of individual destiny: worked 123 weeks in pictures, making about $55,000 to $60,000 with interest."[24]

All in all, the 1930s were good years for him and assured him a comfortable income in his bleak years, the 1960s. A closer look at just what Fergusson accomplished during the 1930s as a writer in attempting to juggle book publication with the picture business entails looking at his three books of the period and his one extant film script. The three major writing projects, outside his movie jobs, to which he devoted most of his attention after *Rio Grande* were a serial novel, *Proud Rider*, which he worked on for about two years and which was published in *Blue Book Magazine* in 1935–36; the reissue of three of his novels as the *Followers of the Sun* trilogy in 1936; and his "view of the cosmos," *Modern Man*, also published in 1936. Had he not been involved in the picture business, perhaps he would have written more books, but had he not been in involved in Hollywood, he might well have been penniless by the time he was sixty. He knew that three books in ten years was not exactly prolific, but he eased his mind by realizing that at least his books were being written and published, and were being read by new and different publics. If nothing else, the picture business allowed him some normalcy and comfort of life, and growth in the process.

PROUD RIDER

Fergusson's next sustained serious writing after *Rio Grande* was a novella which he entitled *Proud Rider*. It evidences his grandfather Huning's and his own lifelong interest in horses and horsemen, combined with his researches into upper Rio Grande Valley history during this period of his career. He conceived of it as another attempt at serial writing. His arrangements with Knopf and Mencken for both the serial and book publication of *Rio Grande* worked out relatively well, given the economic conditions of the time. Serial writing, Fergusson also felt, would allow him to alternate assignments for film scripts, as they came in, with a sustained writing project which had some integrity and would still bring in some money. Horses had been an impor-

tant part of his life as a boy; and in most of his books up to that time
the horseman as a proud rider, a man who was transformed into more
of a man when mounted on horseback, had always figured into his
fictions.

He combined his similar fascination with Spanish aristocrats, the
"ricos," with his love of horses and with his reading and research on
New Mexico history and came up with the basic subject for *Proud
Rider*. Although he did not succeed in placing the novella with a
prestigious publisher, *Blue Book Magazine*, a publication devoted to
popular fiction, did run it—complete with romantic, stylized illustrations by Jeremy Cannon. Today it is virtually inaccessible. It is,
however, a significant work because it is representative of the influence of *Rio Grande*, which continued into the 1930s for Fergusson,
and because it anticipates—as a kind of first draft—Fergusson's last
published novel, *The Conquest of Don Pedro*.

Fergusson's 1933 and 1934 diaries document that he was trying
to work out a schedule that would allow him to make maximum creative use of his time and still realize maximum profits. His entry
under "work plan" in 1934 indicates how *Proud Rider* fit into such a
schedule:

Finish Proud Rider. . . . *Do no further work unless there is a strong
obsession [or] impulse. . . . Devote time to notes, outlines, reading, trips.
If I do write, spend about half time in trips. I have never spent a period of
full energy in reading and trips. . . .* Rio Grande *was in 1933. I could
create a serial early in 1935, a novel in 1936, and publish again in 1937.
There is little use of publishing a serious book oftener than every two years. I
could well afford to write a serial one year, a book the next. The serial
would generally be a light job—four months. I would thus alternate a light
year with a heavy one, and perhaps make some money. This program [is]
subject to many conditions: (1) It seems useless to resist an obsessive impulse
to write, regardless of [the] character of [the] book. (2) It remains to be
seen whether serial writing is a waste of time. Will P[roud] R[ider] sell?
(3) Movie writing might well make serial writing [worthwhile].*[25]

The serialization of *Rio Grande* had its obvious effect. But the *Mercury*
was not *Blue Book Magazine*. Even so, in keeping with his long-range

plan, Fergusson listed his work principles simply: "Take your time. Don't get tired." The "pressures" of the picture business and the physical and emotional conflicts of middle age did have the tendency to "run him a little ragged." He took his time with *Proud Rider*—the better part of two years—and published it in two installments in December and January of 1935 and 1936.[26]

The story concerns the antagonisms between the ricos of early-nineteenth-century New Mexico, their peon slaves, and the rancheros and Pueblo Indians of Rio Arriba. Specifically, the time is 1837, although it is never dated as such during the story—that is, around the time when Governor Albino Perez was killed in the rebellion of Pueblos and rancheros against the Mexican government. Thus, the setting and the overall atmosphere of the novella is the Rio Grande Valley from Taos down to El Paso during the period between 1821, when New Mexico became a political subdivision of the Mexican Republic, and 1846, when Colonel Stephen Watts Kearny occupied Las Vegas and took possession of the region. It is a time just prior to the 1870s and 1880s of *Conquest*.

It is an era and a culture which occupies more than one chapter in *Rio Grande*. Besides the antagonisms between the ricos, rancheros, and Pueblo Indians, *Proud Rider* dramatized the role of the bandidos in the whole upheaval; the conflicts between old and young generations, *viejos* and young wives; between old and new manifestations of primitives, savagery, and civilization wherein both forces take on ironic forms and definitions, based on various assumptions about pride, honor, and humanity.

The proud rider of the title is a nineteen-year-old Navajo named Juan who—first as a stable boy with a talent for training and riding horses, then as a runaway slave in union with a group of bandidos, and eventually as the proud protector of womanhood and justice—lays claim to his heritage as a man of principle, a self-respecting individual who marries Adelita Chacon Montoya. She is the fourteen-year-old second wife of the old rico, Don Pascual Jose Montoya y Penalosa, who as Juan's owner denies him his name and his dignity under punishment of the whip. Juan's earning of the title "proud rider" at each of the stages of his brief, rapid maturation is the major thrust of the narrative. Mutability again becomes a major theme—change within the individual, human maturation, reflected in the larger social and historical changes of revolution.

The scope of the story is both sweeping and speedy, given its length of fifty-one pages: a young man grows up overnight, a rico grows old and dies in battle, a very young girl blossoms into ravishing womanhood (as in *Conquest* and *In Those Days*), and we also see the ending of one frontier and the beginning of another one.

Some might view such a sweeping chronicle in so few pages as presenting an insurmountable problem of verisimilitude. This is one limitation of the work—ironically so when one remembers that Fergusson labored on it as long as he did. But it confirmed again that he could not escape the true chronicle form. Only in a longer, more leisurely work like *Kingdom* or *Conquest*—texts with sufficient scope to allow more time and space for fuller, more psychological, less superficial character development and more descriptive passages to establish setting—does Fergusson successfully reconcile the sweeping convergences of history and humanity. *Proud Rider*, however, does not invite or need intense critical analysis. It is entertainment—but it nevertheless shows that a popular Western can still achieve a degree of art and integrity as historical fiction. A case could be made for *Proud Rider* as a political allegory which, in the context of the American West, offers a kind of moral commentary on the forces of Fascism building in Europe toward World War II. But there is little indication in the diaries or the correspondence that such was Fergusson's intention. Such allegorical interpretations would add to the stature of the novella, but they remain oblique. Even so, *Proud Rider* no doubt made Fergusson all the prouder of his accomplishment in *Kingdom* and *Conquest*. And it, along with *Rio Grande*, helped lead the way to those successes.

Fergusson demonstrates that all of the racial, ethnic, and cultural frontiers merge in the larger frontier of the Southwest over a period of three centuries. He faced up as honestly as he could to the paradoxes of human nature, of savagery become civilization and civilization become savagery. Although *Proud Rider* is an obscure and admittedly minor popular literary effort, infused with a heavy dose of the conventions of the Western novel, it nevertheless occupies an important moment in Fergusson's middle years and the decade of the 1930s as history moved toward the cataclysm of another world war and is an instance of a novella bridging his early and later years as a lone rider become proud writer.

FOLLOWER OF THE SUN

Fergusson's *Followers of the Sun: A Trilogy of the Santa Fe Trail*, along with *Proud Rider*, appeared in 1936. In 1942 Grosset and Dunlap reissued the trilogy under the title *The Santa Fe Omnibus*. As the titles and subtitles of these various editions seek to emphasize, Fergusson's three early novels—*Conquerors* (1921), *Wolf Song* (1927), and *In Those Days* (1929)—are joined together by a common theme, westering to Santa Fe along the Santa Fe Trail. The 1942 edition is a significant reissue for Fergusson and emphasizes in the most explicit ways that the era associated with the end of the frontier, and the changes which came to Santa Fe and the upper Rio Grande regions as a result of the Santa Fe Trail's hastening the means and the end of the frontier through commerce and settlement, remained Fergusson's grand theme.

The three novels in *Followers of the Sun* make a belatedly obvious collection of books: they are all in the same realistic/chronicle vein and all deal with various aspects of the frontier as encountered by characters who are imaginative extensions of Fergusson's grandfather Huning or his father, H. B. Fergusson, or Fergusson himself. The three books taken as a trilogy, just like the characters they portray, are in a sense both a substitution for and a reiteration of what was much easier to write a decade or more earlier. His attention in the mid-1930s was splitting into separate but still related compartments of historical fiction and fictionalized history, with history remaining the common mode but a mode which also split off into philosophy in the guise of a personal inquiry about the why and the wherefore of "modern man," and later of "people and power."

In his introduction to the *Omnibus* edition Fergusson states that he believes the trilogy has more significance than any of the novels if taken separately—a sentiment which might also apply to the total body of his work. That he thought of his trilogy as a continuing history of the frontier is explicitly stated in such commentary: "They all deal with the same region and the same impulse. Taken together, they tell the story of a great migration from the time when hunters invaded a wilderness until the frontier had been pushed into the ocean and the westward flow of human energy had come nearly to a stop. They also cover almost a hundred years in the history of the racial and cultural border where the Spanish-American of the South meets the northern Anglo-American in the contact that is still a vital thing."[27]

Fergusson's introduction is actually another retrospective look at the first half of his writing career. All of the introductions and retrospectives of this period are interesting for what they reveal about Fergusson's writing and his attitude toward it, but the fascinating thing about this particular introductory essay, with its disarmingly simple title, is that it traces Fergusson's own development in relation to the ending of the frontier and describes how that particular "energy" shaped his perspectives as a novelist and a regional historian.

In identifying his two great novelistic themes as the western movement and racial and cultural contact, Fergusson is careful to insist that he does not presume to be definitive on either subject. His use of the two themes is intended mainly to provide the dramatic conflict of his novels, "to reduce themes of social significance to terms of individual destiny and so to give them life" (p. vi). His qualifications to do so he identifies once again under the heading of native son. The genesis of the three novels he equates with growing up in the shadow of "the end of the pioneer period" as a youth of action—as a rider of horses rather than as a reader or as a writer of ideas: "Most of my life has been spent in the Southwest, where I was born in 1890— the year that historians have chosen as the one that marked the end of the pioneering period. What is probably more important to the genesis of these stories, much of my youth until the age of twenty was devoted to a kind of play pioneering in an environment which was only a few years removed from the frontier condition" (p. vi).

Here Fergusson comes as close as anywhere in his writings to explicitly acknowledging Turner and his frontier thesis. His identification of himself as a "play pioneer" applies not just to his childhood but to his novels and histories as well, for that is his dominant persona, a voice which pervades virtually everything he wrote and, by implication, how he "saw" life. In elaboration of this point, he says further that although he played at pioneering, he knew something of its reality as a youth and that even in middle age he still considers himself a frontiersman and still maintains something of the romanticism associated with that state, although tinged in advancing years with a degree of skepticism: "A true pioneer I never was, but I believe I inherited and developed the pioneer psychosis in an acute form. The naive romanticism of the pioneer, his hatred of physical restraint, his impulse of social avoidance, his aversion to routine, and his love of action and excitement all were in me. In fact, they are in me still, but I have come to regard them with some detachment and a growing skepticism as to their social value" (p. vii).

That this kind of skepticism approximates the same tone and includes some of the same vocabulary as *Modern Man* (1936) and *People and Power* (1947) is no coincidence. Fergusson wrote this particular introduction almost at the same time he was writing his "cosmic" inquiry. His temperament was such that he never had a particularly easy or prolonged happy time at any phase of his life, unless it was his youth. But he perceived his middle and old age as even more of an ordeal to persevere through than perhaps they really were. Admittedly, his later years were physically and not just emotionally and psychologically painful because of arthritis. Yet even in the relatively happy 1930s, when the movies were beginning to pay off and he was able to squeeze out another three books, the skepticism almost turned to despair. This is seen in his diaries as well as in his other autobiographical novel of the period, *Riley*, the only one of his fictions to deal explicitly with the contemplation of suicide. Like his hero, Morgan Riley, and Riley's friend, Sally Conner, Fergusson decided to hold on. Things did get better, at least artistically, before they got worse.

In his 1942 diary Fergusson confessed to himself, "I have a temperamental need to see the worst."[28] Few diary entries allude to the events of World War II, and the ones that do refuse to believe that

Hitler will triumph. But Fergusson's own notes are couched in a vocabulary which reflects the greater world conflict and tragic consequences which faced America and the world. The war, middle age, a diffusion of energy into and then away from scriptwriting for films while still trying to write the kind of books represented by *Followers of the Sun*—all of these things are sensed in the 1941 and 1942 diaries as Fergusson tried to hold on.

Under a diary heading "Facts to Face at 51," Fergusson predicted that his working power would decline steadily for the next ten years, that it would be harder to write and to do the things he liked, and harder to finish anything he did start. He vowed to work for the sake of working and, if nothing else, to put into order his accumulation of notes. He was certain that the war would force all of his books out of print, that publication of two or three might retard the process, but that "none of my work has enough hold on the market to survive war and subsequent depression."[29] He was confident that his work had some future use but felt that he would never know about it.

By the end of 1942 he faced what seemed to be defeat, something close to the "end," insofar as all of his books were out of print except *Rio Grande*. He faced considerable difficulty in publishing and felt he might not be able ever to publish again. There was the ever-present money trouble even in the face of what the picture business brought him. He attributed what he considered his dire straits to the plight of all writers after the age of fifty: "Defeat or a feeling of defeat . . . , this is the normal fate of a writer after fifty. It is the final ordeal. It is not necessarily more than the ordeal of youth. . . . The important thing is to see it for what it is. Life is always ordeal and the measure of its value is the way it is endured."[30] Given such a mood, only *Home in the West* and *People and Power* saw publication in the 1940s.

Skepticism balanced with belief, despair mixed with hope—such ambivalence is also found in Fergusson's own changed and changing attitudes toward the past. He states it simply but eloquently in the trilogy introduction: "I began by worshipping the past. I thought of it as that home of my soul. It seemed to me that, like Minniver Cheevey, I had been born too late. Now the past interests me chiefly for the light it sheds on the present. I began by looking backward with longing.

Now I look forward with hope. I began as a romantic, in the simplest sense of the word—as one who longed for an escape and believed that escape is possible. I have become a realist, at least in thought and intention" (pp. vii–viii).

In Fergusson's view, as reflected in this period of taking stock, the past is always two things: an ideal and thus a kind of dream, but also a reality and thus something which actually happened. And these two aspects of the past are always in conflict as the need for myth-making and the need to know. The longer an individual thinks about the past, the more ideal it becomes in its remembering.

In the twentieth century and particularly at the time of Fergusson's middle age, he believed Americans longed for the "real" in reaction to idealized recreations of the past. The problem, he knew, is that "reality" is forever elusive—a theme he tries to work through in *Hot Saturday* and in *Riley* in particular. Thus, the new need for reality, the new history, must be tempered by the knowledge that history and its related component, biography, carry with them the inbuilt fictions of their creators: "The new history and biography are made in the images of their creators hardly less than the old. . . . This endless retelling of our story is supremely necessary, but it is also necessary to remember that the past remains a myth, as surely as it is anything more than a lifeless pile of facts. The debunkers in due course will be debunked, the 'truth' will be endlessly rediscovered and then found false again" (p. ix). Fergusson tried to place each of his *Followers of the Sun* novels into their respective functions relative to such a context of historical and autobiographical assertions.

Wolf Song, the first in the chronological sequence, represents, in Fergusson's motive and mind, the past as romantic impulse, in the form of a typical Western romance, with "pioneer melodrama" taken deliberately as the pattern because that very pioneer melodrama was the true stuff of pioneering in its beginning. Westerns as a literary form do not suffer because they are melodramatic, he says; rather they are an "infantile" literary form because their heroes and heroines are lifeless. Even if the stories are taken from life, the characters are taken from the chivalric and genteel literary past, as represented by Sir Walter Scott and James Fenimore Cooper. In *Wolf Song* he tried to unite melodrama with realism, refusing to sacrifice one element because of the other. *In Those Days* represents Fergusson's attempt to portray the forces of "spectacular and unprecedented change" over a fifty-year period. In this instance the hero, Robert Jayson, is more the antihero than the hero, something of a pawn in the sweep of events around him, a man shaped by the events in his lifetime and the place in which he finds himself—or so explains Fergusson. Jayson's fictional life is admittedly patterned on the real life of Fergusson's grandfather Huning and his experiences as a trader on the Santa Fe Trail. *Blood of the Conquerors*, Fergusson says, deals neither with the times he had dreamed about or read about, but the times in which he himself had lived. It is the story of Albuquerque and his boyhood there.

Taken all in all, there is more romanticism, more heroism, and more mythologizing of the West, westering, and westerners in *Followers of the Sun* than Fergusson would have it in his retrospective introduction. He was proud of all three novels—at the time he wrote them and nearly two decades after he wrote them, as represented by his essay and explanations. It is not a boastful kind of pride. Rather, it is the pride of a writer who wrote what he had to write out of an inner necessity, and wrote in the most honest way he could as a lifelong imagining and real follower of the sun. If life was always an ordeal for him, and the measure of its value the way in which it is endured, writing was, all along, initially and after the fact, his way of holding on.

OUT OF VOGUE

Modern Man represents a similar kind of impulse to the impulse behind the novels in *Followers of the Sun;* that is, it was written from an inner necessity and in the belief that it was worthwhile even in the face of unlikely or at least difficult publication. And yet the impulse has its difference in that it represents what Fergusson regarded as "systematic" thinking, which, although it "[took] the bloom off some intuitional fruits," nevertheless made him think through some of his own positions—a process he found at once challenging and painful, but refreshing.[31] In addition to marking at least a temporary departure from "intuitional fruits," *Modern Man* also marked an end of an era, insofar as it was Fergusson's last book published by Knopf.

Mencken left his position as editor of the *Mercury* in 1933 but still retained his influence with Knopf in lining up manuscripts for publication. Fergusson wrote to Mencken during 1933, 1934, and 1935 informing him about *Modern Man* and soliciting his help in recommending publication to Knopf. In August 1934, Fergusson wrote to Mencken asking permission to quote a sentence from Mencken's "Treatise on Right and Wrong" and notifying him that he had completed the first draft, which, Fergusson said, "runs to nearly 90,000 words and represents the most painful and sustained explosion of literary energy which I have so far suffered. I hardly know what to make of it. It seems to prove either that I am nutty or that everyone else is, and I anticipate that weight of opinion will favor the former view."[32]

Mencken responded by giving his consent to quote and offering encouragement. In September Fergusson wrote an unusually long letter to Mencken about the project, his energy, and his expectations and apprehensions. *Modern Man* was creating quite an upheaval in Fergusson's intellectual life, a process he not altogether humorously refers to as a "thinking spasm": "If Alfred [Knopf] finds the book too bewildering, I may suggest that he send it to you as a referee. I would ordinarily hesitate to impose upon your time in this way, but since you are probably going to take a look at it sooner or later anyway, I assume you would not mind seeing it in Mss."[33]

Mencken, in turn, responded by saying he would be more than willing to read the manuscript and offer suggestions as usual. Fergusson replied on October 1, 1934, informing Mencken that the manuscript would be submitted to Knopf in the middle of November. By January 6, 1935, Mencken had finished reading it and told Fergusson that he liked it. Fergusson was grateful and answered in these words: "I have no illusion that I have solved any fundamental problem, or that any is soluble. I tried only to state an attitude that seems workable to me, and so must have some pragmatic validity. My chief doubt was whether I had made it comprehensible and plausible.[34]

As discussed in an earlier chapter, *Modern Man* did have its support—from Mencken, from the Guggenheim Foundation, and from Knopf, who decided to publish it fully aware that it was not going to be a best seller, or, as Fergusson realized, "not exactly a red hot commercial asset under present conditions." Horgan was impressed with the book and wrote a nine-page critique of it which he decided not to publish but sent to Fergusson in January 1937. Some months earlier, shortly after publication, Fergusson had written to Horgan that the New York "chatter" about *Modern Man* was "more or less mangled," and that "the book is nothing so stupid as a study of freewill and predestination in abstract terms. It is an attempt to do a portrait of modern western man from the anthropological viewpoint."[35] But not everyone shared Horgan's and Mencken's enthusiasm for the book. Reviews were decidedly mixed, a fact which prompted Fergusson to observe, "one finally comes to understand that all opinion is prejudice and that the praise he gets, no less than the blame, sheds more light on the source than on the subject."[36]

In general, Fergusson's apprehensions proved right. Knopf hesitated before publishing it, not confident that it would even begin to break even—a lack of confidence which, complicated by other factors, caused Fergusson to look for another publisher. Audiences were not as interested in such a work of systematic thinking as they were in novels or in the movies for which Fergusson was turning out treatments and screenplays. He tried to adjust to the fate of being a writer who never really quite caught on in the public's taste. Even his writings which he hoped would prove "popular"—his serial, *Proud Rider;* his trilogy, *Followers of the Sun;* his history, *Rio Grande*—just did not sell in great numbers. Whether as a popular novelist or as a more systematic philosopher, Fergusson began to solidify his ever-present image of himself as an outsider, out of step with his times, "out of vogue." His diaries reflect his disappointment—and yet his seemingly rationalized pride—that he was what he was and that disappointment went with the territory. At one point some years later, he looked at the sales totals of his books and formed some conclusions:

[In] 1936, '37, '38 I published two new books and three reprints. I got much publicity. Much of it favorable. All this did not stimulate the role

of sold books or cause any continuity. . . . [For example], Riley, '37 had little or any effect on [the] sale of F[ollowers of the] S[un], *'36; or* R[io] G[rande], *1933. On the other hand, sale of both books increased a little, 1941, '42, '43, despite I published nothing. . . . Because of [the] sale of books in general some things are evident: Only vogue will sell books. Neither publicity or advertising will sell books. . . . Vogue is unaccountable. . . . It probably grows by talk. . . . A writer may have vogue years after he is dead. . . . A book that had no vogue may nevertheless have some life—sell a few copies in libraries. This is definitely true of* Rio Grande. *. . . There is such a thing as reputation without vogue but it is never profitable.*[37]

Amidst his disappointments, he nevertheless had the right intuition about his future reputation.

THE "GOOD" LIFE REMEMBERED

Following the nonfiction departures of *Rio Grande* and *Modern Man* and the serialized *Proud Rider*, Fergusson returned again in the latter 1930s to fiction with *The Life of Riley* (1937). Not surprisingly, it was another novel about the modern West, more in the vein of *Conquerors* and of *McGarnigal*. The appearance of the trilogy and of *Modern Man* no doubt influenced the conception and execution of *Riley;* it is a look at "modern man" in the West—a man like Ramon Delcasar who, in *Conquerors*, struggles with the forces of progress and primitivism. But this "typical" autobiographical novel contains some old ingredients with a new twist, and one new fictionalized but not autobiographical ingredient: suicide. Passion, love and hate, battles of will, eroticism, the lure of solitude and communion with nature, the march of change and modernity, small-town prejudice and small-mindedness, wanderlust—all of these themes appear again in *Riley*, but with a noticeable difference.[38]

That difference seems attributable to Fergusson's at times despairing state of mind in middle age. Fergusson is consistently nostalgic to one degree or another in all phases of his writing, but here the nostalgia passes into despair—and then beyond that to resignation. None of Fergusson's novelistic analogs ever get so low as to consider killing themselves. Fergusson's father committed suicide. Morgan Riley comes close to doing it. So does starlit Sally Conner. But the possibility of suicide and the tone of depression is eventually abandoned for a more sanguine ending. It is not an ending of unqualified optimism; rather, it is one of resignation to individual destiny and temperament in the face of mutability. Perhaps his own father's suicide gave Fergusson the resolve to conquer any death wish which might have laid siege to him.

There is much to say about *Riley* in the context of Fergusson's other writing. He always has a difficult time unifying the numerous aspects of a story—the particulars with each other and with more universal implications. In *Riley* that difficulty appears again, perhaps reflecting a new doubt related to what he regarded as his waning powers as a writer. Although Fergusson always displays a tendency to overextended digression in his plotting, he usually succeeds at integrating his many subplots, minor characters, and disparate settings. In *Riley*, however, he fails to truly unify all of the elements he attempts to develop. He writes here one of his least controlled chronicle novels, trying to make of *Riley* both a journalistic novel like *Capitol Hill* and a "day-in-the-life" concentration of story like *Hot Saturday*. The two modes tend to work against each other. The failure is, paradoxically, a fortunate one. If the digressions and interpolated stories reach a fragmentary extreme here, they are all the more successfully realized in what would be his next novel, *Grant of Kingdom* (1950).

Even so, *Riley* is an important novel in several respects: it incorporates some of Fergusson's new Far West experiences and his ability to grow as a man and an author even in the face of the disillusionments of middle age and of what he feared might be his defeat as a writer; he assimilates new themes with old ones around the central theme of frontier's end; and he dramatizes the dreams and disappointments of Hollywood.

In overall structure, *Riley* may be read as a series of extended character sketches. The central character is, as the title indicates, Riley—Morgan Riley. Still relying on picaresque conventions, Fergusson follows Riley on his journey of life: his parents are introduced;

he is born; he grows up, falls in love, marries, separates, goes into business, fights in World War I, falls in love again and again and again, nearly loses his business, thinks of suicide, then rallies and reunites with his former wife.

Fergusson's writing and rewriting of his own life and loves is apparent throughout. Through its rise, fall, and rise, the life of Riley/Fergusson crosses the lives of many other individuals, each of whom has a life story to tell. And Fergusson as author has a hard time resisting writing what amounts to a short story about each of Riley's relatives, friends, lovers, and acquaintances. Certainly Riley lives a full and zestful and, for a time, happy life. In this respect he is like Franz Huning and his counterpart Robert Jayson; and he is like most of Fergusson's other fictional characters, including Jean Ballard and James Lane Morgan (a nineteenth-century version of Morgan Riley) recreated in *Kingdom,* and like Leo Mendes in Fergusson's last published novel, *Conquest.* In effect, "the life of Riley," complete with the ironies incorporated in the novel, is one more rendition of "the life of Harvey."

The table of contents of *Riley,* in the elaborately overstated tradition of picaresque novels like *Joseph Andrews,* underscores the spirit of wanderlust which informs the patterning of the novel. There is some degree of irony in this insofar as the plot is not a comic plot. The novel ends happily, taken all in all. But whatever happiness exists is anything but complete. Insofar as the title connotes a life of ease and comfort, that lifestyle continues only up to a point—and that point is adulthood and approaching middle age. Life after the glory of college athletics and trench combat during the war has much sobering disappointment for Riley. This is made all the more apparent by the similar rise and fall, innocence and experience of the novel's life stories, stories which collectively reinforce the irony of the title as it affects Riley's happiness. Not only the title but also the older narrative tradition of the intrusive narrator referring repeatedly to Riley as "our hero" take on a decidedly ironic, at times satiric, cast as Fergusson uses it. If the good life is remembered, it is not without regret—for what it was, was not, and for its passing.

Characteristic to form, Fergusson begins *Riley* in the days of the frontier. This time it is the 1880s, just as the railroad arrives in a southwestern town which, although not named, is again recognizable as Albuquerque, the prototypic frontier / modern town in Fergusson's viewpoint. In individual terms, it is with a look into the life of Morgan Riley's father, James Warden Riley, that Fergusson starts his story. The father is Irish and, as just plain "Jim," makes a name for himself as a friendly, competent bartender who before long owns his own saloon. The surname, the outgoing nature, and the saloon become part of the father's legacy to the son. The son, nicknamed "Lucky," is born into a new era of promise at the turn of the century, a "modern man," appearing at a time after the boom-town era of his father and of the town, a time of the train and the automobile rather than the horse and buggy.

The father, Jim Riley, faces the violence and lawless enthusiasm of the wide-open days and soon becomes a walking legend for his strength, the power of his hands to keep the peace, and his reluctance to carry or even keep a gun. The characters which cross Jim Riley's life, such as the Sicilian Pietro De Angelis, are again fictional counterparts of individuals and types which Fergusson himself knew when he was growing up in Albuquerque and which he profiles not only in *Rio Grande* but also in *Home in the West* (1944), Fergusson's next book after *Riley*.

Fergusson works in his own genealogical ties with the Old South in the characterization of Mary Chase Morgan, a woman who emigrates to the Southwest, where she meets Jim Riley and marries him. Mary Chase Morgan (whose name is similar to that of Fergusson's mother, Clara Mary Huning) is a schoolteacher from Mobile, Alabama, who finds the frontier of New Mexico at first too harsh for her refined sensibilities. Here, Fergusson combines his own family myth with the stereotypical Western-novel convention of schoolmarm meeting virile westerner and attempting to domesticate him.

The class-region conflict thus established carries on through the novel. In the case of Morgan Riley, the class issue is complicated by race, for Morgan is (again in keeping with the racial patterns of Fergusson's other fiction) attracted to sensuous Mexican-American women as well as to refined, although sometimes wild and willing,

Anglo women. Fergusson's formula in this respect is elemental and erotic: men need women and are attracted by "the bond of nascent desire that stops at no boundaries and ignores all differences, that works against a thousand perils to make all men one kind" (*Riley,* p. 19).

Typical of another pattern which Fergusson uses without fail in his fiction is the scene of courtship by either buggy or automobile—horse or horsepower. Fergusson's love of horses turns Jim Riley into another "proud rider" figure, like Huning, Jayson, and the supreme horseman, Juan. The importance of the car in Fergusson's fiction reaches its greatest emphasis in *Hot Saturday;* however, the role of the automobile and its seclusion and rapid mobility down the streets of town, out to the mountains or mesa, is again used throughout *Riley* in counterpoint with Jim and Mary's courtship by buggy. While there is nothing particularly profound about the car as character in Fergusson's fiction, it is an emblem of modernism and mechanism. In his life, diaries, and writings, he views the car as a major means of change in social history, allowing a wider touring of the West, sexual seclusion, and relative anonymity. Many of Fergusson's diary entries during the twenties record his automobile trips in and around northern New Mexico; in the 1930s and later, his diaries record his many automobile trips in the Far West. The car was more than an incidental machine; it was a way of life and a welcome means of the mobility he loved.

To anyone who reads Fergusson's books in sequence, *Riley* does not begin on a fresh note. It is formulaic to the point of cliché. At times it is simply boring as Fergusson labors futilely to find a fresh form for this themes and structures. In this sense the opening pages read not like Dreiser's *Carrie,* but like a more sexually explicit Western version of Howells' *Lapham.* Jim Riley in more ways than one—his hands, his love of his horses, his awkward manliness and ambition—seems like another Silas, not as paint manufacturer but as western businessman and saloon keeper. Of course, Fergusson's love scenes are far from Howellsian. The original eroticism of Fergusson's descriptions of Morgan Riley's parents merely sets the stage for a long series of erotic, oftentimes idiomatically profane love scenes, as Morgan moves through life involved with one woman after another, very much like Ralph Dolan in *Capitol Hill*. James Hart, in an early review, observed, "Each chapter introduces a new . . . [woman] to satisfy his urge, and the succession of blondes, brunettes, and redheads becomes monotonous."[39]

In keeping with his conviction that there are two kinds of women, or two sides to all women—saint and sinner—Mary Riley is the tenderest of mothers and conditions her son's attitude to woman as eternal mother. Moreover, this offers credence to viewing her as a composite character, part Rebecca McCann, part Clara Mary Huning. In the romance of the father and the mother is found the future romances of the son as the eternal drama of human sexuality, and Freud's "family romance" plays itself out generation after generation. Mother and son fix upon a special place on the mesa, and throughout Riley's life it serves as a shrine to womanhood and the life force.

Mary Riley dies an early death and leaves her son to grow up in the freedom of Jim Riley's well-intended neglect. But she is replaced by all the women Morgan Riley loves during the course of his life. Fergusson's account of his own mother and the freedom she gave him to traipse over Huning's marshlands, hunting, and to explore the river, swim in its muddy currents, and roam through the dense cottonwood forests of its banks—all of this as told in *Home in the West* is previewed in *Riley*. Freudian theories aside, Fergusson's description of Jim and Mary Riley's marriage and their son's relationship to it seems like Fergusson's own projection into fiction of what marriage might be under the right circumstances and with the right combination of personalities. It reaches toward a greater degree of marital satisfaction and success than marriage in *Women and Wives* or the real-life marriage of Fergusson and Rebecca McCann. Jim and Mary's marriage anticipates the more accepting model of individual will working freely within these structures of marriage which is found both in *Kingdom* and *Conquest*. Perhaps it is the tuberculosis that is killing Mary which determines her understanding and love for her husband, and perhaps it is his reciprocal recognition of his wife's disease and dying which endears her to him. Perhaps Mary's tuberculosis is Rebecca's pneumonia, and another attempted purging of Fergusson's guilt. Amidst the melodrama of the novel's beginning and its ending is evidenced the possible arrangement which Fergusson longed for in two marriages and in countless relationships with women and seemingly found most completely in his old age and his companionship with Quail Hawkins. It is within this satisfied state that Morgan Riley's parents' marriage exists after his mother's illness. Her approaching death quickens her love for her son, the land she once despised, and her ungainly husband, who in all his awkward manliness treasures her above all else.

If such a marriage seems to favor the husband, it is well to observe that *Riley*, like Fergusson's other novels, strives to incorporate his feminist perspectives, such as they were. Similarly, although he tries to break out of strictly ethnocentric attitudes about Mexican-American women in particular, he never quite succeeds by today's standards. In this respect he remains captive to the prevailing values of the 1930s and earlier.[40]

Most of the chapters dealing with Morgan Riley's boyhood and early manhood read like *Home in the West*. It is easy to see how these two volumes appeared in sequence, though separated by seven years. Both *Riley* and *Home* originate in Fergusson's middle-age nostalgia for his youth as a free-spirited "proud rider." Riley takes on his nickname of Lucky, and his carefree days, without any restrictions imposed on him by his father, are the stuff of idealized boyhood dreams. He is a born leader; he is at home along the river and on the mesas; and he is precocious in sex, in his imaginings and in his experiments. The first girl to interest him, although she remains inaccessible to him for a time because she is a local aristocrat, is Anne Bledsoe, the daughter of a banker. Lillian Kringle, the "lower-class" daughter of a German immigrant, temporarily replaces Anne as the object of his affection. Although she is relatively more available than Anne, she is nevertheless still too well-mothered, and Riley turns his attentions next to Consuelo Alcatraz. She is older than Riley and initiates him into the mysteries of sexual intercourse one day in a weed patch. When Consuelo moves away, Lillian replaces her as Riley's girl.

Arcing back to the episodic pattern of plotting which he used in *Capitol Hill*, Fergusson pursues Riley's love exploits with Anne and

Lillian for the central portion of the book and digresses into interpolated stories about his various other loves. If Consuelo is the incidental love of Riley's adolescent years, then Sally Conner, a failed Hollywood actress, and Shirley Skeen, a runaway ranch girl, represent the incidental loves of Riley's later adulthood in the last third of the novel. Consuelo drops out of the novel completely (only to partially reappear as Consuelo Coronel in *Kingdom*), and Sally and Shirley, passionate loves for a time, remain Riley's good friends.

Anne and Riley carry on an intense and sincere love affair after she completes her schooling in California and returns to her hometown for a year or so, and before she heads east for a more exciting, fulfilling life. In this respect she is very much like Catherine Larue in *Women and Wives*. When Anne returns from California, she finds that Riley is a star football player, captain of the local university team, and one of the town's best tennis players. He has worked one summer for the forest service (yet another example of the impact Fergusson's forest service experience had on him and how it recurs in his fiction). Anne likes to drive—and so does Riley—so they travel back and forth between the roadhouse in the canyon and Riley's special hilltop spot on the mesa overlooking the river and the town. They have their childhood and high school memories in common as well as a strong physical attraction for each other. Anne's schoolgirl dreams of a lover and her theory that "virginity was ridiculous and marriage was something you could take or leave" (p. 84) are soon verified in her affair with Riley. On the hilltop, in the car, she gives herself to him. Fergusson was forty-seven when *Riley* was published. All his talk in his diaries of celibacy and an old age without women began and ended there. Whatever the cause, whether Fergusson's nostalgia for youth, sublimation, or zest for life, Riley's libido is stronger and more explicitly dramatized than that of his kindred characters—the virile Fergusson hero and male ideal.

Fergusson's treatment of war in *Riley* is significant in that it is one of the few places in his fiction where he either comments on or dramatizes death. In terms of his biography it is also revealing because Riley's combat experiences are related to news of the death of Riley's father. Fergusson did not attend the funeral of his own father and wrote nothing about it in his diaries. But in *Riley,* some of Fergusson's feelings and associations seem to come out, distanced and mitigated by passing decades and by middle age. When the United States enters World War I, Riley, being of the right age for service, puts thoughts of football and love aside and joins the fray. He gets more than he bargained for, as is so often the case in his idealized projection of the good life. In the gruesomeness of the death which surrounds him, with his feet deep in mud and a .45 automatic beside him to shoot rats rather than Germans, Riley experiences a flood of memories about his boyhood and about his father and mother. It is not sorrow but these memories which color his reaction to hearing about his father's death. (Riley's father, unlike Fergusson's, dies peacefully in his sleep. In his fiction, at least, Fergusson attempted to undo the anguish of the suicide which ended H. B. Fergusson's life.)

That frontier, the old times of his father, and Riley's own youth end in that war scene and memory of his father's death. He returns to his hometown a changed man. He is happy for a time, but in a more sobering way. Innocence has left him and the "shades of the prison house" start to descend up to the point of almost committing suicide. Thus in the last few chapters of the novel, the peaceful death of Riley's father is seemingly influenced by the suicide of Fergusson's own father. That event from his own life he then projects onto the character of Riley. Ironically, it might have been his resolve not to be like his father, to be his own kind of rebel's son, that prevented Fergusson from committing suicide himself. There is no record that Fergusson contemplated suicide. There are notes of depression in the diaries he wrote in middle age and certainly those written in old age, when ailments of various kinds, especially arthritis, assailed him; but he always resolved to go forward. There is evidence that although he did tend to see the worst of things, he never allowed his slumps of despondency to get the best of him. In his love of life and pride in his writing Fergusson, like his fictional counterpart, Riley, continued to face the future and affirm it just as he had the past.

When Riley returns home after the war he finds that the cigar store and the pool room of the Lucky Spot are about all that is left from his father's estate. Like Riley, Fergusson's inheritance was much less than it might one day have been before his father's dreary end. Riley enters a business similar to his father's and marries his high school girlfriend, Lillian Kriegel; he hunts more than he ever did before; he takes short trips. Riley's interest is almost entirely in the past, in his carefree youthful days. The future does not really interest him. He is not a reflective man and lives mainly for physical pleasures. He especially likes to hunt. While he views the struggles for money and social position and "sexual satisfaction" that make up the activity of the town as somehow trivial in comparison to the larger struggles of the war, he is glad to be home. Fergusson makes the point that, above all, Riley is a westerner, held heart and soul by the land.

For Riley, as for Fergusson, the country does not really change. Riley knows he would never be truly happy anyplace else. Even Anne Bledsoe, who has made a way for herself in New York during the war years, must also return to the hometown, if only for a vacation. Anne is much the fictional counterpart of Rebecca McCann. Like Rebecca, she works in New York in the fashion department of a woman's magazine, paints and hopes to exhibit.

While Anne is moving and living, Riley faces a kind of dead-end existence in a small town which suffers from postwar depression, with one business after another facing bankruptcy. If the land, the country itself, has not changed, the opportunities afforded by business in the town have changed. The boom-town days when a fortune could be turned in real estate are over. Whereas Jim Riley made three times his money buying and selling land, Morgan Riley cannot. And, by implication, whereas Franz Huning had bought and sold much of old and new Albuquerque, Fergusson faced tight times as a writer, never to earn what he might have had he finished law school and returned home to practice law with his father. This possibility is reflected in Fergusson's descriptions of the conditions and related options for the future which face Morgan Riley after the war, including a scheme to corner the soft-drink business proposed by Riley's old schoolfellow Gilbert Hill. While Riley's reason urges him to accept the proposal his instinct says no.

If hunting is an inevitable part of Riley's life, so are women. And while he can say no to Gilbert Hill's get-rich-quick proposal, he cannot say no to the attraction he feels for Lillian Kriegel when he sees a chance to meet her on the street. Lillian's family has moved to El Paso and wants her to come there also. Lillian eventually moves to El Paso, back to her family, after a brief period of happy marriage to Riley and then separation because of his infidelity. Relatively few scenes in the novel take place to the south, but Fergusson does provide Riley with a place to head when troubles close in on him. He heads for that almost mythical escape—the border. Part of his luck is that Lillian is in El Paso, still loves him, has forgiven him his transgressions, and helps him find his way back to his old life, including marriage to her. But Riley must work himself out of numerous involvements with other women before he can resign himself to a presumably long and merely tolerable life with Lillian. It is part of Riley's nature not to be able to focus his attentions on one woman—except for Anne. And he realizes that even in his marrying Lillian, Anne will always be present as a third, ghostly presence.

Fergusson draws on some of his Hollywood impressions at this point in the novel. During Riley's separation from Lillian, the first woman he becomes involved with is Mrs. Sylvia Carlson, formerly Sally Conner, another old acquaintance from Riley's youth and school days. Mrs. Carlson opens a new beauty shop across from Riley's cigar store and poolroom, the Lucky Spot, and brings much-needed new business. An extra attraction for Riley is all the women who enter the shop. But it is Mrs. Carlson who catches his attention most of all.

After Riley recognizes Mrs. Carlson as his high-school classmate Sally Conner, he also learns just how she came to have her "battle-scarred" look. It is a result of life in Hollywood, where she went to make it big and failed. Her "biography," as Fergusson tells it, is one of the most interesting in the novel, if for no other reason than what it tells us of the material Fergusson found for his fiction during the decade he spent off and on as a scriptwriter. It is one of the few times Fergusson chooses to write about Hollywood. While his time in Washington and in New York provided the material for two full novels in the 1920s, his time in Los Angeles and Hollywood is almost missing from his fiction. He might have written an entire novel about Sally Conner, or someone like her and the people she meets. He might have written about some extension of himself as a scriptwriter, or about a director or producer or production assistant or some "type" from the film industry. But the interpolated story about Sally Conner in *Riley* is all that resulted, in fiction, from his Hollywood era. Even a screenplay like "Stand Up and Fight" confirms that Fergusson's imagination was most stimulated by his own past in New Mexico and by the lives of his family and the accounts of their frontiers.

Sally's Hollywood story is revealing too in that it is actually another pioneer story, for it begins in the days of silent films. And its dynamism is that of myth demythologized, for Sally's grand and romantic hopes are soon dashed by the stark and disappointing realities of the place. Thus, the progression of things parallels Riley's own life—from potential and expectation to disappointment, prolonged but final. Sally and Riley, like their creator, endure life's ordeal because they choose to affirm life rather than deny it.

Fergusson's account of Sally's and Riley's lovemaking is the most explicit in the novel and in any of his other published novels. The erotic descriptions Fergusson attempts in *Riley* seem self-consciously daring for their time, but restrained in comparison with the kind of eroticism he wanted to write, as represented by *The Land of Lonely Women*. All in all, however, Fergusson's contribution to eroticism in the literature of the 1930s represents a strike against Puritanism in Mencken's sense of the word.

When Sally and Riley have intercourse with each other, they do so out of love as well as lust, and Fergusson communicates their mutual human sensibility and need of the "sexual impulse." As a novelist Fergusson felt his own great need to portray sexuality as one of the most important motives of human life. Certainly his own need for women was equivalent to Riley's, and essential to his will to live and work. If eroticism placed him outside the accepted literary conventions of some audiences, he perhaps cared, but he could not deny its honest portrayal. His own conception of what he was about as a novelist and as a man ruled his aesthetic. Whether a partial sublimation or as a result of his own remaining but tapering lust for life, Fergusson's descriptions of Riley and Sally's union has its own kind of restraint and even beauty in the context of the novel.

In the process of telling the stories of Clarence Weston, Shirley Skeen, and Breezy Holt, Fergusson works in more of his Hollywood impressions combined with the flavor and many of the conventions of Western romance and the Western films of the Tom Mix–Hoot Gibson era. Although it might stretch credibility to find so many locals heading west to become film actors, Breezy Holt, like Sally Conner, has done just that. And like Sally, although he enjoyed a limited success in his film career, he is now back home in Matlock, a typical west Texas, southeast New Mexico plains town, trying to bum a meal from his friend Ed Calloway and winding up robbing a bank out of desperation (and, seemingly, for the sake of Western romance).

Ed, Breezy, and Buck Shultz (another hometown boy who has returned from his adventures in distant points, not as an actor or movie star but as a criminal), and the town of Matlock itself, are all remnants of the Old West—of a frontier ended. Matlock is no longer the cow town it was in its heyday in the 1880s: the open range land is now all fenced by either the railroad or the government; homesteaders are now trying to raise beans on what few sections of arable land exist; and Jim Holt, Breezy's father, is no longer the county sheriff cleaning up rustlers. His legacy to Breezy was a valuable stock saddle, a pair of .45 Colt "Peacemaker" revolvers, and eleven dollars in cash (p. 229).

Breezy's (and perhaps Fergusson's) disillusionment with Hollywood is summed up in these words describing the drugstore cowboys: "They'd wrestle the blondes and we'd wrestle the broncs—when we did anything" (p. 236). One theme is common in Fergusson's portrayal of Sally Conner and her experiences with sham and in Breezy's experience working with drugstore "softies," and that is Fergusson's identification with the outsider or the underdog. He held no sympathy for illusion and fraud which Hollywood fostered in the turnings of the wheels of its dream machine. In a certain sense it is ironic for a fiction writer to feel at odds with illusions. But in another sense, a human sense, the people attracted by Hollywood were flesh and blood and not ink. The fictions of *Riley* make use of Fergusson's own treatment as a mere writer (not a star), and the treatment of other behind-the-scene personnel, to set the record straight by means of satire and exposé, even though it means two major digressions from the central plot.

As convoluted as the plots and subplots are throughout the novel, Fergusson attempts to tie things together by the associations and interrelationships of his characters. Riley shares the disappointments and failures of characters like Sally Conner and Breezy Holt. But with them he also shares an all-important resiliency. He will not give up. Clarence buys him out but then restores him in the business. Lillian takes him back as her husband and lover. He gives Shirley Skeen back to Breezy and helps them both to confirm what they already know: love will out. There are no solutions in the half-pint bottle of whiskey he buys, nor in the old short-barreled .45 caliber Colt revolver he buys in an El Paso pawn shop, nor in the lonely room where he almost pulls the trigger. Whatever the life of Riley is or is not—comfort or pain, success or failure—it is a life and not an unusually bad one at that, Riley finally decides; not as long as one endures the "ordeal," as Fergusson regarded his own struggles as a writer and as a person. Middle age, in particular, was no glory road, Fergusson was finding out. He was not a literary or a Hollywood heavyweight. But he was still involved in the struggle, still alive, and there was always the hope of what the future might mean for his writings. His writings, both in the process and the result, mattered most of all.

"Nuts," Riley says finally when he decides he is not going to kill himself. And if he is not going to bump himself off, he has to go on living. The long pages of reflection which Riley goes through as he looks back at his life and tries to assess his future have certain parallels to Fergusson's own life and its changes; his reflections deal with the nature of change itself and what a person's individual history means in relation to the life histories of other individuals and of whole societies. Riley decides to ask Lillian to take him back. Fergusson decides to go on and write, struggle that it might be. Riley comes to a conclusion which will see him through: "His life was not a passion or a tragedy after all. It was just a compromise" (p. 327).

Such a conclusion might also apply to the novel's author. Riley longs for someone to talk to and someone to understand his compromises. Fergusson has the consolation of writing about his own life and compromises through the maskings of the novel. Such a catharsis, given Fergusson's temperament and destiny as a writer, probably saved him from the real and tragic fate of his own father, who ended his life when the imagined changes of the future could not hold out against the glories of the past and of the excitement and successes of frontiers begun if not realized.

SHOW TIME

The Life of Riley sits squarely between *Modern Man* and *Home in the West* as fiction representative of the doubts and depressions of Fergusson's middle age. Riley, like the modern man Fergusson theorizes about in *Modern Man*, lives his life under the illusion of choice—but only to a certain extent. He is conditioned by his past and by his perceptions of the past and does act out his own destiny as prompted by large environmental and historical forces. But he chooses to keep on living, in a kind of compromise with the forces which have shaped him.

In the one extant film script which Fergusson worked on, "Stand Up and Fight," we find many of the same themes, much more melo-dramatically presented, which inform *Riley* and others of his works— as Fergusson never tired of writing about historical and individual change, both playing themselves out in the context of the ending and recurrent beginnings of the frontier.

Fergusson worked on "Stand Up and Fight" with a team of four scriptwriters which was headed up by James M. Cain, a journalist with past associations with Mencken who had, like Fergusson, published in the *Mercury*. It is difficult to establish just what portions of "Stand Up and Fight" Fergusson was responsible for, but the overall conception of the plot and some of the characterization, if not Fergusson's doing, were very compatible with the kinds of things he had been writing and would write. Cain is not associated with the frontier and the American West. Fergusson is. And "Stand Up and Fight" is a frontier picture— not a Western in the conventional sense because it deals with the opening of the trans-Mississippi West, takes place in Maryland and Ohio, and only points to the opening of the Far West.

The development of the West and its opening to the railroad is the major theme of the script. The concluding scene contains echoes of *McGarnigal* and some of Huning's memories of the railroad's entrance into Albuquerque. Sheer melodrama that it is, the action takes place at a key historical moment, when stage lines were about to be made obsolete by the railroad. The script does not concern itself with the abrupt end of the stagecoach as a means of transportation and the abrupt beginning of the railroad; rather, it deals with a transitional time when locomotives, in their first awkward attempts at heading West under the power of wood-fueled steam engines, were beginning to compete with horses and stages.

In this sense, much of the transition between horse and buggy and machine found in *Riley* are also found in "Stand Up and Fight." Another theme found in *Riley* and others of Fergusson's novels—to persevere and to be true to one's own sense of right and to one's friends—also pervades the screenplay. It is difficult to ascertain just which of Fergusson's treatments and scripts actually made it to the screen. But this one did. The film was directed by Luis Van Dyke and was released by MGM Pictures in 1939. It starred Robert Taylor, Wallace Berry, and Florence Rice, and has a running time of 105 minutes.[41]

Fergusson's diaries do not reveal much interest in theories and formulas for scriptwriting. There are random entries, but they by no means match the number of entries devoted to his theorizing about fiction. His 1940 diary, however, does reveal some theorizing about techniques for success in writing for films. Mainly he was interested in formulas for melodrama, and the kinds of comments he records fit a script like "Stand Up and Fight." In Fergusson's view, no melodrama is any better than its menace—whatever threatens its good characters. Fergusson agreed with Samuel Goldwyn, whom he admired, on this point. What Fergusson sought first when incorporating melodrama into film was first to find the menace—"not a banal heavy," but a moderate menace—and then to find a girl who is an organic part of the

story and is directly threatened by that menace. Fergusson was heart-
ened by Goldwyn's approval of some of his treatments—presumably
scripts like "Stand Up and Fight." Goldwyn was gracious and good-
humored, offered approval to the stories Fergusson worked out, and
"felt [he] had ideas and knowledge of the background." This excited
Fergusson, for he liked Goldwyn, for whom "Stand Up and Fight"
was developed.[42]

Fergusson's days as a scriptwriter were numbered. He received
fewer and fewer offers and reconciled himself to that fact. Other than a
few comments about *The Sea of Grass* (based on Conrad Richter's
novel), for which Fergusson wrote the treatment on which Vincent
Lawrence based his screenplay, and which starred Katherine Hep-
burn, Fergusson takes little credit for his work which actually made it
to public viewing.[43] He missed the money but much preferred to write
for himself, what he had cared about and had done since he decided to
move to New York in the early twenties.

Whether correctly or incorrectly, Fergusson attributed the end of
the Hollywood phase of his life to the war and the change in the cycle
of films associated with the war. Furthermore, he felt he was older
than most of the other scriptwriters in Hollywood and that calls for
scriptwriters in their late fifties would not materialize. At the end of
the 1942 diary he recorded this entry: "Remember my paramount
need is to finish two books and try to publish them regardless of result.
I cannot escape this necessity or sacrifice it to anything else. I have had
three calls in 18 months—all bad jobs for bad producers; not my kind
of stuff. I will probably not have much chance in pictures until after
the cycle changes. Probably until after the war."[44]

The two books which occupied Fergusson's time during the
1940s were *Home in the West* and *People and Power*. He gave up his
temporary residences in Los Angeles (1845 North Gramercy Place in
the early 1930s, and 5611 Carlton Way, Hollywood, in the late 1930s),
and settled in for good in Berkeley, taking up residence at 2427
Hilgard Avenue after keeping a large, sunny, but inexpensive flat at
2711 Virginia Street in the 1930s, and continued his routine of hunting and taking short trips whenever he could. He developed close
friendships with a few select people. In the early 1950s he moved to

2627 Benvenue Avenue in Berkeley. Only one more move was in the offing.

A CHANGE OF PUBLISHERS

During the early 1940s Fergusson's arrangements with Alfred Knopf began to deteriorate. In 1983, at the age of ninety, Knopf only had vague memories of just why Fergusson switched publishers for his last four books, beginning with *Home in the West* (1944): he was certain about the quality of Fergusson's books but uncertain as to the reasons for the switch.[45] Correspondence between Fergusson and Knopf after 1944 indicates that Knopf felt Fergusson treated him badly in deciding to change publishers after the publication of *Modern Man* and *The Life of Riley*. Fergusson wrote to Knopf in early January 1946 to ask about the status of the plates for his books with Knopf and to clarify his understanding of their contract whereby all rights of all books done for Knopf reverted to the author. Fergusson assumed those same conditions applied to *Modern Man* and to *The Life of Riley*. He hoped for a reprint of *Riley* and for a revised edition of *Modern Man*. By January 13, Knopf had not replied, and Fergusson wrote him for the second time asking the same questions, along with an order for one copy of the regular edition of *Rio Grande*.[46] Knopf responded just days later, on January 17, 1946, and opened curtly by saying, "I did not reply to your last letter because I didn't feel that there was anything pleasant that I could say since I thought, and still think that you treated us badly." Knopf continued with an item-by-item list of the status of each of Fergusson's books. *Rio Grande* was the only book in print and with existing plates; *In Those Days*, *Footloose McGarnigal*, *Wolf Song*, *Followers of the Sun*, *Blood of the Conquerors*, *Capitol Hill*, and *Women and Wives* were all out of print; *Modern Man*, *The Life of Riley*, and *Hot Saturday* had all been cancelled in June 1946; and all plates were melted except for *In Those Days*, *Wolf Song*, *Followers of the Sun*, and *Blood of the Conquerors*. Knopf also informed Fergusson that the contract for *Modern Man* would be cancelled, "so that you will be quite free to make other arrangements for its publication."

The reason for the falling-out, such as it was, was due to Fergusson's feeling that Knopf did not give *Home in the West* the kind of consideration Fergusson felt it deserved. Fergusson tried to explain his point of view in another letter a month later on February 26, 1946:

I am truly sorry you feel I treated you badly. I greatly value your friendship and had hoped and believed it would survive what I thought was an unavoidable break in our business relations. Because there seems to be some misunderstanding, on my part if not on yours, I would like to explain my own point of view a little further. When you offered to reconsider my book, in 1942, it was my impression that you did so largely as a matter of friendship and because you thought I had been unable to find another publisher. I had had so much trouble with the book that I had largely lost faith in it myself. I felt an urgent need to get some fresh readings of it, find a more favorable reaction [if] possible, lay it on the shelf if not. I did not feel sure I would publish it at all, and I did not see how I could ask you to publish it when there was so much doubt of it's [sic] value, in my own mind as well as in yours and those of your associates. In the light of our correspondence about the book, I was confident that you would understand how I felt. At any rate, I had no intention of treating you badly and no feeling that I was doing so. I still hope that I may count on your tolerance in the matter, as I have so often in the past.

Knopf responded in a conciliatory letter within a matter of days. On March 4, 1946, he wrote to Fergusson:

I have your letter of February 26th. There's not much use worrying over spilled milk and I certainly don't want to bear any grudge against you and am quite willing to let bygones be bygones. However, just to complete the record I need only say that it always seemed clear to us here in the office, and does still, that you should have put your cards frankly on the table and told us just what was in your mind before sending the manuscript to and signing a contract with another publisher. Of course I dealt with that manuscript as with all of yours "largely as a matter of friendship." How could it be otherwise when, quite obviously, neither of us ever made any particularly noticeable amount of money out of the other? I know quite well that when a publisher doesn't sell an author's books but believes in them, he thinks he is placing the author under a certain obligation to him, whereas the author usually feels the exact opposite. Probably both are right. The dilemma, it seems to me, can never be resolved altogether happily, but the unhappiness can be kept to a minimum if both parties are entirely frank.

And there the matter lay for the rest of their lives, Fergusson believing that Knopf had not expressed enough faith in his work, and Knopf believing that he had continued to have faith in Fergusson as a writer until Fergusson pulled out and sought another publisher. Fergusson apologized and seemed chastised in one last letter of March 12, 1946, saying, "It probably would have been better if I had had a frank discussion of the situation with you. My failure to do so the last time we met was due largely to my own uncertain state of mind. I didn't know what I wanted to do or whether I wanted to do anything." Fergusson's diaries reveal, however, that he never really quite forgot the flap with Knopf over *Home in the West*. As late as the 1960s he remained bitter over the entire matter, appending accusatory notes to some of the correspondence and justifying why Knopf was out.

Fergusson placed *Home in the West* (1944) with the publishing firm Duell, Sloan and Pearce and then worked out an agreement with William Morrow and Company for *People and Power* (1947). William Morrow would remain his publisher until his death and have the privilege of bringing out the products of Fergusson's "second wind," including two of his most acclaimed works, *Grant of Kingdom* (1950) and *The Conquest of Don Pedro* (1954).

The person most responsible for Fergusson's changing to William Morrow was Jesse Carmack. Carmack had met Fergusson in Albuquerque on visits but never came to know him as a friend until just after World War II. William Morrow was publishing H. L. Davis, and Carmack considered Davis and Fergusson as among the best fiction writers of their day in the West. As Carmack remembers it, he was passing through Albuquerque on a trip to New York and stopped to see Jim Threlkeld, then owner of the New Mexico Book Store. Threlkeld informed Carmack that Fergusson had broken off relations with Knopf with no further commitments and suggested that Fergusson might be interested in signing up with Morrow. When Carmack reached New York, he brought up the matter with Thayer

Hobson, then president of Morrow. Hobson had, it seems, also long been an admirer of Fergusson's work and quickly arranged a contract by mail with Fergusson in Berkeley. Hobson later traveled to Berkeley to meet Fergusson and be sure that he was wholly satisfied with the deal. Carmack became a "damn good friend" of Fergusson's during the ensuing years and visited with him off and on throughout the 1950s and 1960s. Ten years after Fergusson's death Carmack remembered some of their good times from the vantage point of his own eighty-second year: "Harvey was a thoroughly honest, intelligent, charming companion, with a touch of old-fashioned courtesy in all his behavior."[47]

As Carmack suggests, Fergusson's life after World War II and into the 1950s and 1960s consisted of writing and visiting with his sister Lina Fergusson Browne, her husband, and their children (Lina outlived Harvey by only three years and died in October 1974 of a quick and painless stroke) and with his friends. Heading the list of Fergusson's friends in Berkeley was Quail Hawkins, with whom he formed one of the most enduring relationships of his many involvements with women. It was Hawkins who gave Fergusson companionship and generally took care of him or saw that he was tended to during his last few years, when he was immobilized by arthritis. Other friends included Carmack; Canadian author Howard O'Hagan and his wife, Margaret, who was a professor of art at the University of California–Berkeley; Lincoln Fitzell, who worked on the San Francisco waterfront as a longshoreman; and his wife, Edith; and Paul and Stanleigh Carey. In addition to visits with such special friends, Fergusson received occasional visits from his sister Erna, who lived in Albuquerque, and from his brother, Francis, who lived in New Jersey. From the outside, Fergusson's later life seems much more congenial, social, and satisfied than his diaries reveal. Often he writes in his diaries of having an empty, monotonous time, particularly on special occasions such as Christmas and New Year's, when, after all the family festivities, he would return to his solitude.

His friend Paul Carey described him during these years: "Harvey was a loner who enjoyed the company of a few good friends. He was rugged physically and an outdoors man, but he was tied to a type-

Harvey Fergusson, ca. 1950. Courtesy of The Bancroft Library.

writer." According to Carey, Fergusson lived for his writing and for his trips, which he would take when he came to a break in his writing or when he had completed a novel: "When he finished a novel he would take to the back roads in the most remote areas of California with his rifle, swimming any stream that guaranteed privacy and, no doubt, shooting squirrels or tin cans."[48]

One negative note in the early fifties was the death on September 3, 1950, of Fergusson's mother, Clara, always an important figure in his life and treated fondly in his diaries, autobiography, and fiction (especially in *Lonely Women*). She died September 3, 1950, a few months after her eighty-fifth birthday. This was the first family death he had faced since his grandfather's, father's, and, on a different plane of relationship, Rebecca McCann's. Most of Clara's estate was bequeathed to her first-born child and Harvey's elder by two years,

Erna. According to the will Clara made in 1944, Harvey's portion of
her total estate amounted to $16,098.62. As far as can be determined,
he found the terms of the estate acceptable. It was his mother's death
and not the conditions of her will which affected him.[49]

Counting his friends and his new-found companion and "nurse,"
the balance sheet of Fergusson's final phase recorded more in the plus
column than in the negative. Not only was he able to endure his life's
ordeal as it intensified in his later years, but he was also able to carry
out his own kind of personal conquest.

FRONTIER KINGDOMS

If one approaches Fergusson's books in the sequence in which they
were written and in the context of his life, two things become obvious:
first, he wanted to write a novel like *Grant of Kingdom* (1950) almost
from the day he started writing, and was, in effect, writing versions of
it in his other novels and in *Rio Grande* all along; and second, *Kingdom,* as the novel he was destined to write, is a compendium of his
other books and a masterwork wherein he flawlessly matches subject
and structure, theme and style, with the result that this novel comes
nearest to realizing Fergusson's talent as a writer. Whatever *Kingdom*
is and whatever order of aesthetic perfection it achieves, it is difficult
to see how it could be anything other than what it is. It represents the
best work Fergusson was capable of doing and stands as a testimonial
not only to his fulfillment as an artist but to his will to live and by so
doing defeat the debilitating forces which he thought were, and which
in fact were, closing in on him and bringing to an end his personal
frontier.[50]

In *Kingdom* things converged in a most auspicious if not triumphant way. This is so much the case that it is possible to say that even if
Fergusson had written nothing else, *Kingdom* would be enough,
would tell all that he had written or could write. Seen in this sense, the
"kingdom" about which he writes serves as a metaphor for the domain of his writing, of how his life conditioned what he wrote about,
how he wrote about it, how he saw the worlds of "reality" and of

"imagination," and how these two "kingdoms" worked together to shape his "world."

Although the kingdom about which Fergusson literally writes in *Kingdom* appears again and again in most of his earlier works as the Cimarron country in northeastern New Mexico, it is more figuratively all of northern New Mexico and, by extension, all of the Southwest and West. Beyond geography, Fergusson's kingdom is the idea and the motive, the symbol of the frontier, of frontiers and all it takes to make up their beginnings and their endings. Typically, the characters who so grandly people this novel are yet again composites of himself, his grandfather, and his father, of historical personages and prototypes, and of anyone willing to face or turn away from a frontier. *Kingdom* is history, fiction, autobiography, biography, and myth all operating in fascinating patterns of plot and episode—a chronicle requiem for the passing of the frontier.

In this context, Fergusson's foreword to *Kingdom* is illuminating. He traces his inspiration for the novel to visiting a beautiful valley at the foot of the Rocky Mountains "more than twenty years ago." Fergusson's imagination was stirred when he saw the great house of Lucien Maxwell, counted nearly forty rooms, and learned that one man had built that house, thanks to the dowry land bestowed by marriage to Luz Beaubien from Taos, and had, in addition, founded a new society. In his ensuing research he pinpointed the history and the story behind such doings as the 1850s, nearly the end of the epoch which he identifies as "primary pioneering" and which was stopped by the Santa Fe railroad (*Kingdom*, p. xiii). He insists that the intervening years mitigated some of the historical truth behind what he saw, felt, and learned about that place and the people—going all the way back to the Spanish king and his subjects who had first occupied it as a Spanish land grant, a virtual "grant of kingdom," and extending to the episodes which the novel reconstructs during the American settlement of the area at mid-eighteenth century. He issues a disclaimer about the historical veracity of his novel saying, "This book is a fiction and neither its characters nor its incidents are to be identified with real ones" (p. xiv). It is, of course, impossible not to acknowledge the historical veracity behind Fergusson's new, composite fictional veracity and impossible not to see how historical source can motivate transformations of the imagination. But Fergusson insists that the purpose of the book is to portray four types of individuals who settled the West, not just those historical personages involved with the set-tling of the Maxwell Land Grant and the town of Cimarron.

In terms of the overall epic scope and drama of the novel, most readers will be attracted to the four major characters: Jean Ballard, the autocratic "conqueror"; Major Arnold Newton Blore, the egoist "usurper" and destroyer of Ballard's benevolent order; Daniel Laird, the idealist and "prophet" cast into exile who must redeem his good name against false accusations and defamations; and Clay Tighe, the Dodge City lawman and gunslinger sent for to enforce the new order of capitalism and exploitation. Readers might be drawn next to the two supporting women in the novel: Consuelo Coronel, the beautiful daughter of Don Tranquilino Coronel, the rico who passes on the vast lands in the Cimarron grant to his daughter as a wedding present; and Betty Weiss, the daughter of German immigrants who, though osten-sibly a prostitute and opportunist, comes to love Laird as devotedly and deeply as Consuelo loves Ballard.

Even the intermediary, Padre Matinez of Taos, and the loyal Ute chief, Kenyatch, might gain, in their minor but necessary roles, a goodly portion of reader interest. But it is James Lane Morgan, the lawyer whom Ballard depends on to close the most important real estate deal of his life and one of the biggest in the history of the region, that should bear closest scrutiny. For it is Morgan (another variation of Morgan Riley) who narrates the story and who, because of his relative youth when he enters events midway, is able to editorialize and offer a retrospective judgment of what such a panorama of change, over several generations, might mean in the larger plan of national and human history. In this capacity, as narrator and interpreter, Morgan shares duties with Fergusson—whose unnamed persona handles nar-ration before Morgan appears and while he is off-stage. In these ways Morgan is the most intriguing of all the characters, at least from the perspective of Fergusson's biography, for he is Fergusson's closest counterpart and spokesman—his scribe.

The first two parts of the novel, dealing with the meeting and the marriage of Jean Ballard and Consuelo Coronel, and the establishment of their "kingdom" in the north, is another version of *Wolf Song* and the love of Sam Lash and Lola Salazar. There are also echoes of the interracial pairings of numerous Anglo and Spanish-Mexican characters who engage in "love" relations in *Conquerors* (e.g., Ramon Delcasar, Catalina Archulera, and Julia Roth), in *In Those Days* (e.g., Robert Jayson, Doña Nina Aragon-Ortiz, and the servant Maria), in *Footloose McGarnigal* (e.g., Alec McGarnigal and Lucretia Bullard), and in *The Life of Riley* (Morgan Riley and Consuelo Alcatraz). What is worth noting is not only Fergusson's borrowings from past patterns in his previous novels—patterns that were in turn borrowed from his own impressions and experiences growing up in New Mexico—but also the degree of variation within each pattern as it reappears. In the instance of his new decision to introduce a narrator who is also a character in the action, Fergusson also draws on past personae, such as that of his grandfather as heard in his own memoir and as applied to the voice of the narrator in *In Those Days*. The appearance of Morgan and his "recollections" in part 2 of the novel and again in his retrospective "epilogue" seems to be a result of Fergusson's voice as historian in *Rio Grande*. Whatever the reasons, Fergusson does a fine job of utilizing the full potential of structures he had attempted before. And in the context of his previous work, *Kingdom* reads like a best and final draft.

There is little doubt that the very place where Sam Lash and Black Wolf engage in their life-or-death struggle is the same locale that the Coronel family gives to Ballard upon his marriage to Consuelo and the place where he takes possession of vast land holdings for which he does not truly know the boundaries (a fact which works as the melodramatic menace in the conflict between Ballard and Major Blore). The locale, special as it is to both Lash in *Wolf Song* and Ballard in *Kingdom,* is for Fergusson the means by which he makes the point again that although cultures, societies, and governments change, the land remains relatively unchanged.

For over a century the Coronel grant has amounted to nothing more than a piece of parchment signifying a wilderness where animals and Indians have roamed at will. Few civilized people dared to enter the region because of the threat to their scalps. On the map, the Santa Fe Trail passed just a few miles east of the foot of the mountains, and that promised the coming of civilization if the land could be settled. That is just what Ballard proposes to do: bring civilization to the wilderness known as the Dark River Valley, a mythical as much as a topographical name. It is a place described in terms of other crucial life-bestowing places, like the fertile crescent or the Garden of Eden. When the Don describes it to Ballard, he recognizes it immediately as the place where he had camped ten years before when he roamed the land as a mountain man. What he recognizes is not just a past encounter with a place but also his destiny, his future.

Because of his vision, his ability to act upon what his life has brought him up to that point, he is able to go beyond the end of whatever frontier his life as a mountain man had meant and cross over into the potential of the future, to merge past and future in a new present for him and for Consuelo. Ricos like Don Tranquilino are at the end of their era, and so are the Ute Indians whom Ballard must pacify. Ballard, too, will outlive his own transitional role as a civilizer, but die like most of Fergusson's heroes, satisfied that he has lived fully, to the limits of his own identity. Until that time he will capitalize on who he was—a mountain man who knows the region and knows the Indians who live there—in order to become who he must be. He will span the frontier of his own biography. The glories of the Indians, of the ricos, and of the mountain men all converge in Ballard's opportunity; and he is celebrated by Fergusson because he can turn the endings of those great frontiers into new frontiers of promise and potential.

Fergusson presents Ballard's individual thoughts and actions with epic flair. Ballard is no more heroic as a fictional creation than his historical counterpart, Lucien Maxwell. What Fergusson accomplishes is the joining of the two. Those were majestic times and places, and there were individuals ready and able to meet the occasion, rise up to it, and make it manifest. Ballard's allies in the enterprise—especially Consuelo, but also the Moache Ute chief, Kenyatch, and later his lawyer and scribe, James Lane Morgan—are admirable and convincing.

Consuelo is the epitome of her kind, the stuff of legend. She, too, crosses her own cultural frontier in adamantly declaring her love and loyalty to Ballard against the traditions and wishes of her father and family. Like Betty Weiss she is not just "behind her man" but joined with him and in large measure the cause and inspiration of whatever successes Ballard knows. Consuelo's beauty and irresistibility as we come to know them from Ballard's perceptions are all the more real and vivid because of the high romanticism of their meeting, courtship, and marriage. After she has helped Ballard tame the land and the elements and make the necessary agreements with Kenyatch and the Moache people, she is even more alluring as a grand señora of the Ballard kingdom. She is in the background during the end of her husband's life and their time together but still romantically present in the legends which Morgan relates. And this kind of exposition, filling in the passing of years and the gaining of reputation by hearsay, is a most effective device, worth more in narrative terms than pages of "showing."

Consuelo's regrets when she comes to the end of her life are that she loved the past too much—and her own beauty when she was young. The scene which finds Consuelo asking Ballard to forgive her her vanity and at the same time raising "the music of the unforgotten past" which carries Ballard all the way back to the first moment of their love (and the moment which more or less begins the novel) is another set scene in Fergusson's fiction. It is also a stock scene in Fergusson's diaries, for at the end of each year he invariably included a retrospective look at his own recent past and sometimes his distant past. In *Kingdom*, Morgan does the honors of placing even Ballard's long look backward in a larger social and historical context and of passing his own kind of judgment on it.

Just as Ballard is an interesting version of Fergusson's grandfather Huning, Morgan seems modeled after Fergusson's father, H. B. Fergusson—western lawyer, negotiator, politician—but with a strong measure of Harvey Fergusson, Jr., as well. Morgan heads west to Ballard's kingdom on call for his legal skills to help Ballard arrange his affairs and resist complete takeover by Blore and his syndicate of Denver backers. As was the case with H. B. Fergusson's call to White Oaks, Morgan combines the right sensitivity and shrewdness to provide Ballard with some relative profit.

By the time Morgan has explored Ballard's kingdom, looked at his accounts, and pieced together the family history, he becomes an advocate not just for Ballard but for the West itself and a "proud rider" in his own right. Morgan is of a different generation, Harvard-educated, and a New Yorker by birth, so he shares little of the rough-and-ready Kentucky and Ohio river valley pioneer background known to Ballard. But they do share a feeling for the land's claim to permanence in the face of the changes which come as a result of westering and the forces of manifest destiny behind it. Morgan, familiar with the relative calm of nineteenth-century Europe, regrets the commotion he meets on his stagecoach ride west in 1870. He has caught up with a spirit as much motivated by destruction as by construction and settlement: "Everyone was rushing, frantically somewhere—to Colorado or California or Santa Fe—in search of gold or a quick profit, cursing every delay, sparing neither man nor beast, fighting the very earth as a prostrate but unyielding enemy" (p. 92). The prose is more Fergusson's than Morgan's, and this is confirmed in the description of the Ballard house. It is, in effect, Fergusson seeing again his grandfather Huning's castle in Old Albuquerque transposed to the Rio Oscuro: "Then suddenly half a mile away I saw a great house topping a low hill beside a stream—a house large enough to be called a castle, with heavy earthen walls, steep shingled roofs and dormer windows, giving it a resemblance, which many had remarked, to some of the chateaux of northern France" (p. 92).

It is Morgan who, in finding out all he can about Ballard and his holdings, also briefs the reader—saving Fergusson the need to actually dramatize much of Ballard's life while he was building his kingdom. Morgan thus functions not only as Ballard's lawyer but as a social and historical commentator whose task is to make sense out of, chronicle, and "balladize" this complex and in many ways contradictory and multitudinous kingdom in the West.

Morgan discovers that it is Ballard's store which holds the whole complicated enterprise together. What the reader discovers is that Ballard, and the pride he takes in stocking, selling, and trading, and in operating his store, is very much another fictional embodiment of not just Lucien Maxwell but also Franz Huning. The operations of the store and what Joseph Anker's, the bookkeeper's, ledgers represent— that is, more credit outstanding than cash received—show Fergusson's adaptation not only of his grandfather's store but of the overall social and economic forces at work in Old and New Albuquerque in the late 1800s. Albuquerque was, for Fergusson, a type of town as well as a particular town which was able to attract the railroad, just as Cimarron was a type of town destined to be left in its remoteness. And just like the other frontier town Fergusson profiles in *Kingdom*— Dodge City, Kansas—Cimarron was destined to remain at the end of the line.

Morgan's first conceptions of the solution to Ballard's problems excites Morgan as it falls into place. Rather than try to raise a loan, Morgan proposes that Ballard survey the holding, incorporate the grant, parcel out the land into smaller lots, and sell the lots to settlers and maybe the railroad, thus carrying Ballard's large debt. From a hilltop he sees the land's potential as a site for a large city. Morgan's hilltop vision is all predicated on the surge of settlers to the West and on the arrival of the railroad. Morgan knew at the time of his telling that such was never to be the case: the future would not work out that way. Paradoxically, what he offers are some once enthusiastic, now disappointed "memories of the future."

Morgan is inspired by his plan, and whereas Ballard had felt a similar burst of insight and energy when he contemplated what his wedding gift meant to him, Morgan equates his own vision of the future with his destiny as a man able to extend Ballard's kingdom, end its isolation, walled away by the wilderness, and "master the new forces of money and machinery which were transforming the whole world" (p. 108). Morgan places his bets with what he thinks of as "necessary change" and the logic of "history."

Morgan thus has a conscious, intellectual sense of history which Ballard lacks. They share their own individual senses of what they hope to become as their particular life histories merge with national history; however, Morgan as scribe allows Fergusson to participate in the "sweep of change"—not just as a narrator, but as a participant, someone who might not only describe the effects of change but cause them. In reality, Fergusson is only playing the games of fiction in his attempt to engage the changes of the historical past more directly. But his invention of Morgan might be seen as a necessary if not quite inevitable choice of an author writing with the benefit of many years' knowledge of his own books and his variations on the same motif.

In this context it is noteworthy that as Morgan recounts his youthful enthusiasm and his vision for change and his role in it, Ballard is serene and slow, enjoying his friends—like Kenyatch, who has deteriorated into an Americanized parody of a chief, and Laird, who is an enjoyable conversationalist and not eager to talk business with Morgan. Morgan attributes Ballard's enigmatic serenity to his middle age and his middle-distance look at change. The situation of Morgan's impatience and Ballard's seemingly calm detachment is made all the more ironic by Ballard's nearness to death, a puzzling paradox for Morgan. Fergusson knew the mood in his diaries, too.

In reaction to Ballard's mood as he faces certain death (just as he had faced possible death so often in his past), Morgan backs away from his plan for the future. He has second thoughts which in the end deny his ambition and his business sense and reconcile him to Ballard's way of seeing things and to the synthesis which Fergusson kept coming back to as he looked back at what might have been had he become a lawyer or a businessman. Even his father and his grandfather both ultimately denied what their lives had been or become—H. B. Fergusson through his suicide, and Franz Huning through his final reclusive refusal, whether deliberate or not, to continue to wheel and deal in Albuquerque real estate.

What Morgan is, denies, and affirms amounts to the same value system as Fergusson's. That Fergusson is on the side of Ballard and Morgan and all of their cohorts—and not on the side of the "menace" in melodramatic terms, Major Blore—is obvious throughout. Morgan allows Fergusson an outlet for philosophizing about history and biography—his own and his characters'—that either an exclusive narrator, remote from the action, or an exclusive character, observing or passing through, could never have accomplished in as fine a way.

Yet Fergusson's exposition through Morgan is not without its dramatic implications. One such implication, of considerable thematic significance as well, is that Morgan is young and Ballard is old; Morgan has his future before him (and behind him, given the retrospective, "recollective" nature of his position), and Ballard has only the present, a very brief future—albeit cherished and thus slowed down—and a very full and long past. Morgan occupies a crucial buffer zone, a narrative and dramatic frontier, which sees the end of Ballard and the beginning of Blore's and Laird's era (their "biographies"); and he has the Janus-faced opportunity and omniscience to look both ways.

At this juncture, Fergusson takes the opportunity to work in one of his pet themes—the transforming power of the West on the individual, whereby an easterner, and usually a sickly one, becomes a westerner, in attitude and in health. This is part, also, of the explanation behind the mellowing of Morgan's attitude as he tries to fathom Ballard's serenity as the final change of death approaches. Morgan— like Huning, like Robert Jayson, like Alec McGarnigal and almost the entire dramatic personae of Fergusson's fiction—blossoms in the fresh air and sunshine. He puts on weight; his skin tans to "the color of a Mexican"; he adopts cowboy fashion, complete with half-boots, jeans and faded shirt, and wide hat—he, in effect, "takes on the color of the country" and is completely assimilated, no longer a stranger anywhere. He frequents the Mexican dances, always an invigorating, life-affirming event in Fergusson's novels; he sits by the stove in the store and swaps gossip and tall tales. He is change personified, experiencing "the rare delight, possible only in youth, of becoming part of a new environment, living a new life, seeming to [himself] another person" (p. 115). In short, Fergusson instills Morgan with his own, and his grandfather's, myth of the West as an out-of-doors rehabilitation sanitarium—something also reflected in the tourism promotions and image of New Mexico as a hospital for tuberculous patients. Morgan rides into the mountains, hunts deer and turkey, gets lost, keeps his own solitude, becomes primordial.

It is Morgan who explains why Ballard has to gamble against Blore's money and the highest stakes of all—the Ballard kingdom. Ballard knows it will take a lawyer to negotiate with Blore for the highest possible price, and he wagers that Morgan will be able to do just that. It is Morgan who realizes that it is money, and large amounts of it, that has brought an end to the frontier as Ballard found it. The "thrust of the rails across the continent" has put an end to "free wealth," to the open cattle range as communal property, and to the freedom to cross virtually all land without thought of tolls or ownership. The end of Ballard's frontier as explained by Morgan (and behind him Fergusson) fits the theories and expositions of Turner as well.

Morgan is up to the task of dealing with Blore because he comes from "a race of traders, of men who win their victories on the pages of a ledger, who fear nothing but the figures in red" (p. 145). In this respect, Morgan is a character in anticipation of Fergusson's supreme trader, the peddler and storekeeper Leo Mendez in *The Conquest of Don Pedro* (1954), published four years after *Kingdom*. With his talents for negotiation and outright bluff, Morgan is able to raise the price of Ballard's properties fifty thousand dollars and obtain Blore's consent to give Ballard a full year to order his business and prepare for death.

Morgan leaves the Ballard grant a year after Ballard's death, but the stories of Blore and Laird more or less tell themselves, which is to say that the original narrator—Fergusson's voice before he introduces the recollections of Morgan which piece together Ballard's life history against the backdrop of his final year or so before his death—resumes the telling of the story. The narrators merge. The details of just what happened to Morgan are not really known until the brief epilogue offered by Morgan. In a sense this transition is something of a visible seam in Fergusson's attempt to stitch the two narrative stances, the two voices, together; for he has Morgan admit that the reader might be surprised to learn that when he returned to the Taos Valley in the spring of 1906, he had been away from that particular part of the West since Ballard's death. But the scheme works well and gives an even more panoramic sense of the magnitude of the West and its appeal.

When Morgan sees Taos, he sees what the mountain men must

have seen sixty years before when they hit town for their spring rendezvous for love and liquor and trade. He returns after a life as a vagabond for a few years, roaming the West as a hunter and a prospector. The outlines of Fergusson's own life literally explode through the portrayals of Laird and of Morgan. Morgan identifies his youth with the West. Like Fergusson and like McGarnigal, he goes east and there makes his living—unlike Fergusson, becoming a successful lawyer, a husband, and a father. Like Fergusson, Morgan becomes a writer in his later years, never able to shake the impressions of the West on his soul and imagination. In his epilogue he has become an amateur historian, a collector of Western Americana, and a contributor to the pages of journals published by historical societies. His motive in returning to northern New Mexico is to research and write something about Ballard and the Dark River Valley. The device is not a new one for Fergusson, who used it first in *Capitol Hill* (1923); in the ending of that novel, Ralph Dolan's friend Henry Lambert informs him that he is writing a "portrait of Democracy in action" and that Dolan is his central character—thereby turning their mutual experiences, in fiction, ironically back into fiction again.

Morgan's admission that he has become a writer thus comes as no real surprise, since what the reader has read all along in the novel is what Morgan has written—or will write, or might have written. The device of history within a history, fiction within a fiction, is not really, in and of itself, as intriguing as Fergusson's decision to use it. One can only surmise that as he grew older and was able successfully to bring to conclusion two of his best efforts in fiction, the lines between his own life and the lives of his characters became ever more blurred—despite his remonstrances to the contrary. His final novel—the one he labored on so long during his later years after *Conquest*—as probably his most autobiographical fiction of them all, tends to confirm such a conjecture.

Whatever Morgan writes, the novel assumes its shape from his at least seeming to share the role of author-narrator with Fergusson. Morgan's research allows him to revisit the Ballard grant, talk to some old timers, and find out just what happened to Major Blore, Clay Tighe, and Consuelo. He is able to locate Laird and spend a few hours talking with him and with his wife, Betty. They are the survivors, and successful ones.

The Ballard grant, Morgan learns, passed from one land syndicate to another, bankruptcy to bankruptcy. And the railroad missed the village by twenty miles, sealing its fate. When Morgan actually rides to the Ballard house, he finds it in ruins. Only the landscape and the surrounding mountains have remained the same, and Morgan takes pleasure "in the fact that their massive resistance had saved something from the sweep of change, the corrosion of human greed" (pp. 310–11). Thus it is that Morgan's epilogue is also an elegy to past glories. Thereby the epilogue and the foreword merge: the ruins which Fergusson saw more than twenty years before he wrote *Kingdom* and the ruins which Morgan revisits become one.

Fergusson, too, merges with the voices and characters and legends he himself has momentarily recreated in writing about an epic story which had motivated his whole career as a writer—in youth and now again in age. The novel's final sentence echoes this thought, and Morgan's voice merges with Fergusson's one last time: "In the days when I had known it and before, a great gust of passion and energy had struck this place and blown itself out and left in its wake the ruin of a proud house and a legend in the memories of aging men" (p. 311). Fergusson was one of those men.

CONQUEST

Fergusson followed *Kingdom* with a second aesthetically successful novel in 1954. This time his efforts were commercially successful as well. With *The Conquest of Don Pedro* he alleviated some of the persistent worry that increased as he faced middle age and the transition into the final years of his life. At the age of sixty, with *Kingdom,* he published one of the best books he had written—and then followed it with a second, some would judge even a better book, at the age of sixty-four. He had slowed down in the amount of writing he was able to do in a year's time, but he nevertheless was writing at the top of his form. *Conquest,* like *Kingdom,* seems a book he began to write at the very beginning of his career. As early as 1928 he had interviewed

W. A. Keleher in Albuquerque about the arrival of Jewish merchants like Leo Mendes; and *Rio Grande* renewed his attention to this topic. *Conquest* is another novel which synthesizes and reshapes some of his earlier novels, allowing him to realize his fullest potential as a writer. In a sense it is his last hurrah, for the novel on which he worked over the next seventeen years which were left to him, *The Land of Lonely Women*, was to remain, although finished, unpublishable and a disappointment to him and to many who knew him and were allowed to read it in manuscript.

Conquest, however, had a different fate—and served as a kind of "conquest" of his own as a writer—and a more than sufficient capstone for his four decades as a writer. It brought him fifteen thousand dollars and more popularity than he had achieved with any of his other books. *Kingdom* had brought him greater recognition and the prestige of that particular kind of "conquest." With *Conquest* there was another kind of prestige: the novel was selected as the July 1954 Literary Guild selection. That meant national marketing and sales on a scale that had previously been denied him.

Part of the explanation behind the appeal of *Conquest* is implied in the publicity which the Literary Guild gave to the novel as "selection of the month." John Beecroft, the editor-in-chief of the guild, saw to it that the membership magazine, *Wings*, included colorful illustrations done by Roswell Keller. The illustrations surrounded a synopsis of the novel with emphasis on the characters (curiously written in the past tense and thus furthering the illusion of the story as "history"), a commentary of Fergusson's about the novel, and a biographical profile of Fergusson. These were pretty much standard ingredients in the guild's promotion of its books, and it is not how the publicity took shape but what it said that is of most interest thirty years later. The synopsis makes the novel into a rags-to-riches story about how an unknown peddler rises to a position of power—a "penetrating story, set against its leisurely background of adobe houses, rare trees, and gentle people."[51]

Fergusson's own essay in the guild magazine[52] is a long one and at odds, at least in tone if not in purpose, with the slickness of the sales-pitch synopsis. He attempts to link the novel of his own family history: the freighting days of his grandfather Huning; the arrival of his father as a frontier lawyer the year Pat Garrett killed Billy the Kid; and the birth of his mother in Albuquerque as "the first blue-eyed baby ever seen there." He calls the setting of *Conquest*—that is, New Mexico in the 1870s and 1880s—"the blood and soil from which my own life sprang" (p. 3). He also places the setting of the novel in an autobiographical context—that of the village of Don Pedro (based partially on the town of Mesilla) and the Jewish merchants who settled in New Mexico, including, presumably, the Spitz family: "I . . . knew well several of the pioneering Jewish merchants who came to New Mexico in the early days. Some of these, like Leo Mendes, who came to the town of Don Pedro, began as peddlers. Most of them prospered and became citizens in Albuquerque and Santa Fe. A son of one of these families was my best boyhood friend" (pp. 3–4).

The turn of the plot toward witches and the "witchcraft" of predicting the future Fergusson attributes to childhood memories and the stories of superstition he heard throughout New Mexico. What today could be regarded as a shift to "magic realism," Fergusson sees as the portrayal of a woman—Dolores Pino—who like many of her kind practiced their occult arts with some sense of humor and play rather than taking themselves and their witchery too seriously. In a sense, Fergusson also resists taking Dolores Pino and her part in the novel too seriously. He develops the life of Mendes in such a way that Pino's prophecies of change do come true. But Fergusson insists that he keeps the magic and superstition to a minimum almost as if such a thing, although worth introducing and in a sense satirizing, had been against his very nature for so long that he was not about to change stylistic modes this late in his career and sell out his aesthetic credo. There is, nevertheless, even more magic and witchery in the novel than he attests.

The fact that he does give as much time as he does to introducing Dolores Pino and developing her sexual liaison with Leo suggests that in his last published novel he could allow a little more play to a style and mode he had always had some feeling for but resisted. What he actually strikes upon with a character like Pino is a new form of one of his favorite characters, and a variation of such narrators as James Lane

Morgan and even of his own persona as narrator and Rio Grande historian. Pino's predictions about Leo's future as one of change do come true. It is one of the safest predictions Fergusson or any of his characters could make about the fictions in which they moved.

Fergusson insists in his guild magazine essay that he is not Leo Mendes—just as he insists that his pioneering family and the early Jewish settlers in Albuquerque do not really provide specific real-life models for his fictions (p. 8). But his insistence is at the same time undercut by ambivalence. He did know such people and places first-hand, and there is something of himself in his characters. His point is that his fictional creations are composite and reflect universal processes of change and need. Even so, more of Fergusson himself comes through than he will admit, all of his equivocation notwithstanding.

It is hard to conceive of Fergusson's puzzlement at imagining a character like Leo—a character he says is so unlike himself in many ways—and of feeling complete sympathy for someone who is such an alleged opposite. Leo is not that much unlike Fergusson. In truth, he is very much like him, or at least one idealized part of him, and very much like many of the other characters Fergusson repeatedly created over the years to inhabit his novels—characters modelled on his own family and experiences.

In a sense, Fergusson takes his grandfather Huning and his already created fictive counterpart, Robert Jayson, the hero of *In Those Days*, and something of himself as a writer-adventurer-wanderer, and reassembles them as a Jewish peddler named Leo Mendes. But, as Fergusson states in the Literary Guild's promotional booklet, there are other sources for his character and his locale. This time, rather than make the action follow the east-west vectors of the Santa Fe Trail and manifest destiny, as he had in the *Followers of the Sun* trilogy and in *Kingdom*, he takes the historic El Camino Real, north-south vectors of travel and settlement—the directions which the Conquistadors and not the Yankee pioneers had utilized, and particularly the infamous "Jornada del Muerto" along that route—and builds his drama around the geographical and cultural conflicts associated with that dangerous passage. Fergusson had hinted at such a possibility in *McGarnigal*, wherein Alec McGarnigal's southern swing takes him through Loui-

siana and Texas and then north through New Mexico to Taos before he
finally decides to return to New York.

The vagabond is an omnipresent character in Fergusson's writings, reflecting his own, his grandfather's, and his father's westering.
And Leo is the natural consequence of that impulse. The plot of
Conquest takes its form from these geographical and cultural tensions.
In much of the novel we see him as a free, wandering peddler, finding
his health and his freedom in his move west from New York; then in
the rest of the novel we follow the intrigues of his life as he starts a
store in Don Pedro, "conquers" the local opposition there—opposi-
tions of race, gender, and religion—and then finally conquers those
forces which would tie him to one place and thus, according to Fergusson's assumption, to the past forever. In the end, he makes a choice
not so much for the welfare of his young wife and her newly found
Texas lover, both of whom are Leo's friends, as he does for himself and
for change and the future. It is a pattern familiar to Fergusson's
novels, his film scripts, his histories, and his life. *Conquest* may thus be
read as one of Fergusson's last statements about the end of freedom
which he still dreams of and champions in his later years just as he had
in his youth. It is no small irony, and probably a factor in the concep-
tualizing of the novel, that Leo remains mobile and opts for the free
over the stationary life in the end, whereas his creator, Fergusson,
faced greater and greater immobility due to crippling arthritis and
increasing age.

The first menace which Leo faces as Fergusson structures the
novel is the land and its history. These two factors are compressed and
made representative in the town of Don Pedro, both in its nature and
in its location. Fergusson uses this method of dramatizing the nodality
of a place in his various accounts of Taos and of Albuquerque as
emblematic old and new towns, places of the past and of the future.
The town of Don Pedro is "historic" in its way generally, and for Leo
specifically. It is located on the eastern edge of the lower Rio Grande
Valley. It is close to the Mexican border and to the towns of El Paso
(sketched out by Fergusson in *McGarnigal*), Mesilla (its prototype),
and Las Cruces. It takes on its ambiance from Mexico, New Mexico,

and Texas. When Leo first sees it sometime in the late 1860s it is at least two hundred years old, with "a history . . . more a matter of legend than of record."[53]

Leo reaches Don Pedro from the north, no easy matter, for he must cross the "Jornada del Muerto," the "dead man's journey" of over sixty-five miles which marks the most sinister leg of the trip from Santa Fe to El Paso. When he first discovers Don Pedro, he is not fresh from the East. He has, in fact, been doing business as a traveling peddler in New Mexico for several years. He has already changed, but only in a preparatory way, since his arrival in the West and is now ready for another challenge, a major one, which Don Pedro represents. He is something of an anachronism, choosing to travel by foot along with his burro even though a stage runs once a week between Santa Fe and El Paso. Change is accelerating, and Leo is of the past yet has an eye toward the future. He is at another transitional point, a social and individual frontier, as well as a geographical one. Thus, he finds himself in the ironic position of being the representative of mutability, of change made incarnate in the form of one man discovering a lost kingdom. In this respect he is like so many of Fergusson's characters, a kind of mythological embodiment of the first man (or the last man) on earth face to face with a new world but simultaneously an old, lost world.

Leo is not a conqueror in armor—he is the ironic inversion of such forces—but he is another kind of conqueror, another kind of pioneer, whose task is not so much to conquer the wilderness of mountain and desert, though he must do that to some extent, as to overpower an "old and ingrown civilization . . . even more resistant to change and penetration [than the wilderness]" (p. 3). Fergusson sees Leo's gifts as more suitable for penetrating human society.

By the time Leo is ready to lay siege to Don Pedro—not as a fortress but as a potential new market for his goods and a location for his long-forming dream of a store—he has the look and the speech of a native. He has already experienced the transformation which Huning experienced, which Robert Jayson and others in Fergusson's fiction experience; he has learned Spanish, has been darkened by the sun, and has assumed the fashion of that place and time, including a dark hat and Apache boot-moccasins. But like others in Fergusson's fiction (and to an extent Fergusson himself) he is a perennial stranger.

His penetration of the society of Don Pedro puts him up against the head of one of the oldest rico families in the area, that of Augustín Vierra. To conquer Augustín and the Vierras he shrewdly enlists the aid of the hunter Aurelio Beltrán, a survivor of another remnant rico family who are ancient enemies of the Vierras. By appealing to Beltrán's sense of pride and the traditions of his family in standing up to the Vierras, and by tempting him with a new Hawken rifle, Leo is able to rent rooms to house his store.

Augustín Vierra represents the first male menace in Leo's conquest of the town because it is Vierra who provides the town with its goods before Leo engages him in competition. But Leo's courage in standing up to Vierra's intimidations, and Vierra's own greed for knives and other items of Leo's merchandise, soon have him in Leo's debt. Leo's subjugation of Vierra is made complete in the course of events when Vierra's wife, Doña Maria Guadelupe, and subsequently her niece, Magdalena, both fall in love with Leo, making Vierra a cuckold on two levels.

Leo's conquest of the two women—the aunt, Lupe, and the niece, Magdalena—is preceded, however, by an affair with another woman that is also typical in Fergusson's fictive patterns. Dolores Pino is one of the presumed lower social class, a Mexican-American rather than a Spanish American. She is, in fact, completely at the other end of the spectrum of social respectability, for she is an outsider, ostracized as a witch. She is the first woman to show any real interest in Leo after his arrival in New Mexico from New York, and she is responsible for awakening his sexuality and ushering him into the kind of manhood which the West requires. She also enables him to function in a way that is closer to the tradition of the picaro and carry out the episodic escapades associated with novels of the picaresque tradition. Dolores is a woman out of Leo's past in Santa Fe, and in dramatic terms, she allows him to arrive in Don Pedro as an experienced lover and ready for his involvements with Doña Lupe and Magdalena.

In many ways, Dolores Pino is the most intriguing character in *Conquest* and by far one of the most interesting of Fergusson's female characters generally. Her mother was a Navajo captured by a scion of the Pino family, and Dolores is supposedly born of rape and nursed on hatred. The Pino family finds it impossible to tame her, and like her mother before her, she runs away. To the disgrace of the Pino family, Dolores keeps their name and makes it notorious because of its association with her practice of witchery. She is thus reminiscent in some ways of the characterization of Juan's mother in *Proud Rider* and is as close as Fergusson comes to portraying a woman out of Mexican-American mythology rather than superficial stereotype. She is, in outline at least, something of a *la llorona* figure, the mysterious good/bad woman of Mexican folklore who, with the crying and wailing of her siren song, is ready to bring promise and disaster, immortality or death, to all males.

Fergusson's rendering of Dolores is that of a maligned woman, a good and pious woman who is wronged by lies and evil gossip. So he attempts to satirize the superstitions of folklore and legend on the one hand, and yet, he leaves enough mystery surrounding Dolores to make the stories about her seem possibly true. It is an old trick in the portrayal of witches, involving the ambiguities of the female mystique as well as of romance. Is she or is she not what she seems to be? Is she woman or spirit? Leo goes to her because she looks at him and entices him to visit her—as much a result of her female wiles as her witchery. Her seductions succeed, and the two of them find solace in each other as solitaries, if not pariahs to the society in which they find themselves. In some ways, Dolores is a female counterpart of the preacher and prophet Daniel Laird in *Kingdom*—but with a greater aura of mystery and mysticism.

It is Dolores, with her gift of "second sight," who intuits and predicts the changes that are in store for Leo as a man of "many lives." Since Fergusson dramatizes Leo and Dolores's affair in retrospect, after Leo has already begun to establish himself in Don Pedro, her predictions take on total credibility when the reader first encounters them: Leo has already acted on them and helped to realize Dolores's prophecy. Her means of making her prophecies are appropriate enough, for she sees the future in a bowl of water into which she pours a little ink. It is a superstition as well as, perhaps, Fergusson's way of commenting on the prescience of the writer as magician, a prescience and omniscience which he had already begun to give form in the opening pages of the novel: "I am sure that you are a man of power" (p. 64).

Leo takes such predictions as a sign of good fortune. But Dolores is quick to inform him that people soon hate a man for what he has and for what he can do. She herself is the victim of such hatred and is eventually driven out of town. But her persecution is treated ambiguously, for she simply vanishes one night from her house, leaving no clues as to where she might have gone. It is stretching the evidence a bit to draw parallels with Shakespeare's presence in Prospero and his witchery in the Bard's final drama. But Fergusson does tease the imaginative reader into seeing certain symbolic meanings in the means Dolores uses to "write" Leo's future life story. Fergusson had no way of knowing that *Conquest* was to be his *Tempest*, and that he too, like Dolores, would figuratively "vanish," leaving the subject of his prophecies, characters like Leo, to live on in the inked pages of his books. Nevertheless, he must have felt his power working in ways that evidenced their own kind of witchery.

In addition to predicting Leo's future as a powerful businessman, Dolores awakens his sexual desire. Fergusson describes this awakening in mystical terms, and although his imagery at times borders on silliness, his attempt at describing the end of the peddler's celibacy is well-intended. The inauguration and development of Leo's sexual prowess must precede his overall change into a man of power. He can wield his power financially and without the characteristic violence associated with the old West, but before he can rightfully claim this power, he must prove himself a man sexually.

Sexual prowess is a constant value, whether in the old or the new West. It is one primal force which insures continuity and, ironically, the permanence of change. Any concept of transition or frontier would be impossible without libido enough, strength enough, to move on and through. A totally celibate man is a sterile man, and in Fergusson's value system, any individual who hopes to affect human society must be virile and affirm the life force. This is somewhat ironic insofar as Fergusson had no children. Leo has no children either—at least not during the course of the novel. But he does create, he is a builder, and his potential for success in such areas is established in his response to the womanly powers of Dolores. Moreover, Fergusson equates his creative power as an artist with the sexual impulse.

The spell Dolores casts on Leo is her best witchery. And thus she is not so much a dark lady or diabolical temptress as she is a kind of earth mother—but in a more mystical sense than most of Fergusson's other females, who are characterized by carnality and regarded by the general populace as fallen, sinful women. Fergusson was, by nature and in his own sexual exploits, outside the traditional puritanical strictures against promiscuity and adultery. So there is much authorial approval in what Dolores, as primal woman, does for Leo.

Fergusson goes as far as he can to make Dolores into a kind of mysterious, demon lover, but, such a magical-mythical basis of character is ultimately at odds with the prevailing realism of the novel and thus at times evokes laughter where none is intended. In such places one senses that even Fergusson was more in tow to puritanical values and taboos than he perhaps realized. The no-holds-barred daring of *The Land of Lonely Women* confirms this. Such is the case when Leo is called by some sixth sense, some primal silent force (the mystery of lust), to the home of Dolores.

After he first meets her and talks with her, he eagerly waits for darkness to follow his growing desire. Fergusson intends the description of such an urge to be taken seriously; he describes the need of men for women many times in his fiction and their necessary leaving of the solitude of nature or the isolated companionship of men. Usually there is nothing particularly funny about the way such things happen. But in his description of the pull Dolores has on Leo, Fergusson lapses into unintended bathos, a kind of unconscious parody of one of his own most common scenes and formulas. Witness these examples: "He had endured celibacy for a long time with a good deal of equanimity, even with some slight disdain for men who could not live without women, but now that a woman had tossed him a challenge, raised his hope, he seemed to be only a walking phallus in search of a home" (p. 66). Silly as this "walking phallus" imagery might seem, it may be associated with Fergusson's reawakening creative powers in both *Kingdom* and *Conquest* and his discovery of a willing lover in his later years when he met Quail Hawkins in 1949. It seems natural to assume, given Fergusson's own belief in the close correspondence between the sexual impulse and the artistic impulse, that some of the creative surge which his last two novels represent might be related to one of the most significant emotional and personal relationships of his life.

Leo fears that what Dolores really feels and wants to express, her need, is hatred for men and that he will reap the whirlwind. Again, this is a characteristic theme in Fergusson's portrayals of men and women, involved as they are in a true and brutal battle of the sexes. But in his description of Leo's rendezvous with Dolores he introduces a new element for him, though one common to high romanticism. And that is the element of Gothicism. Demon lovers like *la llorona* traditionally haunted remote and dark spots, often along the rivers and ditches, and such is the case this night:

Something strongly impelled him to push the door open and enter. He stepped into solid darkness and a silence in which he could hear his own quick breathing. Then, after she had enjoyed his suspense for a full minute he heard her laugh softly. He did not say anything but went groping toward the sound with slightly tremulous hands. She had made down her pallet and lay there naked, and when he put his hands on her she did not laugh any more or say a word, but when he had stripped and mounted her she made a continuous guttural sound deep in her throat. It seemed to have in it nothing of her usual voice or of any human voice but to be subhuman music of desire, of the pure and innocent lust that is common to man and beast. (p. 67)

The scene is common in Fergusson's fiction. But nowhere is it related with such arch romanticism. It fails because it is so much at odds with the prevailing tone and style of the novel. Some might regard this burst of relatively uninhibited talk of Leo as a "walking phallus," penetrating the home and the body of Dolores, who is transformed into some kind of primal (but innocent) animal, as Fergusson beyond the pale. But the silliness of the scene might also be seen as a noble foolishness, whereby an author who has struggled with erotic description throughout his career, has the daring to throw previous restraint to the wind and try to approach sexual intercourse in something like the way the high romantics had in their tales of lamia and demon lovers.

Whatever Fergusson's motive or result, Dolores Pino disappears from the novel as abruptly as she enters it. She is described as a "flame only in the dark" who promises to intuit when Leo needs her again if only he will sit in the plaza whenever he is in Santa Fe. Her reputation, her legend, which she shares with Leo, is that she holds the powers not only of prophecy but of life and death. When he returns to Santa Fe again, all he finds is her deserted house, stripped of everything and feeling like a tomb. Dolores mysteriously disappears, but her words stay with Leo and in some mysterious way contribute to his destiny. She has been both an end and a beginning in his life.

Fergusson was no outright mystic. He did, however, have a mystical side, and as age seemingly brought him more questions than answers, the mystery of his own destiny seemed even more marvelous and baffling. Leo at least has the prophecy of a "witch" to help him understand the motive and method of his conquest of Don Pedro. Fergusson had the "power" of women.

The episode dealing with Dolores Pino is a flashback and, in terms of Leo's life, occurs just before the scenes which open the novel, which dramatize the founding of his store, alliance with Aurelio Beltrán, and the opposition of Augustín Vierra. When the narrative resumes after the flashback, Leo's store is flourishing, and his business extends into Texas, Arizona, and Mexico. The historical basis for such an enterprise is sound enough, for numerous Jewish merchants who settled the Southwest in the middle and later 1800s rapidly expanded their businesses. Such was the case as well for the Huning brothers and other non-Jewish immigrants in the mercantile business.

As Leo becomes more and more successful, he gives up his burro for a good horse, and much like Robert Jayson in *In Those Days*, Jim Riley in *The Life of Riley*, and Juan in *Proud Rider*, he enjoys both the horse and the pride it brings him. As Leo's prestige grows, so does the

number of his social contacts, extending even to the local priest, Padre
Orlando Malandrini, who is Archbishop Lamy's chief assistant in the
south and whom Leo supports. Clara Huning had enjoyed Archbishop Lamy's kindness while at the Loretto school. Franz Huning
had known Lamy's Albuquerque assistant, Joseph Machebeuf, had
purchased property from him, and had generally been his friend, and
Fergusson builds upon this friendship between merchant and priest in
his characterization of Padre Orlando. A similar alliance is also dramatized in *Wolf Song* and in *Grant of Kingdom,* and one chapter of *Rio
Grande* is devoted to the events surrounding Padre Antonio José
Martinez and his power struggle with Archbishop Lamy. So the priest
figure is a recurrent character in Fergusson's writings through his last
published novel.

Padre Orlando also reveals something more of Leo's destiny to
him—or rather, allows him to reveal it to himself. Thus, the padre is
the sacred "confessor" and complement to the profane "prophet,"
Dolores Pino. It is through Leo's talks with the padre about spirit of
place, about the "spell" of the Southwest and particularly this southern speck of it known as Don Pedro, that Leo comes to appreciate his
role in the larger system of things. The padre believes that Don Pedro,
if not the entire Southwest, nourishes a kind of satisfaction and contentment which borders on complacency. The citizens of Don Pedro
have no real ambition. Even the padre is content merely to think about
the ambitions and pursuits of the Conquistadors and their quest for
the Seven Cities of Cibola—content to write a book which he never
expects to finish. For an ambitious man, a man used to mobility,
settling in too deeply in such a place might mean ultimate defeat. Leo
has replaced the Vierras as the head of power, and such a victory is
dangerous. The padre tells Leo, "The longer you stay the harder it is
ever to leave, . . . ever to face life again where life is hard" (p. 92).

Leo's predicament, the decision which faces him with increasing
urgency during the remaining course of the novel, is a reflection of the
predicament which faced Fergusson in the last three decades of his
life, had faced him his entire life as a writer: continue or give up?
Write yet another novel or stop? Insofar as Fergusson wrote the book
of his southwestern life over and over again, and yet refused to return

to his beloved Southwest to live, he wrote to live. Leo ultimately chooses to give up all he had created in Don Pedro and move on to a newer challenge, a harder life in the north. Thus Leo must enjoy the climate and the landscape of Don Pedro but avoid letting its satisfactions conquer his spirit. It is a strange ambivalence which reveals more about Fergusson's attitudes and his decision to be a lifelong exile, never returning to New Mexico to live permanently.

Like Fergusson's other fictive analogs, Leo begins to be involved in more complicated relationships with women. As he advances in business he similarly advances in love. When Augustín Vierra's wife, Doña Maria Guadalupe, flirts with Leo at a dance held at one of the rico homes, he is ready for the encounter: he has the courage of his experience with Dolores Pino to shore up his confidence, and he has read Josiah Gregg's *Commerce on the Prairies* (1844), the most popular book in Santa Fe when Leo lived there. Gregg's commentary on the morals of the ricos has prepared Leo to accept what he knows to be their practice of adultery. Fergusson included a chapter about Gregg in *Rio Grande*, and it is his practice to introduce historical figures in his fiction. So there is some small degree of verisimilitude in his imprinting Leo with Gregg's observations and assumptions about rico morality. Fergusson, presumably, never deeply questioned either Gregg's or his own ethnocentrism, for he tends to portray Mexican-American women as passionately promiscuous and always ready for an affair with Anglo men behind the backs of their husbands or fiances. Leo benefits from the roving eyes and inclinations of Lupe, but later suffers from the cuckoldry committed against him by Lupe's niece and, in the course of events, his wife, Magdalena, when she develops a fondness for Leo's friend, the Texan Robert Coppinger.

Leo plays by the rules of the rico morality as sketched out by Fergusson—at least he plays by them in his affair with Lupe. But when Magdalena culminates her liaison with Coppinger while Leo is in Santa Fe on business, it is not quite so easy to accept the role of a Mexican gentleman. The temptation to rationalize, however, is strong—particularly in light of the possibility of taking many more women to replace Magdalena: "After all, adultery was just as old an institution as marriage and just as necessary, and many of the very best and even greatest men had endured cuckoldry with dignity" (p. 218). Leo, in the final analysis, does not accept cuckoldry in the way he thinks a Mexican gentleman might. He annuls his marriage to Magdalena, setting her free to marry Coppinger. In this way he frees not only his own conscience but frees himself physically to leave Don Pedro and head north for the "harder" life he and Padre Orlando had discussed. In one sense it is to both Leo's and Fergusson's credit that Leo does not succumb to the alleged double standards of the ricos and remains true to himself. He would appear more heroic, alas, had he also refused the rico values when Lupe "seduces" him and together they make a cuckold out of Don Augustín, notwithstanding her status as "property."

As with Dolores Pino, Leo discovers a new strain of primitivism within him and with this relatively more sophisticated rico woman. He still experiences a kind of animalistic atavism which finds him lying naked with Lupe telling her about his life, on one level so different from hers but made similar by their lust. The atavism which Fergusson seeks to convey is captured in one image; after their passion is spent, "a faraway dog howled his feelings at the moon" (p. 117).

Since mutability works its way with everyone, Leo's supremacy is in turn challenged. The challenge comes over a number of years and is connected to the maturation of Lupe's niece, Magdalena. Leo first knows her as a child and encourages her freedom to roam the town and its environs as she pleases. She is a free spirit whose first relationship with Leo places him in the role of an uncle or an indulging father. In some ways she is a reincarnation of Dolores Pino and *la llorona*. She too frequents the ditches and waterways, not magically like *la llorona* or a witch but more like a tomboy in search of turtles and frogs, water snakes, lizards and horned toads. Leo encourages her interest in nature and also, noting her growing facility with English, obtains for her some of the Ned Buntline dime novels beginning to appear in New Mexico. Magdalena blossoms into a young woman before Leo's eyes and, in keeping with her culture, is sent away to school in Santa Fe. Only a watchful Lupe, Fergusson suggests, prevents Leo and Magdalena from violating the taboo which, because of the vast differences in their ages, speaks against their lovemaking.

But their eventual union and marriage is destined. And so is Leo's rivalry with Robert Coppinger both for control of the nearby and strategic source of salt, so important to the harmony of the area, and for the love and loyalty of Magdalena. Coppinger comes out of the Anglo cowboy tradition which Fergusson so often writes about—in *McGarnigal*, in *Riley*, in *Kingdom*, and in other novels, and in *Rio Grande*. Part of the era and world associated with Billy the Kid in that part of southern New Mexico, Leo's hospitality extends to everyone, Coppinger and William Bonney included.

Fergusson's account in *Conquest* of the end of the frontier in New Mexico is not all that different from accounts in his other novels, especially *In Those Days*, and in his memoir of his early youth and manhood, *Home in the West*. Las Vegas is just another version of Albuquerque, with its Old Town and New Town. When Leo visits Las Vegas on the fateful business trip which allows Magdalena her first opportunity to be alone with Coppinger, the new town and the railroad astonish him. He felt "suddenly that he was an old timer, a part of the past, confronted by challenge and disturbance" (p. 207). He first resents the change that disrupts his life—the railroad most symbolically and a short time later, his wife's infidelity when he discovers it. Leo has become almost totally assimilated into the slower ways of his border town, but not entirely. He can still identify with the gringos and their money, and their railroad, and progress. Leo yields to the opportunity which the boom town represents and accepts the proposition offered to him by his Santa Fe suppliers. They need "a good man to go East" and buy goods for them, someone knowledgeable enough to take advantage of the increased speed allowed by rail shipments. When he learns that Magdalena's affections, like the times, have changed, his decision is made. He will go north to Santa Fe and Las Vegas, and then maybe to the East as a buyer for Heine and Kelly. He is, after all, a man of many lives, as Dolores Pino foretold.

It is significant that Fergusson ends *Conquest* with Leo on the road again, as in the old days, between Don Pedro and Santa Fe. He returns the way he came, close to nature, out-of-doors, at first riding his horse, and then sleeping underneath the stars. In coming full circle, however, he is paradoxically saying good-bye to what was his beginning.

His trip across the "Jornada del Muerto," is, in effect, his last one. He will make final arrangements for selling his store and disposing of his property in Don Pedro once he arrives in Santa Fe. As he searches for some rainwater in an arroyo and just before he falls into a deep and dreamless sleep, he becomes for a moment his own historian—as Riley does, as Ballard does, as Fergusson does repeatedly across the years in his diaries and through the transpositions of imagination in his fiction. Leo looks back at the chapter in his life now ending. He has reached the end of a phase of his life and the end of the day. But he is still in transit, still between his past life and his future one. He is alive and facing another individual frontier of man in time before the ultimate end or maybe beginning: the frontier of death. There is little doubt that Leo's life will continue past the expansive final page of the novel, that he will awaken the following morning and proceed on his way to his next phase. In one sense, he advances the struggles of his author, who remained convinced that he had still another book to write, more life to live.

RUBBED OUT

The publication and reception of *Conquest* represents the zenith of Fergusson's career as a writer. Never had one of his books had the publicity and national distribution that the Literary Guild's selection of *Conquest* allowed him. He was to live another seventeen years, to the age of eighty-one, but even at the age of sixty-four in 1954 he was feeling the discomforts and inconveniences of the aging process. As he began the struggle with arthritis and the deterioration of his overall physical condition—the stiff hands, the inability to concentrate, the tapering off of the libido, all problems that would interfere with his writing—dramatic changes were also taking place in society. His grandfather had seen change brought by the coming of the railroad to the Southwest; Fergusson himself had seen the difference that the automobile made in many aspects of the society, but especially in geographical mobility and the sexual relationships between women and men. He had written about the endings and beginnings of technological and social changes as he had seen them: two world wars;

economic, social, and political upheaval in the wake of those wars; and the crash of 1929. He had written novels and histories which incorporated his grandfather's past and his own youth and adulthood—that is, his own present. But as *Kingdom* and *Conquest* confirm, Fergusson was, increasingly, more caught up in the past than in the present. The changes which faced him during the 1950s and 1960s evidenced more than anything in earlier stages of his life that time had passed him by, that—in his own words—he was not in "vogue." The Korean War, nuclear testing, Vietnam, the Cold War—none of these dramatic events get much attention in his diaries or, more significantly, in his fiction. The social change associated with the late fifties and the whole decade of the sixties struck a deep nerve in his being. He had lived through the "new morality" of the twenties and had written about it, interjecting and extrapolating the revolution it caused in sexual mores into his novels about the later nineteenth century. But as man in his sixties and seventies he was now more an observer than a participant and was drawn druing his final twenty years to even greater reminiscence and nostalgia. In his last two works of any real significance, *The Land of Lonely Women* and "The Enchanted Meadow," he essentially rewrote, in the form of autobiographical fiction, the first thirty years of his life. Thus, both of these works are similar in outline to *Capitol Hill* (1923), *Women and Wives* (1924), *Hot Saturday* (1926), *Footloose McGarnigal* (1930), *The Life of Riley* (1927), and *Home in the West* (1944).

But Fergusson's last two attempts at fiction are considerably different in tone. This is surprisingly true of *Lonely Women*. Although this work reads, in general outline, like a telescoping of all of the works listed above—with similar characters and themes, all of which parallel Fergusson's own adolescence and young adulthood—it is considerably more explicit in its descriptions of the sexual impulse, lust, and love. Perhaps it represents Fergusson at his most authentic, stripped of any and all concern about convention, decorum, and restraint in the handling of erotic subject matter. Ironically, if such is the case, it offers testimony, by comparison, of just how puritanical and Victorian Fergusson's published novels really are. Perhaps *Lonely Women* represents Fergusson's lifetime preoccupation with sexuality and eroticism carried to its raunchiest and earthiest extreme and, many sensibilities judged, in response to the manuscript, its most vulgar.

Both *Lonely Women* and "Meadow" are decidedly lesser literary efforts. "Meadow" might have been publishable as a juvenile novella had Fergusson ever finished it under the title of *The Adventures of Mark West* (or an earlier variant, *Clouds of Glory*). The manuscript is unfinished, but Fergusson did work out a 5,000-word section which was published as the autobiographically revealing short story "The Enchanted Meadow."[54]

One can only speculate what the publication of *Lonely Women* might have done to Fergusson's reputation. Seen in the total context of his life and work, it has a certain truth and frankness about it which cannot be denied. As an account of the new morality of the first two decades of the twentieth century, it has certain merit as well. Even as an example of "x-rated" romance (although quaint), it also is of interest. But as a quality novel it is a failure, suggesting little which would bespeak the achievement of Fergusson's talent at its best. It is a somewhat embarrassing product of his sunset years even though it evidences his resolve to continue on according to his lights. For present purposes, however, these two works must be viewed in relation to Fergusson's last years, his relationship with Quail Hawkins, his physical ailments, and his death.

QUAIL

Throughout his life Fergusson loved to walk, drive, move about, and travel, and these activities, along with westering generally, are reflected in the ubiquitous journey structures of his novels. He walked daily in and about Berkeley for five- and sometimes ten-mile stretches. But arthritis in his hips made it more and more difficult and eventually impossible for him to walk. His residence was up a flight of stairs, and he eventually could not negotiate the climb owing to the deterioration of the cartilage in his hips. He had first met Quail Hawkins in 1949, and their friendship grew during the 1950s and early 1960s, so that it became both logical and convenient for him to live for the last six years

Quail Hawkins, ca. 1950. Courtesy of The Bancroft Library.

of his life in closer companionship with and in the close care of Quail. The proximity of Quail's garden cottage to her home made such an arrangement possible and was ideal for both of them—especially for Fergusson. When Fergusson and Quail met, he was fifty-nine and she was forty-four. When Fergusson moved into the Hawkins cottage he was seventy-five. Although their relationship was not without its own love and romance, Fergusson's physical need for women had more or less been spent by the time they met.[55]

Quail's life up until she met Fergusson was very much devoted to books and literature. The head of the children's book department of a large local bookstore, she belonged to the California Writers Club and wrote "easy-reading" children's books before Dr. Seuss. When Quail's father died in 1935, her mother came to live with her, after a successful career as a newspaperwoman. Both women liked people, and they entertained as often as possible, often giving informal Sunday-night suppers for as many as twenty-five guests.

The circumstances of Quail's meeting Fergusson centered, appropriately enough, on books and writing. The two met through Jesse Carmack, who was a salesman for Morrow as well as for Duell, Sloan and Pearce, publishers of *Home in the West*, and who was instrumental in Fergusson's shift from Knopf to Morrow. Carmack was also a good friend of Quail's and of her mother, Hannah, and whenever he was in the Berkeley area, he was always invited to their home for a meal. One Sunday afternoon, Carmack, having been invited to the Hawkins' Sunday-night supper, called from Fergusson's apartment to ask if he might bring Harvey Fergusson and another of Carmack's authors, Western writer H. L. Davis, as guests also. Quail readily agreed: two well-known authors would be more than welcome, especially since Quail had recently read and liked *Home in the West*, knew that Fergusson lived in Berkeley, and hoped to meet him some time.

Quail remembers with a smile that her friendship with Fergusson was based on her good cooking as evidenced in that first supper. According to Quail, Fergusson arrived on time, but Davis could not find the address, and Fergusson left to bring Davis back. The two of them arrived after everyone else had eaten, and one of Quail's earliest memories of Fergusson is of him and Davis alone at the table together

Howard O'Hagan. Courtesy of The Bancroft Library.

eating and talking. Subsequently, she encountered Fergusson again at a meeting of a group of members of the California Writers Club who splintered off to form their own group. At the first dinner of the splinter group, Canadian novelist Howard O'Hagan and Fergusson happened to be seated across the table from Quail. Interesting conversation ensued. Fergusson was a marvelous interviewer, Quail remembers, drawing her out on first one topic and then another. Later, as she was returning to the bookshop after lunch, Quail again ran into Fergusson, who asked her out for a drive. When they did take the ride, they discussed Quail's plans for a new book about cats.

Although Quail had published most of her books before meeting Fergusson, he gave her the idea for *Mountain Courage* (1957) and actually rewrote several paragraphs dealing with the hero's fishing and near-drowning (another of Fergusson's attempts at dealing with the drowning of his young friend Frank Spitz). Quail dedicated the book to Fergusson and gave him a quarter of the royalties for his help.

It was a relationship with nothing especially sexual about it—at least not initially. Fergusson's diaries tend to confirm that by his late fifties he had been celibate for some time. Quail had never been married, knew that marriage with Fergusson was unlikely, but knew also that she liked him very much. So after a few months their friendship developed into an affair for a few years—until 1954—and eventually into love. They knew each other as friends and lovers for nearly twenty-two years. They never married but remained devoted to each other. Fergusson was rather laconic; his letters to Quail were never love letters, and all his diary references to Quail are offered in the most matter-of-fact terms. But when he went on trips, he would always write her short notes letting her know where he was.

Fergusson's Benvenue apartment was quite spacious, but as his arthritis worsened, he could no longer use the second floor. At this point Quail suggested that he move into her cottage until something else turned up. But he could find nothing as good. In addition, Quail had arranged for a cleaning woman, Emma, for about two hours every morning, and Emma would care for Fergusson at first. As time went on, Quail would go over and cook for him. And other persons helped both with the housework, cooking, and errands, and with secretarial chores like correspondence and typing.

By 1954 their physical affair was over. It is perhaps merely coincidental that 1954 was also the year *Conquest* was finished and published. However interesting or possible such a linkage of writing and libido might be, Fergusson's prostate and kidney surgery within a period of three months early in 1955, and his weakened post-operative condition, were primal causes in the waning of his sexual impulse. Fergusson had been troubled by backaches and a worsening prostate condition for three years prior to surgery in January 1955. On their many trips during the 1960s Fergusson and Quail would take two cabins, one with a kitchen, with Quail paying for her cabin and Fergusson for his. So their trips were ones of companionship.

Fergusson was quite a solitary person, spending three-quarters of his time alone, Quail guesses. He had "slumps," spells of depression

Harvey Fergusson (*standing, left*), Quail Hawkins (*kneeling*), and friends in California, 1960. Courtesy of Quail Hawkins.

which would last three or four weeks, during which time he would see no one but Quail. For most of the last decade of his life he took large amounts of Empirin-codeine as a pain killer. Even so, his diaries show that his moments of painless comfort were few and far between.

Fergusson's relationship with Quail probably would not have occurred had it not taken place when it did—in the later years of both their lives when their individual needs coincided, or at least Quail guesses as much: "When he met me, . . . it was almost a case of all passion spent." Fergusson told Quail that over the years he had slept with approximately eighty women, and she was very much aware, more from his writings than from discussions, that he was something of a libertine or a womanizer. Fergusson was discreet and never told Quail more than the most general facts about the many women in his life, and especially about his wives. Up to a point, this same discretion is reflected in his diaries, though he does express there the guilt he felt regarding his relationship with Rebecca McCann.

According to Quail, Fergusson had an explanation if not a theory for such relationships: "He had a very strong feeling that men were inadequate for women. This really was a feeling that he had—men not being as sexual as women. That women were on the whole more sexual than men and they had been badly betrayed by men who simply didn't give them what they needed. And he was one who gave them what they needed." This is the rationale behind *Lonely Women*. The land was full of them, all on the lookout for a man like Fergusson—or his fictive counterpart in that novel, John Dennis. This theory, which is implicit in virtually all of Fergusson's novels, is also underscored by the fact that he was planning a nonfiction book on sex just before he died and had gathered and annotated several men's magazines as part of his research.

During his last years, as his mind began to slip and he read less and could not concentrate enough to write, he talked to Quail about the guilt he felt over the death of a male friend (presumably Spitz), as well as about regrets about a woman he referred to only as D., whom he had known in his college years at Washington and Lee. Fergusson had been in love with her, and she wanted to marry him, but he refused, saying only that he had no money, when in truth he knew that marriage would interfere with his wish to become a writer. Over and over again he lamented that he had not been candid with her in refusing marriage. In Fergusson's mind, marriage would have resulted in children, and providing for them and a wife would have blocked out the freedom required for writing. The assumed prevalence of lonely women and the responsibility of marriage and children are two beliefs strongly held by John Dennis in *Lonely Women*.

ORDEAL

In the 1950s and 1960s Fergusson wrote shorter and shorter entries in his diaries. These entries almost without exception indicate how much discomfort his arthritis and his slumps of depression were causing

Harvey Fergusson, ca. 1957. Courtesy of The Bancroft Library.

him. Instead of writing about the pain he was experiencing, he turned to editing his diaries, scratching out names of women and preparing glosses which indicated the value he attached to some of the entries. Except for his adenoid surgery in 1922, Fergusson's correspondence and letters had offered testimony to his relatively good physical health and his luck in avoiding hospitals. But in 1954, at the age of sixty-four, health worries begin: "I may face some serious ill-health, first time in my life. I find it hard to believe this, but feel I must go through . . . [a] complete check up."[56] Throughout 1954 he felt out of sorts, recording such things as "Life is energy. I have none." By August 1954, his doctor recommended that Fergusson undergo prostate surgery.

In January of 1955 he had the surgery and recuperated at the home of his sister Lina Browne. The first part of 1955 he suffered from illness and postoperative weakness. But by the last four months of that year he rallied long enough to begin sorting his papers, selecting what he wanted to deposit in the Bancroft Library, and writing nearly 17,000 words, by his calculation.[57] During the late 1950s he became more and more bothered by lameness in his leg, but 1958 he regarded as a relatively good year. In the main, his days were spent in weekly dinners with Lina and her family, and with Erna during the time she stayed with Lina. As was his custom at the beginning of every year, on January 2, 1959, he took a retrospective look back at his life and its motives. The entry for 1959 was colored by the worries of his operations and his arthritis.[58]

He faced a new and prolonged crisis in 1960s: a comparative inability to write and thus add to fulfillment in his final years. But he continued to struggle. As he continued to rethink his growth as a writer, he recorded in 1963, "My own growth seems to have been measured by my ability to portray women."[59] *Lonely Women* is his last, sustained attempt to do just this, to portray women—in relation to the kind of man his protagonist, John Dennis, represents.

One character in that novel is obviously modeled on Fergusson's elder sister, Erna. Although versions of Erna also appear in *Hot Saturday* and to some extent in *Women and Wives*, she came to occupy even more of his attention in the 1960s, by virtue of her temporary move to Berkeley for the first of her hip operations. Interviews, correspondence, and Fergusson's diaries indicate that their relationship included some degree of rivalry as siblings and as authors. On July 30, 1964, Erna died, leaving an estate valued at $52,000.[60] Fergusson recorded in his diary his understanding that most of her estate would go to him and his brother, Francis, and when that did not happen, he expressed his puzzlement about her motives. He remained convinced, however, that "she had a right to do what she did."[61] Thus, Fergusson gained no great wealth from either his mother's estate or his sister's. It was the earnings from the picture business which saw him through his final years. He was destined to be outlived by both his sister Lina and his brother, Francis.

During the last ten years of his life Fergusson found it difficult to focus on any one project. He still had more ideas for projects than he could ever hope to bring to completion. He kept notes for a new version of *Modern Man* to be called *The Meaning of Freedom;* read and jotted down ideas for a long work on sexuality; continued to edit and sort his life's accumulation of notes, manuscripts, letters, clippings, and diaries; and kept returning to his juvenile novella, *The Adventures of Mark West* (out of which he was able to complete "The Enchanted Meadow") and *Lonely Women.*

Insofar as his diaries are an indication of his condition, it was a wonder he was able to write anything. One entry during this period seems to sum up how he felt: "My life is an ordeal by pain and fatigue."[62] Life had always been an ordeal for him—but without the pain and fatigue of old age. His pain was such that he could sleep only in short stints. Where he had once enjoyed automobile trips, hunting, long walks, and invigorating swims, he now looked forward to a bath and a rubdown and a few moments of sun and air on the deck of his cottage, He still attended family dinners at his sister's home, and she came to dinner at his place from time to time. But, judging from his diaries, he apparently took less and less pleasure in such things, though he was grateful for food when it tasted good to him—and sleep, when it came. In his diaries he grumbles about his "illusive" doctors, about ineffective medication, and most of all about his inability to concentrate—his muddle. But he records his gratitude when he is able to work, and when what he is writing seems to take form before him and grow. Through all the grumblings in his diaries of what life is like as a tired, infirm old man whose destiny is, above all else, to write, one cannot help admire Fergusson's determination to continue to work until, like Sam Lash, he is "rubbed out." Through the pain one sees recorded, as the entries get shorter and shorter and less and less legible, one also sees certain situations that prompt a smile—like this one, tinged as it is with a certain pathos but illiciting admiration as well: "Laboriously self-sufficient day. Got my own breakfast, dictated three letters . . . from penciled drafts. . . . Some peaceful times on the deck. With Q[uail] to dinner at Lina's. Quite good. I was very tired and felt arthritic pain about six hours. I had a peculiar burst of mental activity and my mind swarming with ideas. I made some notes and could have made many more. My feet got so cold I had to put them in hot water. This was a kind of paroxism of mental activity."[63]

And there is humor of a kind. About social engagements and conversation during this period, Fergusson observes: "Smile and nod but keep your mouth shut."[64] During the last three years of his life he became visibly more and more discouraged, feeling that his social life consisted of "listening to jibberish" amounting to "tough meat" and "noisy boredom."[65] By February of 1970, even the diary entries give out. It is there one sees the reflection of the end: "I cannot get back into the habit of keeping a daily record of my life. But I will try to cultivate the habit of writing in this book every day if I only write a sentence."[66]

Such a failing, the visual disappearance of the word in the life of a person to whom the word had meant so much—not just as an end in itself but as a way of bringing meaning to a man who loved to travel, who loved the outdoors, who loved women—makes *Lonely Women* and "The Enchanted Meadow" all the more significant as final fictions.

FINAL FICTIONS

Fergusson began working on *Lonely Women* in the late 1950s under the various titles of *The King of Terrors* and *A Man Who Liked Women*. As the manuscript took shape, it took on the subtitle of "The Moral Education of John Ethan Dennis" and carried as an epigraph on the title page a quotation from Montaigne: "My art and trade is to live my life." The early title, *The King of Terrors,* was taken from Job 18:14: "His confidence shall be rooted out of his tabernacle, and it shall bring him to the king of terrors." That Fergusson would identify with the anguish and persecutions of Job is no surprise. Fergusson continued to insist in his diaries that he was not his characters, that Dennis had a life of his own and a universality beyond his author/creator. Dennis was to be "the archetypal human male, fairly highly sexed, filled with sexual curiosity, sensuous and adventurous": "He feels sex as a persistent physical desire, creating a large part of his relationship to life, not only to women but to society as a whole. . . . This is a historic type of man in western civilization. He is Ovid and Montaigne, Benvenuto Cellini, Pepys and Casanova."[67]

What is ironic is the disparity between the grandeur of the allusive motivation for the character and the ordinariness of Dennis. He faces life with a lust for living and for women and is faced with one "life on the edge" situation after another, but there is nothing archetypal about him. Moreover, Dennis's commonness, at least on first impression for most readers, is not that of everyman on life's highway but that of a fellow on the low road. This is apparently what several publishers felt in their rejection of the manuscript. The assumption seems to have been not only that it would not sell, but also that it would prove an embarrassment to both publisher and author. Something of a curmudgeon in his rationalization of why the novel kept meeting with rejection after rejection, Fergusson attributed it to a puritanism which supported conventional values—values which he felt were false. Fergusson went so far as to enumerate three such dominant myths which he believed ruled the conventions of fiction: "(1) The angel-devil myth of woman . . . Stendahl and Maupassant did most to dispell it. (2) The Victorian myth of the almost always happy marriage, that feminine monogamy is 'natural,' that adultery is always evil. This dominated most of American-British fiction for 50 years. (3) The current myth which associates all forms of sexual freedom with various forms of misery, disease, violence, and personal deterioration. Publishers are always dominated by the myth more so than the readers. I am convinced the book will not be published by any American publisher."[68]

Fergusson threw convention to the wind in *Lonely Women*, using words like "fuck," "prick," and "twat," and depicting wet dreams, masturbation, fellatio, and sexual violence. His fiction generally incorporates some form of mild violence, slapping, biting, or "mauling" when he depicts intercourse. But in *Lonely Women* he is shockingly explicit relative to his own norm. The regrettable thing is not his frankness, his attempt at honesty—far from it. Rather, it is that the novel itself is weakly structured with relatively little conflict in the plot and with a string of characters who seem totally undifferentiated.

The central male character has sex with one woman after another, and in between these episodes talks with other male characters about women and sexuality. Moreover, the protagonist goes one step further and talks with the women he has sex with about their sex lives. The whole novel reads like a series of confessionals or letters to the editor such as might be found at the front of any of the men's magazines Fergusson took to reading and annotating during this period. And if one has read Fergusson's other autobiographical novels, editorializing by the narrator grows tedious and, in light of the issues and the politics of sex in the 1980s, sexist.

This is ironic, given Fergusson's intention to propagandize for the sexual freedom and equality of both men and women. In the end, *Lonely Women* amounts to an x-rated tract against marriage and for adultery—all cloaked in high-sounding ideals. Thus, in a curious sense, Fergusson's last novel finds him lost between the past and the future, attempting to sound avant-garde but seeming terribly old-fashioned.

Despite the disclaimer in the foreword that all of the novel's characters are imaginary and that the novel is in no way intended as a portrait of the artist as a young man, *Lonely Women* is clearly an autobiographical novel. Fergusson insisted that it was a study of the process of change. Actually, it is both: a study of how he, as a man and as an author, came to know change, and a study of how change itself explained the process of his own life.

Fergusson's fictive counterpart, John Ethan Dennis, is fifteen when the novel opens in 1912 and thirty-two when the novel ends in 1929. So there is a seven-year discrepancy between Fergusson's own experiences and his dramatization of them through Dennis, and there are other discrepancies between Fergusson's own life and that of Dennis. But most of Dennis's outlook and what happens to him can be seen as paralleling Fergusson's outlook and life. In a similar way what happens to Mark West in *The Adventures of Mark West* and "The Enchanted Meadow" dramatizes Fergusson's growing love of the outdoors and his identity as a westerner.

In *Lonely Women* Aubrey Weyer functions as the friend and fictional manifestation of Fergusson's mythologized friendship with Frank Spitz. Weyer becomes a naturalist and museum director, and shadows Dennis, first as a boyhood adventurer in the outdoors and then through his attempts to find a livelihood as a journalist and publicist. Dorothy, the elder sister of Dennis in *Lonely Women*, becomes Diana, Mark West's younger sister in "The Enchanted Meadow," a composite of both Erna and Lina. Both the Dennis and West families strongly resemble Fergusson's family. The mother in *Lonely Women* is a Germanic blonde with blue eyes and perfect white skin who allows Dennis the run of the house and the river—as does Mrs. West in *Mark West*. And although Mrs. Dennis is the former Matilda Lemke, born of Russian-German immigrants in North Dakota, Mrs. West's father is Franz Honig (variantly Honing), a man who was born near Hamburg and at twenty-one sailed to America and then worked his way over the Santa Fe Trail, settled in Albuquerque, and eventually built "the Castle," a big white house across the road from the West house. Mark West is born in the old adobe house, which was given to his parents as a wedding gift. Mark's home is on the edge of "Old Town," and he rides his bicycle to school in "New Town," traveling between "two worlds." John Dennis lives in and must leave the small town of Albuquerque, with its river, its volcanoes to the west, and its mountains to the east. By the end of the novel he must return to that same town and face his past and see again some of the people out of his youth.

It is on the Honig (Huning) grounds that Mark West discovers his "enchanted meadow." And it is that meadow which functions implicitly as metaphor for both West's and Dennis's idyllic childhood. While Dennis has his first sexual experiences in the maid's back room, West experiences his first epiphany of landscape and solitude when he stumbles across the secret meadow on his grandfather's property. Both Dennis and West are expert swimmers and relish frequent swims in the river. Some of the most erotic scenes in *Lonely Women* take place on the banks of the river after swims which, not surprisingly, are also described by Fergusson in his diaries of the 1920s and 1930s.

Both Dennis and West are initiated into their respective worlds of sex and spirit of place by Mexicans. Dennis is lured to the small attic room used as living quarters for the family maid by Adelita Sanchez, a married, older woman and mother of a young son. Dennis likes Indians and Mexicans because they live close to the earth, and he likes Adelita because of her beauty and earthiness. She has no qualms about accepting his advances and time after time welcomes him to her room, where they have intercourse to the rhythm of Judge Dennis's snores in an adjacent bedroom.[69] In "The Enchanted Meadow" the gardener, Juan Ramirez, another mythic manifestation of transcendental experience and earthiness, directs young Mark to the big irrigation ditch located at the outer edges of the Honig property, where he talks with West about his own fears of being lost in the mountains and quiets the boy's apprehension about striking forth along the dim animal paths of his grandfather's land. Juan is Mark's first friend and a man who knows everything about the Honig lands. When West reaches the big irrigation ditch, he climbs a giant cottonwood tree and from there first sees the meadow where the cows of both his father and grandfather graze. It is, for a boy, the discovery of an "enchanted meadow," one that he returns to and explores repeatedly in his youth and in the rememberings of maturity. It is in the meadow, both in the day and at night, that he first feels at one with the earth, "alone but . . . not lonely."[70]

After his discovery of the meadow, West realizes that he is not like other, more socially inclined boys. He goes beyond passively viewing the meadow and begins to make pencil drawings of many of the birds he sees there. And he finds the river and begins swimming in it. Mr. West is portrayed as a man who understands his son's love of nature and shares with him a story or two about his own boyhood in Alabama. As West continues to frequent the meadow during that first summer, a mystery bird begins to possess his mind and imagination. Soon, because of his readings about birds, he identifies it as a jacksnipe. And with the realization that his mystery bird is a common one, some of the enchantment of the meadow diminishes for him.

In his self-knowledge, West identifies with author Ernest Thompson Seton, whose books he begins to read, and makes the further leap of knowledge and prophecy that he too would become a man like Seton—a man of the earth writing about his adventures, about the earth, and about his loneliness on it and love for it. West will write about the earth and draw pictures, like his bird drawings. When he returns home for evening dinner, his parents realize that he looks changed. He simply states that he had an "idea." In truth it was a revelation which started him toward his destiny.

Lonely Women, Mark West, and "The Enchanted Meadow" are accounts of the process by which Fergusson learned not only that he wanted to write but also what he wanted to write about. What Fergusson learned and relearned was that his art and trade were to live his life. Autobiography—whether as fiction or history—became its own means of improving on the art of life and reciprocally improving life through art.

Fergusson lived the last years of his creative imagination in memories of his own past, idealizing what nature and the outdoors meant to him as a boy and what sex and the love of women meant to him as a young man. In his portrayal of both phases of his life he laments their passing while insisting that he welcomed change. He was able to accept the changes brought to his life by the frontiers associated with unmarried life in big cities as he experienced them in his young adulthood, and he welcomed the changes in sexual patterns and in outright mobility associated with the automobile. In both these contexts he saw himself as a champion of individual sexual freedom and bachelorhood. Mutability as it affected his life and American society in the first three decades of the twentieth century after the closing of the western frontier became his controlling theme. But that theme was colored by his belief that mountains, rivers, and the wilderness were not affected by the same forces of mutability which affected an individual life or a society and that the outdoors and nature as he had learned to love it as a child were as unchanging as his memories of his childhood.

TIMBER LINE

Fergusson died August 27, 1971, at the age of eighty-one. Quail Hawkins was with him during his final hours, and he had the support of his sister Lina and her family as he faced his final ordeal. It was a peaceful death accepted by a man who expended great effort in fulfilling the epiphany first known in his grandfather Huning's fields: to live and to write. Fergusson suffered much during his old age, especially with arthritis and depression. But he died of a heart attack.

According to Quail, three or four days before his death he was exhausted from the travail of his medication and treatment of his arthritis.[71] Fergusson called her early one morning just before his death and told her he had a severe stomach pain. Neither she nor Fergusson had any way of knowing that it was a pain manifesting itself in a different spot than the precise one affected. The pain was severe. Subsequently Quail called the doctor. Hospital arrangements were slow in making, since rooms were scarce, but an ambulance finally arrived and took Fergusson to the hospital. The next morning, August 27, about 1:30 P.M., while he was still undergoing diagnostic tests, Fergusson experienced multiple heart attacks on the x-ray table. No heroic measures were taken to try to prolong his life. Quail remembers that he never opened his eyes, but upon hearing her call his name, he squeezed her hand and hung on. Within the hour his breath grew shorter, and he died.

Fergusson was cremated, and his ashes were taken to Oakland. He had instructed that at his funeral Whitman's "The Last Invocation" be read, as well as a poem of his own composition entitled

"Timber Line." It was in such a place—the timber line high above the forests of New Mexico, overlooking the Rio Grande Valley where he was born—that he saw his spirit residing. In his words, it was there "where man is seldom seen" that life was "perfect strong, and lean," there "none grows old . . . or draws breath / but those too strong or swift for death."[72]

Appendix: Critical Views of Fergusson

Nearly a century after his birth in 1890, Harvey Fergusson is recognized as one of the most significant of Western American writers. Some may regard such recognition as damnation with faint praise, and it would probably be much more to the liking of Fergusson's spirit, hovering somewhere around the timber line, to be recognized as an American writer, or perhaps just as a writer. American writers generally dislike regionalist classification. And the label "Western American" writer tends to rankle more than other designations. In part, this is because Western novels are associated with a tradition of magazine-rack pulp fiction, "popular" fiction born of suspect commercial motives and ethnocentric, racist, and sexist assumptions about the nature of men and women, power, and violence.

Designation as a Western American writer, however, is not necessarily demeaning. As Turner argued in conjunction with the closing of the frontier, the West was one of the most significant factors in American history. Whatever the West was or is, it is the very incarnation of dynamism, change, mutability, and quest. The cultural and historical conflicts and issues which it embodies make it one of the most exciting places, one of the most stimulating and controversial "ideas," which anyone interested in understanding the literature and history of America could hope to contemplate. Certainly the idea of "frontier," is rife with puzzlement, inviting ever-expanding perceptions and applications.

This is in part why a lesser, if not relatively obscure American writer like Fergusson is gaining the increased attention of readers interested in the literature of the American West. It bears mentioning too, that Fergusson chose to name one of his final fictional counterparts "Mark West," a name every bit as eponymic as "Mark Twain." If Mark Twain's domain was the Mississippi and the taking of its measurement, its mark, then Fergusson's domain and world view is represented by the West and its marking. Even if Fergusson wanted to escape the West, he could not. Fergusson did not live to see any major recognition for his work. But his reactions to the time and place of his birth and the forces they worked throughout his lifetime illuminate the West and things western in fascinating ways. As long as the West is in any of us, regardless of portion, good or bad, Fergusson's life and writing can speak to us. The attempt here to come to a greater understanding of who Fergusson was, what made him that way, and how he interpreted his experience for himself and for others, is only one such attempt, one "version" of his life.

Fergusson's recognition as a writer during his lifetime came mainly in the form of reviews. Most of the major dailies, including the *New York Times*, reviewed his books as they were published. Many of the reviewers were—like H. L. Mencken, J. Frank Dobie, Paul Horgan, and others—authors in their own right. In the middle and later phases of his career a few critical articles appeared in literary journals. Before his death interest in his writings began to gain momentum, owing mainly to the efforts of a half-dozen individuals who began compiling bibliographies, writing critical and retrospective essays, conducting interviews, and writing booklets and books. In 1971, the year of his death, he was recognized by the Western Literature Association with a distinguished service award and honorary life membership.

A survey of some of the reader response and critical recognition afforded to Fergusson, both during his lifetime and posthumously, helps in attaining a fuller understanding of his accomplishment. In a sense this amounts to a bibliographic essay, but I have attempted to go beyond mere listing and annotation. If this is possible, it is because many of the individuals who have taken a published interest in Fergusson met him during the course of their research and thus became partially absorbed in his biography, thereby helping to identify Fergusson the writer and Fergusson the man.

Aside from book reviews, serious criticism of Fergusson did not appear until the 1950s—and then the recognition was sparse. What is fascinating about the reactions his books have elicited is agreement about the topics and issues but disagreement about the answers. As this study tries to show, this is not surprising, since the essence of Fergusson's temperament and times was transition and ambivalence. His life and writings were an attempt to come to grips with "middleness" and mutability. Should we regard Fergusson as a heroic quester always facing up to the tests of his talent, or as a sycophant, unable to stand alone? Was he a realist or a romantic? A historical novelist, a satirist, a novelist in the tradition of the comedy of manners, a novelist in the picaresque tradition? An optimist or a pessimist? Did he prefer solitude or society? Was he a sympathetic force for reconciling Anglo, Hispanic, and American Indian cultures, or was he ethnocentric to the point of being an unwitting racist? Was he best at rendering male or female characters? Was he an early advocate of women's rights or was he a crypto-chauvinist? Was he a mythologizer of the West or a de-mythologizer? Did his novels move toward allegory, didacticism, and sermonizing? Were his heroes in favor of change and the future and his antiheroes lost in nostalgia for the past—or vice versa? Was he restrained in his portrayal of human sexuality, or might his novels be regarded as gratuitously erotic?

Such questions point again to the intrinsic nature of Fergusson as a bundle of contradictions. Many readers view him, as he seemed to view himself as "progressive," iconoclastic, liberal. But as the distance for retrospective assessment grows, and as times change, he seems somehow conservative if not reactionary. He simply cannot be explained in terms of either-or questions. Actually, he passed through phases and was at one time or another something of all of these things—trying to adapt to his times as they changed, trying to know himself but unwilling to face up to needed adaptations; always called back into the past and into himself. Partially an optimist and partially a pessimist, he was ultimately perhaps more the meliorist. All of which is to argue that it is through a reciprocal attempt to understand his life and his literature, to attempt to see how one influenced the other, that one comes to a better portrait of just how his "art and trade" did indeed amount to the living of his life.

An article by Lorene Pearson led the way for the flourish of attention which came to him most forcefully in the 1960s and extended to the 1970s in the decade after his death. Pearson's article appeared in the *New Mexico Quarterly* in the fall of 1951.[1] The *New Mexico Quarterly* had long been a friendly journal; it ran reviews of his work almost automatically, and in 1936 devoted a dozen pages to a symposium on *Modern Man*.[2] Pearson went so far as to claim that Fergusson was "the first and foremost novelist native to New Mexico" (p. 334). The occasion for her article was the publication of *Grant of Kingdom*, which she reviewed as somehow rounding out the tragedy of the artist encountering, in the West, a centuries-old civilization inimical to individualism and egocentrism. In New Mexico and in Fergusson's settings Pearson saw the crossroads of the continent and of the opposing forces of the individual and the community. Pearson was talking about Fergusson and the frontier theme, although she called it "crossroads," and she struck at the heart of the issue of whether or not Fergusson sided with the past or the future. It is significant that all of Fergusson's novels except *The Conquest of Don Pedro* had been published by the time of Pearson's assessment. In effect, she was considering his total work, exclusive of *Lonely Women* and "The Enchanted Meadow." All novels through *Kingdom* are surveyed; however, she views *Wolf Song* as his most notable. Pearson adroitly hit upon Fergusson's transitional stance and attempted to place him in the larger context of American intellectual and social history, a writer whose first novel in 1921 was published in "an era that too soon tired of facing the irreconcilable elements in our society that the closing of the frontier had set in antagonistic conflict" (p. 337).

In her sequential analysis of Fergusson's books, Pearson wrote what can only be regarded as one of the most important articles ever written about him. It is assuredly a seminal article, one which all subsequent critics gratefully acknowledge, whether in agreement or opposition. Her contention that Fergusson fails to ally himself with the right character, the right idea (i.e., Ballard and his individualism), sells Fergusson's intent if not his achievement in *Kingdom* a bit short. Although Fergusson idealizes Ballard as a lone hero and does romanticize, if not sentimentalize, him, Fergusson does place him in his time—a past time before the ending of the frontier when such heroism and self-reliance were most grandly possible. Pearson faults Fergusson for not arguing more forcefully that an "atavism" such as the "benevolent autocracy" Ballard represented is unworkable in the modern world (p. 354). In fact, Fergusson through his narrator, James Lane Morgan, makes it clear that Morgan has led another, "modern," conforming life and that he must reinvent Ballard from memories. In short, Pearson hits at the center of Fergusson's ambivalence as a "transitional" man but is too categorical in seeing him as giving up and siding completely with the past. He did eventually side almost entirely with the past and with the strange condition of what might be called "static change," change stopped by his own youth and boyhood, but he did so grudgingly and, for all practical purposes, unknowingly. In his final phase as a novelist he did stop time, but within his rememberings was much lip service to the need to acknowledge mutability.

In 1963 University of Arizona professor Cecil Robinson published *With the Ears of Strangers: The Mexican in American Literature*.[3] *Strangers* soon became a classic work not only about the Mexican in American literature but about the literature of the Southwest. And Robinson gives considerable attention to Fergusson as one of several writers who helped further Whitman's prophecy of "a continental culture enriched by Mexican sensibility" (p. viii). In this context, Robinson was one of the first critics to attempt to place Fergusson in a national as well as a regional context. Much of Robinson's attention focuses on Fergusson's portrayal of the ricos and on the penitentes, but he touches also on such topics as racial conflicts, sex conventions, family, the passing of feudal society, primitive virtues, and cultural synthesis. Robinson sees Fergusson, along with such contemporary writers as Paul Horgan, as part of a tradition which is working toward merging and synthesizing East and West, Anglo and Mexican perspectives, and places him in the context of a racial dialectic that might be viewed as Fergusson's own special aspect of the larger issues of the West as frontier. Thus, in his consideration of *Followers of the Sun*, Robinson attempts to isolate themes of racial conflict. Sam Lash, Robert Jayson, and Ramon Delcasar are considered in turn, for each of them enters into a cross-racial, cross-cultural love relationship. Robinson raises the issue of Fergusson's assumption, as presented by Tom Foote in *In Those Days*, that Mexican women reinforce if not encourage complacency: lazy country, lazy women, lazy man. When he comes to *The Conquest of Don Pedro*, Robinson shifts topics and emphasizes Fergusson's historical charting of the rise and fall of the feudalistic Mexican aristocracy; here, he chooses to see Fergusson as less of a moralizer about the process than a social scientist (*Strangers*, pp. 80–81).

Ultimately, Robinson hedges his bets and sees Fergusson as less the ethnocentric moralizer than he really is. For although Fergusson is perhaps comparatively less prone to stereotyping Mexican-American women as passionate, lustful and loose, if not animalistic, his novels imply that Mexican-American women would give anything to have an Anglo man or that, conversely, a Hispano male almost by nature prefers an Anglo woman. In a sense Fergusson is working toward a synthesis of the two cultures and races—but at the expense of an implicitly dying and inferior Hispanic culture. The case can be made—though Robinson does not do so—that Fergusson subscribed very much, and not entirely in spite of himself, to Turnerian, wave-of-the-future, Anglo-American assumptions about Anglos and their inevitable and justified displacement of Hispanics. If Fergusson moves toward merger and synthesis of Spanish/Mexican and Anglo cultures in the Southwest, the Anglos get the best part of the deal, for assimilation is directed toward their culture more than toward 50-50 reciprocity.

Robinson followed *Strangers* with an article devoted exclusively to Fergusson—"Legend of Destiny: The American Southwest in the Novels of Harvey Fergusson"—and another, "A Dedication to the Memory of Harvey Fergusson," written two years after Fergusson's death.[4] In his 1967 essay, "Legend of Destiny," Robinson argues that Fergusson is overdue for recognition as a regionalist writer. Robinson admits a "literary lag" in writing about the American West, a lag that is even behind the similar "frontier-and-cowboy" writing of Latin America's similar region, the northeast of Brazil. Robinson holds up the novels of Brazilian novelist Guimaraes Rosa as the kind of subtle work yet unequaled by Western American writers, but he contends that Fergusson is at the forefront of the "bulk of western writers" (p. 16).

In comparing Fergusson's portrayals of the Southwest to the portrayal of the Snopes clan of Faulkner's trilogy, Robinson sees Fergusson caught in a clash of values between class and social status, and sees his siding with Anglo settlement and Anglo versions of history as more "sympathetic" on Fergusson's part than regrettable or suspect ("Legend," p. 18). Fergusson's ambivalence toward wilderness and civilization Robinson seeks to explain in terms of Henry Nash Smith's *Virgin Land*. Like the paradox represented by the myth of Daniel Boone as a force of both primitivism and civilization, "Fergusson, like the writers of the Boone legend, shows both strains in his work" (ibid.). In all, Robinson sees Fergusson's accomplishment as that of combining social realism with "the aura of the legendary," of being a vitalizer of that period in history when manifest destiny broke upon the Southwest—in other words, of being a novelist of the southwestern frontier.

In his "Dedication to the Memory of Harvey Fergusson," Robinson wrote by far the most cogent account yet to appear of Fergusson's life and achievement. Here Robinson lays claim for Fergusson as a "major interpreter of the Southwest," a man who transcended the restrictions of the Western novel: "In a genre where the lone hero traditionally kissed only his horse, he dared to treat the theme of sexuality realistically and in some detail" (pp. 311–14). Robinson insists that although Fergusson's great concern was history, he did not view the past with nostalgia. His ambivalence, such as it was, ultimately pointed toward the condemnation of "clinging to an older way of life when such a way had clearly ceased to be functional" (p. 313).

Robinson's interest in Fergusson's portrayal of Anglo and Span-

ish- and Mexican-American racial relationships was continued in the
1970s by two articles: Sue Simmons McGinity's "Harvey Fergusson's
Use of Animal Imagery in Characterizing Spanish-American Women"
and Arthur G. Pettit's "The Decline and Fall of the New Mexican
Great House in the Novels of Harvey Fergusson."[5] McGinity is rather
matter-of-fact in her discussion of fifteen of Fergusson's female Spanish American characters from six novels, saying mainly that his
"highly sensuous descriptions of both the physical and emotional
natures of Spanish-American women appeal especially to the reader's
visual and auditory imagination" (p. 46). She laboriously establishes
that not only do such female characters look and act and sound like
animals, but they are also treated as such by other characters. The
result, she judges, is multifold: "First, it is an effective device of
characterization; secondly, it is in keeping with the social attitudes of
time and place of the novel's setting; and thirdly, it creates tone and
atmosphere for the entire novel, especially in matters of character
relationships" (p. 49). Today, most readers would question such stereotyping and speculate about its ethnocentric assumptions.

Arthur Pettit, both in his essay about Fergusson and in his book,
which incorporates that essay, is the most explicit critic thus far to
struggle with Fergusson's ethnocentricity.[6] Both in his original essay
and in his longer study Pettit rightfully makes no attempt to label
Fergusson a racist, consciously working out his prejudices in his
fiction; rather, he sees *Followers of the Sun, Kingdom,* and *Conquest* as
"classical example[s] of Anglo-American ethnocentricity; that is, they
are novels which convey the emotional attitude that one's own race,
nation, or culture is superior to all others. For Fergusson, the economic and cultural superiority of the Anglo-American over the native
New Mexican was a basic assumption" ("Decline," pp. 188–89).
Pettit contends that "the focus of Fergusson's work remained his
conviction that the New Mexican 'rico' lacked the competitive spirit
Fergusson viewed as an Anglo-Saxon monopoly" (*Images,* p. 105). In
short, Pettit's commentary reflects the attitudes about civil and human
rights of the 1960s and 1970s; furthermore, he asserts that Fergusson
would have been appalled at what he would doubtless have regarded
as the "economic lassitude and social decay" of great numbers of
"young Anglos" (hippies) across the country during that period.

Shortly after Cecil Robinson's discussion of Fergusson's writings in *With The Ears of Strangers,* two other advocates of Fergusson appeared in print: John R. Milton and Saul Cohen. Milton, editor of the *South Dakota Review,* ran in his journal an important symposium on the Western novel, including comments by Harvey Fergusson.[7] And Cohen, a book collector and lawyer, compiled the first checklist of Fergusson's work, which was published as the winning entry in the Robert B. Campbell Student Book Collection Contest, sponsored by the UCLA Library in 1965 (with the assumed endorsement of Lawrence Clark Powell), when Cohen was a practicing attorney in Los Angeles.[8] Both Milton and Cohen became friends of Fergusson during his final years, and both continue into the mid-1980s to champion Fergusson as a quality Western writer.

Milton's association with Fergusson grew over the few years he knew him and includes, in addition to Fergusson's answers for the *South Dakota Review* symposium, much correspondence "of a personal nature" and a taped interview of some two-and-a-half hours duration at Fergusson's home in Berkeley—part of which was edited and appeared in the *South Dakota Review* in 1971 as a "Conversation With Harvey Fergusson"; "The Enchanted Meadow" also appeared in the *South Dakota Review* as a posthumous short story.[9] Milton followed the publication of his "Conversation" with an extended chapter on Fergusson's writings in *The Novel of the American West,* a work which brings together many years of Milton's interest in Western writing and his interviews and discussions with many modern Western writers.[10] All four instances—the symposium, the conversation, the posthumous story, and the chapter on Fergusson's novels—reflect Milton's view that Fergusson "did not indulge in the gimmicks, tones, or stylistic quirks that make many other writers stand out and easier to label."[11]

In his symposium, Milton posed ten questions to eight contemporary Western novelists. Fergusson answered only four of the questions, supporting the view that during his last three years in particular he was somewhat curt with questioners. The tone, if not the substance, of his answers indicates some degree of impatience. Fergusson disavowed any regional label, saying "Every time I find myself designated in print as a Western writer, or worse yet as a writer of Westerns,

I feel like quoting the immortal words of the Virginian: 'When you call me that, smile.' " In answer to a query about his favorite Western novel, he demurred, saying he had read none. He admitted to liking *Kingdom* and *Conquest* best among his own novels because "the first book is my best attempt to record the heroic aspect of pioneer life, while the second is anti-heroic, being a portrait of a non-violent man in a violent and romantic world." Concerning the cause for limited recognition of Western novelists, Fergusson attributed it to the "cowboy romance," which he described as possibly "the feeblest product of American imagination with the possible exception of the comic strip" (p. 24).

Fergusson's crotchetiness disappears, however, in his more talkative "conversation" with Milton. Among the points established in the conversation: Fergusson's early short stories had no part in his later novels; Mencken believed *Wolf Song* a "vastly more immortal book than [Cather's] *Archbishop*"; in Fergusson's opinion, Cather did not know the West at all; Paul Horgan, as friend and writer, was in Fergusson's eyes an "indoor" boy; Fergusson could only write about a country that he knew intimately—like New Mexico; Fergusson once offended Mabel Dodge Luhan by joking about Tony's ballroom dancing; as a writer Indians were beyond his knowing as individuals; and he regarded *Kingdom* as his best novel, in part because of the varying narrative points of view ("Conversation," pp. 39–45).

In *The Novel of the American West* Milton continues to lobby for the respectability of the Western novel and particularly for the kind of "serious," "literary" Western novel written by Fergusson, Vardis Fisher, Frederick Manfred, and Frank Waters, among others. Although Milton resists labels when it comes to more specific identification of Fergusson, he finally applies the designation of "sociohistorical," saying that racial compromise rather than conquest is central to Fergusson's novels and that "social conflicts that are more subtle than conflicts of physical force provide much of the drama" (p. 233). Milton considers *Followers of the Sun*, *Kingdom*, and *Conquest* in relationship to each other and in relation to the Western novel more generally. Finally he sees Fergusson as a realist who depended on his own native knowledge of the West and of the land for his motive and material. Myth and romance thus take a back seat in Fergusson's novels, for Milton sees him as a demythologizer—and as ironic in whatever romanticism or melodrama that appear. If ever Fergusson found an ideal reader, it is Milton, in that he finds advantage and justification in ninety-five percent of Fergusson's choices and stated intentions. Regarding Fergusson's conception of history (in effect the "crossroads" issue Pearson first raised), Milton sees Fergusson as decidedly on the side of the future and accepting of change and not nostalgic about a lost golden age. For example, Milton says that *In Those Days* makes the point "that the West is not the Garden of Eden, it does not solve all problems, and regret and longing for one's past are a natural part of moving into the future" (p. 241). The Seven Golden Cities of Cibola might make a more apt utopian symbol of either the past or the future in the context of Fergusson. Even so, Milton overstates his case in arguing that Fergusson does not present a romantic idealization of the past and does portray Hispanics objectively. He says in relation to *Blood of the Conquerors:*

> *Fergusson, as usual, does not take sides. He chronicles the changes, accepts them, but does not pass judgment on the people whose values come from the past unless they are utterly false values, romanticized and sentimentalized and used entirely for escape from the reality. The line between the struggle to retain old values and the inability to accept new ones is often thin. This means that the tone of Fergusson's fiction is of utmost importance and must be handled with great skill, avoiding sentimentality and the expression of regret for a lost past but also resisting the temptations of cynicism and satire. Fergusson accomplishes his purpose as a sympathetic realist by maintaining a dispassionate attitude most of the time, with occasional—and apparently deliberate—lapses into either the romantic or the cynical responses to his material. (p. 244)*

The number of qualifications in Milton's argument suggests that the issue is open to more debate, even in Milton's thinking—and certainly in the thinking of other critics—for in the total body of his work Fergusson's longing for and identification with the past outweighs his insistence that he accepted, if not preferred, change and whatever the present and the future entailed. He was a "hereditary pioneer" and a "modern" Anglo, living, at least in mind and intellect, in the present and a hostage to change; but his heart, one feels, was with not just his own youth and Anglo culture, but also with the times before the closing of the frontier, with the native peoples too, American Indian and Hispanic, whose glory days were ostensibly over. His ambivalence in tone, style, and theme reflects a radically divided conflict in his own temperament and suggests a romantic/realist rather than a "sympathetic realist." Milton's article demonstrates just how tantalizing Fergusson's "old"/"new" selves really are when it comes to identifying the person behind the personae in fiction.

Saul Cohen, who identifies himself as a "semi-impecunious" collector, started in the early 1960s what is now the most complete collection of Fergusson's writing because Fergusson was worth reading as a "good" author, enjoyable reading, and not in demand by collectors and thus inexpensive.[12] Cohen met Fergusson in 1964 and described their visit at Fergusson's home in Berkeley as a delight: "It is easy to be disappointed at meeting an author in the flesh, but over a bourbon and water, two hours of good talk passed like fifteen minutes. He gave me a Czech and a Swedish translation of his first novel."[13] In the comments which prefaced his UCLA "Checklist" Cohen predicted that "the day is not far off when Fergusson will be 'discovered' and the work of an important American writer will receive deserving but overdue recognition" (p. 1). In 1968 and again in 1974 Cohen published articles placing *The Conquest of Don Pedro* at the top of his list of the ten best novels of New Mexico.[14]

William T. Pilkington's "The Southwestern Novels of Harvey Fergusson" appeared in the Winter 1965–66 issue of the *New Mexico Quarterly*. This essay is important on its own terms and as a precursor of Pilkington's later critical and analytical study *Harvey Fergusson*, in the Twayne United States Authors Series.[15] During the course of his research on Fergusson, Pilkington visited Fergusson in Berkeley in July 1968 and discussed Fergusson's life and writings with him. Following his critical study of Fergusson in the Twayne Series, Pilkington wrote a series of introductions to reprints of *Wolf Song*, *In Those Days*, and *The Blood of the Conquerors*, and has written the chapter on Fergusson for *A Literary History of the American West*.[16]

What lends force to Pilkington's praise of Fergusson is his refusal to worship at Fergusson's feet, uncritically and blindly. Pilkington's insights are tough-minded and honest. He thinks Fergusson a fine novelist—not just a Western novelist—but he also calls Fergusson's failings as he sees them. In his *New Mexico Quarterly* article, his book-length critical study, and his introductions, Pilkington sees Fergusson improving over his career as a writer and thus regards *Kingdom* and, above that, *Conquest* as his best books. There is not much disagreement among Fergusson's readers that such is the case; however, *Blood of the Conquerors* and *Wolf Song* are nearly as good, and in terms of plot and lyricism the latter two novels win out. Pilkington, in a simple, straightforward manner, sees Fergusson's career reaching its zenith in its second stage—after *The Life of Riley*, and beginning with his autobiography and his last two novels. Pilkington does not consider Fergusson's writing after *Conquest* and is consistent with other critics in this regard. He enters more controversial territory when he argues that Fergusson did not fully sympathize with Alec McGarnigal and Morgan Riley, who as drifters represent "almost a laboratory specimen of the Fergusson antihero" ("Southwestern Novels," p. 337). Pilkington sees the conqueror and not the drifter as the prototype of the Fergusson hero. Thus, he judges Fergusson more sympathetic to Jean Ballard and Leo Mendes. An equally debatable assertion is that Fergusson's descriptions of sexual encounters "are tastefully detached and restrained. They are never designed for erotic titillation, but are prompted by and are integral to the demands of character and plot" (p. 332). Pilkington also observes that Fergusson lapses into unfortunate stereotypes of Spanish Americans and "does not possess the deep sympathy for the less-exalted Spanish American that other Southwestern writers have displayed" (p. 335).

In his book, Pilkington labels Fergusson both a philosophical novelist and a novelist of manners. He believes that the philosophical precepts of *Modern Man* and *People in Power* dictated Fergusson's rendering of character and incident, but that these ideas, as components of a system formulated early in his career, resulted in a half-century of inflexibility in Fergusson's attitudes (*Fergusson*, p. 144). As a novelist of manners, Pilkington believes Fergusson excelled to the extent that "he was one of the most accomplished writers in the

Realistic vein . . . that America has so far produced" (p. 146). Moreover, Pilkington places Fergusson in the tradition of Ralph Waldo
Emerson. "Like Emerson, Fergusson is a cosmic optimist, who is
confident of man's continued growth and progress" (p. 38).

Certainly Fergusson's attitudes toward nature are identifiable
with Emerson's; and certainly his novels might be regarded as novels
of manners, tinged with the irony and satire usually associated with
such a tradition. But there is a sense in which if he was both a realist
and a romantic, he was neither one nor the other. Pilkington's final
opinion is that Fergusson is not a typical Western writer insofar as he
"was not in any menaingful sense a romantic. While many Western
writers . . . are anti-rational and aspire to the 'blood consciousness'
espoused by D. H. Lawrence, Fergusson calmly upheld the efficacy of
human reason and technological progress" (*Fergusson*, p. 148). Pilkington's assertion is too categorical. Fergusson was a man between
two worlds, two sensibilities. He aspired to be modern, on the side of
human reason and technology, of Anglo notions of "progress," but his
heart lay buried on the boundary created by the closing of the American frontier.

Today, James K. Folsom's 1969 booklet on Fergusson, *Harvey
Fergusson*, is a first point of departure for anyone interested in critical
response to Fergusson and Western writing. Folsom followed his
original work on Fergusson with an important chapter on him in the
1982 volume *Fifty Western Writers.*[17]

Folsom takes issue with some of the assertions Pilkington made in
his 1965 article, although he draws heavily on Pilkington's discussion
of Fergusson's notion of destiny as self-fulfillment. For one thing,
Folsom states that one of Fergusson's deepest beliefs was that people
should be flexible, or "balanced," as presented in *Modern Man*.
Whereas Pilkington views Fergusson's philosophy as a confining su-
perstructure for his fiction, making him "inflexible" for over half a
century, Folsom says, "Inflexibility, as shown in Fergusson's fiction
by inability or unwillingness to change, is not so much a fault because
it renders a character unable to survive in a world of constant flux
(although Fergusson would admit that this is in fact the case) as
because inflexibility makes it impossible for a character to fulfill him-

self" ("Harvey Fergusson," p. 104). To the degree that such is the case—and Folsom illustrates how it is so in *Blood of the Conquerors*—then, by the same argument, Fergusson, if Pilkington is right, did not fulfill himself. Another point of disagreement between Folsom and Pilkington centers on the issue of Fergusson's optimism. Whereas Pilkington describes Fergusson as a "cosmic optimist," Folsom refuses to see Fergusson as a "simple optimist" and spends considerable effort establishing that Fergusson's fiction—especially *Grant of Kingdom*—has an identifiable "tragic dimension" to it, assuming in his shift of terms that pessimism and tragedy have something in common (p. 106). In Folsom's view, backed up by his reading of *Kingdom* and by Fergusson's oft-quoted belief that "only the land lasts forever," tragedy for Fergusson was the human "longing for . . . permanence in a world of flux" (p. 107).

The present study of Fergusson's life and literature, taking as its context the end of the American frontier and Fergusson's longing for modern substitutes, agrees with two of Folsom's major points: Fergusson is an autobiographical writer, and his writings are tinged with, if not outright tragic strains, then certainly elegiac ones. Folsom agrees with John R. Milton's essay on Fergusson and thinks the "metahistory" Milton extracts from Fergusson's writings is argued brilliantly. But what Folsom regards as Milton's explanation of Fergusson's "combination of different levels of historic truth into a kind of 'metahistory' " is not as clear as Folsom assumes. In turn, one of Folsom's most intriguing readings of Fergusson's novels is his contention that *Conquest* is the most "parabolic" of all ("Harvey Fergusson," p. 106).

The critic regarded most highly by Fergusson as a friend and as a publicist for his work—or so it would seem, judging by many of Fergusson's letters—is Lawrence Clark Powell, long-time dean of the School of Library Service at UCLA, and a novelist and follower of southwestern literature. In Fergusson's mind, Powell did "more than any other one man to make [his] books more widely known."[18] Fergusson felt Powell's commentary, as it appeared in *Books West Southwest* and in the *Westways* columns Powell wrote for several years, was the most useful publicity he could get, "for the good reason that your books go to the libraries and the English departments of the West states' universities."[19] It was Powell's opinion that Fergusson sought concerning *The Land of Lonely Women* as a novel about sex and as a publishing problem when Fergusson finished his final revisions in May 1965.[20] Even after Powell read the manuscript and reported negatively to Fergusson in the most forthright of terms, Fergusson continued to correspond cordially with Powell, although he failed to comprehend how Powell could so thoroughly miss the point of *Lonely Women*.

Powell wrote an especially important *Westways* piece in January 1972, the year after Fergusson's death, in which he took a retrospective look at his friend's life and accomplishment. Singling out *Wolf Song, Grant of Kingdom, The Conquest of Don Pedro, Rio Grande,* and *Home in the West,* Powell says, "In these five books is the quintessence of New Mexico. No other writer equalled this achievement."[21] Powell's focus in this article is on *Wolf Song,* a novel he sees as a love song not to Rebecca McCann but to the Sangre de Cristo Mountains and the mountain men who traversed them. Powell agrees with J. Frank Dobie, whom Powell quotes as saying, "Nobody will ever surpass the rhythm of *Wolf Song.* It is a classic in the purest sense of the word" (p. 41). *Kingdom* Powell sees as Fergusson's second creative peak after *Wolf Song* and regards *Conquest* as "his ripest book, his last harvest" (p. 59).

Powell came to know Harvey Fergusson in 1953. And it was partially as a result of Powell's mentioning of Fergusson's works during a panel he served on in 1954 with Fray Angelico Chavez and Laura Gilpin, that George P. Hammond, then head of the Bancroft Library, realized that Fergusson resided in Berkeley and invited Fergusson to leave his papers to the Bancroft.[22] Powell had extended a similar invitation to Fergusson on behalf of UCLA and had collected some materials which were later relinquished. Powell had first visited Fergusson when Fergusson lived alone at his Benvenue address. He remembers Fergusson as a bitter man in his later years who felt he had been born too early for what evolved in the liberalization of morality and who thought his name as a writer and reader interest in his books were not lasting long enough; that he had long "outlived his successes."[23] Powell, of course, knew Fergusson during his saddest years. Even at the first he was severely crippled and walked with a cane; and on some of their final visits Fergusson would be found crying, a near-invalid. But as Fergusson insisted in correspondence in May 1967, he always looked forward to Powell's friendship: "I am enough of an invalid to need a nurse for eight hours a day five days a week just to keep me cleaned up and fed, but I am not too weak to enjoy seeing you very much."[24]

It was an ending with its own special pathos. But it was also a beginning, as this survey attempts to show. Mortality claimed Fergusson with the same inevitability that it had claimed Franz Huning, H. B. Fergusson, Frank Spitz, Rebecca McCann, Clara Huning Fergusson, Erna—all the dear ones in his life—and with the same finality he had written about in the lives of their counterparts and composites in his fictional/historical characters. Each phase of his life, each locale of residence, each friendship, each love, each book he had first imagined and then produced, represented a frontier he had dared to know, to "cross." And in such crossings he staked out a bit of immortality, left his own mapping of where he had been—for others to follow if they sought again to know whence he had gone as Harvey Fergusson (or as his fictive aliases Ramon Delcasar, Ralph Dolan, Jim Royce, John Strome, John Romer, Morgan Riley, Alec McGarnigal, Robert Jayson, Sam Lash, Jean Ballard, James Lane Morgan, Leo Mendes, John Ethan Dennis, and Mark West), a man whose destiny it was to be born in the American Southwest, in a sleepy but rising old/new town on the Rio Grande in 1890, a year said to represent the frontier's end.

Notes

PREFACE

1 Leon Edel, *Literary Biography* (Garden City, N.Y.: Doubleday & Co., 1959).

2 Marc Pachter, ed., *Telling Lives: The Biographer's Art* (Washington, D.C.: New Republic Books, 1979); Dennis W. Petrie, *Ultimately Fiction: Design in Modern American Literary Biography* (West Lafayette: Purdue Univ. Press, 1981). Less recent but still innovative theoretical studies include Daniel Aaron, ed., *Studies in Biography* (Cambridge: Harvard Univ. Press, 1978); James L. Clifford, ed., *Biography as an Art: Selected Criticism, 1560–1960* (New York: Oxford Univ. Press, 1962). A commendable recent interdisciplinary look at biography is L. L. Langness and Gelya Frank, *Lives: An Anthropological Approach to Biography* (Novato, Calif.: Chandler and Sharp, 1981). See also Richard Ellmann, "Literary Biography," in *Golden Codgers* (New York: Oxford Univ. Press, 1973), pp. 1–16.

3 Matthew Arnold "Stanzas from the Grande Chartreuse," in *The Oxford Anthology of English Literature* (New York: Oxford Univ. Press, 1973), 2:1136.

4 Alfred Kazin, "The Self as History: Reflections on Autobiography," in Pachter, *Telling Lives*, p. 75.

CHAPTER I

1 Lina Fergusson Browne to Phil Flangman, March 14, 1970 (letter in possession of Lawrence Clark Powell).

2 Lina Fergusson Browne to Lawrence Clark Powell, Aug. 25, 1971 (letter in Powell's possession).

3 Marilynne Robinson, "Writers and the Nostalgic Fallacy," *New York Times Book Review*, Oct. 13, 1985, p. 1.

4 See Richard Slotkin, *Regeneration through Violence: The Mythology of the American Frontier, 1600–1860,* (Middletown, Conn.: Wesleyan Univ. Press, 1973); Henry Nash Smith, *Virgin Land: The American West as Symbol and Myth* (Cambridge: Harvard Univ. Press, 1970); Leo Marx, *The Machine in the Garden: Technology and the Pastoral Ideal in America* (New York: Oxford Univ. Press, 1964); Roderick Nash, *Wilderness and the American Mind* (New Haven: Yale Univ. Press, 1982); John G. Cawelti, *Adventure, Mystery, and Romance* (Chicago: Univ. of Chicago Press, 1976).

5 *Oxford Universal English Dictionary,* ed. C. T. Onions (New York: Oxford Univ. Press / Doubleday, Doran & Co., 1937), p. 755.

6 Edwin Fussell, *Frontier: American Literature and the American West* (Princeton: Princeton Univ. Press, 1965), p. 6.

7 Frederick Jackson Turner, *The Significance of the Frontier in American History,* ed. Harold P. Simonson (New York: Frederick Ungar Publishing Co., 1983), p. 27. For a casebook look at Turner's essay and the ensuing flap among American historians, pro and con, see Ray Allen Billington, ed., *The Frontier Thesis: Valid Interpretation of American History?* (New York: Holt, Rinehart and Winston, 1966).

8 Erna Fergusson, *Our Southwest* (New York: Alfred A. Knopf, 1946), p. 375.

9 Interview with Quail Hawkins, July 16, 1981, Berkeley, Calif.

10 Turner, *The Significance of the Frontier,* p. 28.

11 Richard Hofstadter, "Turner and the Frontier Myth," *American Scholar* (Autumn 1949), p. 442.

12 T. M. Pearce, "The 'Other' Frontiers of the American West," *Arizona and the West* (Summer 1962), p. 105.

13 Harvey Fergusson, *Modern Man: His Belief and Behavior* (New York: Alfred A. Knopf, 1936); idem, *People and Power: A Study of Political Behavior in America* (New York: William Morrow & Co., 1947).

14 See William T. Pilkington, *Harvey Fergusson* (Boston: Twayne Pub-

lishers, 1975), pp. 31–35. Also, William T. Pilkington, Introduction to *Grant of Kingdom*, by Harvey Fergusson (Albuquerque: Univ. of New Mexico Press, 1950), pp. v–xi. Relevant reviews include "Snark-Hunter," *Time*, Feb. 10, 1936, pp. 75–76; *Journal of Philosophy* (July 1936), pp. 388–89; *American Journal of Psychology* (Oct. 1936), pp. 701–2; *New York Times*, Jan. 26, 1936, p. 2. See also "Modern Man and Harvey Fergusson—A Symposium," *New Mexico Quarterly* (May 1936), pp. 123–35.

15 Pilkington, *Harvey Fergusson*, p. 44.

16 Smith, *Virgin Land*, p. 58; Slotkin, *Regeneration through Violence*, p. 23.

17 Harvey Fergusson, Diary, April 15, 1906, Fergusson Papers, Bancroft Library.

18 An interesting companion book to read all these years later is Marilyn French, *Beyond Power* (New York: Summit Books, 1985). French's point is that the power structure is predominantly paternalistic and masculine—and mistakenly so. Fergusson is concerned with the common man in his study of power—not woman—making the pairing with French's book even more ironic and illustrative of her point.

19 Book jacket, *People and Power*.

20 Pilkington, *Harvey Fergusson*, p. 44. Pertinent reviews include *New York Times Book Review*, Oct. 5, 1947, p. 7; *New York Herald Tribune Weekly Book Review*, Sept. 21, 1947, p. 2; *San Francisco Chronicle*, December 21, 1947, p. 19.

21 Harold P. Simonson, *The Closed Frontier: Studies in American Literary Tragedy* (New York: Holt, Rinehart and Winston, 1970).

CHAPTER 2

1 Paul Horgan, "A Castle in New Spain," in *Figures in a Landscape* (New York: Harper & Row, 1940), pp. 160–82.

2 Taped interview with Paul Horgan, Middletown, Conn., Nov., 1981.

3 Franz Huning, *Trader on the Santa Fe Trail: Memoirs of Franz Huning*, ed. Lina Fergusson Browne (Albuquerque: University of Albuquerque, in collaboration with Calvin Horn Publisher, 1973).

4 Horgan, "Castle," p. 170.

5 Harvey Fergusson, *Home in the West: An Inquiry into My Origins* (New York: Duell, Sloan and Pearce, 1944).

6 *The New Yorker*, Jan. 27, 1945, p. 67. R. L. North insisted that after reading the book he still did not know the answer to the question "Who is Harvey Fergusson and what is he?" (*Saturday Review of Literature*, Feb. 24, 1945). See also *New York Times Book Review*, Feb. 4, 1945, p. 7; *New Republic*, Jan. 19, 1945, p. 398; *Commonweal*, March 2, 1945, p. 500. *The*

Nation, Feb. 24, 1945, p. 227, called *Home* and Fergusson's psychologizing "the feeblest of wolf songs."

7   James K. Folsom, *Harvey Fergusson* (Austin: Steck Vaughn, 1969), pp. 7, 8.

8   Folsom, *Fergusson,* pp. 8–9. Marc Simmons, *Albuquerque* (Albuquerque: Univ. of New Mexico Press, 1982), p. 284, sees Huning as representative of Old Town (past) and H. B. Fergusson as representing New Town (future).

9   See note 3, above. Furthermore, the reminiscences of Lina Fergusson Browne which acccompany Huning's memoir are an added source of information about the childhood of the Fergusson children—Erna, Harvey, Lina, and Francis—in early Albuquerque. Lina married Spencer C. Browne, Jr., the grandson of J. Ross Browne (1821–75), mining commissioner, southwestern traveler, and humorous commentator on the early California scene; and she edited letters, journals, and other writings of J. Ross Browne's. See Lina Fergusson Browne, ed. *J. Ross Browne: His Letters, Journals and Writings* (Albuquerque: Univ. of New Mexico Press, 1969); also see idem, ed., "J. Ross Browne in the Apache Country," *New Mexico Quarterly* (Spring 1965), pp. 5–28.

10 Lina Fergusson Browne, ed., *Trader on the Santa Fe Trail,* p. xi. In her genealogical notes, Erna Fergusson dates that dissolution as 1871.

11 Interview with Fred D. Huning, Jr., Los Lunas, N.M., July 9, 1981. See Browne's Appendix 1 to *Trader,* pp. 149–51.

12 Huning, *Trader on the Santa Fe Trail,* p. 19.

13 For an interesting comparison of description dealing with similar scenes as seen by James Pattie, refer to Richard Batman, *American Ecclesiastes: An Epic Journey through the Early American West* (New York: Harcourt Brace Jovanovich, 1984).

14 William Jackson Parish, *The Charles Ilfeld Company* (Cambridge: Harvard Univ. Press, 1961), p. 309.

15 Marc Simmons picks up on this metaphor of conquest and kingdom, naturally enough, and refers to Huning and others like Ilfeld and Rosenstein as "Albuquerque's new merchant princes" during the 1850s (Simmons, *Albuquerque,* p. 156).

16 Huning Papers, Special Collections, Univ. of New Mexico Library. See also Byron A. Johnson, *Old Town Albuquerque, New Mexico: A Guide to Its History and Architecture* (Albuquerque: Albuquerque Museum, 1980), p. 87. Johnson says that Huning bought the property from Father Machebeuf in 1861 and built his store between 1863 and 1864. The cornerstone bore the legend "August 31, 1864. Fourth Year of the American Civil War. General Grant trying to take Petersburg and Richmond. Gold at 260%. Indians on the Santa Fe road to the United States very hostile. We

built this house and the steam mill in Rancho Seco at the same time."

17   See typescript, Huning Papers, Univ. of New Mexico Library; Huning, *Trader*, pp. 73–75.

18   Simmons, *Albuquerque*, pp. 217–20, 224–28.

19   Howard Bryan, "Railroad Avenue," *Albuquerque Tribune*, Feb. 22, 1984, p. A-2.

20   See Huning, *Trader*, p. 104; also see Barbara Young Simms, "Those Fabulous Fergussons," *El Palacio* (Summer 1976), p. 43.

21   Oliver La Farge, *The Mother Ditch* (Santa Fe: Sunstone Press, 1983).

22   Sylvester Baxter, "Along the Rio Grande," in *New Mexico 100 Years Ago*, comp. Skip Whitson (Albuquerque: Sun Books, 1977), p. 32. Baxter, referring to Huning as "an impassioned tree planter," reports that in 1881 Huning planted 1,500 trees. The pen-and-ink drawings which accompany Baxter's article emphasize the romantic qualities of the mill and the house. While the mill looks so Germanic as to be out of place in its general surroundings, the house captures a thoroughly New Mexican atmosphere with three native women in shawls and flowing dresses, a naked baby playing in the dirt beside one of the women, doves on the edge of the flat adobe roof and flying into the placita, and a cage of canaries (presumably Ernestine's) adorning one of the inner placita walls. In *Home* (p. 40), Fergusson records that some of the trees around the mill served as hanging trees for the lynching of three rowdies. After a brief parley among Huning and other citizens, Huning rode with the crowd into the night. In the morning the "professional bad men" were found dangling from the trees.

23   Huning, *Trader*, pp. 107–9.

24   Clara Huning, Memoir, Huning Papers, Univ. of New Mexico Library.

25   Browne, ed., *Trader*, pp. 106–7.

26   Virginia F. Gillespie, "This Old House," *New Mexico Magazine* (Feb. 1967), p. 4.

27   See Simmons, *Albuquerque*, p. 218.

28   Bainbridge Bunting, "A Glimpse into the Past: Huning Castle, Albuquerque," *New Mexico Architect* (March–April 1960), pp. 16–19.

29   Huning, *Trader*, p. 105.

30   Bunting, "A Glimpse," p. 16.

31   Huning, *Trader*, p. 138.

32   Ibid., p. 139.

33   *Albuquerque Evening Citizen*, Nov. 4, 1905.

34   Clara Huning Fergusson, Memoir, Huning Papers, Univ. of New Mexico Library.

35   Franz Huning, July 16, 1904, Huning Papers, Univ. of New Mexico Library.

36 Interview with Irene Fisher, Albuquerque, July 9, 1981. See also William A. Keleher, *New Mexicans I Knew: Memoirs, 1892–1969* (Albuquerque: Univ. of New Mexico Press, 1969). In 1890 Keleher delivered telegrams to Huning on a weekly basis. Huning and his wife, "Grossmutter," are portrayed as playful and good-natured teases, always initiating a game with Keleher about saving the ten-cent New Town delivery charge by standing on the Old Town side, or the west door, of the double-door entrance: "Franz Huning would take a telegram in Old Town or New Town, as he chose, but always rewarded the boy with a a twenty-five-cent tip" (p. 54).

37 Erna Fergusson to Francis Fergusson, Jan. 9, 1955 (letter in possession of Francis Fergusson).

38 *Albuquerque Tribune,* Jan. 21, 1955, p. 1.

39 Simmons, *Albuquerque,* p. 281.

40 Bunting, "A Glimpse," pp. 16–19.

CHAPTER 3

1 Simmons, *Albuquerque,* p. 284.

2 Sampie Fergusson Taliaferro, in her memoir (1937), identifies Patrick Ferguson as a major; Harvey Fergusson identifies him as a general in *Home.* Memoir of Sampie Fergusson Taliaferro, Huning Papers, Univ. of New Mexico Library.

3 Sampie Fergusson Taliaferro, Memoir, p. 9. The Clay Fergusson Society of North America offers a somewhat different genealogy than that understood by H. B. Fergusson and Harvey Fergusson. The belief that Sampson N. Ferguson descended from a brother of the General Ferguson killed at the Battle of Kings Mountain is described as something of a "legend." Perhaps Col. James Fergusson was Patrick's nephew. "Col. [*sic*] Patrick Ferguson, who was killed at Kings Mountain, never married. Militia Col. James Ferguson (Tory) was killed at the Battle of Huck's Defeat, one of the skirmishes leading up to the Battle of Kings Mountain. James did marry and have a family and we believe [Harvey Fergusson] descended from James" (Shirley Ferguson Doran to Harvey Fergusson, II, Feb. 12, 1984; letter in possession of Harvey Fergusson, II).

4 Sampie Fergusson Taliaferro, Memoir, p. 41.

5 Erna Fergusson guessed that her grandfather Sampson Noland Ferguson got his title of doctor by rolling pills in an apothecary shop. She was dissuaded from that notion, however, by local Alabama historian and attorney J. J. Willett, who insisted that Fergusson "practiced medicine in Pickensville, Alabama, which he could not have done unless he had been a licensed physician from some college. The old south believed strongly

in educating its doctors" (Willett to Erna Fergusson, June 28, 1948, Fergusson Papers, Univ. of New Mexico Library). Sampie records in her memoir that Ferguson "was graduated from a medical school in Nashville" (Sampie Fergusson Taliaferro, Memoir, p. 29).

6 Erna Fergusson to Clara Mary Fergusson, Feb. 21, no year, Erna Fergusson Papers, Special Collections, Univ. of New Mexico Library.

7 Sampie Fergusson Taliaferro, Memoir, pp. 42–43.

8 *Dictionary of Alabama Biography,* Fergusson Papers, Univ. of New Mexico Library.

9 Sampson Noland Fergusson to H. B. Fergusson, April 20, 1864, Fergusson Papers, Univ. of New Mexico.

10 See Scottie King, *Listen to the Wind: Ghost Towns of New Mexico* (Santa Fe: New Mexico Magazine, 1978), p. 26.

11 Harvey Fergusson, "Billy the Kid," *American Mercury* (June 1925), pp. 224–31. Fergusson makes much of the ending of the frontier in this biographical sketch, saying that Billy's death signified an end of an era: "The brief day of the hero-bandit in the Southwest was over" (p. 231). See also Fergusson, *The Life of Riley* (New York: Grosset and Dunlap, 1937), pp. 227–56.

12 William A. Keleher, *The Fabulous Frontier* (Albuquerque: Univ. of New Mexico Press, 1982), p. 36.

13 Ibid., pp. 208–32; also see Howard R. Lamar, *The Reader's Encyclopedia of the American West* (New York: Thomas Y. Crowell Co., 1977), pp. 359–60. David Townsend's research on Fall's background and the events surrounding Teapot Dome (e.g., "To the Peak" and "The Dark Valley," papers delivered at the 1985 annual meeting of the New Mexico Historical Society, Las Cruces, N.M.) is exemplary in its objectivity and detail. Hough's novel *The Land of the Heart's Desire* includes a character purportedly based on H. B. Fergusson.

14 Keleher, *The Fabulous Frontier,* p. 39.

15 Ibid.

16 Morris B. Parker, *White Oaks,* ed. C. L. Sonnichsen (Tucson: Univ. of Arizona Press, 1971), p. 88.

17 Clara Mary Huning, Memoir, Huning Papers, Univ. of New Mexico Library.

18 In 1852 six Sisters of Loretto left their order's house in Kentucky and traveled to Santa Fe under the direction of Bishop Jean Baptiste Lamy. "Only four arrived . . . and in January 1853 Our Lady of Light, the first boarding school for girls, opened" (Syntha Motto, *Albuquerque Journal,* Feb. 1, 1976, p. H-12). See also Paul Horgan, *Lamy of Santa Fe* (New York: Farrar, Straus and Giroux, 1975), pp. 160–65, 318–19.

19 One of the first things which struck Sylvester Baxter about New Town

was "the sidewalk, to use a Hibernianism, it being actually in the middle of the broad Railroad Avenue, for the street-car track was planked over between the rails and used as a walking place, while the rest of the street was a bed of soft sand" (Baxter, "Along the Rio Grande," p. 32).

20 Calvin A. Roberts, "H. B. Fergusson, 1848–1915: New Mexico Spokesman for Political Reform," *New Mexico Historical Review* (July 1982), p. 242.

21 See Robert W. Cherny, *A Righteous Cause: The Life of William Jennings Bryan* (Boston: Little, Brown, 1985). Bryan played a key role in H. B. Fergusson's political career from beginning to end. He visited La Glorieta and became a family friend and, when things grew rough, supported H.B. when he truly needed support. H.B. probably attached his political career too closely to Bryan's. William A. Keleher, *New Mexicans I Knew: Memoirs, 1892–1969* (Albuquerque: Univ. of New Mexico Press, 1969), pp. 38–39, tells of his impression of Bryan's visit to H. B. Fergusson and Albuquerque on January 20, 1895. The two had served in Congress together, and Bryan came to Albuquerque "as a gesture of friendship" and to give a speech on free silver.

22 The key issue in the 1896 presidential election was the free coinage of silver at a ratio of 16:1 with gold, which Bryan, the Democrat, favored and McKinley vehemently opposed. "In an election marked by sharp sectional divisions McKinley triumphed 271 electoral votes to 176" (*Encyclopedia of American Biography* [New York: Harper & Row, 1974], p. 715).

23 Roberts. "H. B. Fergusson," pp. 237–55; also Robert W. Larson, *New Mexico's Quest for Statehood, 1846–1912* (Albuquerque: Univ. of New Mexico Press, 1968), pp. 189–90, 192–94.

24 Simmons, *Albuquerque*, p. 283.

25 Roberts, "H. B. Fergusson," p. 252.

26 Larson, *New Mexico's Quest for Statehood*, pp. 193–94.

27 Estimates of the acreage given to the territory range from 100,000 to 4.25 million: see Simmons, *Albuquerque*, p. 283; Roberts, "H. B. Fergusson," p. 247; and Larson, *New Mexico's Quest for Statehood*, p. 193. Also see *Congressional Record—House*, 55th Cong., 2d sess., vol. 31, pt. 2 (Jan. 25, Feb. 22, 1898), pp. 1369–74.

28 Roberts, "H. B. Fergusson," p. 246.

29 An example of H. B. Fergusson's stand against the state constitution as drawn up at that time may be found in H. B. Fergusson and Frank W. Clancy, "Addresses on the Making of a Constitution," *Bulletin of the University of New Mexico*, no. 57 (October 1910): 6–15.

30 Certified copy of vital record, Vital Statistics Bureau, State of New Mexico.

31   *Lakewood Progress,* June 11, 1915, p. 1.
32   H. B. Fergusson to William Jennings Bryan, September 15, 1911, Fergusson Papers, Univ. of New Mexico Library.
33   H. B. Fergusson to H. H. Pierce, November 16, 1911, Fergusson Papers, UNM Library.
34   H. B. Fergusson to Clara Fergusson, July 28, 1912, Fergusson Papers, UNM Library.
35   Ibid.
36   William Jennings Bryan to Clara Fergusson, June 11, 1915, Fergusson Papers, UNM Library.
37   Roberts, "H. B. Fergusson," p. 252.
38   Francis Fergusson to Robert Gish, October 2, 1981; interview with Francis Fergusson, Kingston, N.J., May 13, 1982.
39   Petition to the Court, Albuquerque–Bernalillo County Probate Court, July 1922 term, Fergusson Papers, UNM Library.
40   Francis Fergusson, interview, May 13, 1982.
41   Erna Fergusson to Francis Fergusson, November 4, 1950, Fergusson Papers, UNM Library.
42   Francis Fergusson, interview, May 13, 1982.
43   Ibid.
44   Ibid.
45   H. B. Fergusson, Diary, December 3, 1869, Fergusson Papers, UNM Library.

CHAPTER 4

1   Robert E. Spiller, *The Cycle of American Literature: An Essay in Historical Criticism* (New York: New American Library, 1957), p. 107. For a capsule summary of the general effect or influence of the closing of the frontier on American literature, see Bartholow V. Crawford, Alexander C. Kern, and Morris H. Needleman, "The Triumph of Realism: 1865–1914," in *American Literature* (New York: Barnes & Noble, 1965), pp. 158–59.
2   Harvey Fergusson, "Albuquerque Revisited: A Preface to the Apollo Edition of *Rio Grande*," *Rio Grande* (New York: William Morrow & Co., 1967), p. xi.
3   Quoted in "Harvey Fergusson," in *Twentieth-Century Authors,* ed. Stanley J. Kunitz and Howard Haycraft (New York: H. W. Wilson Co., 1942), p. 445. See also Harry R. Warfel, *American Novelists Today* (New York: American Book Co., 1951), pp. 150–51.
4   Fergusson to J. Frank Dobie, May 2, 1951, Alfred A. Knopf Correspondence, Humanities Research Center, Univ. of Texas at Austin.
5   Jim Acosta (associate registrar, UNM) to Robert Gish, Dec. 26, 1985.

6   Quoted in Kunitz and Haycraft, *Twentieth-Century Authors*, pp. 445–46.
7   See J. R. Kelly, *A History of New Mexico Military Institute, 1891–1941* (Albuquerque: Univ. of New Mexico Press, 1953), pp. 40, 43.
8   Harold S. Head (registrar, Washington and Lee University) to Robert Gish, June 13, 1985.
9   Fergusson's perceptions of Washington and Lee seem biased, to say the least. For more reverent and accepting perceptions revealing biases on the other side, see John E. Hughes, *A Solitary Man* (Lexington, Va." Washington and Lee University, 1974); and *Washington's Gift to Liberty Hall* (Lexington: Washington & Lee University, 1975).
10 Warfel, *American Novelists Today*, p. 150.
11 U.S. Department of Agriculture Library, 1910–13, *Forest Service Field Program*, no. 404827, p. 11.
12 See Edwin A. Tucker, "The Forest Service in the Southwest" (Albuquerque: U.S. Forest Service, n.d.), 4:1368 (typescript). See also Edwin A. Tucker and George Fitzpatrick, *Men Who Matched the Mountains: The Forest Service in the Southwest* (Washington, D.C.: U.S. Government Printing Office, 1972).
13 Tucker, "The Forest Service in the Southwest," 1:118.
14 Ibid., p. 179.
15 Ed C. Groesbeck to Robert Gish, June 12, 1984; telephone interview with Lou Liedman, June 15, 1984.
16 *Who's Who in America*, 32 (1962–63): 985.
17 *The National Cyclopaedia of American Biography* (New York: James T. White & Co., 1947), p. 297.
18 Donald S. Dreesen, "Directory of Albuquerque Settlers" (unpublished, 1972).
19 Susan Dewitt, *Historic Albuquerque Today* (Albuquerque: Historic Landmark Survey, 1978), p. 102.
20 *Washington Star*, March 23, 1918; *Albuquerque Morning Journal*, March 23, 1918, p. 4.
21 Fergusson Papers, Bancroft Library (hereafter FPBL).
22 Fergusson, Diary, Jan. 2, 1959, FPBL.
23 Harvey Fergusson, "Mencken," typescript, Bancroft Library (also see Fergusson's rememberings of Mencken published in "Bouquets for Mencken," *The Nation*, Sept. 12, 1953, pp. 211–12); Mencken to Fergusson, Aug. 20, 1919, FPBL.
24 "Mencken," typescript, p. 3.
25 Ibid., p. 4.
26 "Bouquets for Mencken," p. 212.
27 David Remley, "Pieces from a Gaudy Age," *Impact*, Sept. 24, 1985, p. 14.

28 See *Encyclopedia of American Biography*, ed. John A. Garraty (New York: Harper & Row Publishers, 1974), p. 121.

29 Remley, "Pieces from a Gaudy Age," p. 14.

30 *Encyclopedia of American Biography*, p. 752.

31 Daniel Aaron, Foreword to *Letters of H. L. Mencken*, ed. Guy J. Forgue (Boston: Northeastern Univ. Press, 1981), p. vi.

32 Carl Bode, *Mencken* (Carbondale: Southern Illinois Univ. Press, 1969), pp. 103–5.

33 Ibid., p. 105.

34 Ibid., p. 107.

35 Ibid., p. 125.

36 See Robert E. Spiller, *Literary History of the United States* (New York: Macmillan Co., 1968), p. 1132.

37 See Bode, *Mencken*, pp. 220–21; also Spiller, *Literary History*, p. 1132.

38 Mencken to Fergusson, Aug. 6, 1924, FPBL.

39 Harvey Fergusson, *Blood of the Conquerors* (Boston: Gregg Press, 1978).

40 Erna Fergusson, *Our Southwest*, p. 375.

41 In 1922 Fergusson conducted a series of interviews with Fred Huning, Jr., visited the Huning family sheep camps, and took over fifteen pages of notes on those discussions. But his fascination with sheep ranching can be traced to even earlier times and Kit Carson's and Uncle Dick Wooton's dealings with sheep. Fergusson planned to include much of this information in *Rio Grande* but decided against it (FPBL).

42 Fergusson, Diary, April 23, 1921, FPBL.

43 Fergusson, Diary, Oct. 13, 1967, FPBL.

44 Fergusson to Mencken, Dec. 19, 1921, Mencken Correspondence, New York Public Library (hereafter MC).

45 For reviews of *Conquerors* see the following: *The New Republic*, Jan. 11, 1922, pp. 186–87; *New York Times Book Review*, Oct. 30, 1921, p. 19; *The Bookman*, Dec. 21, 1921, p. 395.

46 Fergusson to Mencken, July 19, 1920, MC.

47 Mencken to Fergusson, June 5, 1922, FPBL.

48 Fergusson to Mencken, July 25, 1922, MC.

49 Harvey Fergusson, *Capitol Hill* (New York: Alfred A. Knopf, 1923).

50 Harvey Fergusson, "The Washington Job-Holder," *American Mercury* (March 1924), pp. 345–50.

51 Fergusson to Mencken, June 8, 1922, MC.

52 See Harvey Fergusson, "National Woman's Party Backing New Amendment to Give Sex Equal Rights," *Baltimore Evening Sun*, April 6, 1923, p. 1. Fergusson observes, "Whatever may be thought of the party's program, it must be admitted it pursues its end with admirable singleness of purpose" (p. 2).

53 H. L. Mencken, review of *Blood of the Conquerors, Baltimore Evening Sun*, Jan. 14, 1922.

54 H. L. Mencken, review of *Capitol Hill, Baltimore Evening Sun*, April 7, 1923.

55 Harvey Fergusson, notes on *Capitol Hill*, n.d., FPBL.

56 Fergusson, Diary, Aug. 26, 1922, FPBL.

57 Forgue, *Letters of H. L. Mencken*, p. 219.

58 Ibid., p. 231.

59 H. L. Mencken, *Prejudices: Fifth Series* (New York: Knopf, 1926), p. 222.

60 Fergusson, General Notes, Diary, 1923, FPBL.

61 Forgue, *Letters of H. L. Mencken*, p. 464.

62 Editorial, *American Mercury*, Vol. 1, no. 1 (January 1924): 28.

63 "American Portraits: The Washington Job-Holder," *American Mercury* (March 1924), pp. 345–50; "Billy the Kid," ibid. (June 1925), pp. 112–13; "The New Englander," ibid. (Feb. 1926), pp. 187–95; "Seen and Heard in Mexico," ibid. (June 1930), pp. 164–71; "Rio Grande," ibid. (May–Aug. 1931), pp. 1–10.

64 Fergusson to Mencken, Aug. 12, 1923, MC.

65 Fergusson to Mencken, Nov. 29, 1923, MC.

66 Fergusson, Diary, Aug. 27, 1922, FPBL.

67 Fergusson, Diary, July 13, 1928, FPBL.

68 Fergusson, Diary, Sept. 11, 1922, FPBL.

69 Fergusson, Diary, Aug. 27, 1922, FPBL.

70 Fergusson, Diary, June 28, 1924, FPBL.

71 Harvey Fergusson, *Women and Wives* (New York: Alfred A. Knopf, 1924), pp. 294–95. Representative reviews of *Women and Wives* include the following: *The New Republic*. Aug. 13, 1924, p. 336; *Times Literary Supplement*, Oct. 16, 1924, p. 648; and *New York Times Book Review*, April 20, 1924, p. 8.

CHAPTER 5

1 Fergusson, Diary, Jan. 31, 1923, FPBL.

2 Fergusson, Diary, Aug. 2, 1922, FPBL.

3 Fergusson, Diary, July 27, 1922, FPBL.

4 Fergusson to Mencken, July 13, 1923, MC.

5 Fergusson to Mencken, Aug. 2, 1923, MC.

6 Fergusson to Mencken, Aug. 2 and Sept. 21, 1923, MC.

7 Fergusson to Mencken, Aug. 28, 1923, MC.

8 Fergusson, Diary, May 1, 1925, FPBL.

9 Fergusson, Diary, Sept. 5, 1924, FPBL.

10 Fergusson to Mencken, July 20, 1924, MC.

11 Fergusson to Mencken, Oct. 12, 1924, MC.

12 Fergusson, Diary, Sept. 9, 1924, FPBL.

13 Fergusson, Diary, Sept. 5, 1926, FPBL.

14 Harvey Fergusson, *Hot Saturday* (New York: Alfred A. Knopf, 1926), pp. 5–6.

15 Fergusson, Diary, July 13, 1928, FPBL.

16 Fergusson, Diary, April 18, 1924, FPBL.

17 For reviews at the time of publication see the following: *New York Times Book Review*, Aug. 22, 1926, p. 7; *Saturday Review of Literature*, Oct. 22, 1926, p. 86.

18 Fergusson to Mencken, May 21, 1925, MC.

19 Fergusson to Mencken, Sept. 30, 1926, MC. Also, Fergusson, Diary, Jan. 30, 1925, FPBL.

20 Mary Graham Bonner, "Memories of Rebecca McCann," in *The Complete Cheerful Cherub*, by Rebecca McCann (New York: Covici, Friede, 1932), pp. 3–9.

21 Ibid., p. 7.

22 Ibid., p. 9.

23 Fergusson, Diary, Jan. 26, 1927, FPBL.

24 Ibid., May 29, 1927.

25 Ibid., Aug. 14, 1927.

26 Ibid. Reviews of *Wolf Song* include *The Nation*, Sept. 14, 1927, pp. 263–64; *Times Literary Supplement*, Sept. 22, 1927, p. 650; *Saturday Review of Literature*, Oct. 22, 1927, p. 242; *New York Times*, Aug. 7, 1927, p. 12.

27 Bonner, "Memories of Rebecca McCann," p. 9.

28 Interview with Irene Fisher, Albuquerque, July 9, 1981.

29 Fergusson, Diary, July 13, 1928, FPBL.

30 Delbert E. Wylder, Mountain-Man Novels as Literature of the Last Frontier" (paper presented at the annual meeting of the Western Literature Association, Reno, Nev., 1984). John R. Milton, *The Novel of the American West* (Lincoln: Univ. of Nebraska Press, 1980), p. 234, compares *Wolf Song* with Guthrie's *Big Sky* and Manfred's *Lord Grizzly* as the best of fictional treatments of the mountain man.

31 David Stouck, "The Art of the Mountain-Man Novel," *Western American Literature* (Nov. 1985), p. 215.

32 Ibid.

33 Frank Waters to Robert Gish, Sept. 21, 1984. See also Robert W. Smith, "Standing Tall: An Essay/Conversation with . . . Frank Waters," *Bloomsbury Review* (Sept. 1984), p. 20.

34 William T. Pilkington, Introduction to *Wolf Song*, by Harvey Fergusson (Boston: Gregg Press, 1978), p. ix.

35   Harvey Fergusson, *Wolf Song* (Boston: Gregg Press, 1978), p. 2.
36   Fergusson to Mencken, March 26, 1928, MC.
37   Harvey Fergusson, *In Those Days* (Boston: Gregg Press, 1978), p. 6.
38   Harvey Fergusson, "Solons Swallow Theory of the Vanishing Blond," *Baltimore Evening Sun*, Feb. 23, 1923.
39   Fergusson to Mencken, Feb. 16, 1929, MC.
40   Fergusson to Mencken, Feb. 12, 1927, MC.
41   Harvey Fergusson, "Seen and Heard in Mexico," *American Mercury* (June 1930), pp. 165–71.
42   Fergusson to Mencken, Feb. 6, 1929, MC.
43   Fergusson, "Seen and Heard in Mexico," p. 169.
44   Fergusson, Diary, March 27, 1925, FPBL.
45   Harvey Fergusson, *Footloose McGarnigal* (New York: Alfred A. Knopf, 1930), p. 14.
46   Fergusson, general comments, 1923 Diary, FPBL.
47   See *Saturday Review of Literature*, Jan. 26, 1930, p. 682; *Bookman*, March 1930, p. 99; *New York Times*, Feb. 2, 1930, p. 8.
48   Fergusson, Diary, Sept. 6, 1924, FPBL; also ibid., Sept. 2, 1922.
49   Fergusson, Diary, July 16, 1924, FPBL.

CHAPTER 6

1   Fergusson, "Billy the Kid," *American Mercury* (June 1925), pp. 112–14; "The New Englander," ibid. (Feb. 1926), pp. 187–95. Other periodical pieces about New Mexico written by Fergusson preliminary to *Rio Grande* include an essay concerning his sister Erna's Koshare Tour business, "New Mexico: An Old Land of New Delights," in *The Koshare Book* (Albuquerque: Koshare Tours and the Albuquerque Chamber of Commerce, c. 1922), pp. 3–6; an essay about the U.S. Forest Service, "Out Where Bureaucracy Begins," *The Nation*, July 22, 1925, pp. 112–14; another short story similar to "The New Englander," about the rise and fall of a gifted young musician, Jim Runyon, who leaves Albuquerque with much promise of a career as a violinist only to return to sell insurance, "The Gifted Lad," *Scribner's Magazine* (June 1927), pp. 650–56; a travelog-tourism essay, "The Lure of the Southwest," *American Motorist* (Dec. 1927), p. 10; and "The Cult of the Indian," *Scribner's Magazine* (Aug. 1930), pp. 129–33, another nonfiction look at "the contemporary worship of the primitive," but in the context of literary history in addition to American popular culture of the time.
2   Fergusson to Mencken, June 15, 1930, MC.
3   Fergusson to Mencken, March 6, 1931, MC.
4   Fergusson to Mencken, December 13, 1930, MC.

5 Fergusson to Mencken, January 5, 1931, MC.

6 Fergusson to Mencken, January 28, 1931, MC.

7 Fergusson, Diary, Jan.–March 1931, FPBL.

8 Fergusson to Mencken, March 6, 1931, MC.

9 Fergusson, Diary, June 13, 1931, FPBL.

10 See Carl Bode, *Mencken* (Carbondale: Southern Illinois Univ. Press, 1969), pp. 209, 236.

11 Fergusson to Mencken, March 22, 1931, MC.

12 Fergusson, "Rio Grande: The River, the Valley, and the People," *American Mercury* (May 1931), p. xxii.

13 Edwin L. Sabin, "The Old Southwest," *Saturday Review of Literature*, Aug. 12, 1933, p. 41.

14 Maxwell Anderson, *The Nation*, Aug. 16, 1933, p. 191.

15 Paul Horgan, review of *Rio Grande, Yale Review* (Sept. 1933), pp. 211–13. For a more detailed comparison of Horgan and Fergusson as Rio Grande novelist-historians, see Robert Gish, "'Pretty But Is It History?': The Legacy of Harvey Fergusson's *Rio Grande*" *New Mexico Historical Review* (Spring 1985), pp. 173–92.

16 Harvey Fergusson, *Rio Grande* (New York: William Morrow and Co., 1955), p. 293. Text references are to this edition.

17 See Harvey Fergusson, "Albuquerque Revisited," in *Rio Grande* (New York: William Morrow and Co., 1967), pp. vii–xiii.

18 Harvey Fergusson, "Timber Line," *New Mexico Magazine* (July 1957), p. 28.

19 Harvey Fergusson, "Retrospect," 1940 Diary, FPBL.

20 See Pilkington, *Harvey Fergusson*, p. 29.

21 Pilkington, *Harvey Fergusson*, p. 28, says, "He went to California for the first time in 1931." *Hot Saturday* was produced by Paramount in 1932.

22 Fergusson to Horgan, n.d. (letter in Horgan's possession). Horgan dates it as ca. 1930; it was probably written in 1932, perhaps late in 1931.

23 Fergusson, Diary, May 7, 1940, FPBL.

24 Fergusson, Diary, Dec. 24, 1942, FPBL.

25 Fergusson, "Work Plan," 1934 Diary, FPBL.

26 Harvey Fergusson, "Proud Rider," *Blue Book Magazine* (Dec. 1935), pp. 18–41; (Jan. 1936), pp. 28–56. See also Robert Gish, "Cruelty and Civility in Harvey Fergusson's *Proud Rider*," *Southwestern American Literature* (Spring 1985), pp. 5–11. Also see Sue Simmons McGinity, "Harvey Fergusson's Use of Animal Imagery in Characterizing Spanish-American Women," *Western Review* (Winter 1971), pp. 46–50.

27 Harvey Fergusson, Introduction to *The Santa Fe Omnibus* (New York Grosset and Dunlap, by arrangement with Alfred A. Knopf, 1942), p. v.

28 Fergusson, general comments, 1942 Diary, FPBL.

29 Fergusson, general comments, 1941 Diary, FPBL.

30 Fergusson, general comments, 1942 Diary, FPBL.

31 Fergusson to Paul Horgan, Jan. 31, 1937 (letter in possession of Paul Horgan).

32 Fergusson to Mencken, Aug. 19, 1934, MC.

33 Fergusson to Mencken, Sept. 10, 1934, MC.

34 Fergusson to Mencken, Jan. 6, 1935, MC.

35 Fergusson to Horgan, Feb. 14, 1936 (Letter in Horgan's possession).

36 Fergusson to Horgan, Jan. 31, 1937 (letter in Horgan's possession).

37 Fergusson, general comments, 1944 Diary, FPBL.

38 Harvey Fergusson, *The Life of Riley* (New York: Grosset & Dunlap, 1937). Representative reviews include James D. Hart, "Too Many Ladies," *Saturday Review of Literature,* July 3, 1937, p. 6; Charles Poore, "The Story of a Man Who Enjoyed Life," *New York Times Book Review,* July 4, 1937, p. 4.

39 James Hart, review of *The Life of Riley, Saturday Review of Literature,* July 3, 1937, p. 6.

40 As early as 1921 Fergusson recorded in his diaries his interest in Clement Wood's belief in the "biological law" that "woman chooses a mate superior to herself." In response to such an axiom Fergusson exclaimed that it "explains a lot." "It is not always a determining factor in choice, but it is probably always present. The tendency of women of an inferior race to give themselves to men of the superior, and the lack of a corresponding tendency" (notes, 1921–24, FPBL).

41 *Stand Up and Fight,* directed by Luis Van Dyke, Sept. 6, 1939, script writers: James M. Cain, Jane Murfin, Harvey Fergusson, and Forbes S. Parkhill; UCLA Theater Arts Research Library and Metro-Goldwyn-Mayer/United Artists Film Library.

42 Fergusson, Diary, April 29, 1940, FPBL.

43 Fergusson to Clara Mary Fergusson, n.d., Fergusson Papers, University of New Mexico. Fergusson's mother recorded on Aug. 9, 1937, "Harvey came with Mr. and Mrs. T. Jennings to look for a setting for Conrad's [Richter's] *Sea of Grass* which they are going to write for a movie" (Clara Huning Fergusson, Memoir, Fergusson Papers, Univ. of New Mexico Library). Fergusson worked first with Jennings and then with his replacement on *The Sea of Grass.* Fergusson and Jennings apparently spent several days in Santa Fe working on the project in 1937.

Fergusson kept no detailed lists of the treatments and scripts he worked on during his years as a Hollywood screenwriter. In his diaries he talks more about months devoted to scripts and money earned. The files of the Academy of Motion Picture Arts and Sciences have no information on Fergusson other than substantiating that he was screenwriter for two films that were actually produced, *It Happened in Hollywood* (1937) and *Stand Up and Fight* (1939). Two of Fergusson's novels, *Wolf Song* and *Hot Saturday,* were made into movies, but Fergusson had little to do with the scripts.

44 Fergusson, 1942 Diary, FPBL.

45 Alfred Knopf to Robert Gish, Aug. 1, 1983.

46 Fergusson to Knopf, Jan. 13, 1946, Alfred A. Knopf Correspondence, Humanities Research Center, Univ. of Texas at Austin. The subsequent Fergusson-Knopf correspondence cited in the text is located in this collection.

47 Jesse Carmack to Robert Gish, Aug. 8, 1981.

48 Paul Carey to Robert Gish, Aug. 19, 1981.

49 Last Will and Testament of Clara Huning Fergusson, Erna Fergusson Papers, Univ. of New Mexico Library. Judging from her memoir and other evidence, it would seem that the accomplishments of Francis—who attended Harvard, was a Rhodes scholar, and became a well-known scholar of Dante and of drama—pleased Clara more than Harvey's accomplishments as a novelist and writer. She allocates just a few sentences to Harvey: "Harvey went to Washington and Lee University, where he graduated, then went into newspaper work which he followed for a number of years until he decided to write fiction, which was more to his taste" (Clara Huning Fergusson, Memoir, Huning Papers, Univ. of New Mexico Library, pp. 109–11).

Irene Fisher (interview, Albuquerque, July 9, 1981) made this observation: "Harvey loved his mother more than his father. She was very impressed with Francis's being named a Rhodes scholar. I don't think Mrs. Fergusson liked Harvey's novels. She didn't care for that kind of thing. I just don't think she saw any sense in putting things like *Hot Saturday*—that type of thing—on paper." As late as the 1930s and the 1940s, not far from the time of Clara's death, Harvey tried to explain to his mother his "compulsion" to write the kind of novels he wrote rather than attempt to write more popular books or make more money in Hollywood, saying "I can't very well explain this to the public but I can try to explain it to you" (Harvey Fergusson to Clara Fergusson, n.d., Fergusson Papers, Univ. of New Mexico Library).

50 Harvey Fergusson, *Grant of Kingdom* (Albuquerque: Univ. of New Mexico Press, 1975). For reviews on the occasion of the original publication see *The New Yorker,* June 3, 1950, p. 100; *New York Times Book Review,* June 4, 1950, p. 26.

51 "*The Conquest of Don Pedro,*" *Wings: The Literary Guild Review* (July 1954), p. 3.

52 Ibid. pp. 3–8.

53   Harvey Fergusson, *The Conquest of Don Pedro* (Albuquerque: Univ. of New Mexico Press, 1974), p. 1. Early reviews include Lon Tinkle, "Commerce Comes to Mexico," *Saturday Review*, July 3, 1954, p. 14; *The Nation*, July 24, 1954, pp. 77–78; *New York Times Book Review*, June 24, 1954, p. 4.

54   Fergusson, "The Enchanted Meadow," *South Dakota Review* (Winter 1974–75), pp. 7–20.

55   Tape-recorded interview with Quail Hawkins, Berkeley, July 26, 1981. The following discussion of the relationship between Quail and Fergusson, as well as quotations from Quail, are drawn from this interview.

56   Fergusson, Diary, May 4, 1954, FPBL.

57   Fergusson, Diary, Jan. 1, 1956, FPBL.

58   Fergusson, Diary, Jan. 2, 1959, FPBL.

59   Fergusson, Diary, Jan. 1, 1963, FPBL.

60   *Albuquerque Tribune*, June 12, 1965.

61   Fergusson, Diary, Sept. 5, 1964, FPBL.

62   Fergusson, Diary, June 3, 1967, FPBL.

63   Fergusson, Diary, July 16, 1967, FPBL.

64   Fergusson, Diary, Sept. 16, 1967, FPBL.

65   Fergusson, Diary, Jan. 31, 1969, FPBL.

66   Fergusson, Diary, Feb. 22, 1970, FPBL.

67   Fergusson, notes for *The King of Terrors*, March 10, 1960, FPBL.

68   Ibid., March 20, 1960.

69   Fergusson, *The Land of Lonely Women* (typed manuscript), FPBL.

70   Fergusson, "The Enchanted Meadow" (typed manuscript), p. 6, FPBL.

71   Interview with Quail Hawkins, July 16, 1981.

72   Fergusson, "Timber Line," *New Mexico Magazine* (July 1957), p. 28.

APPENDIX

1   Lorene Pearson, "Harvey Fergusson and the Crossroads," *New Mexico Quarterly* (Autumn 1951), pp. 334–55.

2   "Modern Man and Harvey Fergusson—A Symposium," *New Mexico Quarterly* (May 1936), pp. 123–35.

3   Cecil Robinson, *With the Ears of Strangers: The Mexican in American Literature* (Tucson: The Univ. of Arizona Press, 1963).

4   Cecil Robinson, "Legend of Destiny: The American Southwest in the Novels of Harvey Fergusson," *American West* (Nov. 1967), pp. 16–18, 67–68; Cecil Robinson, "A Dedication to the Memory of Harvey Fergusson," *Arizona and the West* (Winter 1973), pp. 311–14.

5   Sue Simmons McGinity, "Harvey Fergusson's Use of Animal Imagery in Characterizing Spanish-American Women," *Western Review* (Winter

1971), pp. 46–50; Arthur G. Pettit, "The Decline and Fall of the New Mexican Great House in the Novels of Harvey Fergusson: A Classical Example of Anglo-American Ethnocentricity," *New Mexico Historical Review* (July 1976), pp. 173–91.

6   In addition to "The Decline and Fall," cited above, see Arthur G. Pettit, *Images of the Mexican American in Fiction and Film* (College Station: Texas A&M Univ. Press, 1980), pp. 86–110.

7   John R. Milton, "The Western Novel—A Symposium," *South Dakota Review* (Autumn 1964), pp. 3–36.

8   Saul Cohen, "Harvey Fergusson: A Checklist" (UCLA Library, 1965).

9   John R. Milton, "A Conversation With Harvey Fergusson," *South Dakota Review* (Spring 1971), pp. 39–45; Harvey Fergusson, "The Enchanted Meadow," *South Dakota Review* (Winter 1974–75), pp. 7–20.

10 John R. Milton, "Harvey Fergusson and the Spanish Southwest," in *The Novel of the American West* (Lincoln: Univ. of Nebraska Press, 1980), pp. 230–63.

11 John R. Milton to Robert Gish, Sept. 12, 1984.

12 Saul Cohen, "The Pleasures of a Semi-Impecunious Book Collector," *New Mexico Quarterly* (Spring 1965), p. 54.

13 Ibid., p. 56.

14 Saul Cohen, "The Ten Best Novels of New Mexico," *New Mexico Magazine* (March–April 1974), pp. 22–27; Saul Cohen, "Harvey Fergusson: 'Smell of River and Pines,'" *Hoja Volante* (Aug. 1968), pp. 6–8, (Nov. 1968), pp. 7–8.

15 William T. Pilkington, "The Southwestern Novels of Harvey Fergusson," *New Mexico Quarterly* (Winter 1965–66), pp. 330–43; William T. Pilkington, *Harvey Fergusson* (Boston: Twayne Publishers, 1975).

16 See the following by William T. Pilkington: Introduction to *Wolf Song* (Boston: Gregg Press, 1978), pp. v–ix; Introduction to *In Those Days* (Boston: Gregg Press, 1978), pp. v–ix; Introduction to *The Blood of Conquerors* (Boston: Gregg Press, 1978), pp. v–ix; "Harvey Fergusson," in *A Literary History of the American West*, ed. J. Golden Taylor (Fort Worth: Texas Christian Univ. Press, 1987, pp. 546–58).

17 James K. Folsom, *Harvey Fergusson* (Austin: Steck-Vaughn, 1969); James K. Folsom, "Harvey Fergusson," in *Fifty Western Writers*, ed. Richard Etulain and Fred Erisman (Westport, Conn.: Greenwood Press, 1982), pp. 100–120.

18 Fergusson to Lawrence Clark Powell, April 18, 1965.

19 Fergusson to Powell, May 29, 1967. See Lawrence Clark Powell, *Books West Southwest* (Los Angeles: Ward Ritchie Press, 1957), and Lawrence Clark Powell, *Southwestern Book Trails: A Reader's Guide to the Heartland of New Mexico and Arizona.* (Albuquerque: Horn & Wallace, 1963). The

latter book is dedicated to Erna Fergusson, "native daughter of New Mexico."

20 On May 31, 1964, Fergusson wrote to Powell asking him if he might read the manuscript and offer an opinion: "I know of no one whose opinion of it, both as a novel and as a publishing problem, would be so helpful as yours, and I greatly need a candid opinion." One year later, May 12, 1965, Fergusson mailed Powell a typescript of *Lonely Women*.

21 Lawrence Clark Powell, "Southwest Classics Reread," *Westways* (Jan. 1972), p. 22.

22 Interviews with Lawrence Clark Powell, Tucson, June 17 and July 1, 1983.

23 Powell, interview, June 17, 1983.

24 Fergusson to Powell, May 29, 1967.

Index